CORBA Programming

Suhail M. Ahmed

SAMS

Unleashed

CORBA Programming Unleashed

International Standard Book Number: 0-672-31026-0

Library of Congress Catalog Card Number: 96-71495

Printed in the United States of America

First Printing: December, 1998

00 99 98 4 3 2 1

Trademarks

All terms mentioned in this book that are known to be trademarks or service marks have been appropriately capitalized. Sams Publishing cannot attest to the accuracy of this information. Use of a term in this book should not be regarded as affecting the validity of any trademark or service mark.

Warning and Disclaimer

Every effort has been made to make this book as complete and as accurate as possible, but no warranty or fitness is implied. The information provided is on an "as is" basis. The authors and the publisher shall have neither liability nor responsibility to any person or entity with respect to any loss or damages arising from the information contained in this book or from the use of the CD-ROM or programs accompanying it.

Executive Editor
Tracy Dunkelberger

Acquisitions Editor
Katie Purdum

Development Editor
Sean Dixon

Managing Editor
Jodi Jensen

Project Editor
Nancy Albright

Technical Editor
Larry Martinez

Indexers
Joy Dean Lee
Rebecca Hornyak

Proofreader
Mona Brown

Software Development Specialist
Andrea Duvall

Interior Design
Gary Adair

Cover Design
Aren Howell

Layout Technician
Susan Geiselman

Contents at a Glance

Contents

PART IV Vendor Extensions and Implementation Issues 271

About the Author

Suhail M. Ahmed has extensive experience as a Senior Consultant with Objective Alliance Group, the leading object technology company in Europe. He became a programmer accidentally after he graduated from Mysore University as a mathematician. It is one accident that has been most profitable for him. While he is not working, he reads history, especially about World War II and the Holocaust. He also pursues an active interest in graphics programming and is currently researching software metrics and methodologies. He lives in Amsterdam, and he is married with one child.

Contributing Authors

Larry Martinez is a Senior Technical Specialist with BSI Consulting in Houston, Texas, where he develops distributed client/server systems using Java, C++, and CORBA. He has developed systems under both UNIX and Windows NT systems for a variety of industries, including NASA's space shuttle program, mutual funds, oil exploration, and natural gas. Larry holds a bachelor's degree in Mechanical Engineering from the University of Texas at Austin, and is an active member of the Houston Java User's Group. He occasionally heads to the Colorado Rockies where he enjoys backpacking, snowboarding, and fishing.

Charles Pace has over 14 years of experience in all kinds of progressive, cutting-edge software development. He has written a vast array of computer programs, from interactive educational games to large enterprise systems. Charles looks forward to enabling developers to deliver applications utilizing the next generation of programming technology.

Dedication

For Aaron

May your future be as kind to you as your past has been to your father.

For Hilde

For being there.

For My Parents

For your faith in me.

Acknowledgments

Innumerable people have influenced this book. Most of the things I learned and came to know are from countless hours of discussions with the people I have had the privilege of working with as a consultant and teacher. But this book would not have been possible without the few good people who somehow crossed my life at the right moment in time. I owe a great deal to Tracy Dunkelberger and Katie Purdum for giving me the chance to write this book. Craig Read was kind enough, in his own way, to make time available for me from my busy schedule. His command of English and history came in handy when he offered his criticisms. I would also like to extend my sincere thanks to Wendy Devolder, who has been a kind friend and brought this opportunity to my attention. Finally, I want to thank Christophe Bon, who read every page, and no matter how scattered the content was at times, he always told me that it was great! Thank you all.

Tell Us What You Think!

As the reader of this book, *you* are our most important critic and commentator. We value your opinion and want to know what we're doing right, what we could do better, what areas you'd like to see us publish in, and any other words of wisdom you're willing to pass our way.

As the Executive Editor for the Programming team at Macmillan Computer Publishing, I welcome your comments. You can fax, email, or write me directly to let me know what you did or didn't like about this book—as well as what we can do to make our books stronger.

Please note that I cannot help you with technical problems related to the topic of this book, and that due to the high volume of mail I receive, I might not be able to reply to every message.

When you write, please be sure to include this book's title and author, as well as your name and phone or fax number. I will carefully review your comments and share them with the author and editors who worked on the book.

Fax: 317-817-7070

Email: `programming@mcp.com`

Mail: Tracy Dunkelberger
Programming Team
Macmillan Computer Publishing
201 West 103rd Street
Indianapolis, IN 46290 USA

Introduction

This book, in many ways, represents everything that I have used from CORBA implementations in my work as a consultant. I started writing the book in the firm confidence that CORBA is a known quantity, which could hold no surprises. To my amazement, I discovered that CORBA held many delightful challenges that still required me to shake off the sense of weariness that had grown on me over years of work with CORBA, both professionally and personally.

The most challenging aspect of CORBA is its promise of interoperability. In my capacity as consultant, I have had to rely on IIOP a number of times. Nowadays, I have come to take it for granted. The other interesting aspect of CORBA was the introduction I have had to dealing with the many interesting ways in which the vendors of CORBA have extended the specification. Some of you might think that such a situation is not an ideal one—especially when it comes to choosing an `ORB` for your application. But you will find that the CORBA vendors have managed to extend CORBA without breaking compliance to the core specification. Surely, that is a giant step toward heterogeneous interoperability of off-the-shelf CORBA implementations.

This book is a thorough exposition of the current implementation of the CORBA standard. It covers the many areas of CORBA that troubled me as a consultant and led to many a mistake that sometimes proved costly. I hope, through this volume, you will know more than I did when I started. *CORBA Programming Unleashed* provides information about the following topics. They may be read in any order you like, and they bear no real interdependencies.

- Chapter 1, "CORBA 2.0: An Architecture for Interoperability"
- Chapter 2, "IIOP and E-Commerce"

These two chapters are really the heart of the book. They demonstrate the twin promise of CORBA interoperability and the potential of IIOP as a protocol for e-commerce.

- Chapter 3, "The Portable Object Adapter"

The Portable Object Adapter is a new addition to the CORBA standard. It promises to bring a new level of abstraction to CORBA.

- Chapter 4, "CORBA Object References and Smart Pointers"
- Chapter 6, "CORBA C++ Memory Management"

These two chapters deal with the arcane issues of using C++ as a language for CORBA implementations. One of the topics that caused me the most grief when I began using CORBA was how to use C++ effectively.

- Chapter 5, "Java/IDL Mapping"

Java is fast becoming a standard language and platform for implementing CORBA applications. This chapter deals extensively with how to use Java with CORBA/IDL.

- Chapter 7, "The Naming Service"
- Chapter 8, "The Trader Service"
- Chapter 9, "The Event Service"

These are what I consider to be the core services that CORBA has to offer. These chapters cover the API and how to effectively use these services in your applications.

- Chapter 10, "The Transaction Service"

With the explosive emergence of the World Wide Web and the potential for exciting opportunities for e-commerce–related businesses, the CORBA Transaction Service is sure to become the cornerstone of many innovative Web applications. This chapter teaches you how to effectively and correctly use CORBA Transactions.

- Chapter 11, "The Security Service"

In a connected world, security is sure to be the one critical component that can make or break an application. The CORBA security specification is one of the most in-depth and complete specifications on distributed security this side of DCE.

- Chapter 24, "CORBA Interface Repository"
- Chapter 25, "CORBA Dynamic Invocation Interfaces"

As applications become more complex while offering new challenges to integration, the CORBA Interface Repository and Dynamic Invocation Interfaces are going to be key components that will enable "the web of objects" to expand the way the Internet did.

- Chapter 12, "CORBA Server Activation Modes"
- Chapter 14, "CORBA and Threads"
- Chapter 16, "Distributed Callbacks"

These three chapters deal with the important issue of server-side scalability. CORBA enables very fine-grained control over scalability issues. These chapters introduce the mechanisms of this control.

- Chapter 13, "Orbix Filters"
- Chapter 15, "Orbix Dynamic Loaders"

These two chapters deal with how IONA has extended CORBA. These two services can widen your options in terms of how CORBA can be further integrated into existing architectures and requirements.

- Chapter 17, "VisiBroker Caffeine"
- Chapter 18, "VisiBroker SmartStubs"
- Chapter 19, "Handling Distributed Events"

These chapters deal with VisiBroker's contribution to adding commercial depth to the CORBA standard. In all, I am sure that many of the interesting mechanisms that the commercial vendors have introduced into CORBA will be incorporated into the CORBA specification. Orbix Dynamic Loaders and VisiBroker SmartStubs are sure to be two that will eventually be added to the CORBA specifications.

- Chapter 21, "CORBA and Java Servlets"
- Chapter 22, "CORBA and Mobile Agents"
- Chapter 26, "Developing CORBABean Wrappers"

These three chapters deal with issues that enable you to integrate the power of CORBA with the flexibility of Java. If an effective distributed-object solution of the Web needs to be constructed with the simplicity of HTML, Java servlets and CORBA will provide the way. Mobile agents, on the other hand, are probably the next evolutionary step in client/server technology; Chapter 22 explores how the technologies can be integrated.

- Chapter 23, "CORBA and Design Patterns"

Over the last couple of years, I have realized that designing distributed systems has many fundamental differences from building desktop applications. Building distributed systems is not just about having objects interacting over networks. Nevertheless, it was heartening to see that the "Gang Of Four" patterns and others still hold true for distributed systems.

- Appendix A, "Annotated ORB Interface API"
- Appendix B, "TIE and BOA"
- Appendix C, "Orbix and MFC"

Appendix A provides you with a reference to the ORB interface API, and Appendix B is a guide to using TIE and the Basic Object Adapter. Appendix C tells you how to use MFC effectively with CORBA.

So, there you have it. Pretty much everything I want to know about CORBA—until the next incarnation of the standard, that is. I wish you luck. Good hunting.

Suhail M. Ahmed
Amsterdam, 1998

The Core Architecture

PART I

IN THIS PART

CORBA 2.0: An Architecture for Interoperability

In This Chapter

CORBA 2.0 specifies a technical framework that allows applications that use different protocols to interoperate. In addition to this, CORBA 2.0 also specifies the means by which protocols such as DCE RPC can interoperate with native CORBA protocols. Although this chapter concentrates on the details of how to achieve interoperability between different CORBA 2.0 implementations, it is instructive to understand the overall architecture for interoperability as defined by CORBA 2.0.

CORBA 2.0 differs from the earlier version in the nature of what the specification defined as interoperability. CORBA 1.0 allowed ORBs from the same vendor to interoperate across multiple platforms. This meant that if you wanted to run CORBA over multiple platforms, you selected an ORB vendor that supported those platforms.

With CORBA 2.0, you were given the freedom to choose any vendor that supported CORBA on the platform of your choice. The specifications guaranteed that applications running on multiple platforms would work together.

The specification defines four broad areas of interoperability. At its highest level, the standard defines an *overall architecture* for interoperability. The architecture defines the ideas used to describe interoperability—the vocabulary, so to speak. Within the context of this architecture, CORBA 2.0 specifies a mechanism known as *bridging* to allow multiple ORBs to communicate and collaborate with each other.

There are a number of reasons why OMG decreed interoperability in the first place. Here are some of the more important reasons:

- Large organizations have a tendency to define applications and services in terms of domains.
- Division in terms of domains results in complex and heterogeneous environments with many different types of platforms and software.
- Diversity of solutions leads to solutions that are optimal for a given problem, but it also introduces tight constraints on how different solutions could coexist.
- Organizations need to have full freedom to choose whatever they like for their domains, but also have the freedom to select solutions that would have the least impact on their existing infrastructure. *This path leads to having different ORBs in different domains—hence the need for interoperability.*

CORBA 2.0 accepts this reality and tries to define an architecture that enables you to define these domains in terms of the roles they play. In a typical organization, you could differentiate them broadly into business domains and technical domains. The technical domains are usually generic enough to be reused by any business domain. Such services include transactions, security, component repositories, and so on.

More Than One ORB?

Within the boundaries of a single domain, it is relatively straightforward to get ORBs to talk to each other. It is when objects in different domains have to work together that a more complex mechanism for interoperability must be defined. For instance, you could define security in terms of domains. You could have high, medium, and low security domains. This is usually how things are defined in complex organizations. In the classical approach to systems design, there is usually little or no interaction between different domains. This means that within the boundary of a single domain, a user usually has a *single systems logon*.

The most important thing to understand about CORBA is the fact that it is a peer-to-peer technology. This means that roles such as clients and servers are just that: roles. A CORBA client could, by design, become a server, and a server could be made into a client. These roles are very arbitrary.

If you consider that an organization would have multiple domains, it means that a server in one domain could function as a client in another. This is a consequence of a CORBA application that can easily integrate object references across many different domains. It is in contexts such as these that broad and general architectures for interoperability need to be defined. The OMG does precisely that with a specification for Inter-ORB Bridge Support running over clearly defined protocols.

Architecture and Protocols

The bridge concept accomplishes a number of functions. The primary one is that when a boundary is crossed, the bridge facilitates the unambiguous translation of the semantics and structure of the call between ORBs. This mediation is accomplished via the application of two protocols: the General Inter-ORB Protocol (GIOP) and the Environment-Specific Inter-ORB Protocol (ESIOP).

The General Inter-ORB Protocol

The GIOP specifies a set of standard messages that can be used to ensure interoperability between ORBs. As such, GIOP is the core of the ORB interoperability architecture.

The GIOP is a simple protocol that facilitates interoperability between different ORBS. It is a *general* protocol that can work over any minimalist connection-oriented transport protocol. It is a very efficient protocol and designed to be as compact as possible. GIOP messages enable object references to change location during runtime. The protocol is designed so that if a change of location does occur, it does so quite transparently for the client.

GIOP-based protocols make a number of assumptions, the most important of which is that GIOP will use a connection-oriented transport mechanism. On top of this, GIOP assumes that this transport will be reliable. Reliability ensures that if a connection is lost due to whatever reasons, the underlying transport will offer some mechanism for notifying that some fault has occurred.

With the CORBA 1.0 implementation, each ORB vendor had its own proprietary protocol to encapsulate invocations across clients and servers. Within the new standard, OMG has made GIOP implementations mandatory. More specifically, OMG specifies the Internet Inter-ORB Protocol (IIOP) as the means to allow an interoperable heterogeneous ORB environment. IIOP is a TCP-based implementation of GIOP. This means that IIOP uses TCP as its transport protocol. It is possible to implement GIOP over other transport protocols such as IPX/SPX, NetBEUI as well.

Environment-Specific Inter-ORB Protocol

CORBA 2.0 also specifies interoperability between CORBA-based implementations and other distributed architectures. What if you have an environment that has applications running on some proprietary transport protocol or even a standard one, such as DCE? This is where the ESIOP comes in. Just as IIOP maps GIOP to TCP, you can use ESIOP to enable interoperability between DCE-based solutions. Implementations of ESIOP allow GIOP messages to be mapped to something like DCE via a *half bridge* so that IIOP objects can interact with ESIOP objects. With bridges, foreign objects appear like native objects.

The Internet Inter-ORB Protocol

IIOP is an implementation of GIOP that uses TCP/IP as its transport protocol. Such an implementation allows CORBA implementations to interoperate over the Internet domain. IIOP is intended to provide an "out-of-the-box" protocol layer over GIOP that allows multiple ORBs to transparently communicate with each other. IIOP is mandatory for any ORB aspiring to CORBA 2.0 compliance.

IIOP is the foundation of interoperability between CORBA 2.0 implementations. If an ORB supports the IIOP protocol, it can communicate transparently to other ORBs. By extension, any service that is implemented on top of a CORBA 2.0–compliant ORB can be used by any other ORB. So it is possible to mix and match services across multiple domains.

As noted, CORBA achieves interoperability by defining bridges. Bridges ultimately make it possible to use object references from one domain in another domain. This is accomplished by defining an unambiguous *information model* for object references known as the *Interoperable Object References* (IORs).

The following information is contained in an IIOP stream:

- Null object reference?—Obviously, null references cannot have invocations operated on them.
- Unambiguously define the type of the object reference—IDL is a strongly typed system. IORs need to contain information about the object reference types so that different implementations of this CORBA object model can treat them in a consistent manner. This enables a uniform object model representation across ORB platforms and languages.
- Protocol support—IORs encapsulate protocol information so that a recipient of an IOR can choose the most efficient available protocol.
- Available ORB services—If an object reference uses various CORBA services to facilitate invocation, this information is encapsulated in the IOR. This is primarily to assist in negotiating the interface to the services using a standard format. This means that a client can unambiguously retrieve an object reference from a service.

Anatomy of an IOR

You can create IORs from object references. Such references are known as *stringified* object references. These references can be passed to a client that requires the services of a server component. At the client side, these stringified object references can be converted back to object references, and operations can be invoked on them.

The Application Programming Interface (API) required for these operations is found in the `ORB` class. Later on, you'll have a detailed look at the protocols offered by the `ORB` class. For the current discussions, two operations, `ORB::object_to_string` and `ORB::string_to_object` are the necessary APIs needed to accomplish the conversion of an object reference to an IOR and an IOR back to an object reference, respectively.

Interoperability in this context is rather simple. Object references running on different ORBs can be converted into stringified references and passed between each other. We will be using this mechanism to illustrate interoperability.

Before we can do that we have to solve the chicken-and-egg problem!

The Chicken-and-Egg Problem

I love these problems. If I have learned anything during my work and my studies, the whole shebang of existence is one big chicken-and-egg problem. It seems that the only way we can deal with this problem is by continually delegating the problem to ever-finer eggs and chickens. The word *delegation* is the key, because that is the approach we are going to use.

Interoperability is rather simple to achieve when you have the IOR. The problem is getting the IOR in the first place. Until that is done, there is no interoperability. But in order to get hold of the IOR, you need to get hold of the ORB on which that IOR is based. Because you need the IOR for that, we arrive at the chicken-and-egg problem.

There really isn't any solution to chicken-and-egg problems. In the context of CORBA, the best we can do is have a potential client and a potential server agree on a standard mechanism to exchange the IOR—the standard mechanism not having anything to do with CORBA itself.

Before we can work on building an application on different ORBs, we first need to build what are known as *infrastructural components*. Most architectures have a number of these. In fact, all the Common CORBAServices are infrastructural in nature. In our example, this component will act as an IOR Registry. CORBA objects that would like to be available over IIOP could register with IORRegistry and should be able to use a simple set of API to achieve this. This means that server objects should be provided with a simple method to do registration management and the client with a method to retrieve an IOR.

WARNING

Ensure that the ORB you are considering in your architecture is 100 percent CORBA 2.0–compliant. The level of interoperability varies from vendor to vendor. Although most CORBA manuals talk about "out-of-the-box" interoperability, some vendors stretch that definition a little too thin.

A Simple IOR Registry

The IOR Registry should be able to provide the following services:

- Enable components to register their IORs
- Enable components to deregister their IORs
- Enable components to retrieve an IOR by passing a component's marker
- Enable components to retrieve all IORs registered with the IORR

Before you specify the interfaces for IORR, you also have to think about how you are going to allow a heterogeneous CORBA environment to use this service. One primary requirement is that a component anywhere should be able to access the IORR's IOR. The trick is to use some unglamorous way to accomplish this. Consider the following possibilities:

- You could stream the IOR to some persistent state. This solution is a good one at first sight. Perhaps you could use something like a small object-oriented database, such as Objectstore PSE, to achieve this. Even traditional persistent stores could be used. The benefit of this is that the search capability of the database could be used to search for IORs.
- You could stream the IOR to a networked file system. This is a simple solution. It is also efficient, because there is very little overhead in streaming to the file system and then retrieving the IOR. Of course, the trade-off you have to make is that you would have to engineer all the search and sort algorithms. Because you live in the age of reuse, however, there are plenty of freely available libraries that do these efficiently. You could use the C++ Standard Template Libraries or the Java Collections that are part of Java Development Kit 1.2, which is also available to JDK 1.1.

  You have to consider that the IORs should be on some type of networked file systems or at least an environment that could provide you with an open means of networked distribution.
- If interoperability is to be achieved on a single machine, a simple Clipboard-based transfer is sufficient. This is an obtuse way of saying, "use cut and paste"!

We are going to try something novel. As a consultant who works with every manner of distributed middleware, I have to keep my ears to the ground, so to speak, for new ways of distributing information. One of the technologies I came across recently is called iBus.

iBus will easily allow us to transmit the IORRegistry's IOR over IP multicast. With Java, the solution is trivial, because the requisite network libraries for UDP-based protocols are built into the JDK. Because iBus is a pure Java implementation, we could easily integrate this solution with Java-based CORBA applications. On the other hand, with C++ it is a little more involved. Trying to implement IP multicast using C++ would be unnecessarily complex, so we shall make a radical design compromise.

With these choices in mind, let's now define the IDL for the IORegistry:

```
IORR.idl
module iorr{
    interface registry {
        exception ObjectAlreadyRegisted { string reason; };
        exception ObjectNotRegisterd { string reason; };
        exception GenralException { string reason; };

        struct entry {
            string object_name;
            string server_name;
            string ior;
        };
```

```
        typedef entry registryEntry;
        typedef sequence<entry> directory;
        void register(in registryEntry t_entry) raises
➥(ObjectAlreadyRegisted);
        void deregister(in registryEntry t_entry) raises
➥(ObjectNotRegisterd);
        void fetch(inout registryEntry t_entry) raise
➥(ObjectNotRegisterd);
        directory fetch_all() raises (GenralException);
    };
};
```

The IORegistry IDL Details

The `struct entry` is the object that will make up the entries in the registry. These entries, of course, have to be held in an array, which is what the following line does:

```
typedef sequence<entry> directory;
```

The API shown in the next three lines are for manipulating the registry:

```
void register(in registryEntry t_entry) raises (ObjectAlreadyRegisted);
void deregister(in registryEntry t_entry) raises (ObjectNotRegisterd);
void fetch(inout registryEntry t_entry) raise (ObjectNotRegisterd);
```

This design also contains exception handling. You will find throughout the book that we will have exceptions wherever appropriate. This should be your standard practice as well. Keep in mind that a CORBA client blocks until an invocation returns. If something goes wrong, the client usually gets some cryptic CORBA exception, which is not helpful in the context of the invocation. It is a small price to pay to make some intelligible exceptions for a client invocation if things do go wrong.

The design is very minimalist, just enough to move IORs around. Let's now move to the implementation of the IORegistry Server.

The following tools and environment will be used in building the solution:

IORegistry Server Environment and Tools

The ORB	Inprise VisiBroker for Java 3.1
IDE	Inprise JBuilder 2.0
Additional Library	iBus 0.7
	Java Generic Library 3.0.1

The Java Generic Library can be downloaded from `www.odi.com`. iBus can be obtained from `http://www.softwired.ch`.

Compiling the IDL

Run the VisiBroker IDL pre-compiler on the `ior.idl` with the following line:

```
C:\> idl2java -strict -no_comments -no_tie iorr.idl
```

The flags are as follows:

- `strict`—This flag ensures that the IDL pre-compiler generates OMG-compliant Java code.
- `no_comments`—Absence of this flag generates comments in the generated file that can then be used by Javadoc to generate code documentation.
- `no_tie`—This flag disables the support code generation.

The IDL pre-compiler generates the following files:

- `Reregistry.java`—This is Java mapping for the IDL interface.
- Various helper files—The helper classes contain various utility functions. The functions are all static so that you don't need to instantiate these classes to access their services.
- Various holder files   These contain utility functions related to mapping Java to CORBA-compliant parameters (more on this later). The functions also contain services for `CORBA::Any`.
- `_registryImplBase.java`   This file contains BOA support for the registry interface implementation.
- `portable_stub_registry.java`   These are stub files for the registry implementation.
- `example_registry.java`   This is skeleton implemenation of the registry interface, which you can fill up and compile. This is the first file you need to work with. You are free to change the name of this file. Remember also to change the class name if you do.

Listing 1.1 shows the example_`registry.java` file.

LISTING 1.1 A SKELETON IMPLEMENTATION OF THE REGISTRY INTERFACE

```
package iorr;
import com.objectspace.jgl.*;
import java.util.Enumeration;

public class _example_registry extends iorr._registryImplBase {

//A Java generic library Hashset to hold all the Registry entries
```

continues

LISTING 1.1 CONTINUED

```
    private HashSet iortable = null;

//Method to check if an entry already exists in the registry
  private boolean CheckEntry(iorr.registryPackage.entry y_entry){
     iorr.registryPackage.entry x_entry;

     Enumeration en = iortable.elements();
     boolean found_it = false;

     while(en.hasMoreElements()){
       x_entry = (iorr.registryPackage.entry) en.nextElement();
       if(x_entry.server_name.equals(y_entry.server_name) &&
        x_entry.object_name.equals(y_entry.object_name) )
          found_it = true;
     }
     return found_it;
  }

  public _example_registry() {
    super("IORR");
    iortable = new HashSet(false);
  }

//Method to register an IORRegistry entry
    public void register(iorr.registryPackage.entry t_entry) throws
iorr.registryPackage.ObjectAlreadyRegisted {

    try{
        iortable.add(t_entry);
        System.out.println("IOR From the Client: " + t_entry.ior);
    }
    catch(NullPointerException e){
       throw new iorr.registryPackage.ObjectAlreadyRegisted(e.toString());
    }
  }

//Method to deregister an IORRegistry entry
    public void deregister(iorr.registryPackage.entry t_entry)throws
  iorr.registryPackage.ObjectNotRegisterd {
     try{
         iortable.remove(t_entry);
     }
     catch(Exception e){
        throw new iorr.registryPackage.ObjectNotRegisterd(e.toString());
     }
  }

//Method to retrieve an already registered IORRegistry entry by passing an
//entryHolder
```

```
    public void fetch(iorr.registryPackage.entryHolder t_entry)
              throws iorr.registryPackage.ObjectNotRegisterd {
    Enumeration e = iortable.elements();
    boolean found = false;

    while(e.hasMoreElements() && found == false )

       iorr.registryPackage.entryHolder _entry =
              (iorr.registryPackage.entryHolder) e.nextElement();
       if(_entry.value.object_name == t_entry.value.object_name
        && _entry.value.server_name == t_entry.value.server_name){
          t_entry.value.ior = _entry.value.ior;
          found = true;
       }
    }
    if(!found)
      throw new iorr.registryPackage.ObjectNotRegisterd("Object not
➥found");
  }

//Method to retrieve the entire contents of the IORRegistry.
//They arereturned as an array of entry elements
    public iorr.registryPackage.entry[] fetch_all( ) throws
                     iorr.registryPackage.GenralException {
    int count = iortable.size();
    if(count == 0)
      new iorr.registryPackage.GenralException("IOR table is empty");

    Enumeration e = iortable.elements();
    iorr.registryPackage.entry[] table =
               new iorr.registryPackage.entry[count];
    for(int i = 0; i < count; i++){
      table[i] = (iorr.registryPackage.entry)e.nextElement();
    }
    return table;
  }
}
```

These are the details of the IORRegistry interface's implementation:

- The Registry entries coming in from clients are to be held in the Java Generic Library (JGL) Hashset. The JGL Hashset stores elements by their hash code by invoking the `hashcode()` on them. The JGL is an extremely efficient set of Java container classes based on the C++ Standard Template Library.
- The client can invoke `register()` on the IORRegistry by passing an instance of the following:

  ```
  iorr.registryPackage.entry t_entry
  ```

On receipt of the entry instance, the implementation adds the entry into the Hashset.

- The following method verifies whether the entry exists in the Registry:

```
public void fetch(iorr.registryPackage.entryHolder t_entry)
              throws iorr.registryPackage.ObjectNotRegisterd {
    Enumeration e = iortable.elements();
    boolean found = false;

    while(e.hasMoreElements() && found == false )

       iorr.registryPackage.entryHolder _entry =
              (iorr.registryPackage.entryHolder) e.nextElement();
       if(_entry.value.object_name == t_entry.value.object_name
        && _entry.value.server_name == t_entry.value.server_name){
          t_entry.value.ior = _entry.value.ior;
          found = true;
       }
    }
    if(!found)
      throw new iorr.registryPackage.ObjectNotRegisterd("Object not
➥found");
  }
```

The object reference's name has to be unique within a server. If this constraint is violated, the exception

`iorr.registryPackage.ObjectAlreadyRegisted`

is thrown to the client.

- Any implementation that has registered with the IORRegistry can use this method to remove its IOR when it is no longer needed. Of course, this implies that the object to be deregistered exists in the registry; otherwise, an exception is thrown.
- Operation for fetching an element from the IORRegistry was defined in IDL as the following:

```
void fetch(inout registryEntry t_entry)
```

The parameter passed into the server was tagged as `inout`. This means that the parameter is passed from the server, and the server can operate on it and return it. In Java, an `inout` parameter maps to a holder class. The implementation is rather simple, because it involves iterating over an enumeration of the elements of the Hashset until a match is found and then setting the requested IOR in the holder class.

- As it should be clear from the interface for the `iorr.registryPackage.entry`, a client is expected to know the name of the server and object before it can request an IOR. In case these are not known, the client can request all the entries. This means that the client needs to figure out which IOR it wants.

We now have to design a solution to allow potential clients to discover the register's IOR so that it can use its services.

iBus IORRegistry Transmitter

The design of the IORRegistry is such that any client that needs to use IOR for interoperability needs to find only the initial IOR for the registry. A good solution that solves this problem would be to decouple the *location* of where this IOR was stored from the potential client. Otherwise, if the location were to change, the client would have to be reinitialized with the new settings.

With Java, such changes could easily be handled with property files. Java property files can be read in by an application, and these files could contain all the necessary parameters to initialize the connection to the IORRegistry. If such a solution could be found, the system has a good chance to be flexible and scalable. One such technology is iBus. In fact, it would be a good solution in some cases to have all servers multicast their IORs over predefined channels. This would result in an architecture that has no need for a centralized naming service.

Using iBus means that any client that has implemented the required callback interface could "listen" to the IOR for the registry being transmitted over the network. Our implementation of iBus uses IP multicast as the transmission protocol. (Information about iBus can be otained at the Softwired Web site.) This does mean the quality of service is rather poor, because the packets have no guaranteed delivery. But this is more efficient in terms of conserving your network's bandwidth.

The `SOAR.infrastructure.transmitter` defines two classes and an interface. The class `iortransmitter.java` defines and implements the requirements for an iBus channel. The implementation is rather simple, because the only thing this class needs to do is transmit the IORRegistry server. The `IORReceiver.java` contains the implementation for the iBus channel receiver functionality. Any client that needs to "tune" into the IORRegistry server's channel can use this class to do so. The only constraint is that such a client implements the `receiver` interface defined in `receiver.java`. Listing 1.2 shows the implementation of the `IORRegistry` IOR transmitter.

LISTING 1.2 THE `IORRegistry` TRANSMITTER

```
package SOAR.infrastructure.transmitter;
import iBus.exception.*;
import iBus.*;
import java.util.*;
import java.net.*;
```

continues

LISTING 1.2 CONTINUED

```
public class iortransmitter extends Thread {

  private String ior_to_transmit = null;
  private iBus.Stack t_stack = null;
  private iBusURL t_url = null;
  private Posting t_posting = null;

 public iortransmitter(String t_ior){

    ior_to_transmit = t_ior;

    try{
     t_url = new iBusURL ("ibus://226.0.0.1/soar/iorrt");
    }
     catch(java.net.MalformedURLException e){
      System.out.println(e.toString());
    }

  t_stack = new iBus.Stack("IPMCAST");
    t_posting = new Posting();

    // put the message into the posting:
    t_posting.setLength(1);
    t_posting.setObject(0, ior_to_transmit);

    // register this application as a talker for the URL:
    try{
      t_stack.registerTalker(t_url);
    }
    catch(iBus.exception.CommException e){
      System.out.println(e.toString());
    }
    catch(iBus.exception.AlreadyRegistered e){
      System.out.println(e.toString());
    }

    System.out.println("Transmitter is initialized for " +
➥ior_to_transmit);

  }

  public void run(){

    for(;;){
      try{
        t_stack.push(t_url, t_posting);
        System.out.println("tick..");
        Thread.currentThread().sleep(10000);
      }
```

```
      catch(Exception e){
        System.out.println(e.toString());
      }
    }
  }
}
```

This implementation is a very simple adaptation of the iBus "hello world" channel application. As stated earlier, we are going to use IP Multicast to "push" our IOR around the network.

The `IORTransmitter` class can be used by any CORBA object that needs to transmit its IOR around. Any class that wishes to do so could launch the `IORTransmitter` on a thread so that it can work in the background and not interfere in the normal workings of the CORBA implementation:

- When instantiating the `IORTransmitter` class, the IOR of the source object can be passed into the class. This is the IOR that is transmitted.
- With iBus, you can use extended URL objects known as iBus URLs to construct a channel. You do so at

  ```
  t_url = new iBusURL ("ibus://226.0.0.1/soar/iorrt");
  ```

  Depending on your IP address, you would have to change the address that you put into this URL.
- You initialize the protocol stack for IP Multicast. iBus offers a number of protocols, including Reliable and even Reliable IP Multicast. Let's choose IPMCAST to conserve the network bandwidth.
- You initialize the posting object, which is to contain the IOR string object. In fact, iBus posting objects can contain any valid Java object (!). Here is the relevant code:

  ```
  t_posting.setObject(0, ior_to_transmit);
  ```
- After you have done all this, you register the talker for the chosen iBus URL. The *talker* is the object that contains the logic that transmits the information over the channel. This is accomplished in the following line of code:

  ```
  t_stack.registerTalker(t_url);
  ```
- Finally, a client class on invoking `start()` on the `IORTransmitter` launches an infinite `for` loop that transmits the posting every ten seconds.

IORRegistry Server Implementations

Now that we have the implementation of the IORRegistry and the iBus transmitter for pushing the IOR for the registry server, we need to implement a Visigenic server to host the `IORRegistry` object, as shown in Listing 1.3.

LISTING 1.3 IMPLEMENTING A SERVER HOST

```
package iorr;
import SOAR.transmt.*;
import org.omg.CORBA.*;
import java.io.*;

public class iorserver {

       public static void main(String[] args) {

         ORB t_orb = ORB.init();
         BOA t_boa = t_orb.BOA_init();

         _registryImplBase t_registry = new _example_registry();

        String t_registry_ior = t_orb.object_to_string(t_registry);

         try{
           File outputFile = new File("ior.dat");
           FileWriter out = new FileWriter(outputFile);

           int ior_length = t_registry_ior.length();
           for(int i=0;i<ior_length;i++){
             out.write(t_registry_ior.charAt(i));
           }
           out.flush();
           out.close();
         }

         catch(IOException ioe){
           System.out.println(ioe.toString());
         }

         t_boa.obj_is_ready(t_registry);
         System.out.println(t_registry + " is ready.");
         System.out.println("IOR is " + t_registry_ior);

         iortransmitter t_transmitter = new
➥iortransmitter(t_registry_ior);
         try{
           t_transmitter.start();
         }
         catch(Exception e){
            System.out.println(e.toString());
         }

       t_boa.impl_is_ready();
       orb.disconnect(registry);
       }
}
```

As I said earlier, most CORBA server implementations are relatively standard. In fact, some ORBs do generate a standard server file that can be used without changes with a wide variety of client implementations. But our server implementation does contain a few changes relating to the steps required to set up the `IORTransmitter` object:

- After instantiating an instance of the registry interface, you invoke the call `object_to_string` on the ORB handle. This call returns the IOR, which is a stringified object reference of the registry.
- After you have returned the IOR to the registry, you can now instantiate an instance of the `IORTransmitter`. The constructor of the `IORTransmitter` requires a string parameter referring to the IOR. The IOR string is passed into the `IORTransmitter` to instantiate it.
- After instantiating the transmitter, the `start` method is called on the object to have the `IORTransmitter` run on a separate thread from the main one.
- The main thread blocks, waiting for incoming requests, in this line:

  ```
  orb.disconnect(registry);
  ```

  Setting the `IORTransmitter` on a separate thread now makes a lot more sense. The server waiting for messages and the transmitter multicasting messages make excellent candidates for threading.

We have implemented the `IORRegistry` and the `IORTransmitter`. You can now run the application to see whether everything functions as intended. Of course, it won't seem to do much, because the only thing that is happening is hidden from your view: On one thread, the blocked BOA call is waiting for any request, and on the other thread, the `IORTransmitter` multicasts the server's IOR every ten seconds. We now need to build some ears!

The IORRegistry Client-Side Implementation

There are some important considerations you have to take into account before constructing a listener. The most important thing is that no matter which client uses a listener, the services that have been implemented cannot change. This means that no matter what type the client is, the implementation of the `IORRegistry` server or the `IORTransmitter` cannot change. The other consideration is that we should have the ability to just reuse the listener without change; after all, this is what object orientation is all about isn't it? This is a valid consideration, because any real-world implementation of such a system would consist of any number of `IORReceiver` clients running. The iBus listener should not have to know all the clients that are using its services. It should be a simple matter of any client requiring the services of a listener to simply "plug in" the receiver and receive transmissions.

We can accomplish this constraint on our design by specifying a generic interface that must be implemented by any client that wishes to be notified on reception of an IOR. We shall specify such an interface, which we call the `IORReceiver` interface:

```
package SOAR. infrastructure.receiver;

public IORReceiver receiver {

public void set_IOR(String t_ior);

}
```

The `IORReceiver` interface specifies only a single operation: `set_IOR(String t_ior)`. This method needs to be implemented by any client that requires notification by the `IORReceiver` object.

The `IORReceiver` Class Implementation

The `IORReceiver` is the ear that listens to a specific iBus channel for reception of the IOR string. Most of the constraints that were imposed on the transmitter also apply to the receiver. For instance, the receiver has to execute on a thread, the receiver has to be shut down when the Registry IOR has been received, and so on. Listing 1.4 shows the implementation of the `IORReceiver` class.

LISTING 1.4 THE `IORReceiver` CLASS

```
package SOAR.infrastructure.receiver;
import iBus.exception.*;
import iBus.*;
import java.util.*;
import java.net.*;
import iorr.*;

public class IORReceiver extends Thread {

  private iBus.Stack t_stack = null;
  private iBus.iBusURL t_url = null;
  private IORTuner t_tuner = null;
  private IORReceiver _temp_ior = null;

  public IORReceiver(receiver t_temp) {

    String args[] = new String[]{""};
    args = Application.init("IOR Tuner", args);
    _temp_ior = t_temp;
  }

  public void run(){
```

```
    t_tuner = new IORTuner(_temp);
    _temp= null;

    try{
      t_url = new iBusURL ("ibus://226.0.0.1/soar/iorrt");
    }
    catch(MalformedURLException e){
      System.err.println(e.toString());
    }

    t_stack = new iBus.Stack("IPMCAST");
    // subscribe the receiver object to the hello world channel:

    try{
      t_stack.subscribe(t_url, t_tuner);
    }
    catch(iBus.exception.CommException e){
      System.err.println(e.toString());
    }
    catch(iBus.exception.AlreadySubscribed e){
      System.err.println(e.toString());
    }

    System.err.println(Application.getAppName() + " is ready.");

    // wait for incoming postings:
    t_stack.waitTillExit();
  }

  public void logout(){
    t_stack.readyToExit();
  }
}


class IORTuner implements iBus.Receiver {

    receiver t_buffer = null;

    public IORTuner(receiver t_temp){
      t_buffer = t_temp;
    }

    public void dispatchPush(iBusURL source, Posting p)
    {
    String t_ior = (String)p.getObject(0);
        t_buffer.set_IOR(t_ior);
    }

    public Posting dispatchPull(iBusURL channel, Posting request)
```

continues

LISTING 1.4 CONTINUED

```
    {
    return null;
    }

    public void error(iBusURL url, String details)
    {
    System.err.println("Error: " + details);
    System.err.flush();
    System.exit(1);
    }
}
```

The `IORRegistry` receiver contains two classes: the `IORReceiver` and the `IORTuner`. Think of the `IORReceiver` class as the radio and the `IORTuner` class as the component that actually receives the signals. Let's look at the internals of the two classes:

- The `IORReceiver` is a subclass of the `java.util.Thread` class. This allows you to run the receiver on a thread. By design, any class that wants to receive IORs over the iBus can use this class by aggregation and simply "start up" the thread.
- iBus requires that you initialize the application. It is not really necessary, but if you want to pass Quality of Service information to iBus, you can do that as parameters to this method.
- In the `run` method, an instance of the `IORTuner` is instantiated. The `IORTuner` is required to be a concrete implementation of `iBus.Receiver`. Let's look a little closer at this class:

  The `IORTuner` accepts any class that implements the `receiver` interface. As mentioned earlier, this interface allows the `Tuner` to be independent of any client using its services by simply invoking `set_IOR(t_ior)`.

  The following method:

  ```
  void dispatchPush(iBusURL source, Posting p)
  ```

  is where posting "pushed" by the `IORTransmitter` is received. On reception, a cast decodes the message. This message is then passed to the client that is waiting.
- The method on this line:

  ```
  t_url = new iBusURL ("ibus://226.0.0.1/soar/iorrt")
  ```

  is where the URL that specifies the iBus channel is constructed.

  Any client that needs to tune into the IOR channel must subscribe to this channel. A perceptive reader will catch on to the fact that the original aim to solve the chicken-and-egg problem hasn't really been solved. It has just been moved to another place. The tuner needs to have the IOR channel's URL a priori. One way to address the problem is to standardize on the URL so that it is an invariant entity.

- In fact, this is the way CORBA addresses the problem. Object references to standard services, such as the Naming Service or Trading Service, is resolved by invoking `resolveinitialreference` on the ORB and passing standardized names to those services. For example `NS` is the required name for the Naming Service.
- IP Multicast is the protocol stack over which the channel is transmitted, so an `IPMCAST` stack is constructed.
- The URL channel is then used to subscribe to an iBus channel that is being broadcast over IP Multicast. Two parameters are passed: a reference to the URL that points to the channel, and a reference to an instance of any class that implements `iBus.Receiver` interface.
- At this point, the tuner is initialized. The `t_stack.waitTillExit()` method blocks, listening on the iBus channel and waiting for incoming transmissions. Because Listing 1.4 uses IP Multicast, the reception is not guaranteed, but it will get there eventually. If reliability is required, you could specify `RELIABLE` as your IP stack.

We are now ready to build clients that can subscribe to the `IORTransmitter` channel. This is to be only a test client that allows us to try on the `IORRegistry`'s API. The client is only a CORBA client. The packages included in the client are standard `org.omg.*` packages, so it should be possible for you to use any ORB implementation.

Before looking at the implementation, the necessary ORB support files need to be generated. Run your preferred IDL compiler on `iorr.idl`. Invoke the IDL pre-compiler with the `-clientstubonly` switch. Different ORBs have different switches. Here are two:

- ORBIXWeb 3.0: `c:\>idl -jC -jOMG iorr.idl`

  The `-jC` is the switch required to generate only client-side files.

  The `-jOMG` generates "pure" OMG-specified code without any value-added proprietary support.
- VisiBroker 3.0: `c:\>idl2java -strict -no_skel -no_comments`

  The `-strict` flag ensures that only OMG-compliant code is generated.

  The `-no_skel` means that only client-side stubs are generated.

  The `-no_comments` switches off code comment generation.

The IDL pre-compiler generates the following files under ORBIXWEB 3.0:

- `_registryStub.java`—This file contains the client-side stub support for the `iorr` interfaces.

- registry.java—The registry.java file contains the interface mapping for the iorr interface to Java.
- The helper and the holder files are the same as for the server. These files contain various utilities.

The OrbixIORTuner Implementation

Everything required to build a test interoperability client is now ready. The implemena-tion has some simple requirements:

- The client needs to have support to the IORReceiver component.
- The client should be threaded for performance.

Listing 1.5 shows the implementation of the OrbixIORTuner.

LISTING 1.5 OrbixIORTuner

```
Package Iorr;
import org.omg.CORBA.*;
import SOAR.receiver.*;
import java.util.*;


public class OrbixIORTuner extends Thread implements iorr.receiver{

  private String t_registry_ior = null;
  private ORB _orb = null;

  public OrbixIORTuner(){

    _orb = ORB.init();
    System.out.println("ORB Client initializing..");
  }

  public void run(){

    IORReceiver t_receiver = new IORReceiver(this);
    t_receiver.start();

    while(t_registry_ior == null){
      System.out.println("waiting..");
      try{
        Thread.currentThread().sleep(10000);
      }
      catch(InterruptedException e){
        System.out.println(e.toString());
```

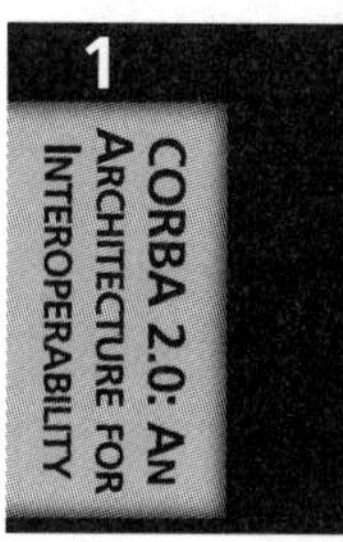


```
}
    }

   t_receiver.logout();
   t_receiver.stop();
   t_receiver = null;
   System.out.println("Registry IOR is " + t_registry_ior );
   this.continueProcess();

  }

  public synchronized void set_IOR(String t_ior){
     t_registry_ior = t_ior;
  }

  private void continueProcess(){
    registry t_registry = null;

    try{
     org.omg.CORBA.Object _temp =_orb.string_to_object(t_registry_ior);
     t_registry = registryHelper.narrow(_temp);
    }
    catch(SystemException e){
      System.out.println(e.toString());
    }

    iorr.registryPackage.entry t_entry =
new iorr.registryPackage.entry();

    iorr.registryPackage.entryHolder r_entry = new
iorr.registryPackage.entryHolder();

    t_entry.server_name = "VisibrokerServer";
    t_entry.object_name = "SomeObject";

    t_entry.ior = t_registry_ior;

    r_entry.value.server_name = t_entry.server_name;
    r_entry.value.object_name = t_entry.object_name;
    r_entry.value.ior = "";

    iorr.registryPackage.entry[] t_allentries = null;

    try{
      t_registry.register(t_entry);
    }
    catch(iorr.registryPackage.ObjectAlreadyRegisted e){
      System.out.println("ObjectAlreadyRegistered..");
      System.out.println(e.toString());
    }
```

continues

LISTING 1.5 CONTINUED

```
    try{
      t_registry.fetch(r_entry);
    }
    catch(iorr.registryPackage.ObjectNotRegisterd e){
      System.out.println("ObjectNotRegisterd..");
      System.out.println(e.toString());
    }

    try{
     org.omg.CORBA.Object _temp =_orb.string_to_object(t_registry_ior);
     t_registry = registryHelper.narrow(_temp);
    }
    catch(SystemException e){
      System.out.println(e.toString());
    }
    try{
      t_registry.register(t_entry);
    }
    catch(iorr.registryPackage.ObjectAlreadyRegisted e){
      System.out.println("ObjectAlreadyRegistered..");
      System.out.println(e.toString());
    }

    try{
        t_allentries = t_registry.fetch_all( );
    }
    catch(iorr.registryPackage.GenralException e){
      System.out.println("GeneralException..");
      System.out.println(e.toString());
    }

    for(int i = 0; i < t_allentries.length; i++)
      System.out.println(t_allentries[i].object_name);

    try{
      t_registry.deregister(t_entry);
    }
    catch(iorr.registryPackage.ObjectNotRegisterd e){
      System.out.println("ObjectNotRegisterd..");
      System.out.println(e.toString());
    }
  }
}
```

The `OrbixIORTuner` is a thread class. It also implements the `iorr.receiver` interface. This means that an instance of this class can be passed into the constructor of the `IORTuner` class:

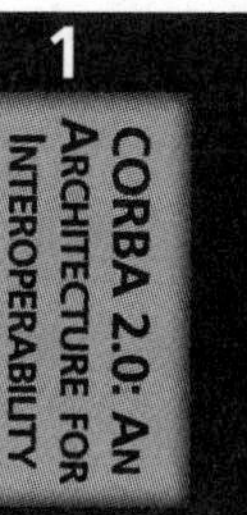

- The constructor for `OrbixIORTuner` initializes the ORB. Because this class is a thread, everything that needs to be initialized once can be done here.
- A number of things are accomplished in the `run` method. An instance of the `IORReceiver` is instantiated and activated. Notice that in this method:

  ```
  IORReceiver t_receiver = new IORReceiver(this)
  ```

  a reference to the `OrbixIORTuner` is passed. Remember from the discussion of the `IORTuner` that its constructor takes an `iorr.receiver` as a parameter. Because `OrbixIORTuner` is an `iorr.receiver`, you can pass an instance of it into the constructor.
- In this line, you go into a busy-waiting loop. This is not the most efficient way for a thread to wait for something, because processor cycles are gobbled up with each loop. Better ways will be demonstrated with other examples. Nevertheless, the busy-waiting tests on the truth of `t_registry_ior`. A null value for `t_registry_ior` ensures that the block will loop. Also note that the thread sleeps for ten seconds so that other threads can also have some CPU time.

  Keep in mind that the `IORReceiver` is also a thread. If the class is to be continuously blocked, the `IORTuner` will not get an opportunity to set the `t_registry_ior` to something else.
- When the busy-waiting block breaks out, the code shuts down the `IORReceiver` and assigns a null value to the object reference. This is how object references can be marked for garbage collection in Java.
- The `public synchronized void set_IOR(String t_ior)` is an implementation of the required method that has to be implemented from the `iorr.receiver` interface. This is the method that is invoked by the `IORTuner` to notify the client class that the IOR has been received. We could have used Java's built-in `even` class to do this work, but for the purposes at hand this method would suffice. Chapter 2, "IIOP and E-Commerce," contains an improved version of the `IORTuner` and `IORReceiver`.
- The `private void continueProcess()` is where the main test block sits. All the operations on the `iorr.registry` interface are tested here. Before that can be done, the appropriate object reference needs to be constructed for the IOR that was received by the `IORReceiver` and passed on to the `OrbixIORClient`. Let's take a deeper look at what this method does:

  The `CORBA.Object` contains the required method that would allow the conversion of the stringified object reference, the IOR to an instance of `CORBA.Object`. This is what occurs in the method:

  ```
  org.omg.CORBA.Object _temp =_orb.string_to_object(t_registry_ior);
  ```

- When the object reference is retrieved from the IOR, it needs to be safely cast into the appropriate object reference. In this case, the `_temp` object reference that is defined in the previous code needs to be cast into an instance of `iorr.registry`. This can be accomplished by invoking `narrow` on the helper class provided for the target class. IDL to Java always generates helper classes for the interfaces. These follow a simple code convention: Take the name of the interface and add the word `Helper` to it, and you have the name for the helper.
- In this case, you need the assistance of `iorr.registryHelper`. Invoking the method `narrow` on the helper returns a safely cast instance of the registry object reference. At this point, you should have a valid instance of the `IORRegistry` object reference. You are now equipped to make your invocations to test the implementation of the registry interface. The remaining methods test the implementation of the registry interfaces. Keep in mind that the `registry.register()` takes an instance of `iorr.registryPackage.entry`, and the `registry.fetch()` takes an instance of `iorr.registryPackage.entryHolder`. This difference is because, for the former in the IDL for the registry, you specified that the parameter is to be passed as an `in` parameter, and for the `fetch` operation, the parameter is specified as `inout`. `inout` support in Java is mapped to a holder class.

TIP

Always ensure that a remote invocation is made in the context of error handling. Of course, this should be standard practice with any implementation that has error support. This is necessary in CORBA, because if something does go wrong remotely, the application must be capable of handling the faulty condition gracefully.

This completes the implementation of the IOR interoperability component.

Summary

CORBA was designed since version 2 for broad-based interoperability. To this extent, a clear distinction is made in terms of its underlying protocols. CORBA 2.0 specified two broad-transport, independent protocols: the GIOP or General Interoperability Protocol, and the ESIOPs or Environment Specific Protocols. A TCP transport that implements GIOP is known as IIOP, the Internet Inter-ORB Protocol. This protocol implementation is mandatory for any CORBA 2.0–compliant ORB.

IIOP allows interoperability between different ORBs. This interoperability can be achieved through bridges. There are two types of bridges: a half bridge and a full bridge. CORBA 2.0 also specifies the mechanism that allows the conversion of an object reference into a string format. This format is known as the Interoperable Object Reference (IOR). Objects sitting on one ORB can be converted to an IOR and exchanged with another ORB to achieve interoperability.

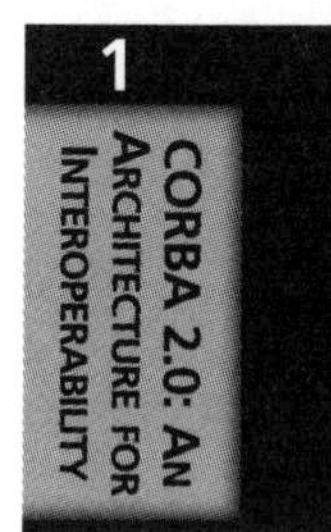

CHAPTER 2

IIOP and E-Commerce

IN THIS CHAPTER

Large organizations have a multiplicity of information technology architectures. Under those circumstances, it is unreasonable to assume a homogeneous ORB environment. It is likely that an ORB most suited for the environment would be present. There could be a specialized ORB for the mainframe, one for the desktop client/server environment, and so on.

If the Internet is taken into consideration, homogeneity should surely be out of the question. The Internet is the most powerful testbed to prove the promise of CORBA interoperability. In this chapter, you use IIOP over the Internet/intranet to connect complex e-commerce solutions over IIOP.

This example will not attempt to build anything as complex as a bridge. Nevertheless, the application will be rather involved and complex. This is by choice, because CORBA solutions are not for the fainthearted or the unskilled. Before we dive into the internals of the problem and the proposed solution, let's look at the environments we are going to use.

The application uses VisiBroker 3.3. The solution will be built using Java. This setup brings to focus a number of CORBA features. This example demonstrates that CORBA is platform-neutral and language-independent. In this context, it is desirable to show the synergy between Java and CORBA.

I will also show how you can use a multiplicity of development environments with CORBA. A number of IDEs will be used to build both client-side and server-side applications.

CORBA and Java

Perhaps inadvertently, there has been some undue confusion about Java and CORBA. Always remember that CORBA is a *cross-platform* technology, and Java is a *multiplatform* solution. CORBA thrives in a heterogeneous environment, and Java aspires to be in a homogeneous one. Java solves the portability problem through the application of its Virtual Machine implementations, and CORBA is adept at solving problems of integration.

If you consider that most information technology problems relate to the ones involving portability and integration, it stands to reason that Java and CORBA are ideal for the vast majority of problems that involve integration and portability. Within this frame work, the example highlights Java's power of *portability* and the potential for clear and transparent *integration* that is inherent in CORBA.

> **NOTE**
>
> All the Java code will be 100 percent pure so that it will run on any Javasoft-compatible JVMs. My own test environment runs on OS2 and Windows NT.

Cookies Cannot Cut It for Long

The Internet is an interconnected Web of HTML and CGI applications. The power and flexibility of the platform comes from its underlying protocol, HTTP. This TCP/IP-based protocol is a connectionless application-level protocol. By this, I mean that the server/client relationship is based on a request/response mechanism, with the server being stateless. That is a roundabout way of saying that the server, in this case a Web server, does not care who the client is or where it is making the request from.

This type of architecture is intentional. The explosive growth (read scalability) of the Internet can be directly attributed to this feature. But there is one drawback. A stateless server is unsuited for complex transactions. Transactions require state, which means that the client can be tracked through various stages of its interaction with the server.

Consider a proto–e-commerce site such as `www.cbooks.com` or `www.amazon.com`. Every time a book is added to a shopping cart, the system has to remember what was bought and who bought it. The system does so admirably. But it does so by delegating the responsibility for maintaining state to the client through the agency of *cookies*. This is not such a bad thing, as demonstrated by the impressive growth of companies offering such services.

Some of you might have noticed that the term *proto–e-commerce* was used to describe such solutions. The term was intentional, considering that such setups become cumbersome and unworkable as soon as an attempt is made to *integrate* such solutions with others.

Consider the scenario of booking and buying an airline ticket over the Web. There are many airlines offering such services right now, using HTTP-based transactions. But such solutions are only partial, because there is little or no integration of the solution beyond the Web server. If you could *componentize* this solution and use CORBA to integrate the components, you could have a wall-to-wall e-commerce solution. A wall-to-wall solution is a system that could be envisaged as a group of subsystems: one for searching, another for booking, yet another for paying, and so forth. These would work all the way from one end of the "wall," where a potential buyer searches for a flight and books a seat, to the other end, with the client paying for it. When it's paid, the transaction is recorded in a number of places: first with the Internet company that provided the service, then with the airline company where the booking was made, and finally with the bank where the money will be transferred from one account into *many*. Such an approach has the benefit of each part being designed by domain specialists, such as Yahoo, offering the search services. Airlines know everything about airplanes, so they would be the perfect party to offer their reservations systems over the Internet. Who knows more about money and transactions than the banks? A clever bank would expose its back-end payment systems to the Web so that monitory transactions components could be reused by anybody willing to pay for it.

SOAR will be a prototype for such a solution. Its goal will be to illustrate the benefits and aesthetics of integrated e-commerce solutions and the power of a platform-independent operating environment. Each section will end with another part of SOAR being built. The hope is to learn about some of the issues that real applications face. The application will be intentionally complex and involved to bring forth the problems that have to be tackled. This complexity nevertheless should not obscure the fact that CORBA development is simple.

Analysis and Design of the SOAR System

A through and robust analysis is a prerequisite for any software project. CORBA does not minimize this. As much as I would like to offer an exhaustive analysis of the SOAR domain, it is best left to another book. But I would like to take the opportunity to emphasize the importance of object-oriented analysis and design (OOA/D)—especially the design.

Although I have stated that CORBA does not impose any new constraints on the analysis phase of software development, it does limit your design. It must be pointed out that CORBA does not specify things such as reliability, fault tolerance, or any other such quality-of-service criteria. These are essentially up to the ORB vendors.

Even then, such things are not givens, but your design should manifest these requirements. A badly designed distributed application has the potential to be your worst nightmare, because, more often than not, you have very little control of things when they do go wrong. This is typical for any piece of software. Imagine if things go wrong on the other side of the world, and your piece of architecture depends on it. You can hardly call up people in the middle of the night and expect support!

ORBs that offer quality-of-service features are coming out, so at least you can look forward to a reasonable level of fault tolerance. Nevertheless, there is no excuse for shoddy design. Enough said about OOA/D. Let's lay down some of the ground rules. SOAR has a number of requirements as well as constraints. Alas, constraint analysis is beyond the scope of this book. I will, nevertheless, mention here what I mean by constraints. These are systems attributes, something that is usually confused with systems functionality. By that I mean, the user friendliness of the GUI, system response time, and so forth. These are worthy goals in themselves, but they don't really have anything to do with SOAR's goals. So for the time being, I will ignore all such constraints and describe the system only in terms of what is required for interoperability and effectively delivering the prototype with the book.

Analysis and Design of SOAR in a Nutshell

As stated earlier, this chapter is meant to be neither exhaustive nor complete, because the primary purpose of this chapter is to show the issues relating to a complex application.

What SOAR Should Do

The SOAR system should offer a number of subsolutions in the context of the overall package. They can be broadly identified as follows:

- Provide the ability for a potential passenger to search the flight schedules by various constraints.
- After a flight has been identified, enable the passenger to book a particular seat on the selected flight.
- Enable a client to pay for the booking using credit cards.

Within the overall architecture for the system, this functionality could be analyzed and designed separately and built independently. This approach will be taken in this book.

The different parts of SOAR correspond to the broad requirements that have been identified previously. They point to the initial requirements of three services that the SOAR back-end would have to provide: one for searching for flights, one for reserving tickets, and one for buying tickets. Let's tackle the reservation requirements first.

The SOAR Reservations

The reservation requirements should do essentially two things: enable a customer to reserve a seat, and, if required, enable the same or some other person to cancel an existing reservation. The following is such an interface:

```
#include "factory.idl"
module Reservations{
    interface Flight{
        enum status{open,full};
        struct seat{
            string id;
            status availability;
        };
        readonly attribute string name;
        readonly attribute float cost;
        readonly attribute string flightNumber;
        readonly attribute string date;
        readonly attribute string time;
        readonly attribute short capacity;
        readonly attribute string from;
```

```
        readonly attribute string to;
        void reserveSeat(in string id,
                         in Factory::Object::Person passenger);
        void cancelSeat(in string id);
    };
};
```

Most of the Flight interface is just read-only attributes. This means that the IDL pre-compiler will only generate accessor methods for these attributes. These attributes will be initialized by some external process; in our case, the server that holds the flight object will do this setup to initialize the state of the aircraft. After the state is initialized, a customer cannot change the state of the flight; he or she can only read it. The only mutable attribute in the preceding interface is the seat. The seat can have an identifier and a flag announcing the status of the seat.

Further on, the interface defines two operations: one for reserving the seat, the other for canceling a reserved seat. Beyond that, the flight interface does not do anything. The interface has to be compiled and implemented. Invoke the following command on the idl2java pre-compiler:

```
prompt$> idl2Java -no_comments -no_tie search.idl
```

We now have the implement the Flight interface.

The Flight Interface Implementation

The Flight interface implementation should adhere to several design constraints. Because the space on the airplane is finite, it is natural that this space can run out. The design should accommodate this aspect. A seat should not be capable of being reserved more than once. This is a requirement that is stated implicitly. Beyond this, the requirements on the interface are modest. These requirements are implemented, as shown in Listing 2.1.

LISTING 2.1 THE RESERVATION COMPONENT

```
package Reservations;
import Reservations.FlightPackage.*;
import java.util.*;

public class Reservations extends Reservations._FlightImplBase {

  private String name = null;
  private String flightNumber = null;
  private float cost;
  private String date = null;
  private String time = null;
  private short capacity;
  private String from = null;
```

```
private String to = null;
private com.objectspace.jgl.Stack aircraft =
                    new com.objectspace.jgl.Stack();
private com.objectspace.jgl.Stack reservations =
                    new com.objectspace.jgl.Stack();
private ReservationListener listener = null;

public Reservations() {
  super();
}

public Reservations(String name,
                    String flightNumber,
                    float cost,
                    String date,
                    String time,
                    short capacity,
                    String from,
                    String to){
  super(name);

  this.name = name;
  this.flightNumber = flightNumber;
  this.cost = cost;
  this.date = date;
  this.time = time;
  this.capacity = capacity;
  this.from = from;
  this.to = to;

  seat[] seats = new seat[capacity];

  for(short i = 0; i< capacity; i++){
    seats[i] = new seat(new Short(i).toString(),status.open);
    aircraft.add(seats[i]);
  }
}

public void reserveSeat(
  java.lang.String id,
  Factory.ObjectPackage.Person passenger
) {
  for (Enumeration e = aircraft.elements() ; e.hasMoreElements() ;) {
    seat temp_ = (seat)e.nextElement();
    if(temp_.id == id){
      temp_.availability = status.full;
      reservations.push(new reservation(temp_,passenger));
      aircraft.remove(e);
    }
  }
```

continues

LISTING 2.1 CONTINUED

```
    ReservationEvent event =
        new ReservationEvent(this,ReservationEvent.SeatReserverd);
    sendMessage(event);
  }

  public void cancelSeat(
    java.lang.String id
  ) {
    for (Enumeration e = reservations.elements() ;
         e.hasMoreElements() ;) {
      reservation temp_ = (reservation)e.nextElement();
      if(temp_.a_seat.id == id){
        temp_.a_seat.availability = status.open;
        aircraft.push(temp_);
        reservations.remove(e);
      }

    ReservationEvent event = new
➥ReservationEvent(this,ReservationEvent.SeatCanceled);
    sendMessage(event);
  }

  public java.lang.String name() {
    return name;
  }
  public float cost() {
    return cost;
  }
  public java.lang.String flightNumber() {
    return flightNumber;
  }
  public java.lang.String date() {
    return date;
  }
  public java.lang.String time() {
    return time;
  }
  public short capacity() {
    return (short)aircraft.size();
  }
  public java.lang.String from() {
    return from;
  }
  public java.lang.String to() {
    return to;
  }

  public void addReservationListener(ReservationListener listener){
    this.listener = listener;
```

```
  }

  public void sendMessage(ReservationEvent anEvent){
      listener.reservationStatus(anEvent);
  }
}

class reservation{
  public seat a_seat;
  public Factory.ObjectPackage.Person a_passenger;

  reservation(seat s_, Factory.ObjectPackage.Person p_){
    a_seat = s_;
    a_passenger = p_;
  }
}
```


The manner in which the `Reservation` application is envisioned is to enable an application to construct as many aircraft objects as required inside the server. Each aircraft object represents an object that can be used to reserve a seat. In this context, a potential passenger should be able to search for an aircraft using some criteria. The search facility implemented later uses a search server. For now, let's look a little closer at the implementation of the `Reservation` interface.

The `Reservation` implementation's primary methods are the `reserveSeat()` and `cancelSeat()` methods. To reserve a seat, a client uses the former; the latter is used to cancel a seat that had been reserved. By some means, every aircraft is allocated a specified number of seats. This means that even though an aircraft has 290 seats, for example, under certain circumstances a capacity less than this number is actually used inside an aircraft.

The seats and the internal data structure of the aircraft are initialized in the constructor. The constructor is the other important method that the reservation object uses. The seats are the key to reservations. The seat is a structure that is represented as the following class, which is generated by the IDL pre-compiler:

```
package Reservations.FlightPackage;
  final public class seat {
    public java.lang.String id;
    public Reservations.FlightPackage.status availability;
    public seat() {
    }
    public seat(
      java.lang.String id,
      Reservations.FlightPackage.status availability
    ) {
      this.id = id;
```

```
      this.availability = availability;
    }
    public java.lang.String toString() {
      org.omg.CORBA.Any any = org.omg.CORBA.ORB.init().create_any();
      Reservations.FlightPackage.seatHelper.insert(any, this);
      return any.toString();
    }
  }
```

When a seat is reserved, its availability status is set to `status.full`; when it is cancelled, it can be set to `status.open`. The seats are initialized in the following manner in the constructor:

```
..
..
seat[] seats = new seat[capacity];
        for(short i = 0; i< capacity; i++){
      seats[i] = new seat(new Short(i).toString(),status.open);
      aircraft.add(seats[i]);
    }
..
..
```

The seats are initialized in an array. They are initialized to the capacity that an external process passes as a capacity parameter inside the reservation server's constructor. When the seats are allocated, they are added to an instance of a JGL stack object named `aircraft`. The `aircraft` object represents the seats that are available in an aircraft.

The `reserveSeat()` method is passed two parameters: a `String` identifier and an instance of a `Passenger` (to be specified later). The client invokes this method to reserve a seat, the identifier being the seat number the client wants to reserve. In terms of the implementation, the reservation object first validates the existence of such a seat in the aircraft. If an instance is present, the implementation reserves this seat by moving the seat, after setting the state of the object, to another stack object called `reservations`. Over time, the number of seats inside the `aircraft` stack should go down, and the number of seats present in the `reservations` collection should go up.

I took this approach because it seems easier to remove an object from the `reservations` stack if a cancel operation is called on the `Reservation` interface. Both `reserveSeat()` and `cancelSeat()` generate an event, the `ReservationEvent`. This enables us to create a loose coupling between some GUI that we are yet to build and this object.

The `ReservationEvent` Class and Interface

The `Reservation` implementation defines a set of event-related classes that is used to couple the GUI with this class. The `Reservation` design specifies a listener interface that can be used by any party to listen in on event when a `ReservationEvent` takes place. The following is the interface:

```
package Reservations;
import java.util.*;

public interface ReservationListener extends EventListener{
    public void reservationStatus(ReservationEvent anEvent);
}
```

In this case, it is the GUI that is going to use this interface so that the `Reservation` implementation can notify it when an event takes place. The corresponding `Event` class is used by the `reservations` object to notify listeners when a `ReservationEvent` takes place. Here is the `ReservationEvent` class:

```
package Reservations;
import java.util.*;

public class ReservationEvent extends EventObject{

  static final  int SeatReserverd = 1;
  static final  int SeatCanceled = 2;
  private  int id = 0;

  ReservationEvent(Object source, int eventId) {
    super(source);
    id = eventId;
  }

  int getID() {
    return id;
  }
}
```

When a `ReservationEvent` takes place—for instance, a reserve event or a cancel event, the aforementioned methods invoke the following method:

```
...
...
ReservationEvent event =
       new ReservationEvent(this,ReservationEvent.SeatCanceled);
    sendMessage(event);
...
...
```

The object will instantiate a `ReservationEvent` object and fire the `sendMessage()` method. `sendMessage` invokes the instances that have registered with the object for notification; in this case, such objects have to implement the `ReservationListener` interface. This code is shown here:

```
public void sendMessage(ReservationEvent anEvent){
      listener.reservationStatus(anEvent);
  }
```

This concludes the implementation of the `Flight` interface. Now, let's construct a server to hold the object reference for service.

The `ReservationServer` Implementation

Listing 2.2 illustrates a typical implementation of a CORBA server. It uses Java Swing class for the GUI. Here, you separate the server from the GUI that acts as a front-end to the server. This can be accomplished if you implement a server class as an object that is capable of running as a thread inside the GUI object. This enables the GUI to respond to interactions with the user at the same time that it is providing service to the client. The server code is shown first and then the GUI code.

LISTING 2.2 THE FLIGHT SERVER

```
package Reservations;

public class Server implements Runnable{
  private ReservationServer gui;
  private org.omg.CORBA.ORB orb;
  private org.omg.CORBA.BOA boa;
  private Reservations[] rs = null;
  Search.TimeTable SearchEngine = null;

  Server(ReservationServer rs_){
    gui = rs_;
  }

  public void run(){
    orb = org.omg.CORBA.ORB.init();
    boa = orb.BOA_init();
    rs = new Reservations[2];
    java.util.Date date = new java.util.Date();
    try{
      com.visigenic.vbroker.URLNaming.Resolver resolv =
      com.visigenic.vbroker.URLNaming.ResolverHelper.narrow(
        orb.resolve_initial_references("URLNamingResolver"));
      org.omg.CORBA.Object obj =
       resolv.locate("http://localhost:15000/timetable.ior");
      SearchEngine = Search.TimeTableHelper.narrow(obj);
    }
    catch(Exception e) {
      gui.DisplayMessage(e.toString());
    }
    for(int i = 0; i < 2; i++){
```

```
      String hour = new Integer(date.getHours() + i).toString();
      String minutes = new Integer(date.getMinutes()).toString();
      String time = hour + " : " +  minutes;
      String[] from = {"London","Los Angles"};
      String[] to = {"Warsaw", "Rome"};

      rs[i] = new Reservations(
"Flight " + new Integer(i).toString()
,"LM"+ new Integer(i).toString()
                    ,(float)450.00
                    ,date.toGMTString()
                    ,time
                    ,(short)150
                    ,from[i]
                    ,to[i] );

      rs[i].addReservationListener(gui);
      boa.obj_is_ready(rs[i]);
      gui.DisplayMessage(rs[i] + " is ready.");
    }
    try{
     SearchEngine.RegisterFlight(rs);
    }
    catch(org.omg.CORBA.SystemException e){
      gui.DisplayMessage(e.toString());
    }
    boa.impl_is_ready();
  }

  public void stop(){
    for(int i = 0; i < 2; i++){
      try{
        SearchEngine.RemoveEntry(rs[i].flightNumber());
      }
      catch(org.omg.CORBA.SystemException e){
        gui.DisplayMessage(e.toString());
      }
      catch(Exception ex){
        gui.DisplayMessage(ex.toString());
      }
    }
    for(int j=0;j<rs.length;j++)
    boa.deactivate_obj(rs[i]);
    orb.shutdown();
    gui.DisplayMessage("Reservation Server Shutdown.");
  }
}
```

The `ReservationServer` initializes the `reservations` objects that implement the `Flight` interface. If a more real-world scenario is required, the `reservations` objects can be initialized using data that is retrieved from a database. In this case, you just hold the `reservations` objects in an array.

```
private Reservations[] rs = null;
```

The following line of code may seem perplexing right now, but the implementation uses VisiBroker URL Naming to locate a search engine to register flight details. Let's implement the `Search` interface next. URL Naming is a simple facility VisiBroker provides that can be used by a client to retrieve an IOR using an URL. VisiBroker URL Naming is covered in Chapter 17, "VisiBroker Caffeine." When the object reference to the search engine is retrieved, the `ReservationServer` can register the flight details with it:

```
org.omg.CORBA.Object obj =
➥resolv.locate("http://localhost:15000/timetable.ior");
         SearchEngine = Search.TimeTableHelper.narrow(obj);
```

Before that can be accomplished, the `reservations` objects have to be constructed. In this case, two such objects are constructed. The first reservation object represents a flight from London to Warsaw and the second, from Los Angles to Rome. Both flights have a capacity of 10 seats:

```
rs[i] = new Reservations("Flight " + new Integer(i).toString()
                               ,"LM"+ new Integer(i).toString()
                               ,(float)450.00 /*Cost*/
                               ,date.toGMTString()
                              ,time
                              ,(short)10 /*capacity*/
                              ,from[i]
                              ,to[i] );
```

When the `reservations` objects are constructed, an instance of the GUI object is registered with the `reservations` object as a `ReservationEvent` listener; then they are registered with with the Basic Object Adapter (BOA), and then with the search engine:

```
rs[i].addReservationListener(gui); //Event Listener
        boa.obj_is_ready(rs[i]); //BOA registeration
    ...
    ...
SearchEngine.RegisterFlight(rs); //Search Registration
```

Finally, the `boa.impl_is_ready()` method is called to notify the BOA that the server is read to receive invocations from a client.

All the preceding implementation takes place inside the `run()` method. This means that it will execute when the `start()` method is called on a thread. Similarly, when the `stop()` method is called on the thread, the reverse of what we did in the `run()` method takes place. First, the flight details are removed from the search engine. Then the object references are deregistered from the BOA, and finally the instance of the BOA is shut down. Now we are ready to build the GUI.

The ReservationServer GUI

Java Swing classes are used to construct a user interface that monitors the internal state of the reservation object references. Primarily, it should display `Reservation` events as and when they occur. This code is shown in Listing 2.3.

LISTING 2.3 THE `ReservationServer` INTERFACE

```
package Reservations;

import java.awt.*;
import com.sun.java.swing.*;
import org.omg.CORBA.*;
import java.awt.event.*;
import borland.jbcl.layout.*;

public class ReservationServer extends JPanel
              implements ReservationListener{
  JButton StartButton = new JButton();
  JButton StopButton = new JButton();
  Thread serverThread = null;
  Server rs = null;
  JPanel jPanel1 = new JPanel();
  JScrollPane jScrollPane1 = new JScrollPane();
  JTextArea StatusArea = new JTextArea();
  PaneLayout paneLayout1 = new PaneLayout();

  public ReservationServer(){
    try  {
      jbInit();
    }
    catch (Exception e) {
      e.printStackTrace();
    }
  }

  private void jbInit() throws Exception {
    this.setLayout(null);
    StartButton.setText("Start");
    StartButton.addMouseListener(new java.awt.event.MouseAdapter() {
      public void mouseClicked(MouseEvent e) {
        StartButton_mouseClicked(e);
      }
    });
    StopButton.setText("Stop");
    jPanel1.setLayout(paneLayout1);
    jPanel1.setBounds(new Rectangle(215, 236, 173, 27));
    jScrollPane1.setBounds(new Rectangle(12, 12, 377, 219));
    StopButton.addMouseListener(new java.awt.event.MouseAdapter() {
```

continues

LISTING 2.3 CONTINUED

```
      public void mouseClicked(MouseEvent e) {
        StopButton_mouseClicked(e);
      }
    });
    this.setLayout(null);
    this.add(jPanel1, null);
    jPanel1.add(StartButton, new PaneConstraints("StartButton",
                   "StartButton", PaneConstraints.ROOT, 1.0f));
    jPanel1.add(StopButton, new PaneConstraints(
              "StopButton",
              "StartButton",
              PaneConstraints.RIGHT,
              0.45679012f));
    this.add(jScrollPane1, null);
    jScrollPane1.getViewport().add(StatusArea, null);
  }

  public void reservationStatus(ReservationEvent anEvent){
    switch(anEvent.getID()){
      case ReservationEvent.SeatReserverd:
 DisplayMessage ("New Reservation Made.");
        break;
      case ReservationEvent.SeatCanceled:
 DisplayMessage("Reservation Cancelled.");
        break;
      default:
    }
  }

  void StartButton_mouseClicked(MouseEvent e) {
    if(rs == null){
      rs = new Server(this);
      serverThread = new Thread(rs);
      serverThread.start();
    }
    this.DisplayMessage("Reservation Server Initialized.");
  }

  void StopButton_mouseClicked(MouseEvent e) {
    if(rs != null){
      rs.stop();
      rs = null;
    }
  }

  void DisplayMessage(String msg){
    java.util.Date date = new java.util.Date();
    StatusArea.append(date.toGMTString() +": "+ msg + "\n");
  }
}
```

The essential nature of the GUI is that it implements the `ReservationListener` interface. It is through this interface that the `reservations` object communicates with the user interface. The implementation of this interface is very simple, depending on the message ID the class invokes the `DisplayMessage` method to output a string to the display area. The corresponding implementation is shown in the following lines of code:

```
public void reservationStatus(ReservationEvent anEvent){
    switch(anEvent.getID()){
      case ReservationEvent.SeatReserverd:
 DisplayMessage ("New Reservation Made.");
        break;
      case ReservationEvent.SeatCanceled:
 DisplayMessage("Reservation Cancelled.");
        break;
      default:
    }
  }
```

The server handles two `ReservationEvents`: `SeatReserved` and `SeatCanceled`.

The user interface uses two command buttons: a Start button and a Stop button. When the `start` command is issued, the class constructs the `ReservationServer` on a thread and launches it:

```
rs = new Server(this);
         serverThread = new Thread(rs);
         serverThread.start();
```

The `stop` command terminates the thread by invoking `stop()` on it.

We have now completed the implementation of the `Reservation` interface. The complete implementation consisted of implementing the `Reservation` interface, constructing a `Server` class to host the objects themselves, and providing a GUI to provide visual cues to the user. The exact manner in which to launch the server will be explained after we have constructed the entire application. Figure 2.1 shows the server running.

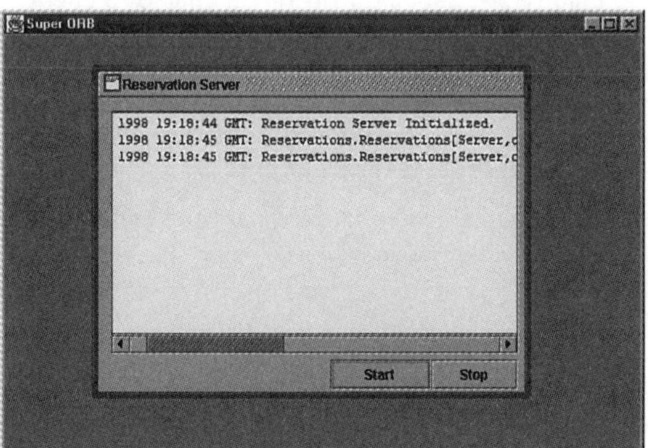

FIGURE 2.1
The `Reservation-Server` *user interface.*

We are now ready to implement the search engine.

The SOAR Search Engine

The SOAR search engine is nothing complicated. On the user end, it should enable a customer to search for a potential aircraft by some criteria. In the ideal situation, a customer would search by whatever criteria seems appropriate to the customer. In this case, you have to keep things simple to not complicate the overall design of SOAR.

You can achieve this simplicity if you narrow down the list of criteria a customer can search by to the barest minimum. In this case, let's enable the customer to search only by the departure point and the destination point. The interface that would enable you to build such a search service is given in the following code:

```
#include "reservations.idl"

module Search{
    interface TimeTable{
        typedef sequence<Reservations::Flight> FlightList;
        void RegisterFlight(in FlightList TimeTableEntries);
        void RemoveEntry(in string FlightNumber);
        FlightList search(in string From,
                          in string To,
                          in string Date,
                          in string Time);
    };
};
```

The `Search` module specifies an interface that is named `TimeTable`. This interface represents the external face of the search engine. The interface itself specifies three operations. The first is `RegisterFlight()`. This operation takes in a sequence of `Reservation::Flight` objects. This enables the instance of `TimeTable` objects to return instances of `Flight` objects to the client that is using its search facility. `RemoveEntry` is another administration operation that enables a registered flight object to be removed from the `TimeTable`. Finally, the `Search()` operation enables a client to search by a number of parameters, such as destination and departure points, dates, time of day, or all of these criteria. Let's look at one possible manner of implementing this interface.

The `TimeTable` Implementation

The `TimeTable` interface is implemented in a class named `Schedule`. Its implementation is given in Listing 2.4.

LISTING 2.4 THE Search COMPONENT

```
package Search;
import java.util.*;

public class Schedule extends Search._TimeTableImplBase {

  private com.objectspace.jgl.Stack timetable =
                     new com.objectspace.jgl.Stack();
  private TimeTableListener listener;

  public Schedule(String name) {
    super(name);
  }

  public void RegisterFlight(
    Reservations.Flight[] TimeTableEntries
  ) {
    for(int i = 0; i < TimeTableEntries.length; i++){
      timetable.push(TimeTableEntries[i]);
      TimeTableEvent event = new TimeTableEvent(this,
         TimeTableEvent.RegisterEvent,"Registering Flight: "
        + TimeTableEntries[i].flightNumber() +
        "Registering From: " + TimeTableEntries[i].from()
        + "Registering To: " +  TimeTableEntries[i].to());
      this.sendMessage(event);
    }

  }

  public void RemoveEntry(
    java.lang.String FlightNumber
  ) {
   for (Enumeration e = timetable.elements() ; e.hasMoreElements() ;) {
      Reservations.Flight temp_ = (Reservations.Flight)e.nextElement();
      if(temp_.flightNumber() == FlightNumber){
        timetable.remove(e);
      }
    }
   TimeTableEvent event = new TimeTableEvent(this,
        TimeTableEvent.DeRegisterEvent,"Removing Flight: "
        + FlightNumber);
   this.sendMessage(event);
  }

  public Reservations.Flight[] search(
    java.lang.String From,
    java.lang.String To,
    java.lang.String Date,
    java.lang.String Time
  ) {
```

continues

LISTING 2.4 CONTINUED

```
    com.objectspace.jgl.Stack tempBag = new com.objectspace.jgl.Stack();
    for (Enumeration e = timetable.elements() ; e.hasMoreElements() ;) {
       Reservations.Flight temp_ = (Reservations.Flight)e.nextElement();
       if(From.equalsIgnoreCase(temp_.from())
               && To.equalsIgnoreCase(temp_.to())){
         tempBag.push(temp_);
       }
    }

    Reservations.Flight[] ret_ = new Reservations.Flight[tempBag.size()];

    if(tempBag.size() > 0){
      Enumeration en = tempBag.elements();
      for(int i = 0; i < ret_.length; i++){
        ret_[i] = (Reservations.Flight)en.nextElement();
      }
      String msg = "Found Flight From:" + From + " To:" + To;
      TimeTableEvent event = new TimeTableEvent(this,
                             TimeTableEvent.SearchEvent,msg);
      this.sendMessage(event);
    }
    else{
      String msg = "Flight From:" + From + " To:" + To + "Not Found";
      TimeTableEvent event = new TimeTableEvent(this,
                             TimeTableEvent.SearchEvent,msg);
      this.sendMessage(event);
    }
    return ret_;
  }

  public void addScheduleListener(TimeTableListener listener){
    this.listener = listener;
  }

  public void sendMessage(TimeTableEvent anEvent){
      listener.TimeTableStatus(anEvent);
  }
}
```

Just like the `Flight` implementation, the `TimeTable` implementation also uses events to couple GUI with its states. Beyond that, let's look at the implementation of the operations in a little detail. The first method that is implemented is the `Register()` method. This method is passed an array of `Flight` objects from the client. This enables a client to construct any number of flight objects at its end and then pass these in an array to the `Schedule` implementation. The implementation is straightforward; it uses a JGL stack to represent a list of flights that are in its schedule. A more efficient and thorough extension of this scheme should also be just as trivial. The stack object in question is named `timetable`. When an element of the incoming array is added to the stack, the `Schedule` object generates a `TimeTable` event that is passed back to registered listeners. You will look at the event-related interface and class a little later in the chapter. The essential statement that deals with the registration is shown here:

```
timetable.push(TimeTableEntries[i]);
```

The next operation that is implemented is the `RemoveEntry()` method. This method is passed an identifier that is used to locate the flight object in the `timetable` stack. The search is carried out by constructing an enumeration and checking whether the parameter that is passed to the implementation matches an attribute of an object in the stack. The following is the associated code:

```
Reservations.Flight temp_ = (Reservations.Flight)e.nextElement();
          if(temp_.flightNumber() == FlightNumber){
            timetable.remove(e);
```


The removal of an entry also generates an `TimeTableEvent` that is fired to all registered listeners. Next is the core of the `TimeTable`—the operation that enables a client to search for an aircraft by some parameter. The `search()` method is passed four parameters. The four parameters correspond to the following lines of code:

```
public Reservations.Flight[] search(
    java.lang.String From,
    java.lang.String To,
    java.lang.String Date,
    java.lang.String Time
  )
```

As with the removal of a registered item, the essence of the search algorithm is similar. The implementation enumerates over the elements of the stack and uses the accessor method in the `Flight` interface to check whether a searched flight if found in the `Schedule`:

```
if(From.equalsIgnoreCase(temp_.from()) && To.equalsIgnoreCase(temp_.to()))
```

The search implementation in this case searches on the departure point and the destination points only. All the elements in the timetable that match this criteria are added to an array. This array constitutes the result of the search. This array is passed back to the client. As with the other two methods, the search also generates a `TimeTableEvent` to the registered listeners. The next sections explain the classes that help specify the events that the `Schedule` class generates.

The `TimeTableEvent` Class and Interface

The event listener interface needs to be implemented by the classes that are interested in receiving events from the `Schedule` object:

```
package Search;
import java.util.*;

public interface TimeTableListener extends EventListener{
    public void TimeTableStatus(TimeTableEvent anEvent);
}
```

The interface uses a `TimeTableEvent` class that encapsulates the event itself:

```
package Search;
import java.util.*;

public class TimeTableEvent extends EventObject{

 static final  int SearchEvent = 1;
 static final  int DeRegisterEvent = 2;
 static final  int RegisterEvent = 3;
 private int id = 0;
 private String msg = null;

  TimeTableEvent(Object source, int eventId, String msg) {
    super(source);
    id = eventId;
    this.msg = msg;
  }

  int getID() {
    return id;
  }

  String toString(){
    return msg;
  }
}
```

The preceding event class is slightly different from the `ReservationEvent` in terms of the internal data structure. This class contains a `String` object that encapsulates the actual event message. The `Schedule` class goes uses the event class in the following manner:

```
String msg = "Flight From:" + From + " To:" + To + "Not Found";
         TimeTableEvent event =
        new TimeTableEvent(this, TimeTableEvent.SearchEvent,msg);
         this.sendMessage(event);
```

The preceding event is generated when the `search()` method is invoked by a client. The event is fired at objects that have registered with the `Schedule` class using the following method:

```
public void addScheduleListener(TimeTableListener listener){
    this.listener = listener;
  }
```

In the case of both the `Reservation` class and the `Schedule` class, only one object is registered as listener. From the design, this notification facility is only used by the GUI to be notified when some interface event occurs. If more than one listener has to be notified, a collection object such as a vector has to be used to hold the reference to all the listeners.

We are now ready to implement the `TimeTable`Server. As with the `Schedule` class, the `TimeTable`Server is also implemented as a thread in a separate class. This enables you to separate the server logic from the presentation logic. The server code is shown in Listing 2.5.

LISTING 2.5 THE `TimeTableServer` THREAD

```
package Search;

public class TimeTableServer implements Runnable{

  private SearchServer gui;
  private org.omg.CORBA.ORB orb;
  private org.omg.CORBA.BOA boa;
  private Schedule timetable = null;

 TimeTableServer (SearchServer rs_){
    gui = rs_;
  }

  public void run(){
    orb = org.omg.CORBA.ORB.init();
    boa = orb.BOA_init();
    timetable = new Schedule("TimeTable");
    timetable.addScheduleListener(gui);
    boa.obj_is_ready(timetable);
    com.visigenic.vbroker.URLNaming.Resolver resolver = null;
    try{
      resolver = com.visigenic.vbroker.URLNaming.ResolverHelper.narrow(
                 orb.resolve_initial_references("URLNamingResolver"));
    }
    catch(org.omg.CORBA.ORBPackage.InvalidName ivn){
      gui.DisplayMessage(ivn.toString());
    }
    try{
      resolver.force_register_url(
        "http://localhost:15000/timetable.ior",timetable);
    }
    catch(Exception e) {
      gui.DisplayMessage(e.toString());
    }
    gui.DisplayMessage("TimeTable Server Started.");
    gui.DisplayMessage(timetable + " is ready.");
    boa.impl_is_ready();
```

continues

LISTING 2.5 CONTINUED

```
  }

  public void stop(){
    boa.deactivate_obj(timetable);
    timetable = null;
    orb.shutdown();
    gui.DisplayMessage("TimeTable Server ShutDown.");
  }
}
```

The `TimeTableServer` class implements two methods from the `Runnable` interface: the `run()` method and the `stop()` method. The `run()` method, an instance of the `TimeTable` interface is initialized. This is the `Schedule` class. The GUI object is then registered with the `Schedule` object. In the next step, the BOA is notified that the object reference is ready. The `TimeTableServer` uses VisiBroker URL Naming to advertise its IOR. This IOR is used by the `Reservation` server to register the entire flight object for the search service. These steps are contained in the following lines of code:

```
    timetable = new Schedule("TimeTable");
    timetable.addScheduleListener(gui);
    boa.obj_is_ready(timetable);
...
...
    resolver.force_register_url(
  "http://localhost:15000/timetable.ior",timetable);
...
...
```

The `stop()` method does the reverse of what is done in the `run()` method. The `TimeTableServer` is to be launched inside the GUI object; this class is shown next. The code, as shown in Listing 2.6, is essentially the same as the `Reservation` GUI.

LISTING 2.6 THE `SearchServer` INTERFACE

```
package Search;

import java.awt.*;
import org.omg.CORBA.*;
import java.awt.event.*;
import com.sun.java.swing.*;

public class SearchServer extends JPanel implements TimeTableListener{
  JButton StartButton = new JButton();
  JButton StopButton = new JButton();
  TimeTableServer rs = null;
  private Thread serverThread = null;
```

```
JScrollPane jScrollPane1 = new JScrollPane();
JTextArea StatusArea = new JTextArea();
JPanel jPanel1 = new JPanel();
PaneLayout paneLayout1 = new PaneLayout();

public SearchServer() {
  try {
    jbInit();
  }
  catch (Exception e) {
    e.printStackTrace();
  }
}

private void jbInit() throws Exception {
  this.setLayout(null);
  StartButton.setText("Start");
  StartButton.addMouseListener(new java.awt.event.MouseAdapter() {
    public void mouseClicked(MouseEvent e) {
      StartButton_mouseClicked(e);
    }
  });
  StopButton.setText("Stop");
  StartButton.setSize(50,30);
  jScrollPane1.setBounds(new Rectangle(7, 5, 428, 209));
  jPanel1.setLayout(paneLayout1);
  jPanel1.setBounds(new Rectangle(256, 226, 177, 24));
  StopButton.addMouseListener(new java.awt.event.MouseAdapter() {
    public void mouseClicked(MouseEvent e) {
      StopButton_mouseClicked(e);
    }
  });
  this.setLayout(null);
  this.add(jScrollPane1, null);
  jScrollPane1.getViewport().add(StatusArea, null);
  this.add(jPanel1, null);
  jPanel1.add(StartButton, new PaneConstraints(
      "StartButton",
      "StartButton",
      PaneConstraints.
      ROOT,
      1.0f));
  jPanel1.add(StopButton, new PaneConstraints(
      "StopButton",
      "StartButton",
      PaneConstraints.
      RIGHT,
      0.5185185f));
}
```

continues

LISTING 2.6 CONTINUED

```
  public void TimeTableStatus(TimeTableEvent anEvent){
    switch(anEvent.getID()){
      case TimeTableEvent.SearchEvent:
        this.DisplayMessage("Client Searching.");
        this.DisplayMessage(anEvent.toString());
        break;
      case TimeTableEvent.RegisterEvent:
        this.DisplayMessage("Entry Registered.");
        this.DisplayMessage(anEvent.toString());
        break;
      case TimeTableEvent.DeRegisterEvent:
        this.DisplayMessage("Entry Removed.");
        this.DisplayMessage(anEvent.toString());
        break;
      default:
    }
  }

  void StartButton_mouseClicked(MouseEvent e){
    if(rs == null){
      rs = new TimeTableServer(this);
      serverThread = new Thread(rs);
      serverThread.start();
    }
  }

  void StopButton_mouseClicked(MouseEvent e){
    if(rs != null){
     rs.stop();
     rs = null;
    }
  }

  void DisplayMessage(String msg){
    java.util.Date date = new java.util.Date();
    StatusArea.append(date.toGMTString() +": "+ msg + "\n");
  }
}
```

As with the `Schedule` server, the `SearchServer` implements the listener interface `TimeTableListener`. This means that it has to implement the `TimeTableStatus()` method. The method is passed an event object, and the implementation passes the string content of the event object to the `DisplayMessage()` method to display the message in the GUI.

The `TimeTableServer` itself is constructed and launched in one of the mouse handling methods of the `start` command button. The following code shows the implementation:

```
void StartButton_mouseClicked(MouseEvent e){
    if(rs == null){
      rs = new TimeTableServer(this);
      serverThread = new Thread(rs);
      serverThread.start();
    }
}
```

That concludes the implementation of the `TimeTableServer` and GUI. The executing application, along with the `ReservationServer`, is shown in Figure 2.2.

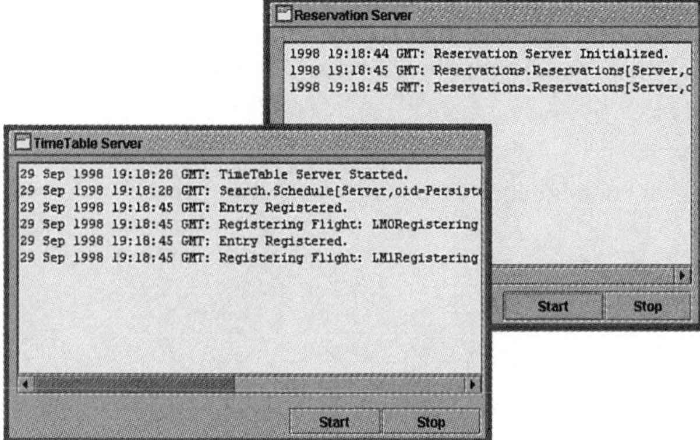

FIGURE 2.2
The `SearchServer` *user interface.*

The SOAR Factory

The SOAR application requires a number of objects to make it work. In the context of making a reservation, for example, you require a passenger object. In making a payment, there are a number of objects that are required. For example, you might require a number of addresses, credit card information, and so forth. It is possible to design all these in the context of the interfaces that have been specified until now; the `Reservation` module could have defined a passenger interface as well. But it might make things a little clearer if I define these things seperately. The following `Factory` interface defines all such concepts:

```
module Factory{

    interface Object{

        struct Person{
            string name;
            short age;
            char gender;
            string email;
        };
```

```
        struct CreditCard{
            string CardType;
            string CardNumber;
            string ExpiryDate;
        };

        struct Address{
            string addressOne;
            string addressTwo;
            string city;
            string stateOrProvince;
            string zipcode;
            string country;
        };
        Person createPassenger(in string name,
                               in short age,
                               in char gender,
                               in string email);
        CreditCard creatCreditCard(in string type,
                                   in string number,
                                   in string expiry);
        Address createAddress(in string addressOne,
                              in string addressTwo,
                              in string city,
                              in string state,
                              in string zip,
                              in string country);
    };
};
```

The `Object` interface defines three structs; `Person`, `Address`, and `CreditCard`. It further specifies three operations. Each of these operations creates and returns an appropriate `struct`. So you have one operation that creates a person, another for the address, and another to create a credit card.

Implementing the `Factory::Object` Interface

The implemetation of these operations is fairly simple. All that an implementation has to do is initialize a `struct` with the parameter that is passed into these operations and return the requested `struct`. The implemention of `Factory::Object` is done in the `Factory` class. The implementation does not maintain any state, so it is very simple, as shown in Listing 2.7.

LISTING 2.7 THE `Factory` COMPONENT

```
package Factory;
public class factory extends Factory._ObjectImplBase {
  public factory() {
```

```
    super();
  }
  public Factory.ObjectPackage.Person createPassenger(
    java.lang.String name,
    short age,
    char gender,
    java.lang.String email
  ) {

    return new Factory.ObjectPackage.Person(name,age,gender,email);
  }
  public Factory.ObjectPackage.CreditCard creatCreditCard(
    java.lang.String type,
    java.lang.String number,
    java.lang.String expiry
  ) {
    return new Factory.ObjectPackage.CreditCard(type,number,expiry);
  }
  public Factory.ObjectPackage.Address createAddress(
    java.lang.String addressOne,
    java.lang.String addressTwo,
    java.lang.String city,
    java.lang.String state,
    java.lang.String zip,
    java.lang.String country
  ) {
    return new Factory.ObjectPackage.Address(addressOne,
                                             addressTwo,
                                             city,
                                             state,
                                             zip,
                                             country);
   }
}
```

OMG IDL `structs` map to Java classes. In terms of the implementation, the `Factory` simply instantiates the appropriate class and returns this class to the client. The code is trivial enough to warrant no further explanation. We can now proceed with the implementation of the `Factory`Server.

The FactoryServer

The `FactoryServer`, like the servers implemented before consists of two classes: one that implements the server itself and the other that just builds the GUI to hold the server. The server code implements the `Runnable` interface so that the GUI class can launch it on a thread. Let's first look at the server code and then the GUI code (see Listing 2.8).

LISTING 2.8 THE `FactoryServer` THREAD

```
package Factory;

class FactoryServer implements Runnable{

  private FactoryServer gui;
  private org.omg.CORBA.ORB orb;
  private org.omg.CORBA.BOA boa;
  private Factory.factory t_factory= new Factory.factory();

  FactoryServer(FactoryServer rs_){
    gui = rs_;
  }

  public void run(){
    orb = org.omg.CORBA.ORB.init();
    boa = orb.BOA_init();
    com.visigenic.vbroker.URLNaming.Resolver resolver = null;
    try{
      resolver = com.visigenic.vbroker.URLNaming.ResolverHelper.narrow(
        orb.resolve_initial_references("URLNamingResolver"));
    }
    catch(org.omg.CORBA.ORBPackage.InvalidName ivn){
      System.out.println(ivn.toString());
    }
    try{
      resolver.force_register_url(
        "http://localhost:15000/factory.ior",t_factory);
      boa.obj_is_ready(t_factory);
      gui.DisplayMessage("Factory Server Started.");
      gui.DisplayMessage(t_factory + " is ready.");
    }
    catch(Exception e) {
      gui.DisplayMessage(e.toString());
    }
    try{
      boa.impl_is_ready();
    }
    catch(org.omg.CORBA.SystemException ex){
      gui.DisplayMessage(ex.toString());
    }
  }
}
```

The code is typical to most CORBA servers. Two things are salient to this code: the instantiation of the `Factory` object and the registration of the `Factory`'s IOR with the VisiBroker URL Naming service. The following shows the instantiation and associated code:

```
private Factory.factory t_factory= new Factory.factory();
...
...
resolver.force_register_url("http://localhost:15000/factory.ior",
                            ➥t_factory);
...
...
```

The URL Naming service is used so that the client can locate a `Factory` using this service to construct the required objects. The `structs` defined in the `Object` interface are primarily going to be used by a client. Next comes the GUI code that launches this server in a thread, as shown in Listing 2.9.

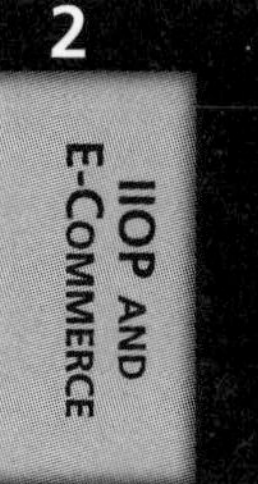

LISTING 2.9 THE FactoryServer INTERFACE

```
public class FactoryServer extends JPanel{
  JScrollPane jScrollPane1 = new JScrollPane();
  JButton StartButton = new JButton();
  JTextArea factoryDisplay = new JTextArea();
  Thread ServerThread;

  public FactoryServer() {
    try  {
      jbInit();
    }
    catch (Exception e) {
      e.printStackTrace();
    }

  }

  private void jbInit() throws Exception {
    this.setLayout(null);
    jScrollPane1.setBounds(new Rectangle(2, 8, 324, 143));
    StartButton.setText("Start");
    StartButton.setBounds(new Rectangle(250, 155, 72, 24));
    StartButton.addMouseListener(new java.awt.event.MouseAdapter() {
      public void mouseClicked(MouseEvent e) {
        StartButton_mouseClicked(e);
      }
    });
    this.add(jScrollPane1, null);
    jScrollPane1.getViewport().add(factoryDisplay, null);
    this.add(StartButton, null);
  }

  void StartButton_mouseClicked(MouseEvent e) {
    FactoryServer factoryserver = new FactoryServer(this);
    ServerThread = new Thread(factoryserver);
```

continues

LISTING 2.9 CONTINUED

```
    ServerThread.start();
  }

  void DisplayMessage(String msg){
    java.util.Date date = new java.util.Date();
    factoryDisplay.append(date.toGMTString() +": "+ msg + "\n");
  }
}
```

The core methods that the GUI implements are again found in the mouse command handler for the Start button. The code instantiates an instance of the `FactoryServer`. This instance isspawned on a thread. Here is the associated code:

```
FactoryServer factoryserver = new FactoryServer(this);
ServerThread = new Thread(factoryserver);
ServerThread.start();
```

This concludes the implementation of the `Factory::Object` interface. The executing server is shown in Figure 2.3.

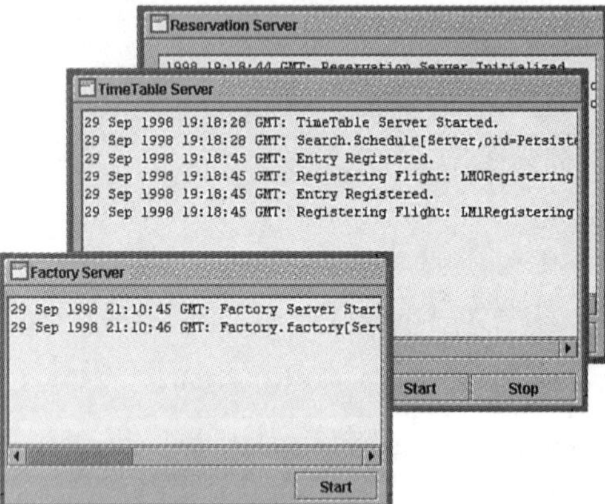

FIGURE 2.3
The `FactoryServer` *user interface.*

The final element of the SOAR application on the server side is to construct a `Payment` server. When a customer has located a flight he or she wants using a `Search` server, the customer will then reserve a seat on the flight. When this is done, a payment needs to be made to confirm the reservation. It is at this point that the `Payment` server kicks in.

The SOAR `Payment` Server

The `Payment` server is the last link in the chain that makes up SOAR. After the user has selected a flight, he or she has to pay for it using a credit card. The `Payment` server supports this facility. When the payment is made, the Payment server should return an invoice as proof of payment. An interface that enables you to do this is given here:

```
#include "factory.idl"

module Bank{

    interface Payment{

        struct invoice{
            Factory::Object::Person from;
            string to;
            string invoiceNumber;
            float amount;
            string date;
        };

        invoice createPayment(
                in Factory::Object::Person from,
                in string to,
                in Factory::Object::CreditCard plastic,
                in Factory::Object::Address billing,
                in float amount);

        void undoPayment(in string invoiceNumber);
    };
};
```

The Payment interface defines a struct named invoice that captures receipt of a payment. It is the invoice that is returned when a client invokes the creatPayment() operation. This operation takes a number of parameters that is used to construct the invoice object. The Payment interface further defines the undoPayment() operation that can be used by a client to roll back a payment instruction in case the user changes his or her mind.

Implementing the Bank::Payment Interface

Ideally, the implementation of the Payments interface would use a transaction service to record the payment in a database. But that is not done here to keep the implementation simple. In essence, the implementation of the next interface is very much in the spirit of how we implemented the Factory::Object interface. The interface is implemented in a class named Payments, as shown in Listing 2.10.

LISTING 2.10 THE Payments COMPONENT

```
package Bank;
import java.util.*;
```

continues

LISTING 2.10 CONTINUED

```
public class Payments extends Bank._PaymentImplBase {

  private com.objectspace.jgl.Stack instructions =
       new com.objectspace.jgl.Stack();

  public Payments() {
    super();
  }

  public Bank.PaymentPackage.invoice createPayment(
    Factory.ObjectPackage.Person from,
    java.lang.String to,
    Factory.ObjectPackage.CreditCard plastic,
    Factory.ObjectPackage.Address billing,
    float amount
  ) {
      int number = instructions.size()+1;
      paymentHolder t_payment =
        new paymentHolder(from,to,plastic,
              billing,amount,new Integer(number).toString());
      instructions.push(t_payment);
      Date today = new Date();
 Bank.PaymentPackage.invoice t_invoice =
       new Bank.PaymentPackage.invoice(from,to,
              new Integer(number).toString(),amount,today.toString());
      return t_invoice;
  }

  public void undoPayment(
    java.lang.String invoiceNumber
  ) {
    for (Enumeration e = instructions.elements() ;
                              e.hasMoreElements() ;) {
      paymentHolder temp_ = (paymentHolder)e.nextElement();
      if(temp_.invoiceNumber.equals(invoiceNumber)){
        instructions.remove(e);
 }
    }
  }
}

class paymentHolder {
    Factory.ObjectPackage.Person from;
    java.lang.String to;
    Factory.ObjectPackage.CreditCard plastic;
    Factory.ObjectPackage.Address billing;
    float amount;
    String invoiceNumber;
```

```
    paymentHolder(Factory.ObjectPackage.Person from,
                  java.lang.String to,
                  Factory.ObjectPackage.CreditCard plastic,
                  Factory.ObjectPackage.Address billing,
                  float amount,
                  String invoiceNumber
                  ){

      this.from = from;
      this.to = to;
      this.plastic = plastic;
      this.billing = billing;
      this.amount = amount;
      this.invoiceNumber = invoiceNumber;
    }
}
```


The package `Bank` defines two classes: `Payments` and `PaymentHolder`. All the invoices that are created by the `Payments` class are stored in a JGL stack. This enables us to insert an invoice into the stack when it is created and remove it from the stack when the client requests that a payment be undone.

The `createPayment()` method does two things. First, it creates an instance of a `PaymentHolder` and inserts it into the stack. The next thing it does is to create an `invoice` object and return it to the client. The following line shows the creation of the `invoice` object:

```
Bank.PaymentPackage.invoice t_invoice =
       new Bank.PaymentPackage.invoice(from,to,
              new Integer(number).toString(),amount,today.toString());
```

In the `undoPayment()` method, the client passes an invoice identifier that is used to locate the `PaymentHolder` instance from the stack and then remove it. This is accomplished by constructing an enumeration on the elements of the stack and iterating over it until the desired invoice is located. When it is located, the instance of `PaymentHolder` is removed from the stack.

The `PaymentServer` GUI

Finally, we are now ready to construct a server to host the `Payments` object reference. Like the three servers that we built earlier, the GUI for the server is separated from the actual server itself. The server is constructed on a thread to allow the GUI to function more responsively. First, you look at the implementation for the server, as shown in Listing 2.11, and then at the implementation for the GUI.

LISTING 2.11 THE `PaymentServer` THREAD

```
Package Bank;

public class Server implements Runnable{

  private org.omg.CORBA.ORB orb;
  private org.omg.CORBA.BOA boa;
  private Bank.Payments payment = new Bank.Payments();
  private PaymentServer gui;

  Server(PaymentServer ps){
    gui = ps;
  }

  public void run(){
    orb = org.omg.CORBA.ORB.init();
    boa = orb.BOA_init();
    com.visigenic.vbroker.URLNaming.Resolver resolver = null;
    try{
      resolver = com.visigenic.vbroker.URLNaming.ResolverHelper.narrow(
                orb.resolve_initial_references("URLNamingResolver"));
    }
    catch(org.omg.CORBA.ORBPackage.InvalidName ivn){
      System.out.println(ivn.toString());
    }
    try{
      resolver.force_register_url(
        "http://localhost:15000/payment.ior",payment);
      boa.obj_is_ready(payment);
      gui.DisplayMessage("Payment Server Started.");
      gui.DisplayMessage(payment + " is ready.");

    }
    catch(Exception e) {
      System.out.println(e.toString());
    }
    try{
      boa.impl_is_ready();
    }
    catch(org.omg.CORBA.SystemException ex){
      gui.DisplayMessage(ex.toString());
    }
  }
}
```

As with the `FactoryServer` implementation, the `Server` class is very typical for CORBA servers. The two methods that are vital to this implementation are constructing the

`Payments` object and registering this object reference with the Visigenic URL Naming Service. The first is accomplished in the following line of code:

```
private Bank.Payments payment = new Bank.Payments();
```

The second is done in the following manner:

```
resolver.force_register_url("http://localhost:15000/payment.ior",payment);
```

All that remains is to construct the GUI which enables you to monitor this server, as shown in Listing 2.12.

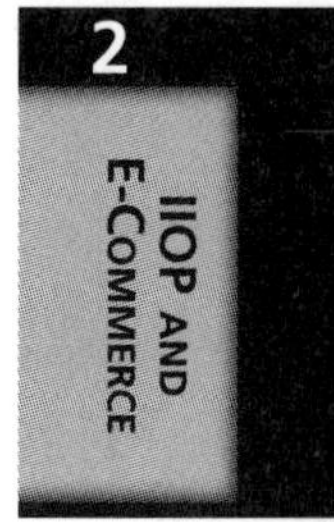

LISTING 2.12 THE `PaymentServer` INTERFACE

```
package Bank;
import com.sun.java.swing.*;
import java.awt.*;
import java.awt.event.*;

public class PaymentServer  extends JPanel{

  JScrollPane jScrollPane1 = new JScrollPane();
  JButton StartButton = new JButton();
  JTextArea factoryDisplay = new JTextArea();
  Thread ServerThread;

  public PaymentServer() {
   try  {
      jbInit();
    }
    catch (Exception e) {
      e.printStackTrace();
    }
  }

   private void jbInit() throws Exception {
    this.setLayout(null);
    jScrollPane1.setBounds(new Rectangle(2, 8, 324, 143));
    StartButton.setText("Start");
    StartButton.setBounds(new Rectangle(250, 155, 72, 24));
    StartButton.addMouseListener(new java.awt.event.MouseAdapter() {
public void mouseClicked(MouseEvent e) {
        StartButton_mouseClicked(e);
      }
    });
    this.add(jScrollPane1, null);
    jScrollPane1.getViewport().add(factoryDisplay, null);
    this.add(StartButton, null);
  }
```

continues

LISTING 2.12 CONTINUED

```
  void StartButton_mouseClicked(MouseEvent e) {
    Server paymentserver = new Server(this);
    ServerThread = new Thread(paymentserver);
    ServerThread.start();
  }

  void DisplayMessage(String msg){
    java.util.Date date = new java.util.Date();
    factoryDisplay.append(date.toGMTString() +": "+ msg + "\n");
  }
}
```

As with the other GUI implementations, the server is launched when the user clicks the Start button. When this event occurs, the following lines of code execute:

```
Server paymentyserver = new Server(this);
ServerThread = new Thread(paymentserver);
ServerThread.start();
```

In the first line, a `Server` object is constructed. In the next line, the thread is constructed, and the last line launches the instance of the `Server` (`paymentserver`) on the thread.

That concludes the construction of the `PaymentServer`. The `Server` executing is shown in Figure 2.4.

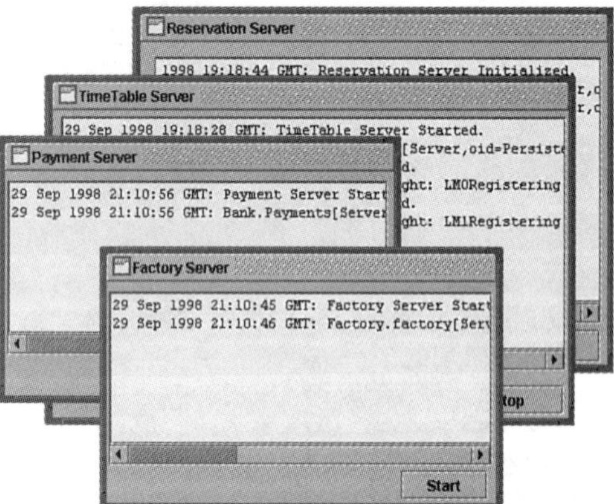

FIGURE 2.4
The `PaymentServer` *user interface.*

Now it's time to actually run these applications. None of the GUI classes defined previously has a `main()` method that would enable you to launch them independently. This was done explicitly. The reason is very simple. Any serious CORBA application should have more than one server to get the job done. If they are all standalone, you have two options of launching them:

- Use a script or a batch file to launch then all in a batch process.
- Launch them all manually.

Both these scenarios tend to clutter your OS workspace with innumerable windows, and besides, it is quite cumbersome. I usually provide a Multi Document interface to all the servers that make up an application. Since the introduction of Swing, this has become possible in Java using `InternalFrames`. So let's use `InternalFrames` to host all the GUI objects in this chapter. In our case, we need to host four GUI objects. The code for doing this is given in Listing 2.13.

LISTING 2.13 THE `SOARServerWindow`

```
package Server;

import java.awt.*;
import com.sun.java.swing.*;

public class SOARServerWindow extends JFrame {

  Factory.FactoryServer factoryServerWindow;
  Bank.PaymentServer paymentServerWindow;
  Search.SearchServer searchServerWindow;
  Reservations.ReservationServer reservationServerWindow;

  JInternalFrame FactoryFrame;
  JInternalFrame BankFrame;
  JInternalFrame SearchFrame;
  JInternalFrame ReservationFrame;


  JLayeredPane layers;

  public ServerWindow() {
    this.setTitle("Super ORB");
    layers = new JDesktopPane();
    setLayeredPane(layers);

    FactoryFrame = new JInternalFrame(
        "Factory Server",true,false,false,false);
    BankFrame = new JInternalFrame(
        "Payment Server",true,false,false,false);
    SearchFrame = new JInternalFrame(
        "TimeTable Server",true,false,false,false);
    ReservationFrame = new JInternalFrame(
        "Reservation Server",true,false,false,false);

    factoryServerWindow = new Factory.FactoryServer();
    paymentServerWindow = new Bank.PaymentServer();
```

continues

LISTING 2.13 CONTINUED

```
    searchServerWindow = new Search.SearchServer();
    reservationServerWindow = new Reservations.ReservationServer();

    FactoryFrame.getContentPane().add(factoryServerWindow,"Center");
BankFrame.getContentPane().add(paymentServerWindow,"Center");
SearchFrame.getContentPane().add(searchServerWindow,"Center");
ReservationFrame.getContentPane().add(
             reservationServerWindow,"Center");

    FactoryFrame.pack();
    BankFrame.pack();
    SearchFrame.pack();
    ReservationFrame.pack();

    layers.add(FactoryFrame);
    layers.add(BankFrame);
    layers.add(SearchFrame);
    layers.add(ReservationFrame);

    this.setVisible(true);
  }

  public static void main(String[] args) {
    SOARServerWindow serverWindow = new SOARServerWindow();
  }
}
```

The code in Listing 2.13 is purely related to GUI. The essence of the implementation is that it uses `JinternalFrame` to display all the `Server` windows that we made to implement the SOAR requirements. As a consequence of this implementation, the process of activating the SOAR application can be accomplished with the following steps:

1. Start VisiBroker Smart Agent.
2. Start VisiBroker GateKeeper.
3. Launch the `SOARServerWindow`.
4. Inside the `SOARServerWindow`, first launch the `TimeTableServer`. Then launch the `ReservationServer`. Next, launch the `PaymentServer`, and finally activate the `FactoryServer`.

When you have finished these steps, the SOAR application is ready for use. The final product is shown in Figure 2.5.

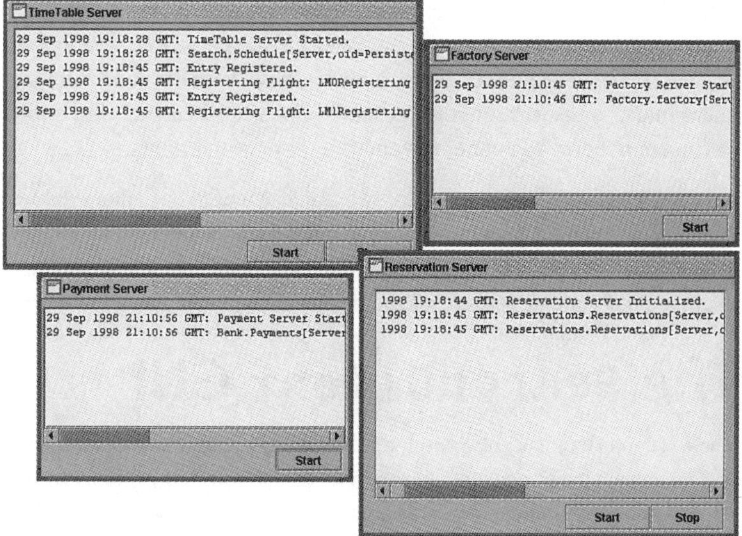

FIGURE 2.5
The SOAR application user interface.

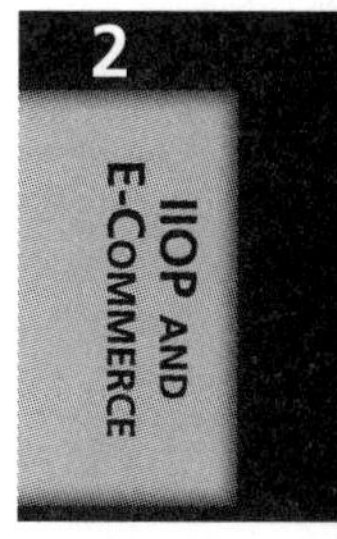

The SOAR Client

Now that you have built all the servers, you are ready to build and deploy clients to use those servers. There is just one requirement in terms of design: The client should be capable of running in a browser. There are some problems that need to be solved. You will look at those problems a little later. First, let's figure out how the client is going to interact with the SOAR servers.

The client basically needs to be able to search for a particular flight. After the flight is located, a client should be able to reserve a seat on that flight. Finally, the client needs to be able to pay for the flight. This sequence of events is depicted in Figure 2.6.

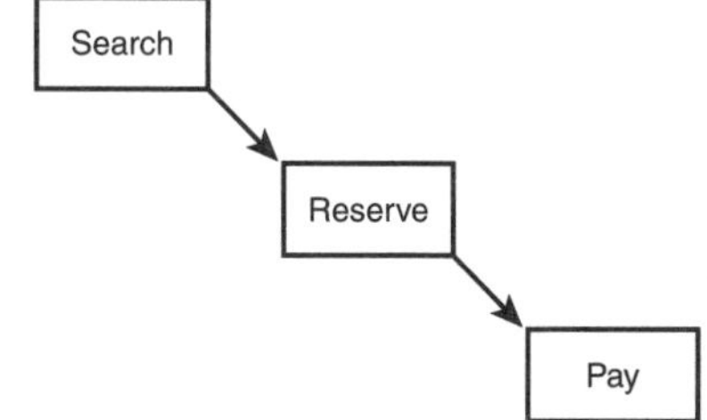

FIGURE 2.6
The SOAR client sequence of operations.

It might be appropriate to implement the client with a Microsoft-like wizard interface in a browser. This means that a client starts off with a Search window. When the client selects a result and presses Next, it could show a Reservation window. Finally, when the client makes a reservation and presses Next in the Reservation window, it is provided a Payments window to enable the client to pay for the ticket.

Java AWT provides a layout manager called `CardLayout` that enables you to do this. `CardLayout` enables you to stack multiple panels. Only one panel or card can be visible at one time. This enables you to construct each step in purchasing an airplane ticket using a panel and then stack all the panels using `CardLayout` in an applet.

The SearchClient GUI

The user interface for the search engine should enable a user to input a departure point and an arrival point and invoke the `search()` operation on the `TimeTable` object reference. The result that the `TimeTable` object provides should be displayed in a grid object listing all the parameters of the flights available. The code that enables you to do this is shown in Listing 2.14.

LISTING 2.14 THE `SearchClient` INTERFACE

```
package SoarClient;

import java.awt.*;
import com.sun.java.swing.table.*;
import com.sun.java.swing.border.*;
import com.sun.java.swing.event.TableModelListener;
import com.sun.java.swing.event.TableModelEvent;
import java.util.Vector;
import com.sun.java.swing.*;


import java.awt.event.*;

public class SearchClient extends JPanel{

  JLabel jLabel1 = new JLabel();
  JLabel jLable2 = new JLabel();
  JTextField FromField = new JTextField();
  JTextField ToField = new JTextField();
  JScrollPane jScrollPane1 = new JScrollPane();
  SearchResultModel tablemodel = new SearchResultModel();
  JTable resultTable = new JTable(tablemodel);
  JButton SearchButton = new JButton();
  JButton Cancel = new JButton();
  JButton Reserve = new JButton();
```

```
private org.omg.CORBA.ORB orb;
private org.omg.CORBA.BOA boa;
private Search.TimeTable searchEngine = null;
private com.visigenic.vbroker.URLNaming.Resolver resolver = null;
private ReservationsClient client = null;
private Soar panel = null;

public SearchClient(org.omg.CORBA.ORB orb,
     org.omg.CORBA.BOA boa,
     com.visigenic.vbroker.URLNaming.Resolver resolver,
                    ReservationsClient client,
                    Soar panel) {
  this.orb = orb;
  this.boa = boa;
  this.resolver = resolver;
  this.client = client;
  this.panel = panel;

  try  {
    jbInit();
  }
  catch (Exception e) {
    e.printStackTrace();
  }
  try{
    org.omg.CORBA.Object obj = resolver.locate(
              "http://localhost:15000/timetable.ior");
    searchEngine = Search.TimeTableHelper.narrow(obj);
  }
  catch(Exception e) {
    System.out.println(e.toString());
  }
}

private void jbInit() throws Exception {

  jLabel1.setText("From");
  jLabel1.setBounds(new Rectangle(8, 14, 41, 15));
  jLable2.setText("To");
  jLable2.setBounds(new Rectangle(173, 14, 41, 15));
  ToField.setToolTipText("Enter Separture Point");
  ToField.setBounds(new Rectangle(173, 31, 149, 19));
  jScrollPane1.setBounds(new Rectangle(7, 58, 452, 154));
  SearchButton.setText("Search");
  SearchButton.setBounds(new Rectangle(286, 222, 84, 23));
  SearchButton.addMouseListener(new java.awt.event.MouseAdapter() {
    public void mouseClicked(MouseEvent e) {
      SearchButton_mouseClicked(e);
    }
```

continues

LISTING 2.14 CONTINUED

```
    });
    Cancel.setText("Cancel");
    Cancel.setBounds(new Rectangle(372, 222, 84, 23));
    Reserve.setText("Reserve");
    Reserve.setBounds(new Rectangle(200, 222, 84, 23));
    Reserve.addMouseListener(new java.awt.event.MouseAdapter() {
      public void mouseClicked(MouseEvent e) {
        Reserve_mouseClicked(e);
      }
    });
    FromField.setToolTipText("Enter Destination Point");
    FromField.setBounds(new Rectangle(7, 31, 149, 19));
    setLayout(null);
    add(jLabel1, null);
    add(jLable2, null);
    add(ToField, null);
    add(FromField, null);
    add(jScrollPane1, null);
    jScrollPane1.getViewport().add(resultTable, null);
    add(SearchButton, null);
    add(Cancel, null);
    add(Reserve, null);
  }

  void SearchButton_mouseClicked(MouseEvent e) {

     Reservations.Flight[] flights;
     flights = searchEngine.search(
       FromField.getText(),ToField.getText(),"","");
     System.out.println("Results " +
       new Integer(flights.length).toString());
     SearchResultModel _model
       = (SearchResultModel)resultTable.getModel();
     java.util.Vector t_ = new java.util.Vector();
     String[] temp_ = new String[5];
     for(int j = 0; j < _model.getRowCount(); j++){
        _model.removeRow(j);
     }
     resultTable.setModel(_model);
     resultTable.tableChanged(
       new TableModelEvent(_model,tablemodel.getRowCount()));
     resultTable.repaint();

     for(int i = 0; i< flights.length;i++){
      temp_[0] = flights[i].name();
      temp_[1] = flights[i].flightNumber();
      temp_[2] = flights[i].date();
      temp_[3] = flights[i].time();
      temp_[4] = new Float(flights[i].cost()).toString();
```

```
t_.addElement(temp_);
      _model.addRow(temp_);
     }
     resultTable.setModel(_model);
     resultTable.tableChanged(
       new TableModelEvent(_model,tablemodel.getRowCount()));
     resultTable.repaint();
  }

  void Reserve_mouseClicked(MouseEvent e) {
     SearchResultModel _model = (SearchResultModel)resultTable.getModel();
     int selectionIndex = resultTable.getSelectedRow();
     String[] temp_ = new String[7];
     for(int i = 0; i < _model.getColumnCount(); i++){
      temp_[i] = (String)_model.getValueAt(selectionIndex,i);
     }
     temp_[5] = FromField.getText();
     temp_[6] = ToField.getText();

     client.setParams(temp_);
     panel.displayPanel(Soar.RESERVATIONPANEL);
  }
}

class SearchResultModel extends DefaultTableModel{

  String columns[] =  {"Airline", "FlightNumber", "Date", "Time", "Cost"};
  String[] row = new String[0];
  Vector rows = new Vector();

  public SearchResultModel(){
  }

  public int getColumnCount(){
    return columns.length;
  }

  public int getRowCount(){
    return rows.size();
  }

  public java.lang.Object getValueAt(int row, int column){
    java.lang.Object temp_[] = (String[])rows.elementAt(row);
    return   temp_[column];
  }

  public boolean isCellEditable(int row, int col) {return false;}

  public void setValueAt(java.lang.Object aValue, int row, int column){
```

continues

LISTING 2.14 CONTINUED

```
    java.lang.Object temp[] = (String[])rows.elementAt(row);
    temp[column] = aValue;
    rows.setElementAt(temp,row);
    fireTableChanged (new TableModelEvent(this,row));
  }

  public String getColumnName(int columnIndex){
    return columns[columnIndex];
  }

  public void addRow(String row[]){
    rows.addElement(row);
  }

  public void removeRow(int index){
    rows.removeElementAt(index);
  }
}
```

The `SoarClient` package implemented in Listing 2.14 specifies two classes. The first class deals with the user interface itself, and the second class defines a `TableModel` that will be used to construct a `Jtable` object to display the results of the search. This discussion highlights only the essentials of the preceding two classes—particularly the code that deals with CORBA.

The constructor is passed five parameters that are required by the search client to do its job. The parameters are constructed in the applet. The constructor is shown in the following code:

```
public SearchClient(org.omg.CORBA.ORB orb,
       org.omg.CORBA.BOA boa,
       com.visigenic.vbroker.URLNaming.Resolver resolver,
                    ReservationsClient client,Soar panel)
```

The five parameters are an instance of the ORB, the BOA, the URL Naming object reference, an instance of the `ReservationClient`, and the container that uses the `CardLayout`.

The first three parameters are used to retrieve the `TimeTable` object reference. The `TimeTable` object reference is registered with the URL Naming server under the name `timetable.ior`. This object reference is retrieved using the URL naming service in the following line of code:

```
org.omg.CORBA.Object obj = resolver.locate(
        "http://localhost:15000/timetable.ior");
      searchEngine = Search.TimeTableHelper.narrow(obj);
```

After the TimeTable object reference (named searchEngine) is retrieved, the client is ready to allow the user to perform searches on the airline schedule that is held in the TimeTable implementation. This search occurs when the user presses the Search button. At that point, the contents of the To and From text fields are retrieved and passed to the TimeTable object:

```
flights = searchEngine.search
➥(FromField.getText(),ToField.getText(),"","");
```

If the searchEngine finds flights that the user is searching for, the flights array will be initialized. When the array of flights are retrieved from the server, the TableModel is modified so that the result can be displayed in the table object that the client uses to display the results. This implementation is shown in the following lines of code:

```
resultTable.setModel(_model);
resultTable.tableChanged(
new TableModelEvent(_model,tablemodel.getRowCount()));
resultTable.repaint();
```

With a successful result, the table object will display all the flights that were returned.

The next step in the chain is for the user to select some flight and invoke the reserve button. At that point, the following code will execute:client.setParams(temp_);

```
panel.displayPanel(Soar.RESERVATIONPANEL);
```

The first line of code initializes the state of the client code. In this case, the client is the ReservationClient that was passed into the SearchClient by the applet. The second line of code invokes the displayPanel on the panel object with the parameter Soar.RESERVATIONPANEL. This causes the panel to invoke the card that is identified by the final attribute—in this case, the ReservationClient. The first panel is shown executing in Figure 2.7.

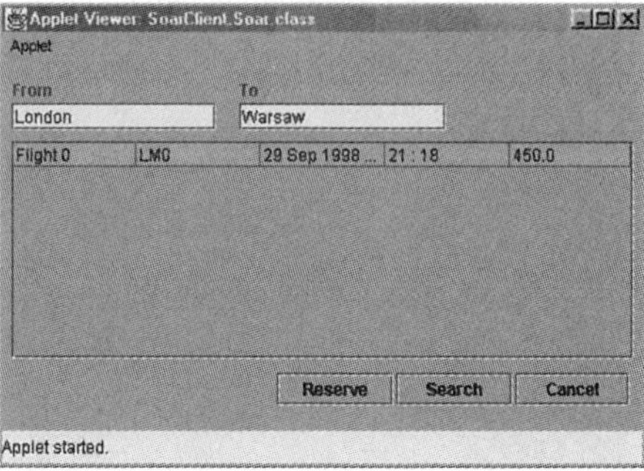

FIGURE 2.7
The SearchClient *user interface.*

That concludes the implementation of the SearchClient application. Next is the ReservationsClient.

The ReservationsClient GUI

When the user clicks the Reserve button in the SearchClient GUI, the ReservationsClient panel is brought into view so that a user can reserve seats on the selected airline. A user can reserve as many seats on the airplane as allowed by the capacity on the airline. The implementation, shown in Listing 2.15, follows similar lines as the SearchClient GUI.

LISTING 2.15 THE ReservationsClient INTERFACE

```
package SoarClient;

import java.awt.*;
import com.sun.java.swing.*;
import borland.jbcl.layout.*;
import java.awt.event.*;
import com.sun.java.swing.table.*;
import com.sun.java.swing.event.TableModelListener;
import com.sun.java.swing.event.TableModelEvent;
import java.util.*;
import org.omg.CORBA.*;

public class ReservationsClient extends JPanel {

  private org.omg.CORBA.ORB orb;
  private org.omg.CORBA.BOA boa;
  private com.visigenic.vbroker.URLNaming.Resolver resolver = null;
  private String[] params;
  private PaymentClient payment;
  private Soar panel;

  JPanel jPanel1 = new JPanel();
  JTextField AirlineField = new JTextField();
  JTextField FlightNoField = new JTextField();
  JTextField DateField = new JTextField();
  JTextField TimeField = new JTextField();
  JTextField CostField = new JTextField();
  JLabel jLabel1 = new JLabel();
  JLabel jLabel2 = new JLabel();
  JLabel jLabel4 = new JLabel();
  JLabel jLabel5 = new JLabel();
  JTextField Name = new JTextField();
  JTextField Age = new JTextField();
  JTextField Email = new JTextField();
  JComboBox Gender = new JComboBox();
  JLabel jLabel7 = new JLabel();
  JPanel jPanel2 = new JPanel();
  JLabel jLabel8 = new JLabel();
  JLabel jLabel9 = new JLabel();
```

```
JLabel jLabel10 = new JLabel();
JLabel jLabel11 = new JLabel();
JButton AddPassengerButton = new JButton();
JScrollPane jScrollPane1 = new JScrollPane();
PassengerListModel tablemodel = new PassengerListModel();
JTable PassengerList = new JTable(tablemodel);
JButton ConfirmButton = new JButton();
java.util.Vector passengers = new Vector();

private Factory.Object factory;
JButton BackButton = new JButton();
public void setParams(String[] params){

  this.params = new String[params.length];
  for(int i=0; i <params.length; i++){
    this.params[i] = params[i];
  }

  AirlineField.setText(params[0]);
  FlightNoField.setText(params[1]);
  DateField.setText(params[2]);
  TimeField.setText(params[3]);
  CostField.setText(params[4]);
}

public ReservationsClient(org.omg.CORBA.ORB orb,
                          org.omg.CORBA.BOA boa,
           com.visigenic.vbroker.URLNaming.Resolver resolver,
                          PaymentClient payment,
                          Soar panel) {
  this.orb = orb;
  this.boa = boa;
  this.resolver = resolver;
  this.panel = panel;
  this.payment = payment;

  try  {
    jbInit();
  }
  catch (Exception e) {
    e.printStackTrace();
  }
  try{
    org.omg.CORBA.Object obj = resolver.locate(
      "http://localhost:15000/factory.ior");
    factory = Factory.ObjectHelper.narrow(obj);
  }
  catch(Exception e) {
    System.out.println(e.toString());
```

continues

LISTING 2.15 CONTINUED

```
    }
  }


  public ReservationsClient() {
    try  {
      jbInit();
    }
    catch (Exception e) {
      e.printStackTrace();
    }
  }

  private void jbInit() throws Exception {
    jPanel1.setLayout(null);
    jPanel1.setBounds(new Rectangle(-1, 5, 469, 85));
    AirlineField.setBounds(new Rectangle(14, 17, 151, 19));
    AirlineField.setEditable(false);
    FlightNoField.setBounds(new Rectangle(177, 16, 296, 19));
    FlightNoField.setEditable(false);
    DateField.setBounds(new Rectangle(13, 56, 151, 19));
    DateField.setEditable(false);
    TimeField.setBounds(new Rectangle(176, 56, 151, 19));
    TimeField.setEditable(false);
    CostField.setBounds(new Rectangle(335, 56, 135, 19));
    CostField.setEditable(false);
    jLabel1.setText("Airline");
    jLabel1.setBounds(new Rectangle(176, 7, 135, 15));
    jLabel2.setText("Flight Number");
    jLabel2.setBounds(new Rectangle(14, 3, 95, 13));
    jLabel4.setText("Time");
    jLabel4.setBounds(new Rectangle(176, 39, 115, 17));
    jLabel5.setText("Cost");
    jLabel5.setBounds(new Rectangle(335, 39, 70, 15));
    Name.setBounds(new Rectangle(0, 22, 175, 21));
    Age.setBounds(new Rectangle(178, 22, 85, 21));
    Gender.setBounds(new Rectangle(265, 22, 47, 21));
    Email.setBounds(new Rectangle(314, 22, 138, 21));
    jLabel7.setText("Date");
    jLabel7.setBounds(new Rectangle(14, 39, 114, 18));
    jPanel2.setLayout(null);
    jPanel2.setBounds(new Rectangle(9, 81, 468, 51));
    jLabel8.setBounds(new Rectangle(0, 5, 114, 18));
    jLabel9.setText("Age");
    jLabel9.setBounds(new Rectangle(177, 4, 42, 18));
    jLabel10.setText("Gender");
    jLabel10.setBounds(new Rectangle(266, 3, 46, 18));
    jLabel11.setText("Email");
    jLabel11.setBounds(new Rectangle(314, 3, 37, 18));
```

```
    AddPassengerButton.setText("Add");
    AddPassengerButton.setBounds(new Rectangle(387, 136, 80, 23));
    AddPassengerButton.addMouseListener(new java.awt.event.MouseAdapter()
{
      public void mouseClicked(MouseEvent e) {
        AddPassengerButton_mouseClicked(e);
      }
    });
    jScrollPane1.setBounds(new Rectangle(13, 165, 455, 94));
    ConfirmButton.setText("Confirm");
    ConfirmButton.setBounds(new Rectangle(387, 264, 80, 22));
    BackButton.setText("Back");
    BackButton.setBounds(new Rectangle(315, 264, 68, 22));
    BackButton.addMouseListener(new java.awt.event.MouseAdapter() {
      public void mouseClicked(MouseEvent e) {
        BackButton_mouseClicked(e);
      }
    });
    ConfirmButton.addMouseListener(new java.awt.event.MouseAdapter() {
      public void mouseClicked(MouseEvent e) {
        ConfirmButton_mouseClicked(e);
      }
    });
    jLabel8.setText("Name");
    setLayout(null);
    this.add(jLabel1, null);
    add(jPanel2, null);
    jPanel2.add(Name, null);
    jPanel2.add(jLabel8, null);
    jPanel2.add(Age, null);
    jPanel2.add(jLabel9, null);
    jPanel2.add(Email, null);
    jPanel2.add(Gender, null);
    jPanel2.add(jLabel10, null);
    jPanel2.add(jLabel11, null);
    add(AddPassengerButton, null);
    add(jScrollPane1, null);
    jScrollPane1.getViewport().add(PassengerList, null);
    add(ConfirmButton, null);
    this.add(jPanel1, null);
    jPanel1.add(jLabel2, null);
    jPanel1.add(jLabel7, null);
    jPanel1.add(AirlineField, null);
    jPanel1.add(FlightNoField, null);
    jPanel1.add(DateField, null);
    jPanel1.add(TimeField, null);
    jPanel1.add(jLabel4, null);
    jPanel1.add(jLabel5, null);
    jPanel1.add(CostField, null);
```

continues

LISTING 2.15 CONTINUED

```
    this.add(BackButton, null);
    Gender.addItem("F");
    Gender.addItem("M");
  }

  void AddPassengerButton_mouseClicked(MouseEvent e) {
    Factory.ObjectPackage.Person passenger = null;
    PassengerListModel _model =
    ➥(PassengerListModel)PassengerList.getModel();
    passengers = new java.util.Vector();
    String[] temp_ = new String[4];
    temp_[0] = Name.getText();
    temp_[1] = Age.getText();
    temp_[2] = (String)Gender.getSelectedItem();
    temp_[3] = Email.getText();

    String gn = (String)Gender.getSelectedItem();
    char Gendr = gn.charAt(0);
    Short age_ = new Short(Age.getText());
    short age = age_.shortValue();
    try{
     passenger = factory.createPassenger(
        Name.getText(),
        age,Gendr,Email.getText());
    }
    catch(SystemException ex){
      System.out.println(ex.toString());
    }
    passengers.addElement(passenger);
    _model.addRow(temp_);
    PassengerList.setModel(_model);
    PassengerList.tableChanged(
        new TableModelEvent(_model,tablemodel.getRowCount()));
    PassengerList.repaint();
  }

  void ConfirmButton_mouseClicked(MouseEvent e) {
    PassengerListModel _model = (
        PassengerListModel)PassengerList.getModel();
    String[] temp_ = new String[5];
    Enumeration ex = passengers.elements();
    Factory.ObjectPackage.Person passenger = null;
    Reservations.Flight flight = null;
    short seatsleft = 0;

    try{
     flight = Reservations.FlightHelper.bind(orb,AirlineField.getText());
     seatsleft = flight.capacity();
    }
```

```
      catch(SystemException excp){
        System.out.println(excp.toString());
      }
      if(seatsleft >= passengers.size() ){
        while(ex.hasMoreElements()){
          passenger = (Factory.ObjectPackage.Person)ex.nextElement();
          try{
            flight.reserveSeat(new Short(seatsleft).toString(),passenger);
          }
          catch(SystemException excp){
            System.out.println(excp.toString());
          }
          seatsleft--;
        }
      }
      String[] param = new String[8];
      param[0] = params[5];
      param[1] = params[6];
      param[2] = params[2];
      param[3] = params[0];


      PassengerListModel model =
      ➥(PassengerListModel)PassengerList.getModel();
      int selectionIndex = PassengerList.getSelectedRow();

      param[4] = new Integer(model.getRowCount()).toString();
      Float f = new Float(params[4]);
      int total_cost = f.intValue() * _model.getRowCount();
      param[5] = new Integer(total_cost).toString();
      param[6] = (String)_model.getValueAt(selectionIndex,0);
      param[7] = (String)_model.getValueAt(selectionIndex,3);

      payment.setParam(param,passenger);
      panel.displayPanel(Soar.PAYMENTPANEL);
    }

    void BackButton_mouseClicked(MouseEvent e) {
      panel.displayPanel(Soar.SEARCHCLIENTPANEL);
    }
  }

  class PassengerListModel extends DefaultTableModel{

    String columns[] =  {"Name", "Age", "Gender", "Email"};
    String[] row = new String[0];
    Vector rows = new Vector();

    public PassengerListModel(){
    }
```

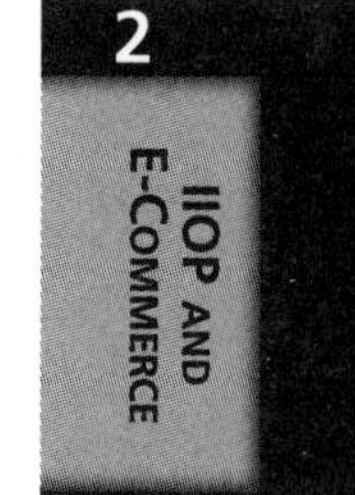

continues

LISTING 2.15 CONTINUED

```
  public int getColumnCount(){
    return columns.length;
  }

  public int getRowCount(){
    return rows.size();
  }

  public java.lang.Object getValueAt(int row, int column){
    java.lang.Object temp_[] = (String[])rows.elementAt(row);
    return   temp_[column];
  }

  public boolean isCellEditable(int row, int col) {return false;}

  public void setValueAt(java.lang.Object aValue, int row, int column){
    java.lang.Object temp[] = (String[])rows.elementAt(row);
    temp[column] = aValue;
    rows.setElementAt(temp,row);
    fireTableChanged (new TableModelEvent(this,row));
  }

  public String getColumnName(int columnIndex){
    return columns[columnIndex];
  }

  public void addRow(String row[]){
    rows.addElement(row);
  }

  public void removeRow(int index){
    rows.removeElementAt(index);
  }
}
```

The important aspects of the code are given in the following snippet. The rest of the code essentially deals with the presentation of information to the user:

```
org.omg.CORBA.Object obj = resolver.locate("http://localhost:15000/
factory.ior");
factory = Factory.ObjectHelper.narrow(obj);
```

In this code snippet, the `ReservationClient` class uses the `Factory` object reference. This reference is retrieved using the VisiBroker URL Naming service. The `Factory` object is used to construct the `passenger` objects:

```
passenger = factory.createPassenger(Name.getText(),age,Gendr,Email.
getText());
```

When the user enters the details for a passenger and clicks the add button, the `Factory` object reference is used to construct a passenger object. This information is further used to add to the `TableModel` so that the user can see what passengers are added to the reservation request. Finally, the user has to select a user from all the users that are shown in the table object and hit the Confirm button. At that point the following code is invoked:

```
flight = Reservations.FlightHelper.bind(orb,AirlineField.getText());
seatsleft = flight.capacity();
```

In the first line of code, the `bind` method is invoked to retrieve the `Flight` object reference. After the reference is retrieved, the capacity is checked. The following code is executed only if the capacity of the flight in terms of seats left is greater than the number of reservations required:

```
flight.reserveSeat(new Short(seatsleft).toString(),passenger);
```

All the passengers that the user input into the `JTable` object are passed into the flight object reference by invoking the `reserveSeat()` operation:

```
payment.setParam(param,passenger);
panel.displayPanel(Soar.PAYMENTPANEL);
```

Finally, the next object in the chain is initialized to the appropriate state—that is, all the state that is common between the `Reservations` server and the `Payment` server. This is done in the first line of code. Then the panel object is instructed to display the `Soar.PAYMENTPANEL` object, which will be used by the user to make the payment.

The executing client is shown in Figure 2.8.

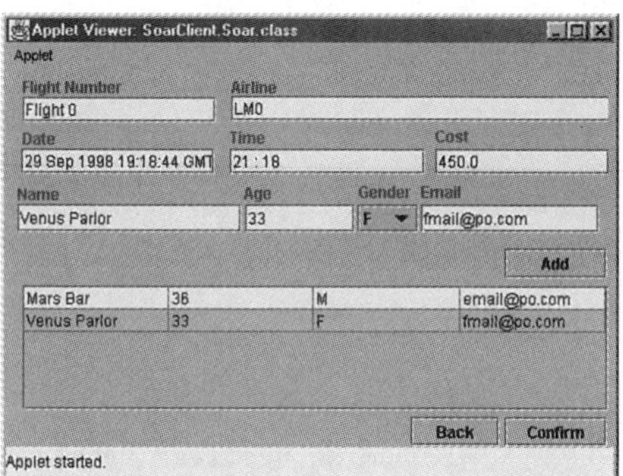

FIGURE 2.8
The `Reservation-Client` *user interface.*

The PaymentClient GUI

After all the required reservations are made—that is, all the passengers are filled in—the user has to select a single passenger from the list of passengers. This passenger will act as the payee for the seats on the flight, and the user has to click the reserve button. Then the screen shown in Figure 2.9 is presented to the user.

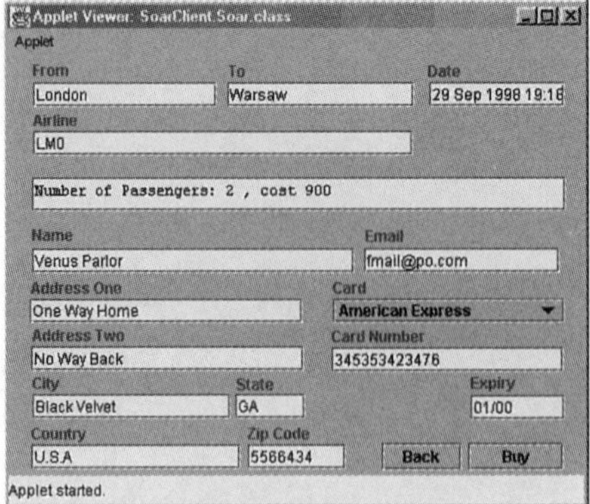

FIGURE 2.9
The `PaymentClient` *user interface.*

This is the `PaymentClient` GUI. The implementation for this class is given in Listing 2.16.

LISTING 2.16 THE `PaymentClient` INTERFACE

```
package SoarClient;

import java.awt.*;
import com.sun.java.swing.*;
import java.awt.event.*;
import org.omg.CORBA.*;
import org.omg.CORBA.ORB.*;

public class PaymentClient extends JPanel {

  private ORB orb;
  private BOA boa;
  private com.visigenic.vbroker.URLNaming.Resolver resolver = null;
  private String[] params;
  private Factory.Object factory;
  private Bank.Payment payments;
  private Factory.ObjectPackage.Person passenger;
  private Invoice invoice;
  private Soar panel;
```

```
JTextField From = new JTextField();
JTextField To = new JTextField();
JTextField Date = new JTextField();
JLabel jLabel1 = new JLabel();
JLabel jLabel2 = new JLabel();
JLabel jLabel3 = new JLabel();
JTextField Airline = new JTextField();
JLabel jLabel4 = new JLabel();
JTextArea Invoice = new JTextArea();
JTextField Name = new JTextField();
JTextField Email = new JTextField();
JLabel jLabel5 = new JLabel();
JLabel jLabel6 = new JLabel();
JTextField AdressOne = new JTextField();
JTextField AddressTwo = new JTextField();
➥JTextField City = new JTextField();
JTextField State = new JTextField();
JTextField Country = new JTextField();
JTextField Zip = new JTextField();
JLabel jLabel7 = new JLabel();
JLabel jLabel8 = new JLabel();
JLabel jLabel9 = new JLabel();
JLabel jLabel10 = new JLabel();
JLabel jLabel11 = new JLabel();
JLabel jLabel12 = new JLabel();
JComboBox CreditCard = new JComboBox();
JTextField CardNumber = new JTextField();
JTextField ExpiryDate = new JTextField();
JLabel jLabel13 = new JLabel();
JLabel jLabel14 = new JLabel();
JLabel jLabel15 = new JLabel();
JButton BuyButton = new JButton();
JButton BackButton = new JButton();

public void setParam(String[] param,
                     Factory.ObjectPackage.Person passenger){

  this.params = new String[param.length];
  for(int i=0; i <params.length; i++){
    this.params[i] = param[i];
  }
  this.passenger = passenger;
  To.setText(params[0]);
  From.setText(params[1]);
  Date.setText(params[2]);
  Airline.setText(params[3]);
  String invoice =
     "Number of Passengers: "
     + params[4] + " , "
```

continues

LISTING 2.16 CONTINUED

```
      + "cost "
      + params[5];
    Invoice.setText(invoice);
    Name.setText(params[6]);
    Email.setText(params[7]);
  }

  public PaymentClient(org.omg.CORBA.ORB orb,
                       org.omg.CORBA.BOA boa,
                       com.visigenic.vbroker.URLNaming.Resolver resolver,
                       Invoice invoice,
                       Soar panel) {
    this.orb = orb;
    this.boa = boa;
    this.resolver = resolver;
    this.invoice = invoice;
    this.panel = panel;

    try{
      org.omg.CORBA.Object factoryObject =
        resolver.locate("http://localhost:15000/factory.ior");
      factory = Factory.ObjectHelper.narrow(factoryObject);
      org.omg.CORBA.Object payementObject =
        resolver.locate("http://localhost:15000/payment.ior");
      payments = Bank.PaymentHelper.narrow(payementObject);
    }
    catch(Exception e) {
      System.out.println(e.toString());
    }
    try  {
      jbInit();
    }
    catch (Exception e) {
      e.printStackTrace();
    }
  }


  public PaymentClient() {
    try  {
      jbInit();
    }
    catch (Exception e) {
      e.printStackTrace();
    }
  }

  private void jbInit() throws Exception {
    From.setBounds(new Rectangle(177, 22, 148, 19));
```

```
To.setBounds(new Rectangle(20, 22, 148, 19));
Date.setBounds(new Rectangle(337, 22, 106, 19));
jLabel1.setText("From");
jLabel1.setBounds(new Rectangle(20, 5, 41, 15));
jLabel2.setBounds(new Rectangle(178, 6, 41, 15));
jLabel3.setText("Date");
jLabel3.setBounds(new Rectangle(336, 6, 41, 15));
Airline.setBounds(new Rectangle(20, 60, 304, 19));
jLabel4.setText("Airline");
jLabel4.setBounds(new Rectangle(20, 44, 41, 15));
Invoice.setBounds(new Rectangle(19, 96, 425, 26));
Name.setBounds(new Rectangle(19, 151, 258, 19));
Email.setBounds(new Rectangle(285, 151, 154, 19));
jLabel5.setText("Name");
jLabel5.setBounds(new Rectangle(19, 133, 41, 15));
jLabel6.setText("Email");
jLabel6.setBounds(new Rectangle(286, 134, 41, 15));
AdressOne.setBounds(new Rectangle(17, 190, 219, 19));
AddressTwo.setBounds(new Rectangle(18, 227, 219, 19));
City.setBounds(new Rectangle(19, 264, 160, 19));
State.setBounds(new Rectangle(183, 264, 55, 19));
Country.setBounds(new Rectangle(18, 303, 169, 19));
Zip.setBounds(new Rectangle(193, 303, 77, 19));
jLabel7.setText("Address One");
jLabel7.setBounds(new Rectangle(18, 174, 88, 15));
jLabel8.setText("Address Two");
jLabel8.setBounds(new Rectangle(19, 211, 80, 15));
jLabel9.setText("City");
jLabel9.setBounds(new Rectangle(19, 247, 77, 17));
jLabel10.setText("State");
jLabel10.setBounds(new Rectangle(184, 249, 48, 15));
jLabel11.setText("Country");
jLabel11.setBounds(new Rectangle(18, 287, 48, 15));
jLabel12.setText("Zip Code");
jLabel12.setBounds(new Rectangle(193, 287, 74, 15));
CreditCard.setBounds(new Rectangle(260, 190, 183, 19));
CardNumber.setBounds(new Rectangle(259, 228, 183, 19));
ExpiryDate.setBounds(new Rectangle(369, 265, 74, 19));
jLabel13.setText("Card");
jLabel13.setBounds(new Rectangle(260, 174, 48, 15));
jLabel14.setText("Card Number");
jLabel14.setBounds(new Rectangle(259, 212, 84, 15));
jLabel15.setText("Expiry");
jLabel15.setBounds(new Rectangle(369, 248, 48, 15));
BuyButton.setText("Buy");
BuyButton.setBounds(new Rectangle(367, 302, 75, 21));
BackButton.setText("Back");
BackButton.setBounds(new Rectangle(299, 302, 63, 21));
BackButton.addActionListener(new java.awt.event.ActionListener() {
```

continues

LISTING 2.16 CONTINUED

```
        public void actionPerformed(ActionEvent e) {
          BackButton_actionPerformed(e);
        }
      });
      BuyButton.addMouseListener(new java.awt.event.MouseAdapter() {
        public void mouseClicked(MouseEvent e) {
          BuyButton_mouseClicked(e);
        }
      });
      jLabel2.setText("To");
      setLayout(null);
      add(To, null);
      add(From, null);
      add(Date, null);
      add(jLabel3, null);
      add(jLabel2, null);
      add(jLabel1, null);
      add(Airline, null);
      add(jLabel4, null);
      add(Invoice, null);
      add(Name, null);
      add(Email, null);
      add(jLabel5, null);
      add(jLabel6, null);
      add(State, null);
      add(City, null);
      add(AddressTwo, null);
      add(AdressOne, null);
      add(Country, null);
      add(Zip, null);
      add(jLabel7, null);
      add(jLabel8, null);
      add(jLabel9, null);
      add(jLabel10, null);
      add(jLabel11, null);
      add(jLabel12, null);
      add(CreditCard, null);
      add(CardNumber, null);
      add(ExpiryDate, null);
      add(jLabel13, null);
      add(jLabel14, null);
      add(jLabel15, null);
      add(BuyButton, null);
      this.add(BackButton, null);
      CreditCard.addItem("American Express");
      CreditCard.addItem("Diners Club");
      CreditCard.addItem("Mastercard");
      CreditCard.addItem("Visa");
    }
```

```
  void BuyButton_mouseClicked(MouseEvent e) {

     String card = (String)CreditCard.getSelectedItem();
     String number = CardNumber.getText();
     String expiry = ExpiryDate.getText();

     String address1 = AdressOne.getText();
     String address2 = AddressTwo.getText();
     String city = City.getText();
     String state = State.getText();
     String zip = Zip.getText();
     String country = Country.getText();
     try{
       Factory.ObjectPackage.CreditCard cc  =
               factory.creatCreditCard(card,
                                       number,
                                       expiry);

       Factory.ObjectPackage.Address address =
                      factory.createAddress(address1,
                       address2,
                       city,
                       state,
                       zip,
                       country);
       Float cost = new Float(params[5]);
       Bank.PaymentPackage.invoice invce =
         payments.createPayment(passenger,
               Airline.getText(),cc,address,cost.floatValue());
       invoice.setInvoice(invce);
       panel.displayPanel(Soar.INVOICECLIENTPANEL);
     }
     catch(SystemException ex){
      System.out.println(ex.toString());
     }
   }

  void BackButton_actionPerformed(ActionEvent e) {
    panel.displayPanel(Soar.RESERVATIONPANEL);
  }
}
```

The payment client uses two object references: the `Factory` object and the `Payment` object. Both these object references are retrieved using the VisiBroker URL service:

```
org.omg.CORBA.Object factoryObject =
resolver.locate("http://localhost:15000/factory.ior");
factory = Factory.ObjectHelper.narrow(factoryObject);
org.omg.CORBA.Object payementObject =
resolver.locate("http://localhost:15000/payment.ior");
payments = Bank.PaymentHelper.narrow(payementObject);
```

The user has to fill in all the fields on the form. After the user has finished filling in all the information, the user can press the Buy button. Then the following code is executed:

```
Factory.ObjectPackage.CreditCard cc  = factory.creatCreditCard(card,
                                                                number,
                                                                expiry);

       Factory.ObjectPackage.Address address = factory.
        createAddress(address1,
                                                                address2,
                                                                city,
                                                                state,
                                                                zip,
                                                                country);
       Float cost = new Float(params[5]);
       Bank.PaymentPackage.invoice invce =
        payments.createPayment(passenger,Airline.getText(),cc,address,cost.
        floatValue());
       invoice.setInvoice(invce);
       panel.displayPanel(Soar.INVOICECLIENTPANEL);
```

In the first two lines of code, the `Factory` object reference is used to construct an instance of a credit card and a billing address. Using this information with the cost, the `Payment` server is requested to create a payment using the `creatPayment()` method. This method is passed all the information that is required by the `Payment` interface to construct an invoice. The invoice itself is displayed in another panel named `Soar.INVOICECLIENTPANEL`. The last line of code essentially displays the invoice panel that tells the information that the `Payment` object reference had passed back to the `PaymentsClient`.

The Invoice GUI

There is nothing spectacular about the invoice GUI. All it does is use a `JtextArea` object to display the state of the `invoice` object that was passed to it from the `PaymentsClient`. The code for this GUI is shown in Listing 2.17.

LISTING 2.17 THE INVOICE CLIENT INTERFACE

```
package SoarClient;

import java.awt.*;
import com.sun.java.swing.*;

public class Invoice extends JPanel {
  JTextArea InvoiceDisplay = new JTextArea();
  JButton FinishButton = new JButton();
  private Soar panel;
```

```
  public void setInvoice(Bank.PaymentPackage.invoice inv){
    this.display("Invoice # " + inv.invoiceNumber);
    this.display("Date # " + inv.date);
    this.display("From # " + inv.from.name);
    this.display("To # " + inv.to);
    this.display("Amount # " + new Float(inv.amount));
  }

  public Invoice(Soar panel) {
    try  {
      jbInit();
    }
    catch (Exception ex) {
      ex.printStackTrace();
    }
    this.panel = panel;
  }

  void jbInit() throws Exception {
    InvoiceDisplay.setBounds(new Rectangle(4, 7, 427, 236));
    FinishButton.setText("Finish");
    FinishButton.setBounds(new Rectangle(342, 248, 87, 26));
    this.setLayout(null);
    this.add(InvoiceDisplay, null);
    this.add(FinishButton, null);
  }

  void display(String msg){
    InvoiceDisplay.append(msg + "\n");
  }
}
```


The final screen of the client sequence is shown in Figure 2.10.

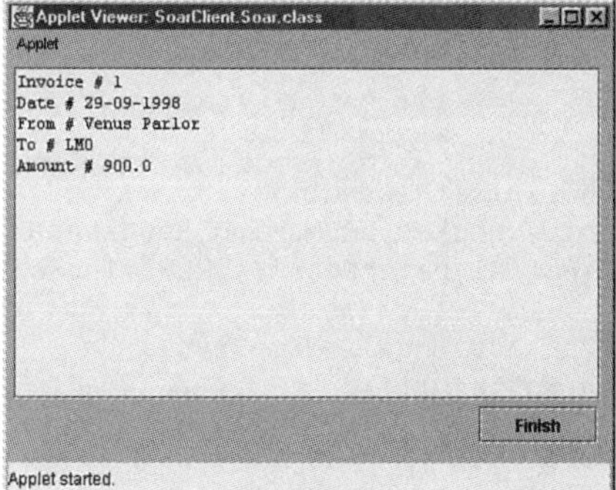

FIGURE 2.10
The invoice client user interface.

The SOARClient Applet

As mentioned earlier in this chapter, the `SOARClient` GUI is presented with a wizard-type interface in an applet. Furthermore, the applet uses the `CardLayout` to achieve a fluid wizard-like execution. The code for constructing such an applet is given in Listing 2.18.

LISTING 2.18 THE SOARCLIENT APPLET

```
package SoarClient;

import java.awt.*;
import java.awt.event.*;
import java.applet.*;
import com.sun.java.swing.*;
import com.sun.java.swing.UIManager;
import org.omg.CORBA.*;

public class SOARClient extends JApplet {
  boolean isStandalone = false;
  CardLayout Layout = new CardLayout();

  final static String PAYMENTPANEL = "Payement";
  final static String RESERVATIONPANEL = "Reservation";
  final static String SEARCHCLIENTPANEL = "Search";
  final static String INVOICECLIENTPANEL = "Invoice";

  private org.omg.CORBA.ORB orb;
  private org.omg.CORBA.BOA boa;
  private com.visigenic.vbroker.URLNaming.Resolver resolver = null;

  Invoice invoice = null;
  PaymentClient Payment = null;
  SearchClient Search = null;
  ReservationsClient Reservation = null;

  public Soar() {

    try{
      orb = org.omg.CORBA.ORB.init(this,null);
      resolver = com.visigenic.vbroker.URLNaming.ResolverHelper.narrow(
               orb.resolve_initial_references("URLNamingResolver"));
    }
    catch(org.omg.CORBA.ORBPackage.InvalidName ivn){
      System.out.println(ivn.toString());
    }

    invoice = new Invoice(this);
    Payment = new PaymentClient(orb,boa,resolver,invoice,this);
    Reservation = new ReservationsClient(orb,boa,resolver,Payment,this);
    Search = new SearchClient(orb,boa,resolver,Reservation,this);
  }
```

```
  public void init() {
    try {
    jbInit();
    }
    catch (Exception e) {
    e.printStackTrace();
    }
  }
  static {
    try {
      UIManager.setLookAndFeel(new
      ➥com.sun.java.swing.plaf.metal.MetalLookAndFeel());
    }
    catch (Exception e) {}
  }

  private void jbInit() throws Exception {
    this.getContentPane().setLayout(Layout);
    this.setSize(400,300);
    this.getContentPane().add(SEARCHCLIENTPANEL,Search);
    this.getContentPane().add(RESERVATIONPANEL,Reservation);
    this.getContentPane().add(PAYMENTPANEL,Payment);
    this.getContentPane().add(INVOICECLIENTPANEL,invoice);
  }

  public void start() {
  }

  public void stop() {
  }

  public void destroy() {
  }

  public String getAppletInfo() {
    return "Applet Information";
  }

  public String[][] getParameterInfo() {
    return null;
  }

  public void displayPanel(String panelname){
    ((CardLayout)this.getContentPane().getLayout()).show(
                               this.getContentPane(),panelname);
  }
}
```

The applet initializes the ORB and the associated resources. This is accomplished in the following three lines of code:

```
orb = org.omg.CORBA.ORB.init(this,null);
      resolver = com.visigenic.vbroker.URLNaming.ResolverHelper.narrow
      (orb.resolve_initial_references("URLNamingResolver"));
```

After this is done, the applet code initializes all the SOAR clients in sequence:

```
invoice = new Invoice(this);
Payment = new PaymentClient(orb,boa,resolver,invoice,this);
Reservation = new ReservationsClient(orb,boa,resolver,Payment,this);
Search = new SearchClient(orb,boa,resolver,Reservation,this);
```

The rest of the code is related to the Java GUI API. You now have to run this applet in a browser so that the application can be potentially enhanced and deployed over the Internet/intranet. In order for you to run this applet in a Web browser, you have to satisfy a couple of criteria:

- You must have access to a Web server.
- You must have a Java Swing–compatible Web browser. Netscape 4.5 is swing-compatible. If you need to have 100 percent Java support on the browser side, one of your best options is to download the Java Activator component and install it to your favorite browser.

NOTE

For the previous application, I used the Java WebServer 1.0.3 and HotJava Web browser. You could use any Web server to hold the client code.

Take the following steps to run the client applet.

To run the client applet, first create an HTML file to load the applet into the Web browser. This is accomplished in Listing 2.19.

LISTING 2.19 THE SOAR CLIENT HTML PAGE

```
<HTML>
<HEAD>
<META HTTP-EQUIV="Content-Type" CONTENT="text/html; charset=iso-8859-1">
<TITLE>
Super Orb Airline Reservartion
</TITLE>
</HEAD>
<BODY>
Super Orb Airline Reservations.<BR>
```

```
<APPLET
  CODEBASE = "."
  CODE     = "SoarClient.Soar.class"
  NAME     = "Soar"
  WIDTH    = 600
  HEIGHT   = 600
  HSPACE   = 0
  VSPACE   = 0
  ALIGN    = middle
>
</APPLET>
</BODY>
</HTML>
```


The two most important parameters in Listing 2.19 are the `CODE` and `CODEBASE` tags. The former identifies the class that has to be loaded into the browser, and the latter indicates where the code is to be loaded from. `CODEBASE` specifies `"."`, which means that the code will be found where the HTML page was found in the Web server.

It is necessary to load the applet from a Web server, because the applet is going to make network connections. Java places the restriction on applets that they cannot connect to servers other than the one on which they were loaded. Therefore, if the applet was just loaded from the hard drive, the Java Virtual Machine security manager throws a security exception.

Additionally, the following steps have to be taken to ensure that the applet will execute properly in the browser:

1. Ensure the Web server is running.
2. Map the Java Class package directory as an alias so that the applet can download the code from the location that is specified in the `CODEBASE` tag. For instance, if you store the HTML page and the code for the SOAR client in a directory `C:\Corba`, map this directory to an alias in the Web server—for example, `/Corba`.
3. Place all the packages in the directory where your page will be downloaded. For the HotJava Web browser, the following class packages are placed in the page directory:

   Unjar the `vbjorb.jar` archive file to the page directory.

   Unjar the `swingall.jar` archive file to the page directory.
4. Load the SOAR client HTML page from the Web server. The applet executing in the browser is shown in Figure 2.11.

That concludes the implementation of the SOAR application. You have built four servers and an applet client. The applications have been built using Java, and extensive uses of the Swing libraries were used to build the GUI.

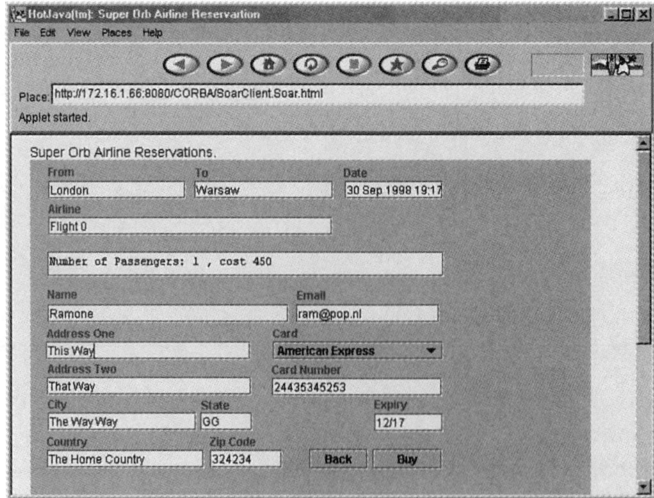

FIGURE 2.11
SOAR client in HotJava.

Summary

CORBA over the Internet has the potential of transforming the nature of applications built over the Internet. The first impact will probably occur when innovative companies use CORBA-based application servers to drive second-generation e-commerce systems. Java will play an ever-increasing role in the drive of what Orfalli and Harkey (Java and CORBA) called the *Object Web*. The true potential of the Internet as a medium to transform our lives will then become evident.

CHAPTER 3

The Portable Object Adapter

IN THIS CHAPTER

A new standard object adapter specification was added to CORBA as of version 2.2. This new adapter is called the Portable Object Adapter (POA). This new adapter is meant to replace the Basic Object Adapter (BOA). The object adapter is a key CORBA architectural component. A server communicates with an ORB through the object adapter. It serves as a central gateway functionality that is common for all implementations.

The BOA was meant to be a minimalist adapter. Over time, the BOA has grown into a multifunctional component. Its primary purpose is to control the life cycle of an implementation. It is the primary interface into an implementation repository. Some implementations of the BOA also add basic security information in the implementation repository, such as granting access privileges. Since CORBA 1.0, the BOA has grown into a behemoth. The problem is that every ORB vendor has its own interpretation of what the BOA is. Consequently, the server-side implementation is not portable between ORBs. These implementations have been many proprietary extensions. In itself, this is not a bad development. The only thing OMG mandates for an implementation is a basic level of interoperability. Various ORBs achieve this to various degrees.

The POA is designed to achieve portability at the server end. It is a breakthrough specification for OMG and is a very tight and precise specification. The overall result should mean that vendors implementing POA would enable the user to move implementations from one ORB to another with minimal hassle.

The Rationale Behind POA

The main goal behind the POA is portability. This would enable plug-and-play ORBs. POA-compliant servers could be deployed on any ORB that supports the POA.

Transparent activation of servers is brought forward from the BOA. Under the BOA, a server that is registered as a shared server is automatically activated when a request comes in. This functionality is also present in the POA.

The POA enables support for persistent object identities. These identities can be spread across multiple server lifetimes. With the BOA, a server's identity is unique for every time the server is activated. The adapter via an adapter activator can ensure that the POA instances are created to handle an incoming client request.

An implementation under POA can have more than one instance. This entails the existence of a servant to support more than one object identity. This is similar to a shared server, except that a single servant can support multiple identities simultaneously.

More than one POA can exist within a server. In conjunction with POA policies, each POA can have a distinct policy.

These are the components of the POA architecture:

- The POA Client

  A POA client is similar to a BOA client. It needs to acquire an object reference before making an invocation.

- The POA Server

  The server is the process that hosts an implementation of some interface.

- The POA Servant

  The servant is the mapping for a given IDL interface. The programmer implements an interface under POA; this implementation is a servant. With POA, an interface can have more than one servant.

- The POA

  Every server contains a POA. Each POA has a set of associated policies. The POA provides a namespace for the objects hosted by the server. If the POA is related to other POAs, namespaces are provided for these as well.

- POA Policy

  Under BOA, the adapter essentially controlled the life cycle of the server. The POA policy provides a coherent and consistent mechanism for specifying these and the other components, such as the POA client, servant, and so forth, that make a POA implementation. Policies provide various options for the management of the objects.

- The POA Manager

  The POA manager controls the life cycle of the POA. It is possible to visualize the POA as integral to the server. Therefore, the POA manager essentially manages the server.

- The Servant Manager

  Every POA server hosts a set of servants. A POA can contain one or more servants. Just as the POA manager controls the life cycle of the POA, the servant manager controls the life cycle of the servant. The manager associates an object with a particular servant.

- Adapter Activator

  The activator is responsible for creating a POA when an invocation comes in.

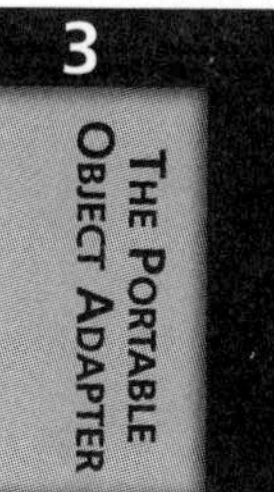

Using POA

POA implementations are only just becoming available. One of the first implementations of POA is from DAIS J2 from ICL. The version used for the examples is a DAIS J2 implementation. As such, the beta release is not a complete implementation of POA. It is nevertheless sufficient to demonstrate the benefits of POA.

The ORB interface enables an application to obtain a POA object. This object is known as a root POA, and it is just like the other CORBA services that are available through the ORB operations. When a POA is created, a specific policy should be associated with a POA. If none is specified, a default policy will be used.

The example demonstrates only the root POA. The root POA has the following default policies:

Thread Policy: `ORB_CTRL_MODEL`

Lifespan Policy: `TRANSIENT`

Object ID Uniqueness Policy: `UNIQUE_ID`

ID Assignment Policy: `SYSTEM_ID`

Servant Retention Policy: `RETAIN`

Request Processing Policy: `USE_ACTIVE_OBJECT_MAP_ONLY`

Implicit Activation Policy: `IMPLICIT_ACTIVATION`

The POA is an active service such as the Naming Service. When the POA is created or acquired, the following steps need to be taken for an application to use the POA:

1. Acquire a servant object.
2. Activate the object.
3. Activate the `POAManager`.
4. Deactivate the object.

Getting Hold of the POA

The POA is just like any other service that runs on top of the ORB—for instance, the Naming service or the Trader service. The POA is acquired by requesting the ORB for an `initial_reference` by passing a string literal `"ROOTPOA"`:

```
org.omg.CORBA.Object poa_ =
            orb.resolve_initial_references("RootPOA");
org.omg.PortableServer.POA poa =
            org.omg.PortableServer.POAHelper.narrow(poa_);
```

CORE object services uder CORBA can always be retrieved using the `resolve_initial_services()` operation. This operation retrieves the object reference. After the object reference has been retrieved, it has to be narrowed. In order to retrieve the POA, you use the same mechanism that was shown previously. The default POA is known as the "RootPOA". After the POA is acquired, the interface needs to be instantiated. This is similar to the activation of an object; the code could look something like this:

```
HangarImpl hangar_i = new HangarImpl("Hangar");
```

After the servant is acquired, the object must be activated. This can be managed through the ActivationPolicy object. There are two policies for activation: IMPLICIT_ACTIVATION and NO_IMPLICIT_ACTIVATION. The former causes the servant to be activated implicitly when an invocation comes in. Implicit activation of an object can be accomplished by invoking the _this() method:

```
Hangar hangar_ = hangar_i._this();
```

After the POA is acquired and activated, the POAManager is activated. The POAManager manages the life cycle of the POA by managing the invocations for the POA. The POAManager is also responsible for the deactivation of the POA. The managers themselves are implicitly activated and deactivated.

Implementing a POA Application

The POA application will use the IDL interface shown in Figure 3.1. The application will model a Hangar interface that maintains aircraft by moving them in and out of a hangar:

```
    interface Hangar{
            exception HangarException {string reason;};
            struct aircraft{
                   long  id;
                   string name;
            };
            void CheckInAirCraft(in aircraft
t_aircraft);
            void CheckOutAirCraft(in long id);
            void kill();
    };
```

The Hangar.idl needs to be compiled using the DAISORB stubgen idl pre-compiler. The following environment is used to implement the Hangar interface:

```
Server Side Orb - Dais J2
Client Side Orb - Dais J2
Java Setup - JDK 1.1.6 With Jbuilder 2
Additional Libs - Swing 1.0.1 and JGL 3.2
```

Run the J2 IDL compiler using the following command:

```
c:> stubgen -ljava -s Hangar.idl
```

The following files are the main ones of interest. The rest of the files are similar to the one generated for pre-POA IDL BOA implementations:

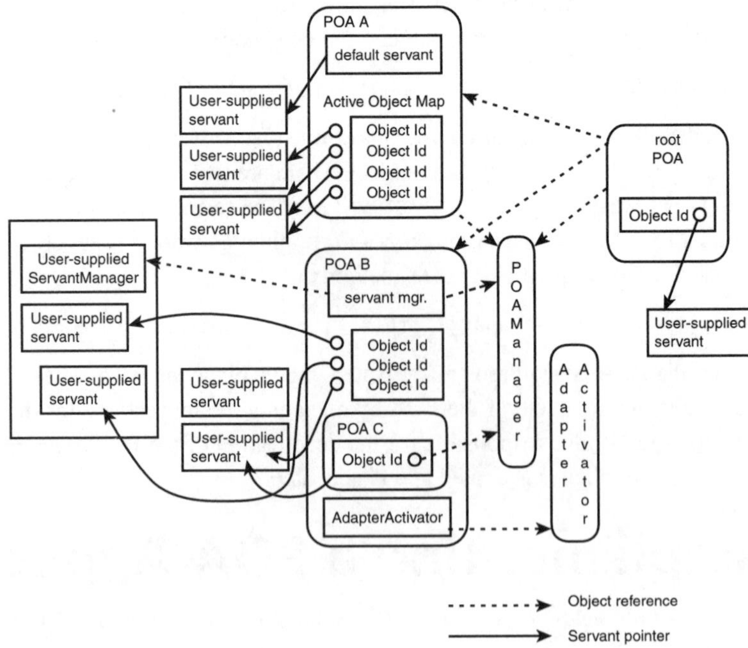

FIGURE 3.1
The IDL interface used by the POA application.

- `HangarOperations.java`—This file contains the Java interface mapping for the `Hangar` IDL interface.
- `POA_Hangar.java`—This file contains an abstract class named `POA_Hangar`. This class needs to be subclassed and implemented. This `POA_Hangar` also provides a skeleton implementation for the `HangarOperations` interface.

Interface Implementation

The interface is implemeted by defining a class, `HangarImpl`, that is derived from the `HangarOperations` class. The code, as shown in Listing 3.1, is very simple and straightforward.

LISTING 3.1 THE `HangarImpl` IMPLEMENTATION

```
import java.util.*;
import org.omg.CORBA.*;
import org.omg.PortableServer.*;
import java.lang.Thread;
import com.sun.java.swing.*;

public class HangarImpl extends POA_Hangar {
```

```
 Vector t_Hangar = new Vector();
 HangarPackage.aircraft t_aircraft = null;
 ORB orb_ = null;
 Trader trader_ = null;
 POA poa_ = null;
 JTextArea HangarStatus = null;

0. public HangarImpl(ORB orb
                   ,Trader trader
                   ,POA poa
                   ,String name
                   ,JTextArea Display){
   super(name);
   orb_ = orb;
   trader_ = trader;
   poa_ = poa;
   HangarStatus = Display;
 }

public void CheckInAirCraft(HangarPackage.aircraft
             t_aircraft ){
   this.t_aircraft = new HangarPackage.aircraft();
   this.t_aircraft.id = t_aircraft.id;
   this.t_aircraft.name = t_aircraft.name;
   t_Hangar.addElement(this.t_aircraft);
   HangarStatus.append("Aircraft:"+t_aircraft.name+"\n");
 }

 public void CheckOutAirCraft(int id ){
   java.util.Enumeration e = t_Hangar.elements();
   while(e.hasMoreElements()){
     HangarPackage.aircraft temp_ =
     (HangarPackage.aircraft)e.nextElement();
     if(temp_.id == id){
        t_Hangar.removeElement(temp_);
        HangarStatus.append("Aircraft Checked Out : " +
                                      temp_.name + "\n");
     }
   }
 }

 public void shutDown ( ){
     try{
       trader_.delete(_this(),"");
       byte[] objectid_ = poa_.reference_to_id(_this());
       poa_.deactivate_object(objectid_);
       new capsuleShutdown(orb_);
     }
     catch(Exception e){
```


continues

LISTING 3.1 CONTINUED

```
            e.printStackTrace();
        }
    }
}

 class capsuleShutdown implements Runnable{
    private org.omg.CORBA.ORB the_orb;
    capsuleShutdown( org.omg.CORBA.ORB _the_orb){
        the_orb = _the_orb;
        (new Thread( this )).start();
    }

    public synchronized void run(){
        the_orb.shutdown( true );
    }
}
```

The constructor takes five arguments. These arguments are passed by the server when it instantiates the servant. These arguments are passed primarily for the `capsuleShutdown` class. This class is invoked when the server is shut down.

The implementations of the operations themselves are trivial. A vector is utilized to store the `Aircraft` structure when one is passed in from the client. Similarly, when a client passes an ID into the `CheckOutAircraft` operation, the given element is removed from the vector.

The server also passes an instance of a `JText` object. This object is used to update the status of the `Hangar`. When the principal operations are called, the `JText` object is updated. The method `shutDown` is not really important right now. It is meant to be called when the servant and the POA are shut down.

The HangarServer Implementation

The `HangarServer` is the heart of setting up POA. All the steps listed earlier in the chapter will be illustrated in the implementation of the server, which is shown in Listing 3.2.

LISTING 3.2 IMPLEMENTING THE `HangarServer`

```
import com.sun.java.swing.*;
import java.lang.Thread;

public class HangarServer implements Runnable{
  ORB orb = null;
  JTextArea Display = null;
```

```
  public HangarServer(String[] args,JTextArea
             HangarStatus,JTextArea Display) {
   try{
   orb = org.omg.CORBA.ORB.init(args,null);
     this.Display = Display;
   org.omg.CORBA.Object pfobj =
            orb.resolve_initial_references( "RootPOA" );
   POA poa = org.omg.PortableServer.POAHelper.narrow(
                                         pfobj );
   org.omg.CORBA.Object trader_obj =
         orb.resolve_initial_references( "DAIS_Trader" );
   Trader trader = TraderHelper.narrow( trader_obj );

 HangarImpl Hangar_ = new
          HangarImpl(orb,trader,poa,"Hangar",HangarStatus);
 Hangar Hangar_ref = Hangar_._this();
 POAManager poamgr_ = poa.the_POAManager();
 poamgr_.activate();
 trader.register("Hangar","/","",Hangar_ref);
   }
   catch(org.omg.CORBA.ORBPackage.InvalidName ivn){
     ivn.printStackTrace();
     Display.append(ivn.toString());
   }
   catch(POAManagerPackage.AdapterInactive iva){
     iva.printStackTrace();
     Display.append(iva.toString());
   }
   catch(TraderPackage.BadType ivt){
     ivt.printStackTrace();
     Display.append(ivt.toString());
   }
   catch(TraderPackage.BadContext ivc){
     ivc.printStackTrace();
     Display.append(ivc.toString());
   }
   catch(Exception e){
     e.printStackTrace();
     Display.append(e.toString());
   }
  }
  public void run(){
      Display.append("Hangar is ready");
 orb.run();
  }
}
```

The following steps describe the POA in action:

1. The ORB is initialized with this line:

   ```
   orb = org.omg.CORBA.ORB.init(args,null);
   ```

The initialization is identical to BOA or other Object Adapter initialization.

2. The "RootPOA" is acquired for the ORB by invoking the `resolve_initial_references()` method. At this juncture, other POAs could have been extracted as well. It's just that the version of DaisORB that was used did not have the complete implementation. Also note the API used. It is identical to those used to resolve other standard CORBA services, such as Naming or Trading. If all goes well, at this point the "RootPOA" should be active.
3. The `resolve_initial_reference` returns a `CORBA.Object`. This object needs to be narrowed (or downcast) to an instance of the POA.
4. The `Trader` object reference is retrieved by another call to the ORB context.
5. `DaisOrb` uses the Trader service. There will be more on how to use the Trader service in Chapter 8, "The Trader Service." `Dais` uses the Trader service as a repository to hold object references. This service is retrieved like any other CORBA service.
6. The Servant `HangarImpl` is instantiated. The required parameters are passed into the class constructor.
7. The object reference is activated at this line:

   ```
   Hangar Hangar_ref = Hangar_._this();
   ```
8. The `POAManager` is attached to the given POA. In this case, because the "RootPOA" is all there is, it is the "RootPOA" that is attached to the `POAManager`.
9. The `POAManager` is activated so that it can from here on control the interaction of the outside world with the "RootPOA".
10. The `Hangar` object reference is registered with the trader. This enables any client to obtain the `Hangar` object reference from the Trader. The `Hangar` is registered with the `rootContext` of the Trader.
11. When the constructor finishes, all the elements of the POA are initialized. The server itself implements the `Runnable` interface. This is a good way to ensure that the class can be initialized and sent off on a thread. The `run()` method is very similar to the `BOA_impl_is_ready()` method.

The Hangar Deactivation Class

The POA and the servants need to be cleanly shut down before exiting. The object references that were registered with the Trader service should be removed from the Trader context. A `Terminator` class accomplishes the removal of the object reference, as shown in Listing 3.3. This class does the reverse of what the server class does. An added benefit might be that the terminator (and the server) might be generalized into an abstract base class. This can then be subclassed and extended by the `Server` and `Terminator` classes, thereby saving implementation time and code.

LISTING 3.3 THE Terminator CLASS

```
import com.sun.java.swing.*;
import java.util.*;

public class Terminator implements Runnable{
  JTextArea display;
  int object_ref;
  org.omg.CORBA.Object object_ = null;
  org.omg.CORBA.ORB orb = null;
  String args[] = null;

  public Terminator(String[] args, JTextArea display) {
    this.args = args;
    try{
      Properties orb_properties = new Properties();
      orb_properties.put("TRADER_ADDRESS","galileo.oa.nl");
      orb_properties.put("TRADER_PORT", "11001");
      orb = org.omg.CORBA.ORB.init(args,
new Properties(orb_properties));
    }
    catch ( Throwable t){
        display.append( "Exception: (Orb)" + t.toString());
        return;
    }
  }

  public void run(){
   Hangar Hangar = null;
   try{
        org.omg.CORBA.Object trader_
           = orb.resolve_initial_references("DAIS_Trader");
        Trader trader = TraderHelper.narrow(trader_);
        TraderPackage.OffersHolder results =
           new TraderPackage.OffersHolder();
        trader.lookup ("Hangar","/","",
        TraderPackage.LookUpPolicy.lookup_random,results );

        Hangar  = HangarHelper.narrow(
                  (results.value[0]).offer_ref );
    }
    catch ( org.omg.CORBA.UserException e ){
                display.append(e.toString());
        return;
    }
    catch ( org.omg.CORBA.SystemException e ){
        display.append( e.toString());
        return;
    }
    catch( Exception e){
        display.append(e.toString());
```

continues

LISTING 3.3 CONTINUED

```
    }

    try{
      Hangar.shutDown();
    }
    catch( org.omg.CORBA.SystemException ex){
        display.append(ex.toString());
    }
    catch( java.lang.Exception exp){
        display.append(exp.toSting());
    }

   Hangar._release();
   orb.shutdown(true);
    display.append("Server Shutdown.. \n");
  }
}
```

The `shutDown()` method on the `Hangar` object reference is called. This causes the `shutDown()` method to execute on the object, deactivating the object reference with the POA.The `Hangar._release()` frees the `Hangar` object reference that was acquired from the Trader. Calling the `shutdown()` on the ORB shuts down the ORB instance that was acquired by the `ORB.init` method.

The Hangar Server GUI

Most often, CORBA servers have boring DOS boxes or UNIX terminals for output display. That might have been appropriate when coding in C or C++, but when using Java, there aren't any excuses for not providing a GUI for the server. Such an interface is provided for the Hangar server, as shown in Listing 3.4. Figure 3.2 shows how the GUI looks.

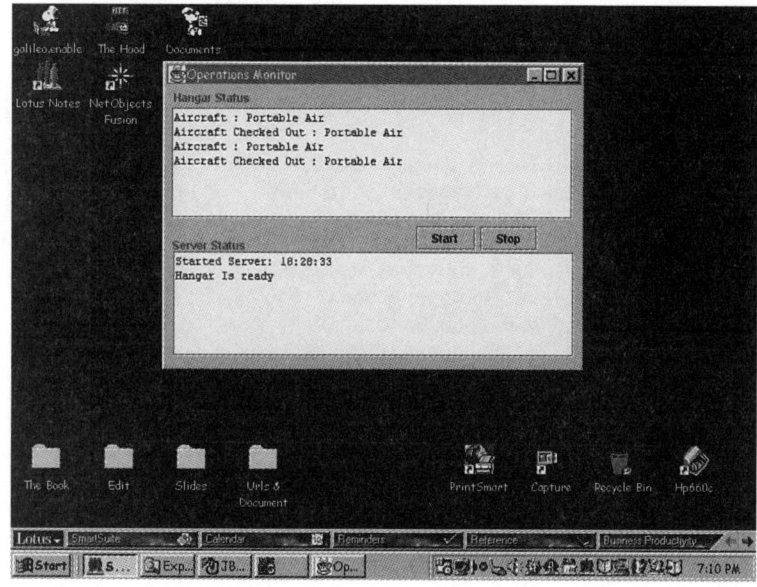

FIGURE 3.2
The Hangar server GUI.

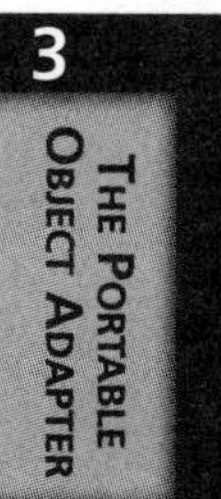

LISTING 3.4 THE HANGARSERVER GUI

```
import java.awt.*;
import com.sun.java.swing.*;
import java.awt.event.*;
import java.util.*;
import java.lang.Thread;

public class OpsMonitor extends JFrame{

  JScrollPane jScrollPane1 = new JScrollPane();
  JLabel jLabel1 = new JLabel();
  JScrollPane jScrollPane2 = new JScrollPane();
  JTextArea ServerStatus = new JTextArea();
  JButton StartBtn = new JButton();
  JButton StopBtn = new JButton();
  JLabel jLabel2 = new JLabel();
  JTextArea HangarStatus = new JTextArea();
  String[] args = null;
  public OpsMonitor(String[] args) {
    try  {
      this.args = args;
      jbInit();
    }
    catch (Exception e) {
      e.printStackTrace();
    }
  }
```

continues

LISTING 3.4 CONTINUED

```
  public static void main(String[] args) {
    OpsMonitor opsMonitor1 = new OpsMonitor(args);
  }

  private void jbInit() throws Exception {
    this.setDefaultCloseOperation(
WindowConstants.DISPOSE_ON_CLOSE);
    this.setTitle("Operations Monitor");
    jScrollPane1.setBounds(new Rectangle(6, 21, 431, 132));
    jLabel1.setText("Hangar Status");
    jLabel1.setBounds(new Rectangle(7, 1, 140, 22));
    jScrollPane2.setBounds(new Rectangle(7, 189, 428,101));
    ServerStatus.setEditable(false);
    StartBtn.setText("Start");
    StartBtn.setActionCommand("StartBtn");
    StartBtn.setBounds(new Rectangle(238, 158, 98, 28));
    StartBtn.addMouseListener(
 new java.awt.event.MouseAdapter() {
      public void mouseClicked(MouseEvent e) {
        StartBtn_mouseClicked(e);
      }
    });
    StopBtn.setText("Stop");
    StopBtn.setActionCommand("StopBtn");
    StopBtn.setBounds(new Rectangle(336, 158, 98, 28));
    StopBtn.addMouseListener(
 new java.awt.event.MouseAdapter() {
      public void mouseClicked(MouseEvent e) {
        StopBtn_mouseClicked(e);
      }
    });
    jLabel2.setText("Server Status");
    jLabel2.setBounds(new Rectangle(7, 169, 142, 18));
    HangarStatus.setEditable(false);
    this.getContentPane().setLayout(null);
    jScrollPane1.getViewport().add(HangarStatus, null);
    this.getContentPane().add(jScrollPane1, null);
    jScrollPane1.getViewport().add(HangarStatus, null);
    jScrollPane1.getViewport().add(HangarStatus, null);
    this.getContentPane().add(jLabel1, null);
    this.getContentPane().add(StartBtn, null);
    this.getContentPane().add(StopBtn, null);
    this.getContentPane().add(jLabel2, null);
    this.getContentPane().add(jScrollPane2, null);
    jScrollPane2.getViewport().add(ServerStatus, null);
    this.setVisible(true);
    this.setResizable(true);

  }
```

```
  void StopBtn_mouseClicked(MouseEvent e) {
    String[] args = new String[1];
    args[0] = "Hangar";
   Terminator theSweeper = new Terminator(args,
ServerStatus);
    Thread terminator = new Thread(theSweeper);
    terminator.start();
  }

  void StartBtn_mouseClicked(MouseEvent e) {
   Date today_ = new Date();
   String msg =   "Started Server: " +
                  today_.getHours() + ":" +
                  today_.getMinutes()+":"+
                  today_.getSeconds();
   ServerStatus.append(msg + "\n");
 HangarServer temp_ =
new HangarServer(args,HangarStatus,ServerStatus);
   Thread HangarThread = new Thread(temp_);
   HangarThread.start();
  }
}
```


The user clicking on the "stop" button instantiates an instance of the `Terminator` class. The Terminator, as mentioned previously, shuts down the POA and associated resources. Here is the relevant piece of code:

```
void StopBtn_mouseClicked(MouseEvent e) {
    String[] args = new String[1];
    args[0] = "Hangar";
   Terminator theSweeper = new Terminator(args,
ServerStatus);
    Thread terminator = new Thread(theSweeper);
    terminator.start();
  }
```

The "start" button starts an instance of the Hangar servant on a new thread. This is the code that handles this function:

```
void StartBtn_mouseClicked(MouseEvent e) {
   Date today_ = new Date();
   String msg =   "Started Server: " +
                  today_.getHours() + ":" +
                  today_.getMinutes()+":"+
                  today_.getSeconds();
   ServerStatus.append(msg + "\n");
 HangarServer temp_ =
new HangarServer(args,HangarStatus,ServerStatus);
   Thread HangarThread = new Thread(temp_);
   HangarThread.start();
  }
```

The HangarClient

Unlike the server, the client code is very low-tech. It just demonstrates that everything functions as it should. The body of code is very similar to that of the server. The Trader plays the central role. The client retrieves the reference to the Trader. From the Trader, the client then resolves the Hangar's object reference. This is shown in Listing 3.5.

LISTING 3.5 THE HangarClient

```
import org.omg.CORBA.*;
import org.omg.PortableServer.*;
import java.util.*;

public class HangarClient {
  Hangar Hangar = null;
  HangarPackage.aircraft checkin_aircraft = new
HangarPackage.aircraft();

  public HangarClient(String[] args) {

  try{
     checkin_aircraft.id = 6001;
     checkin_aircraft.name = "Portable Air";


     Properties orb_properties = new Properties();
     orb_properties.put("TRADER_ADDRESS", "galileo.oa.nl");
     orb_properties.put("TRADER_PORT", "11001");
     ORB orb_ = org.omg.CORBA.ORB.init(args,
                           new Properties(orb_properties));
     org.omg.CORBA.Object trader_ =
            orb_.resolve_initial_references("DAIS_Trader");
     Trader trader = TraderHelper.narrow(trader_);
     TraderPackage.OffersHolder results =
                   new TraderPackage.OffersHolder();
trader.lookup("Hangar","/","",
    TraderPackage.LookUpPolicy.lookup_random,results);
   Hangar =
          HangarHelper.narrow(results.value[0].offer_ref);
   }
   catch (org.omg.CORBA.UserException e ){
     System.err.println(e.toString());
     return;
   }
   catch ( org.omg.CORBA.SystemException e ){
     System.err.println(e.toString());
```

```
        return;
      }
      catch( Exception e){
        System.err.println(e.toString());
        return;
      }
      try{
      Hangar.CheckInAirCraft(checkin_aircraft);
        Hangar.CheckOutAirCraft(6001);
      }
      catch(SystemException ex){
        ex.printStackTrace();
      }
  }
    public static void main(String[] args) {
      HangarClient HangarClient = new HangarClient(args);
    }
  }
```

The `Dais` clients need to have access to the Trader server. Properties enable the client to initialize the ORB reference with the information required to locate the Trader server. The properties are passed to the ORB initialization routines so that when `orb_.resolve_initial_references()` is called, the ORB will know exactly where to look for the Trader server.

The `Hangar` object reference is retrieved from the result set that is acquired from the Trader server.

Once the `Hangar` reference is acquired, the code can treat the object reference as if it's local. Because the `Hangar` has only two operations, these two are invoked on the object reference.

Summary

The Portable Object Adapter is one more step taken by OMG to ensure that CORBA is a modular plug-and-play technology. Over time, OMG has been trying to ensure that a reasonable level of interoperability and integration is possible with any CORBA 2.0–compliant ORB. Although the current ORB implementations leave much to be desired, the matter is progressing to the extent that OMG specifications allow as little dependence on a particular vendor as possible.

The POA is perhaps one of the most important pieces in this strategy. Pre-POA ORB implementations, although IIOP-compliant, did not offer much portability on the server side. By portability, it is primarily portability between ORBs that is intended. The POA will enable this to happen. In conjunction with IIOP, implementations of POA will allow vendors the opportunity to continually innovate their interpretation of the CORBA standard without cornering customers on their platform.

The main benefit of the POA is that many of the innovations vendors have made with their implementations of the BOA are now formalized in very tight specifications. As such, the POA is not a revolutionary step over BOA as much as it is an evolution of the BOA into something that is formal and standard.

IDL Language Mapping

PART II

IN THIS PART

CHAPTER 4

CORBA Object References and Smart Pointers

IN THIS CHAPTER

Object references are the workhorse of CORBA. It is on an object reference that the client invokes an operation. This chapter looks at how these object references can be managed. Particular attention will be paid to the issue of object reference counts and how the ORB interface API could be used to elicit information on the services and objects available on the ORB.

The chapter primarily deals with management of reference counts, which includes passing object references. It will also look at who ultimately has responsibility for disposing an object reference.

Object Reference Mapping in C++

Every interface specified in the IDL maps to a C++ class. This class is implemented as per specification and deployed on some server. This means that the implementation is hosted in a server. This implementation or component can be provided with a name, and the ORB can be notified of an object's initialization. This is accomplished in the `boa.impl_is_ready()` method call to the ORB. The client acquires this object reference in a number of ways. It can acquire an object reference using a `bind()` call. It can retrieve an object reference from a naming service. Where interoperability is an issue, an object reference may be reconstructed by morphing a stringified object reference to a proper object reference.

More importantly, object references can be passed around as parameters to operations. CORBA specifies that an object reference can be mapped to a `T_ptr` and a `T_var` type. The `T_ptr` is usually a normal C++ pointer type upon which operations appropriate to a pointer type may be applied. This is generally true except for pointer arithmetic. Pointer arithmetic cannot be applied to an object reference pointer, because the arithmetic is local in nature but the pointer that is being operated on is a pointer to a remote object.

Memory for `T_ptrs` needs to be allocated. And as with any pointer, memory needs to be deallocated when the variable is no longer required. In many cases, this leads to memory leaks where a programmer forgets to deallocate memory. To lessen the probability of such leaks, CORBA 2.0 specifies the `T_var` type. The `T_var` makes the deallocation a bit painless. This is accomplished by the fact that a `T_var` is automatically deallocated when the pointer falls out of scope. However, the use of the `T_var` type is optional.

Consider the following IDL (`oref.idl`):

```
module objects{
    interface object{
        readonly attribute long dummyvariable;
    };

    interface reference{
```

```
        void setObjectReference(in object anObject);
        object getObjectReference();
        void getOutObjectReference(out object anobject);
    };
};
```

The intention of this exercise is to show the passing of object references between clients and servers. The example will particularly focus on the essential aspects of memory management of object references in CORBA. In the previous interface, you pass an object reference to and from a client. This demonstrates how object references can be managed in terms of memory.

The interfaces need to be pre-compiled. The examples will use Orbix 2.3c. The interface can be compiled with the following command:

```
prompt$> idl -B -S reference.idl
```

CORBA Memory Management for Object References

CORBA does not support distributed memory management. Though the issues might seem complicated to a novice, the underlying principle is rather simple. Memory is managed separately for both client and server. This is accomplished through reference counting. This means that if a copy of an object is made, the effect is only local. It is conceivable that a server object serves a number of clients.

A consequence of this is that, under CORBA, what a particular client chooses to do with its object reference has no impact on another client. This eliminates the overhead of maintaining a global count of the number of object references on the server. This overhead would conceivably impose a severe strain on the scalability of the server. The overhead of servicing the kinds of requests made over the Internet would probably not be possible with an architecture that supports global reference counts.

The whole framework of CORBA memory management of object references is based on reference counting. As an architecture that does not support distributed memory management, this mechanism leads to local management of reference counts.

There are two interfaces in the previous module: the reference interface and the object interface. The object interface is operated upon by the reference interface. Later in the chapter, we shall develop an example implementation that will demonstrate two things, the first being the rules of passing object references around. Just like the other IDL types, standard rules apply to memory management of object references.

Secondly, perhaps more importantly, the example will illustrate the mechanism of reference counting. The example will have two clients that will interact with the server in various ways.

Object References as Parameters

An object reference in CORBA maps to a C++ pointer type. Just as with the other IDL types, care needs to be taken to ensure that the correct semantics of memory management is used. With object references, there is an added dimension to these semantics: an incorrect management of object references might lead to a corruption of object reference count. In theory, this could lead to a premature deletion of the object reference all together. Subsequent calls on the reference will lead to undefined behavior. Ultimately, the goal of correct management of object references is to ensure that the reference count is consistent with the actual reference count.

The IDL pre-compiler for C++ maps interfaces as represented in the following table:

Type	`in`	`out`	`inout`	`return`
interface X	`X_ptr`	`X_ptr&`	`X_ptr&`	`X_ptr`

When you specify an object reference as a parameter to an operation or a return type, this mapping will be used by the IDL pre-compiler to generate the C++ mappings.

When the Object Reference Is Passed In

The object reference passed by the client to the server should be treated as read-only. This means that `CORBA::release(T_ptr)` cannot be called on the parameter. But because the parameter is an object reference, the code can treat it as such and invoke operations on the object reference.

If the application runs in a distributed address space, the object reference is passed as a copy. The underlying ORB will call `release()` on this reference when the method returns.

WARNING

The server does not own the object reference. Therefore, it is deleted when the call returns. The ORB accomplishes this deletion. One of the consequences is that no attempt to use the assignment operator should be made. Both the variables end up pointing at the same area of memory that is marked for deletion.

The only safe way to keep a local copy of the object reference is to use `duplicate()` on the passed reference.

When the Object Reference Is Passed Out

On a distributed address space, the server has to allocate memory for the parameter. The ORB then copies them across to the client and calls `release()` on the references. This also means that assignments should be avoided in initialization of the parameter or the return type, because the ORB will deallocate the memory that is allocated when the method retruns.

When the Object Reference Is Passed Inout

The semantics of inout are very similar to inout for strings. The parameter that is passed in is read/write. This means that the server could treat it as an in parameter. But if the server wishes to change the parameter, it then has to first dispose of the incoming parameter and then reallocate a new one. Here is an example:

```
void someobject::foo(anotherobject_ptr p){

    try{
        p->bar();
    }
    ..
    ..
    CORBA::release(p);
    p = anotherobject_ptr::_duplicate(myinstance);
}
```

Object References and Reference Counts

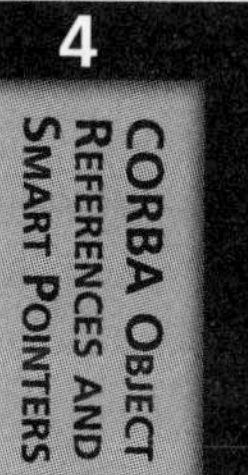

CORBA employs a simple mechanism of localized reference counting for memory management. It is most important to realize that this reference count is only local. The server maintains its own reference count, and the client has a separate reference count.

Deletion of the object reference occurs when the reference count of the object falls to zero. The fact that CORBA does not have distributed garbage collection means that when the client's reference count of an object falls to zero, the object on the client side may be deleted. However, the server has to take care of its own deallocations.

Incrementing and Decrementing the Reference Counts

When a new object reference is allocated, the reference count is incremented to one. This can be accomplished in a number of ways.

On the Server

A server can control the reference count on its end. When a server instantiates a class to create an object, the reference count on the object is incremented by the number of instantiations the server has made. Here is the sample code:

```
objects::object_var dummyobject = new
                    objects::object_i("Object");
```

or

```
objects::object_ptr dummyobject = new
                    objects::object_i("Object");
```

This sets the reference count of the `objects::object` to one. A simple assignment of object reference does not increment the object reference count. Doing this simply means that both the object references refer to the same object.

Care needs to be taken when using the assignment operator with object references. It is conceivable that one of the object references could be released and deallocated, while elsewhere, the implementation could try to invoke an operation on the reference. This would lead to undefined behavior.

The reference count of an object can be decremented by calling the static function `release(T_ptr)` on the CORBA name space. The following statement:

```
CORBA::release(dummyobject);
```

decrements the reference count by one. If the implementation iterates on `T_ptr->_refCount()` and releases all the object references, the object itself will be deallocated. Code such as the following ensures that the object is correctly disposed of when no longer needed:

```
for(long i = 0; i < local_object->_refCount(); i++){
CORBA::release(local_object);
}
```

> **WARNING**
>
> The `T_ptr` is Orbix-specific. Most ORB implementations have such an API—for example, `T_ptr->_ref_count()` under VisiBroker. This API is not CORBA-compliant, so if you use it, isolate the code somewhere so it can be replaced easily if such an API does become CORBA-compliant.

On the Client

When the client does a connect to an object reference using the naming service to initialize the object reference, the reference count goes up by one. Here, the client is using an Orbix `bind` call to retrieve an object reference. This increases the reference count by one:

```
objectRef = objects::object::_bind("Object:ORefManager");
```

On the Server and the Client

If an implementation needs to make a copy of an object reference, it calls `T_ptr::_duplicate(t_ptr)` on the object reference. Calling the `duplicate(t_ptr)` increments the reference count by one. This means that every time `_duplicate()` is called, the reference count goes up by one. A common mistake is to assume that no memory leaks occur when the server exits. This is correct if the reference count is zero for the object, but if the reference count is greater than zero, the destructor for the object will not be called.

The following example illustrates how `_duplicate()` can be used:

```
void objects::reference_i:: setObjectReference (objects::object_ptr
anObject, CORBA::Environment &IT_env) {
    local_object = objects::object::_duplicate(anObject);
}
```

Here, after the `duplicate()` is called, the reference count on the server for the `local_object` object goes up by one.

The Difference Between `T_ptr` and `T_var`

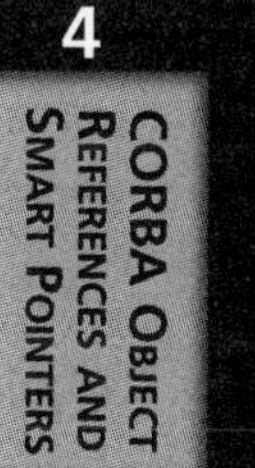

The primary difference between IONA's implementation of the `T_ptr` type and the `T_var` type is that the former is just an alias for a pointer type. Here is an example:

```
typedef objects::object* objects::object_ptr;
```

The `T_var` types are more interesting because they are smart pointers. Smart pointers are interesting in this context because when the destructor for `T_var` type is called, the implementation automatically calls the `CORBA::release()` method on the object being pointed to. The combination `T_var` and `T_ptr` leads to a couple of interesting things to keep in mind.

For example, consider the following:

```
objects::object_ptr ptr_one = new objects::object_ptr();
objects::object_var var_one = new objects::object_var();
objects::object_var var_two = new objects::object_var();
```

This code instantiates three instances of the `objects::object` class. One is a `T_ptr` type, and the others are `T_var` types.

There are two assignments possible with the three variables:

1. `ptr_one = var_one;`

   `T_var` always assumes ownership of the object being pointed to. This means that both `ptr_one` and `var_one` point to the same instance of the object. An assignment of this type also leads to the reference count of the object being pointed to by `var_one` decremented.

   When `var_one` falls out of scope, its destructor will automatically release the object reference count. This means that no attempt should be made to access the `ptr_one` after `var_one` has gone out of scope.

2. `var_one = var_two;`

   This assignment is the safest one, because the overloaded assignment operator calls the `duplicate()` methods implicitly. This means that the reference count on the object reference count will be incremented. This also leads to the release of the object being pointed to by `var_two`. It is only after both objects fall out of scope that the object reference may be deleted.

Implementing the Object Module

Now let's implement the module we specified in `oref.idl`. The object interface specifies only one attbribute. The attribute is defined as a read-only. The method to which it maps will return the object's current reference count. Before examining this, some changes were introduced in the header file to provide a constructor and a destructor as well.

The reference implementation maintains a local instance of the object interface. It is this local object that is operated upon by the client. The reference class also has an overloaded constructor and a destructor.

LISTING 4.1 THE OBJECT HEADER FILE

```
namespace objects{

    class IT_DECLSPEC_oref object_i:public virtual objectBOAImpl {
    public:
        virtual CORBA::Long dummyvariable () ;
        object_i(const char* marker);
        ~object_i();
    private:
        CORBA::Long local;
    };
```

```
    class IT_DECLSPEC_oref reference_i:public virtual referenceBOAImpl{
    public:
     void setObjectReference (objects::object_ptr anObject);
     objects::object_ptr getObjectReference();
     void getOutObjectReference(objects::object_ptr& anobject);

    public:
        reference_i(const char* marker,object_ptr);
        ~reference_i();
    private:
        object_ptr local_object; //Local instance of object
    };
};
```

This header file lists two classes that correspond to the two interfaces specified in `oref.idl`. As an extension of the default mappings provided, we made some changes. First, we added a constructor and a destructor to both the classes. In fact, the constructor in the `reference_I` class is overloaded to take a parameter:

```
reference_i(const char* marker,object_ptr);
```

The reference class also provides a local instance variable, `local_object`.

```
object_ptr local_object;
objects::object_i::object_i(const char* marker):objectBOAImpl(marker){
    local = this->_refCount();
    cout<<"Object's int Ref count: "<<local<<endl;
}
```

The constructor takes a character array as a parameter. This is then passed to the superclass constructor. The parameter is known as a *marker*. The marker allows the naming of object references inside a server. It is possible that there is more than one object inside a server. The marker allows the naming of these objects so that clients can bind to a particular object. The server in our case hosts two objects. The marker is used to distinguish the two objects. Otherwise, the server just returns the default available instance:

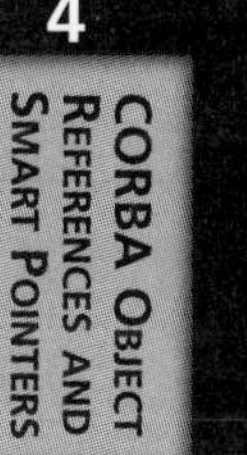


```
objects::object_i::~object_i(){
    cout<<"object_i dtor called"<<endl;
}
```

The destructor will not be called if the reference count is more than zero. Over the course of this object's execution, the reference count should be more than one. These are released in the reference's distructor. When the count is reduced to zero, this method, shown in Listing 4.2, will be invoked.

LISTING 4.2 IMPLEMENTING THE OBJECT MODULE

```
CORBA::Long objects::object_i::dummyvariable (){

    cout<<"Object's int Ref count: "<<local<<endl;
    return this->_refCount();
}

void objects::reference_i:: setObjectReference (objects::object_ptr
anObject, CORBA::Environment &IT_env) {

    local_object = objects::object::_duplicate(anObject);
    cout<<"setObjectReference count is now: "<<
local_object->_refCount()<<endl;
}

objects::object_ptr objects::reference_i:: getObjectReference(){

objects::object_var temp_ref =
objects::object::_duplicate(local_object);
    cout<<"getObjectReference count is now: "<<
local_object->_refCount()<<endl;
    return temp_ref;
}

void objects::reference_i:: getOutObjectReference (objects::object_ptr&
   anobject) {

    cout<<"getOutObjectReference count A is now: "<<
local_object->_refCount()<<endl;
    anobject = objects::object::_duplicate(local_object);
    CORBA::release(anobject);
    cout<<"getOutObjectReference count A is now: "<<
local_object->_refCount()<<endl;
}

objects::reference_i::reference_i(const char* marker, object_ptr
initObject):referenceBOAImpl(marker){
    local_object = objects::object::_duplicate(initObject);
    cout<<"Object's ref count after dunlicate: "<<
local_object->_refCount()<<endl;
}

objects::reference_i::~reference_i(){

    for(long i = 0; i < local_object->_refCount(); i++){
        CORBA::release(local_object);
        cout<<"local Object ref count: "<<
local_object->_refCount()<<endl;
```

```
    }
    cout<<"Reference dstor called.."<<endl;
}
```

The Server Implementation

The server should have only one instance of the reference object. This means that the moment the release method is invoked on it, this destructor should be called. The reference's destructor releases all the reference count on the `objects::object` reference, ensuring that the object is correctly destroyed (see Listing 4.3).

LISTING 4.3 THE SERVER IMPLEMENTATION

```
int main(int argc, char** argv) {

      objects::object_var dummyobject =
new objects::object_i("Object");
    cout<<"Object initialized.."<<endl;
    objects::reference_var referenceobject =
new objects::reference_i("Reference",dummyobject);
    cout<<"Reference initialized.."<<endl;

    try{
        CORBA::Orbix.impl_is_ready("ORefManager");
    }
    catch (CORBA::SystemException &sysEx) {
        cerr << "Unexpected system exception" << endl;
        cerr << &sysEx;
        exit(1);
    }
    catch (...) {
        cout << "Unexpected exception" << endl;
        exit(1);
    }
  cout << "server exiting" << endl;
  return 0;
}
```

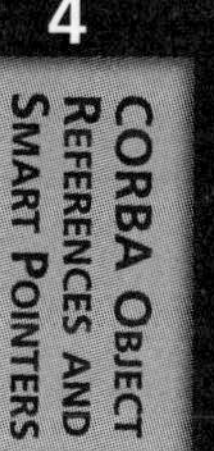

The two objects are constructed with a marker. The server will shut down after the default timeout under Orbix when it should become apparent that the appropriate destructor has been called.

The Client Implementation

The client implementation is straightforward except for the details showing that CORBA really treats memory as local, as shown in Listing 4.4.

LISTING 4.4 THE MODULE CLIENT

```
int main(int argc, char** argv){

    objects::object_var objectRef;
    objects::reference_var referenceRef;

    try {
        objectRef = objects::object::_bind("Object:ORefManager");
        referenceRef =
objects::reference::_bind("Reference:ORefManager");

        //Objects initialized using the marker on the server.
    }
    catch (CORBA::SystemException &sysEx) {
        cerr << "Unexpected system exception" << endl;
        cerr << &sysEx;
        exit(1);
    }

    try{
        cout<<"Object ref count: "<<objectRef->_refCount()<<endl;
        cout<<"Reference ref count: "<<
referenceRef->_refCount()<<endl;
        cout<<"Count on the object server: "<<
objectRef->dummyvariable()<<endl;
        referenceRef->setObjectReference(objectRef);
        objects::object_var tempRef =
referenceRef->getObjectReference();
        cout<<"Object ref count after getObjectReference: "
<<objectRef->_refCount()<<endl;
        CORBA::release(tempRef);
        referenceRef->getOutObjectReference(tempRef);
        cout<<"Object ref count after getOutObjectReference: "
<<objectRef->_refCount()<<endl;
    }
    catch(...){}
    cout<<"Object ref count before exiting: "<<
objectRef->_refCount()<<endl;
    return 0;
}
```

Summary

CORBA does not support distributed memory management. This is true for both the basic types as well as object references. Nevertheless, CORBA specifies the exact semantics of what happens when object references are passed as parameters and/or returns. Memory is managed via the mechanism of reference counts. It should be noted that reference count APIs are not CORBA-compliant but APIs introduced by the vendors.

CHAPTER 5

IDL/Java Mapping

In This Chapter

The OMG ratified the IDL-to-Java mapping specifications on June 24, 1997. I could call the mapping "unintuitive," because some aspects of IDL do not map cleanly to Java. But this would not be entirely correct. Most of the IDL maps almost keyword for keyword, except where parameters are concerned. There are also some other issues where no one-on-one mapping is possible, such as for IDL `typedefs`.

Consider the context of this before accusing me of heresy. CORBA is a cross-platform technology, where Java is not the only game in town. Altering the IDL to make it more Java-friendly would result in issues dealing with backward compatibility with other languages. The IDL is the foundation on which CORBA implementations in different languages talk to each other. To restructure the IDL to make it more intuitive for Java would have meant making it unintuitive for other languages.

Reserved Names in Java IDL Mapping

OMG has reserved several names for the mapping in the specifications:

- The Java class `<type>HelperHelper Java class>Helper>Helper>` is reserved. This type can stand for any IDL user-defined type. So, if some interface named `bingo` is specified in IDL, the IDL2Java pre-compiler will generate a `bingoHolder` class. If you specify an interface `bingoHolder` in your interface, the pre-compiler will generate a `bingoHolderHolder` class while the interface will map to the `_bingoHolder` Java interface.
- The IDL defined `<type>` maps to a Java class `Holder Java class>Holder> Holder>` named `<type>Holder`. These could correspond to your regular IDL types.
- Basic IDL types, such as `short` and `long`, map to `<basicJavaType>Holder`, where `<basicJavaType>` can be any primitive`Holder Java class>Holder>Holder>` built in Java types. For instance, if you have a `long` specified as an `out` parameter in an interface, that maps to a `LongHolder` parameter in Java.

Mapping of IDL Types to Java

There are four categories of IDL types:

- Basic types
- Constructed types
- Template types
- Pseudo Object types

WARNING

There are some fundamental differences between the range of values of Java types and IDL types. Problems can occur when the range of an IDL type is less than that of Java types. An `in` value parameter is checked during runtime. This is particularly important, because Java does not have support for unsigned types in Java. An error during this conversion results in either a `CORBA::DATA_CONVERSION` exception or a `CORBA::MARSHAL` exception.

Table 5.1 shows the fundamental mapping of IDL types to Java.

TABLE 5.1 BASIC IDL TYPE TO JAVA MAPPING

IDL Types	*Value Range*	*Java Types*	*Value Range*
`boolean`	TRUE or FALSE	`boolean`	TRUE or FALSE
`char`	8-bit	`char`	
`wchar`	16-bit	`java.lang.String`	
`octet`	Invariant 8-bit	`byte`	
`string`		`java.lang.String`	
`short`	16-bit	`short`	
`unsigned short`	16-bit	`short`	
`long`	32-bit	`int`	32-bit
`unsigned long`	32-bit	`int`	32-bit
`long long`	64-bit	`long`	64-bit
`unsigned long long`	64-bit	`long`	64-bit
`float`	single-precision floating number	`float`	
`double`	double-precision floating number	`double`	

IDL Module

The *module* denotes a naming scope for a set of IDL interfaces. The module enables you to classify and group sets of related interfaces within a single scope:

```
module mappings {

    //****************

};
```

The IDL module maps onto a Java package of the same name. Everything specified in the module scope maps to associated classes and interfaces within this package:

```
package mappings;
```

Module specifications can occur more than one time within a single IDL definition. This is possible as long as each module consists of different types. In the following example:

```
module com {
    module mcp {
        module library {

        };
};
};
```

maps to

```
package com.mcp.library; in Java.
```

IDL Interfaces

Interfaces denote the public view exposed by an object. The interface of an object represents the functionality required by the client from the server object. The IDL interface maps cleanly to a Java interface with the same name. In addition to this, a `Helper` and a `Holder` class are generated for the interface as well. The following:

```
module com{
    module mcp{
        module library{
            interface catalog{
            };
        };
    };
};
```

maps to

```
package com.mcp.library;
public interface catalog extends org.omg.CORBA.Object {
}
```

Internals of Interfaces

The interfaces defined correspond to the classes identified in an object model. The classes defined in the object model define methods with varied visibilities. By this I mean that methods that are defined in a class can have private, protected, or public visibility. The IDL interfaces expose the public part of the object model. Within this scope, an interface contains the following constructions:

- Attributes—The attributes defined in an interface correspond to the instance variables in a class. The IDL pre-compiler generates accessor and modifier methods for the attributes defined.

  Remember to add support for the attributes defined in an interface, because most compilers do not generate the declarations of the variable in the classes.
- Syntax Modifiers—The `readonly` attribute modifier causes the IDL pre-compiler to generate only the `accessor/get` function.

  The attribute generates the public interfaces for the instance to the instance variables. A properly designed class results in a manageable number of attributes.

The following interface:

```
module com{
    module mcp{
        module library{
            interface catalog{

            attribute string name;
            attribute string address;
            readonly attribute short age;

            };
        };
    };
};
```

generates the following Java interfaces:

```
package com.mcp.library;
public interface catalog extends org.omg.CORBA.Object {

  public void name(java.lang.String name);
  public java.lang.String name();
  public void address(java.lang.String address);
  public java.lang.String address();
  public short age();
}
```

Note that there is only one method generated for the age attribute. The normal attribute definition results in a set of overloaded methods: one that takes a parameter and another that takes none.

Constructed Types in Interfaces

As mentioned, a poorly analyzed concept results in an unnecessary number of attribute definitions. Nevertheless, sometimes requirements necessitate the inclusion of complex data types in an interface. In order to model complex data types, OMG IDL provides a set of types to allow the definition of these types.

struct Types

IDL `struct` maps to a `final` Java class. A Java class that is defined as `final` cannot be subclassed. This class will contain declarations for the members of the `struct` as public instance variables of the class. The class will also contain two constructors. The default constructor contains initialization routines for the entire instance variable. These definitions initialize the instances with their default value, usually zero or null. The second constructor provides a parameterized constructor to enable initialization of the `struct` with external values.

A struct can be passed as a parameter in an interface operation. Returns on an IDL operation can also be a `struct`. Consider the following `struct`:

```
module com{
    module mcp{
        module library{
            interface catalog{

            struct name{
               string first;
               string middle;
               string last;
            };
        };
    };
     };
};
```

This interface will generate the following class:

```
package com.mcp.library.catalogPackage;

  final public class name {
    public java.lang.String first;
    public java.lang.String middle;
    public java.lang.String last;
```

```
    public name() {
    }
    public name(
      java.lang.String first,
      java.lang.String middle,
      java.lang.String last
    ) {
      this.first = first;
      this.middle = middle;
      this.last = last;
    }
}
```

Note the fact that although the definition of the `struct` was inside a `com.mcp.library.catalog` interface, the class was generated in a separate package called `catalogPackage`.

Inside the `catalogPackage` are two additional classes: the `nameHolder` class and the `nameHelper` class. You can find a detailed coverage of the `Holder` and `Helper` class in the later section "IDL Operations."

A `struct` can contain any legal IDL type. This could include references to other interfaces, `struct`s, strings, and so forth.

Enumeration Type

When a set of values is required, it is appropriate to use an `enum` type. This enables you to group related values and assign names to them. As with the constructed type, the IDL maps to a Java `final` class.

The following IDL:

```
module com{
    module mcp{
        module library{
            interface Calender{
                enum Days{Monday,
                        Tuesday,
                        Wednesday,
                        Thursday,
                        Friday,
                        Saturday,
                        Sunday
                       };
            Days getToday();                                  };
        };
    };
};
```

generates the following `final` class (partial listing) for the constructed type:

```
package com.mcp.library.CalenderPackage;

final public class Days {
    final public static int _Monday = 0;
    final public static int _Tuesday = 1;
    final public static int _Wednesday = 2;
    final public static int _Thursday = 3;
    final public static int _Friday = 4;
    final public static int _Saturday = 5;
    final public static int _Sunday = 6;

     ...
}
```

The interface itself maps the operation to the following code:

```
package com.mcp.library;
public interface Calender extends org.omg.CORBA.Object {
  public com.mcp.library.CalenderPackage.Days getToday();
}
```

The implementation can then directly use the static member variables.

Union Type

IDL also supports discriminated unions. The definition consists of a discriminator and a value corresponding to that particular discriminator. Look at the following example:

```
module com{
    module mcp{
        module library{

            interface menu{};

            interface Dietician{
                enum Days{Monday,
                       Tuesday,
                       Wednesday,
                       Thursday,
                       Friday,
                       Saturday,
                       Sunday
                      };

                  union MenuAllocater switch(Days){
                 case Monday: menu MondayMenu;
                 case Tuesday: menu TuesdayMenu;
                 default: menu MondayMenu;
                };

             };
        };
```

```
    };
};
```

The union is named MenuAllocator, and its discriminator is the Days enumeration, which is an int.

The Java mapping produced a final class. A default constructor is also generated, along with accessor and modifier methods for each branch in the union:

```
package com.mcp.library.DieticianPackage;
  final public class MenuAllocater {
    private java.lang.Object _object;
    private com.mcp.library.DieticianPackage.Days _disc;
    public MenuAllocater() {
    }

  public com.mcp.library.DieticianPackage.Days
    discriminator() {
      return _disc;
  }

  public com.mcp.library.menu MondayMenu() {
      if(
        _disc == (com.mcp.library.DieticianPackage.Days)
         com.mcp.library.DieticianPackage.Days.Tuesday ||
        false
      ) {
        throw new
org.omg.CORBA.BAD_OPERATION("MondayMenu");
      }
      return (com.mcp.library.menu) _object;
  }

  public void
  MondayMenu(com.mcp.library.DieticianPackage.Days disc,
  com.mcp.library.menu value) {
      _disc = disc;
      _object = value;
  }
...

(Partial Listing...)
```

Template Types

There are two basic template types in IDL: strings and sequences.

String Type

The string type is the most commonly used complex type in IDL. These are much easier to handle than the chars are. However, strings do place some extra burden on the programmer in terms of memory management.

IDL allows the definition of both bound and unbound strings. Be mindful that Java strings are unbound, which, if not accounted for, could result in conversion error from IDL string to Java string.

The following IDL defines both bound string and unbound strings:

```
module com{
    module mcp{
        module library{
            interface catalog{

                typedef string<20> aName;

            struct name{
                 string first;
                 string middle;
                 aName last;
            };
             };
        };
};
};
```

The IDL defines an alias for a string of 20 characters called `aName`. The `struct` is then defined with the alias as the name for one of its members. It is possible to define the IDL also as the following:

```
module com{
    module mcp{
        module library{
            interface catalog{

               struct name{
                 string first;
                 string middle;
                 string<20> last;
               };
             };
        };
};
};
```

Both the definitions will result in the following Java class:

```
package com.mcp.library.catalogPackage;
  final public class name {
    public java.lang.String first;
    public java.lang.String middle;
    public java.lang.String last;
    public name() {
    }
```

```
    public name(
      java.lang.String first,
      java.lang.String middle,
      java.lang.String last
    ) {
      this.first = first;
      this.middle = middle;
      this.last = last;
    }
  }
```

The generated class uses the original name because Java does not have any support for `typedefs`. Because Java does not have this support, the code generation always maps the `typedef` to its original name.

The fact that both the bound and the unbound versions generate identical code needs attention. Remember the unfixed nature of the Java string class. All Java strings are unbound. Take care when passing a Java string as a bound `CORBA.string`.

Sequence Types

The sequence is reasonably similar to a one-dimensional array. Like the string, the sequence can be either bound or unbound. A bound sequence specifies a maximum number of elements a sequence can contain, and an unbound string has no limit on the number of elements it can contain.

The following IDL illustrates both a bound and an unbound sequence and their associated mappings:

```
module com{
    module mcp{
        module library{
            interface catalog{

              struct name{
                 string first;
                 string middle;
                 string last;
            };

            struct register{
              sequence<name,10> somemembers;
              sequence<name> allmembers;
            };
           };
        };
};
};
```

The interface specifies another `struct` named `register`, which contains both a bound and unbound sequence of another `struct`.

The pre-compiler generates an additional final Java class named `register`, along with the `Holder` and `Helper` classes for the class:

```
package com.mcp.library.catalogPackage;

  final public class register {
public com.mcp.library.catalogPackage.name[]
                                        somemembers;
     public com.mcp.library.catalogPackage.name[]
                                             allmembers;
    public register() {
    }
    public register(
      com.mcp.library.catalogPackage.name[] somemembers,
      com.mcp.library.catalogPackage.name[] allmembers
    ) {
      this.somemembers = somemembers;
      this.allmembers = allmembers;
    }
  }
```

The Java classes contain two open arrays that correspond to the sequences. In every other respect, the class is identical in structure to another `struct` mapping.

Sequences can be made of any legal IDL type. This includes sequence of interfaces, `structs`, basic types, and so forth.

Array Type

Although a sequence enables the definition of a one-dimensional array of sorts, with an array, definitions of multidimensional constructions are possible. Arrays of arrays are a little difficult to grasp at first. But when you master them, they enable you to pass by reference complex collections of data types over IIOP. Just as with the constructed data type described previously, definitions can be of any kind of arrays. It is possible to define arrays of `structs`, arrays of interfaces, basic types, and so forth.

The following IDL generates code almost identical to that of the sequence:

```
module com{
    module mcp{
        module library{
            interface catalog{

              struct name{
                 string first;
                 string middle;
```

```
                string last;
              };

              typedef name theNames[100];

                  struct theWhiteBook{
                   theNames allTheName;
                string   year;
              };
            };
        };
};
};
```

The Java mapping for the register is the following:

```
package com.mcp.library.catalogPackage;
  final public class theWhiteBook {
    public com.mcp.library.catalogPackage.name[]
                                              allTheName;
    public java.lang.String year;
    public theWhiteBook() {
    }
    public theWhiteBook(
      com.mcp.library.catalogPackage.name[] allTheName,
      java.lang.String year
    ) {
      this.allTheName = allTheName;
      this.year = year;
    }
  }
```

An array must be given an alias by a `typedef` before its use. However, because Java does not have support for `typedef`, the Java mapping will contain the real name of the variable instead of the alias.

Although an array seems to do just what a sequence could, there are some differences. They both allow the passing of "collections" between clients and servers. The main difference is that a sequence can be variable, but an array is always fixed. This means that the size of a sequence can shrink or grow. Only the actual length of the sequence is transmitted, whereas an array is always transmitted in its entirety.

Example Illustrating Differences Between Array and Sequence

Run the following through the VisiBroker idl2java pre-compiler (or any other product that supports Java mapping):

```
module com{
    module mcp{
```

```
        module library{
            interface catalog{

              struct name{
                 string first;
                 string middle;
                 string last;
            };

            struct register{
              sequence<name,10> somemembers;
              sequence<name> allmembers;
            };

            typedef name theNames[10];

              struct theWhiteBook{
                   theNames allTheName;
                string   year;
                };

               register getRegister();
            theWhiteBook getWhiteBook();

};
    };
};
};
```

The VisiBroker pre-compiler will generate a file named `_example_catalog.java`. Rename the file to something else if required:

```
package com.mcp.library;
import com.mcp.library.catalogPackage.*;

public class _example_catalog extends com.mcp.library._catalogImplBase {

  public _example_catalog(String serverName) {
      super(serverName);
  }
  public register getRegister() {
  }
  public theWhiteBook getWhiteBook() {
  }
}
```

The `getRegister()` method expects a return of the `register` class. The `register` class contains two instance variables. Both of them are uninitialized Java arrays.

One of the instance variables, `somemembers`, is a bound sequence with ten elements. The variable `allmembers` is an unbound sequence that should be an initialized size during runtime.

The theWhiteBook structure is defined to contain an array of ten name structs. The classes generated for theWhiteBook is also similar to that of the register. The rules for both the bound sequences and array are, in one respect, identical. Both a bound sequence and an array cannot be initialized to a size greater than what was defined and returned or passed back out or inout parameters (refer to the section “IDL Operations”).

The implementation of getregister() follows:

```
public register getRegister() {
    System.out.println("in getregister..");
    name[] bound_names = new name[5];
    try{
      for(int i = 0; i < 5; i++){
        name temp_ = new name();
        temp_.first = "Dennis";
        temp_.middle = "R.";
        temp_.last = new String(new Integer(i).toString());
        bound_names[i] = new name();
        bound_names[i].first = temp_.first;
        bound_names[i].middle = temp_.middle;
        bound_names[i].last = temp_.last;
      }
    }
    catch(java.lang.ArrayIndexOutOfBoundsException e){
      e.printStackTrace();
    }


    name[] ubound_names = new name[10];
    try{
        for(int j = 0; j < 10; j++){
          name temp_ = new name();
          temp_.first = "Dennis";
          temp_.middle = "R.";
          temp_.last = new String(new
    Integer(j).toString());
          ubound_names[j] = new name();
          ubound_names[j].first = temp_.first;
          ubound_names[j].middle = temp_.middle;
          ubound_names[j].last = temp_.last;
        }
    }
    catch(java.lang.ArrayIndexOutOfBoundsException e){
        e.printStackTrace();
    }

    register sequenceType = new register();
    sequenceType.somemembers = bound_names;
    sequenceType.allmembers = ubound_names;
    return sequenceType;
  }
```

In this code, `sequenceType.somemembers` is initialized to only five elements. When a client invokes this method, a sequence with only five elements will be returned to it. The `sequenceType.allmembers` is initialized to 11 members. The implementation illustrates that although the specification of the bounded sequence contains ten elements, the example adds only five elements to the bound sequence. It will not be the same with the array.

The array implementation is found in the `getWhiteBook` method. The array is defined to contain 10 elements. The method illustrates that a sequence is more flexible than arrays for one-dimensional lists. But when multidimensional lists are required or the size of the list is invariant, the array needs to be used:

```
public com.mcp.library.catalogPackage.theWhiteBook getWhiteBook(){
    System.out.println("In getWhiteBook...");
    theWhiteBook arrayType = new theWhiteBook();
    arrayType.allTheName = new name[10];

    try{
      for(int i = 0; i < 10; i++){
        name temp_ = new name();
        temp_.first = "Franklin";
        temp_.middle = "M.";
        temp_.last = new String(new Integer(i).toString());
        arrayType.allTheName[i] = new name();
        arrayType.allTheName[i].first = temp_.first;
        arrayType.allTheName[i].middle = temp_.middle;
        arrayType.allTheName[i].last = temp_.last;
      }
     }
     catch(java.lang.ArrayIndexOutOfBoundsException e){
      e.printStackTrace();
     }
     arrayType.year = "1842";
     return arrayType;
  }
```

With the implementation of the `Register` interface complete, it is required to build a runtime to host the component. The runtime or server will subclass the `DisplayWindow` class and use the `GenericServer` implemented in the Common Utilities section.

The SequenceArrayExample Implementation

The following code shows a sample implementation of using sequences in Java:

```
package com.mcp.library;

import org.omg.CORBA.*;
import java.lang.Thread.*;
import com.javau.utils.*;
import java.awt.event.*;
```

```
public class SequenceArrayExample extends
DisplayWindow implements DisplayWindowAdapter{

  Thread ServerThread = null;
  GenericServer t_server = null;
  catalog t_SeqArray = null;
  private static String[] arg = null;

  public static void main(String[] args) {
    SeqArray _array = new SeqArray();
    for(int i = 0; i < args.length; i++){
        arg[i] = new String();
        arg[i] = args[i];
     }
  }

  public SeqArray(){
    super();
    t_SeqArray = new _example_catalog("Catalog");
  }

 protected void startbtn_mouseClicked(MouseEvent e) {
    t_server = new GenericServer(t_SeqArray, this);
    try{
      t_server.initializeOrb(arg);
    }
    catch(SystemException ex){
      DisplayWindow.append(ex.toString() + "\n\n");
      ex.printStackTrace();
    }
    try{
      new Thread(t_server).start();
      DisplayWindow.append("Server Started.." + "\n");
    }
    catch(SystemException ex){
      DisplayWindow.append(ex.toString() + "\n\n");
      ex.printStackTrace();
    }
  }

  protected void stopbtn_mouseClicked(MouseEvent e) {
    ServerThread.stop();
    this.dispose();
  }

  public void addText(String txt_){
    DisplayWindow.append(txt_ + "\n");
  }
}
```

The `SequenceArrayExample` implementation does not do anything special except initialize the `GenericServer` and the `DisplayWindow`. Besides that, it overrides the mouse handling methods defined in the `DisplayWindow` to handle user-generated events. A running server is depicted in Figure 5.1.

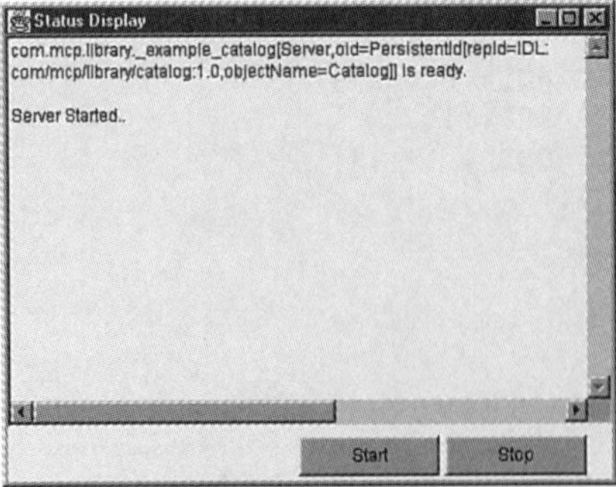

FIGURE 5.1
The SequenceArray server GUI.

After the `SequenceArrayExample` is built, implementing the client is just as straightforward. The `SequenceArrayExampleClient` also subclasses the `DisplayWindow`, enabling it to have a function `GUI` to accept user input. Unlike the `SequenceArrayExample`, the client does contain more specific implementation to interact with the server.

The `SequenceArrayExampleClient` Implementation

The following shows how a client could pass sequences to and from a server:

```
package com.mcp.library;

import com.mcp.library.catalogPackage.*;
import org.omg.CORBA.*;
import java.lang.Thread;
import com.javau.utils.*;
import java.awt.event.*;


public class SequenceArrayExampleClient extends
DisplayWindow{

  private ORB _orb = null;
  private catalog catalog_reference = null;
  private register t_register = null;
  private theWhiteBook t_whitebook = null;
  private static String[] arg = null;
```

```
public static void main(String[] args) {
   for(int i = 0; i < args.length; i++){
      arg[i] = new String();
      arg[i] = args[i];
   }
   new seqArrayClinet(args);
}

public seqArrayClinet(String[] ags){
  super();
  t_register = new register();
  t_whitebook = new theWhiteBook();
}

public void runTest(){
  try{
    DisplayWindow.append("Getting Sequence\n");
    t_register = catalog_reference.getRegister();
    DisplayWindow.append("Number Of Bounded Elements: "+
    new Integer(t_register.somemembers.length).toString()
           + "\n");
    DisplayWindow.append("Number Of Unbounded Elements: "
    + new Integer(t_register.allmembers.length)
.toString() + "\n\n");
    DisplayWindow.append("Getting Array\n");
    t_whitebook = catalog_reference.getWhiteBook();
    DisplayWindow.append("Elements of Array\n");
    DisplayWindow.append("Number Of Elments: "+new
Integer(t_whitebook.allTheName.length).toString()+
"\n");
  }
  catch(SystemException e){
    DisplayWindow.append(e.toString());
    DisplayWindow.append("\n");
  }
}

protected void stopbtn_mouseClicked(MouseEvent e) {
  this.dispose();
}

protected void startbtn_mouseClicked(MouseEvent e) {
  try{
    _orb = ORB.init(arg, null);
    catalog_reference =catalogHelper.bind(_orb,
"Catalog");
    DisplayWindow.append("Catalog Reference
  Retrieved..\n\n");
    runTest();
  }
  catch(SystemException ex){
```

```
            DisplayWindow.append(ex.toString());
            DisplayWindow.append("\n");
        }
    }
}
```

The heart of the implementation is found in the `runTest()`. This method is invoked when the user clicks the Start button. The client invokes the `getRegister()` and `getWhiteBook()` method on the server. The output is shown in Figure 5.2.

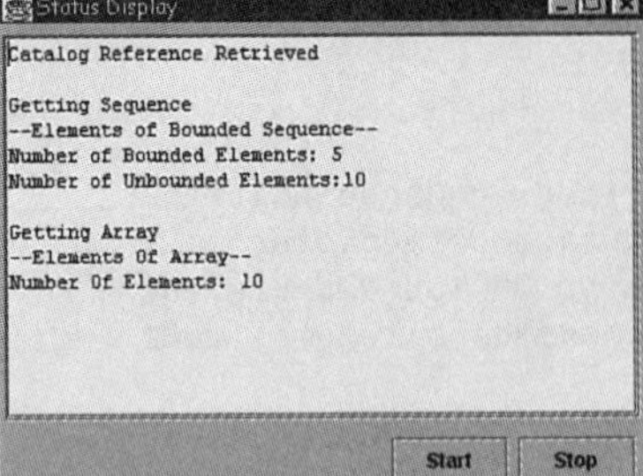

FIGURE 5.2
The SequenceArray client GUI.

typedefs and Constants

Java does not have a `typedef`. Therefore, the original name that you created as an alias for using a `typedef` replaces any `typedef` found in the IDL.

IDL constants are mapped to a static final member field. Java compiler applies normal optimization to the static finals.

Consider the following IDL that defines a `typedef` and a constant:

```
module com{
    module mcp{
        module library{
            interface Invariant{
            typedef long age;
            const long lifeExpectantcy = 76;
            void checkInvariant(in age t_age);

            };
        };
    };
};
```

The idl2java will produce the following mapping:

```
package com.mcp.library;
public interface Invariant extends org.omg.CORBA.Object {
```

```
  final public static int lifeExpectantcy = (int) 76;
  public void checkInvariant(
    int t_age
  );
}
```

The pre-compiler has replaced the `typedef` with the Java mapping for an IDL `long` type, an `int`. The `const` in the IDL has been mapped to a Java final static that has been explicitly cast to a Java `int` type.

IDL Operations

Operations are the heart of an interface. They enable the specification of services offered by an interface. There are a number of requirements to specifying an operation correctly:

- The operation must have a default return type, `void` if none is returned.
- If arguments are being passed into an operation, these parameters must be named and the direction of passage must be specified:

  ```
  void operations_name(in type name
   ,out type name
   ,inout type name
  );

   atype operations_name(in type name
     ,out type name
     ,inout type name
    );
  ```

- An argument specified as `in` is passed from the client to the server.
- An argument specified as `out` is passed from the server to the client.
- An argument specified as `inout` is passed in both directions.
- Return types are passed back by value. Because Java implements them as such, return types map to corresponding Java types or user-defined Java types that correspond to IDL specs defined.
- Parameters passed as `in` in IDL are required to implement pass-by-value semantics. Java allows this type of implementation. Therefore, `in` arguments are mapped to normal Java types. Java passes all parameters by value, so this semantics is simple to implement.
- Parameters specified in IDL as `out` and/or `inout` are a little more tricky. IDL `outs` and `inouts` are passed by reference or call by value/result. Java does not have support for this semantics. In order to overcome this, the IDL-to-Java specifiers came up with `Holder` classes that allow Java to handle IDL pass-by-reference semantics.

Every basic IDL type has associated `Holder` classes. User-defined types and interfaces in specification results in the Java pre-compiler generating appropriate `Holder` classes. These classes can be used where `outs` and/or `inouts` are specified in an IDL specification.

Using `Holder` Classes

The following specification defines `ins`, `outs`, and `inouts` for both primitive IDL types as well as a user-defined type. The example is constructed along similar lines as that of the `SequenceArrayExample` implementations:

```
module com{
    module mcp{
        module library{
            interface params{
            struct parameter{
               string name;
               long version;
            };

            long primitiveParams(in long anumber,
                         out string astring,
                         inout string anotherstring
                        );
            parameter userParams(in parameter inparam,
                         out parameter outparam,
                         inout parameter inoutparam
                        );
            };
        };
    };
};
```

The `primitiveParams()` operation specifies passing IDL types as parameters in all three directions. The `userParams()` passes the user-defined `struct params` as arguments to the operation in all three directions. Both operations return a value.

The associated Java interface generated is as follows:

```
package com.mcp.library;
public interface params extends org.omg.CORBA.Object {

  public int primitiveParams(
    int anumber,
    org.omg.CORBA.StringHolder astring,
    org.omg.CORBA.StringHolder anotherstring
  );
```

```
public com.mcp.library.paramsPackage.parameter
userParams(
  com.mcp.library.paramsPackage.parameter inparam,
  com.mcp.library.paramsPackage.parameterHolder outparam,
  com.mcp.library.paramsPackage.parameterHolder
  inoutparam
);

}
```

Operations with Native IDL Types

All basic IDL types have an associated Java `Holder` class. This is specified in the IDL to Java standard from OMG.

The following Java method:

```
public int primitiveParams(
    int anumber,
    org.omg.CORBA.StringHolder astring,
    org.omg.CORBA.StringHolder anotherstring
  );
```

requires a Java `int` returned by value. The first parameter `anumber` is passed from the client by value. The second parameter `astring` is passed from the server to the client with the help of a `StringHolder` class. The client provides an instance of this class when making the invocation. As such, the `Holder` class is passed by value. The implementation of the mapping will ensure that the instance itself is not modified (that would have been possible if Java supports pass-by-reference). The contents of the `Holder` class may be modified. The semantics is similar for the third parameter `anotherstring`. The only difference is that the parameter is passed from the client to the server where it may be modified and returned to the client.

Operations with Constructed IDL Types

The operation `userParams()` passes the `parameter struct` in all three directions. Before looking at the details of implementing the `params` interface, the IDL pre-compiler generates `Holder` classes for all constructed types as well as the interfaces defined in the module. The IDL pre-compiler will generate two `Holder` classes for the `params` interface; the `paramsHolder.java` contains the implementation of the interface `Holder` class. The source file `parameterHolder.java` contains the mapping for the `parameter struct` to a

Holder class. This is the class that is defined in the Java mapping of the params interface that would allow it to be passed as an argument in an out or inout operation:

```
public com.mcp.library.paramsPackage.parameter userParams(
    com.mcp.library.paramsPackage.parameter inparam,
    com.mcp.library.paramsPackage.parameterHolder outparam,
    com.mcp.library.paramsPackage.parameterHolder
    inoutparam
  );
```

The parameterHolder is in the following class:

```
package com.mcp.library.paramsPackage;
  final public class parameterHolder implements
  org.omg.CORBA.portable.Streamable {

public com.mcp.library.paramsPackage.parameter value;

public parameterHolder() {
}
public parameterHolder(
 com.mcp.library.paramsPackage.parameter value) {
      this.value = value;
}
..
}
```

The implementation of the Holder class is a final Java class. The content of the argument passed in the pass-by-reference semantics is mapped to a public instance field. In this case, the content is a struct (the parameter) which is held in the Holder class.

Example Implementation of the params Interface

Implementing this interface is rather straightforward. Both the client and server inherit from the DisplayWindow class. A slight modification is made to example_params.java to pass a reference to the DisplayWindow control to it so that it can display a message in the TextEdit control:

```
public class _example_params extends com.mcp.library._paramsImplBase {
  private  DisplayWindowAdapter dwa = null;

  public _example_params(java.lang.String name) {
    super(name);
  }
  public _example_params(DisplayWindowAdapter dwa, String
  name) {
    super(name);
```

```
    this.dwa = dwa;
  }
..
```

The method implementing the operation on primitive arguments is as follows:

```
public int primitiveParams(
    int anumber,
    org.omg.CORBA.StringHolder astring,
    org.omg.CORBA.StringHolder anotherstring
  ) {
      dwa.addText("Inside primitiveParams.." + "\n\n");
      dwa.addText("IN Value: " + new
    Integer(anumber).toString() + "\n");
      astring.value = "OutValue is this";
      dwa.addText("INOUT Value: " + anotherstring.value +
    "\n\n");
      anotherstring.value = "InOutValue is that";
      return 1001;
  }
```

The method operates on the three arguments in a simple manner. The `IN` parameter `anumber` is output to the `DisplayWindow` as is, the contents of `astring` is set so that it can be returned to the client, and `anotherstring` is output and reset to a different value.

The operation on constructed types is just as simple as the one on the primitive types:

```
public com.mcp.library.paramsPackage.parameter userParams(
       parameter inparam,
       parameterHolder outparam,
       parameterHolder inoutparam
  ) {
    dwa.addText("Inside userParams.." + "\n\n");
    dwa.addText("IN Values of inparam: "+ "\n");
    dwa.addText("in parameter.name: "+inparam.name +"\n");
    dwa.addText("in parameter.version : " + new
        Integer(inparam.version).toString() + "\n\n");
    parameter outParamVal = new parameter(new String("UD
        Out value"), 1998);
    outparam.value = outParamVal;
    dwa.addText("INOUT Values of inoutparam: " + "\n");
    dwa.addText("inout parameter.name: " +
        inoutparam.value.name +"\n");
    dwa.addText("inout parameter.version: " + new
        Integer(inoutparam.value.version).toString() +
        " \n\n");
    inoutparam.value.name = new String("UD InOut value");
    inoutparam.value.version = 1999;
    parameter ret_value = new parameter("UD Retrun",2000);
    return ret_value;
  }
```

The content of the parameterHolder is parameter. The code shows how arguments passed as an in and an inout parameter can be operated on. The code is similar to that of primitiveParams(). The IN and Return work on parameter itself, but the OUT and INOUT are passed by reference. The code works on the contents of the arguments. Relevant information is output to the DisplayWindow.

The params Client Implementation

The client implementation is similar to the example on sequences and arrays. The initialization and window code is the same. The only difference is in the RunTest() method:

```
public void runTest(){
    try{
       DisplayWindow.append("Testing Primitive
          Params\n\n");
       parameter inParam = new parameter();
       inParam.name = new String("Stings..");
       inParam.version = 5990;
       StringHolder outHolder = new StringHolder();
       StringHolder inoutHolder = new StringHolder("Just
         another String..");
       int primitive_return =
          params_reference.primitiveParams
          (1003,outHolder,inoutHolder);
       DisplayWindow.append("Returned form
          primitiveParams()" + "\n");
       DisplayWindow.append("Return Value" + new
          Integer(primitive_return).toString() + "\n");
       DisplayWindow.append("Out Value"+outHolder.value+
          "\n");
       DisplayWindow.append("INOUT Value" +
          inoutHolder.value + "\n\n");
       parameterHolder outParamHolder = new
          parameterHolder();
       parameterHolder inoutParamHolder = new
          parameterHolder(new parameter(new String("The
          Clueless"), 2000));
       parameter ud_return =
     params_reference.userParams
         (inParam,outParamHolder,inoutParamHolder);
       DisplayWindow.append("Returned form userParams()"+
         "\n");
       DisplayWindow.append("Return Value: " + "\n");
       DisplayWindow.append("Return Name: " +
         ud_return.name + "\n");
       DisplayWindow.append("Return Version: " + new
         Integer(ud_return.version).toString() + "\n\n");
       DisplayWindow.append("OUT Value: " + ud_return.name
         + "\n");
```

```
      DisplayWindow.append("Out Name: " +
        outParamHolder.value.name + "\n");
      DisplayWindow.append("Out Version: " + new
        Integer(outParamHolder.value.version).toString() +
        "\n\n");
      DisplayWindow.append("INOUT Value: " +
        ud_return.name + "\n");
      DisplayWindow.append("Inout Name: " +
        inoutParamHolder.value.name + "\n");
      DisplayWindow.append("Inout Version: " + new
        Integer(inoutParamHolder.value.version).toString()
        + "\n\n");
   }
   catch(SystemException e){
     DisplayWindow.append(e.toString());
   }
```

The operations client GUI is shown in Figure 5.3.

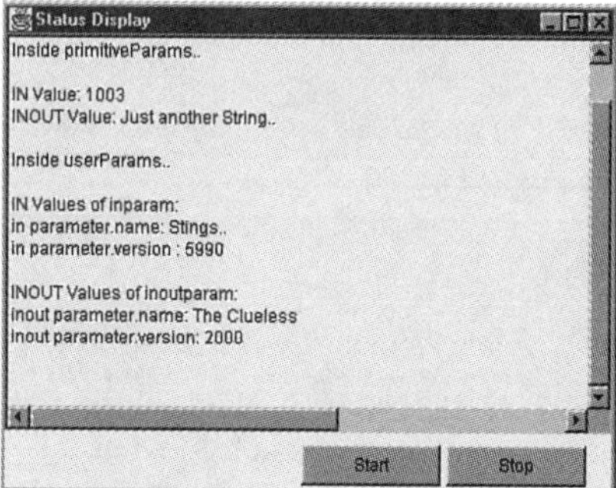

FIGURE 5.3
The operations client GUI.

Here are the complete mappings for `Holder` classes mapping; the first grid lays out the mapping for basic IDL types:

Type	IN	OUT	INOUT	RETURN
		Basic IDL Type		
short	short	shortHolder	shortHolder	short
unsigned short	short	shortHolder	shortHolder	short
long	int	IntHolder	IntHolder	int
unsigned long	int	IntHolder	IntHolder	int
long long	long	LongHolder	LongHolder	long
unsigned long long	long	LongHolder	LongHolder	long

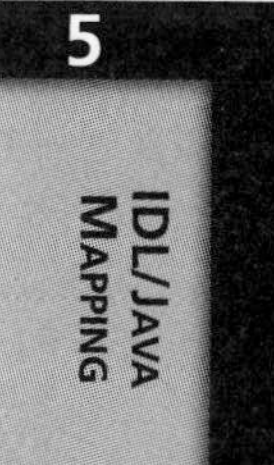

Type	IN	OUT	INOUT	RETURN
float	float	FloatHolder	FloatHolder	float
double	double	DoubleHolder	DoubleHolder	double
boolean	boolean	BooleanHolder	BooleanHolder	boolean
char	char	CharHolder	CharHolder	char
wchar	char	CharHolder	CharHolder	char
octet	byte	ByteHolder	ByteHolder	byte
any	any	AnyHolder	AnyHolder	any
		User-Defined Types		
enum	type	typeHolder	typeHolder	type
struct	type	typeHolder	typeHolder	type
union	type	typeHolder	typeHolder	type
string	String	StringHolder	StringHolder	String
wstring	String	StringHolder	StringHolder	String
sequence	array	typeHolder	typeHolder	array
array	array	typeHolder	typeHolder	array

IDL Exceptions

Exceptions are an integral part of CORBA. When you are designing a system, there are two things that are taken into consideration. One tries to figure out how a solution should work. The other tries to ensure that the solution does not do what it is not supposed to. Meyers called it "programming by contract." It cannot be sufficiently emphasized how important contracts are with distributed systems. When things that are not supposed to happen do happen with the server, the client needs notification. This is accomplished through exceptions.

CORBA specifies two types of exceptions:

- CORBA System Exception

  The ORB will dispatch these standard exceptions when specified standard exceptions occur. These exceptions map to a final Java class named `org.omg.CORBA.SystemException`. This class is inherited from `java.lang.RuntimeException`. Implementers should ensure that this exception is handled on every remote invocation.

- User-Defined Exception

  CORBA enables a designer to construct application-specific exceptions. These exceptions can be attached to any operation. When an invariant condition is violated, these exceptions can be thrown. This would allow the client to trap these violations and handle them correctly and safely.

User-defined exceptions also map to a final Java class. They are derived from `org.omg.CORBA.UserException`, which is a subclass of `java.lang.Exception`. User exceptions are mapped to the scope in which they were defined in IDL. If, for example, an exception is defined in an interface, the Java exception class will be contained within the same scope.

The following IDL generates a `final` class name `Contract`. This class contains the mapping for the user-defined exception:

```
module com{
    module mcp{
        module library{
            interface Contract{
            const short MaleLifeExpectancy = 76;
            exception violation{string condition;
short code;};
            void checkInvariant(in short age) raises
(violation);

            };
        };
    };
};
```

On the server side, using the exception can be as follows:

```
public void checkInvariant(
    short age
  ) throws com.mcp.library.ContractPackage.violation {

    if(age < MaleLifeExpectancy ){
//Implement the use case..
}
else
    throw violation("Expectancy exceed", 1001);
}
```

On the client side, the implementation can be as follows:

```
    try{
    contractRef.checkInvariant(77)
}
catch(ContractPackage.violation v){
    System.out.prinln(e.toString());
```

```
}
catch(CORBA.SystemException e){
    e.printStackTrace();
}
```

Summary

The IDL-to-Java mappings are consistent with other mappings OMG has produced. The mapping ensures that CORBA retains its language neutrality. Aspects of the Java language and its lack of pass-by-reference semantics lead to a certain complexity to the mapping.

All except a few elements of IDL map to Java. IDL modules map to Java packages. IDL interfaces map to Java interfaces. This interface needs to be implemented to construct a CORBA component in Java. IDL enables the specification of complex types and constructed types. Both these elements map to Java final classes.

IDL operations map to methods on the interface that a class has to implement. Parameters passed as arguments introduce a certain artificiality to the Java mapping. Java does not have a pass-by-reference semantics, so it specifies the concept of `Holder` classes. These classes allow passing parameters as `out` and/or `inout` parameters. IDL exceptions integrate naturally with Java's native exception handling capability. Dealing with `Holder` classes is a small price to pay, considering the transparency of Java memory management. It is something to be appreciated—especially if you have a choice between Java and C++ implementations.

CHAPTER 6

CORBA C++ Memory Management

In This Chapter

C++ CORBA implementations are the most popular. This popularity stems from the expressive power of the C++ language. CORBA can be found in the most hard-to-reach places, such as telephone switching systems and industrial process controllers. Most of these environments have a premium on resources. CORBA is also found in environments requiring complex integration of diverse technologies, including legacy systems. In these environments, it is prudent to opt for a solution that imposes the least overhead during runtime. C++ is a good choice in these situations, because designers and implementers of C++ systems have the freedom to ensure that the language imposes as much or as little on their system as they choose.

There is nevertheless a price to be paid for this freedom and flexibility. C++ memory management, although simpler than C, imposes a higher responsibility on the designer and implementer. A carelessly designed and implemented C++ CORBA application, ignoring the conventional practices on safe memory management, is guaranteed to fail.

Issues of memory management affect all levels of the C++ IDL mappings. These issues range from the management of object references to the allocation and deallocation of memory for parameters. At the implementation level, especially dealing with complex IDL types such as IDL `structs` or sequences, these issues present a certain complex subtlety that can be confusing at times. This chapter deals primarily with the issues of memory management pertaining to parameter passing.

IDL Operations

Operations specified in IDL map to C++ member functions. These functions are implemented by a C++ class to enable a C++ component to provide some service.

An example of an IDL operation would be the following:

```
return_type t_operation( in type name,
                        out type name,
                            inout type name);
```

The IDL operation illustrates the four ways a client can exchange information with a server. When dealing with parameters, IDL enables parameters to be passed as `IN`, `OUT`, and `INOUT`. When a parameter is passed `in`, information is passed from the client to the server. When a parameter is specified as `out`, the server passes information to the client. Finally, information can also be passed in both directions. If a parameter is passed as `inout`, the client passes information to the server and the server can use the same parameter to pass information back to the client. The server can also pass information back to the client as a `return` type.

Memory Management for Basic Types

Basic IDL types do not map to any C++ pointers. Therefore, the issue of memory management does not have to be dealt with.

Memory Management for Template Types

There are three template types in the IDL:

- Strings
- Sequences
- Arrays

Sequences and arrays are essentially containers for other types. This introduces a certain dynamic into dealings with sequences and arrays as a byproduct of the memory management of the associated type. This dynamic is a result of the fact that `structs`, sequences, and arrays can be used as *containers* for other types, including other `structs`, sequences, and arrays. Strings are rather straightforward.

Ownership of Memory

Before dealing with the details of memory management, let's look at the principle of CORBA memory management. All of CORBA memory revolves around the concept of memory ownership. I would characterize it as *ownership of memory rests with that which needs to own it*. CORBA specifies the rules of this ownership to establish unambiguously which (the client or the server) owns memory when.

Largely, the rules for defining ownership are consistent across all data types in CORBA. They can be grouped around the direction the parameters are being passed:

- `in` parameters—The client owns the memory for an `in` parameter. The server object has a temporary copy that the ORB eventually deletes when the method returns. With an `in` parameter, the server object only has read access to the parameter provided by the client, and consequently the server cannot change the parameter's value. Memory management for `in` parameters are shown in Figure 6.1.
- `out` parameters—The memory management rules also apply to return values and attribute accessor values. When something is specified as an `out` (or return), the value originates with the server. It is on the server that the variable is allocated. The ORB then copies the variable over the network to the client. On the client side, the ORB allocates memory for the variable. On the server side, the ORB deallocates the memory for the variable. To put it simply, with `out` parameters, the server allocates the memory, and the client is responsible for deallocation of memory. It is

critical to remember that because the ORB deallocates memory, you must return a copy of the variable in question and not the original pointer. Memory management for `out` parameters are shown in Figure 6.2.

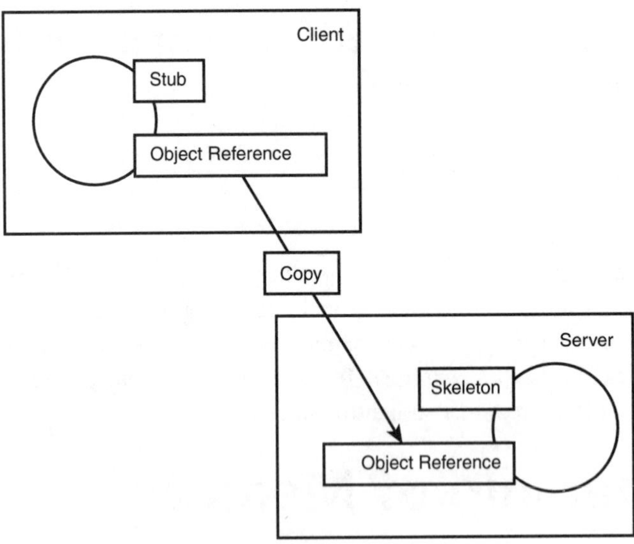

FIGURE 6.1
`in` memory.

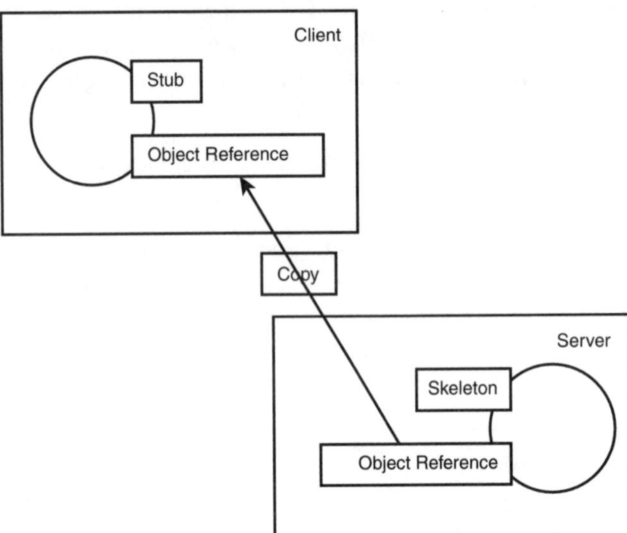

FIGURE 6.2
`out` memory.

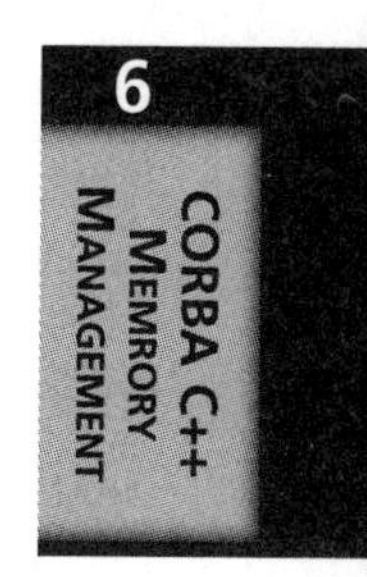

- inout parameters—These types of parameters are passed in both directions. An inout parameter changes the rules of ownership, depending on where the parameter is. The client passes ownership to the server. On the server, the server has the option of either modifying the variable or just treating it as a read-only parameter. A client passes a variable to the server object, and the ORB copies the object over the network. If the server treats the object as read-only, the semantics are similar to that of IN parameters, when the call returning the ORB deletes the object on the server. If the server chooses to change the object, it should free the old copy and make a new copy of the object. When the call returns, the ORB copies the object over the network. The client is then given back ownership of memory. It should then deallocate the memory when it is no longer required. Figure 6.3 shows how memory management for inout parameters are handled.

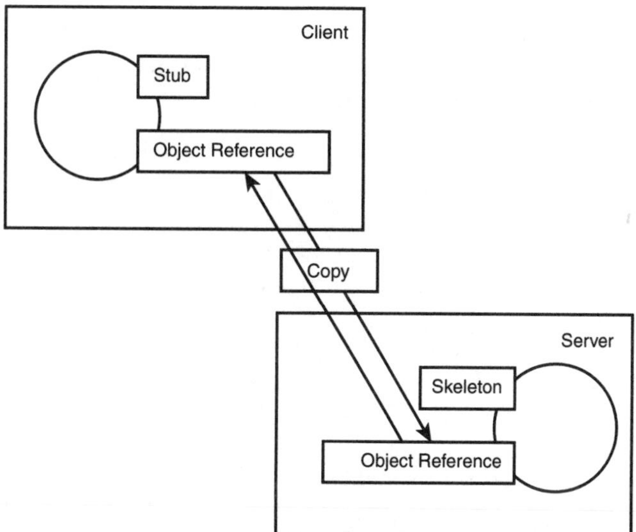

FIGURE 6.3
inout memory.

Memory Management for Strings

IDL strings can be either *bounded* or *unbounded.* In both cases, IDL strings map to char* in C++. The data in the String is null-terminated. The CORBA module defines a class called String_var that encapsulates a char* value. An instance of the class dynamically deallocates memory for the pointer when the String_var destructor executes.

Issues of memory management issues relating to strings are described using the following IDL interface operation:

```
string stringmap(in string inString,
  out string outString,
  inout string inoutString);
```

The C++ IDL pre-compiler will generate the following member function definition:

```
virtual char* stringmap( const char* inString,
     char*& outString,
     char*& inoutString) ;
```

Three operations in the CORBA namespace are essential for the management of strings:

- `char *string_alloc(Ulong len);`
- `char *string_dup(const char*);`
- `void string_free(char*);`

These methods are primarily used when a string is passed as `in`, `inout` or return values to operations. The same applies when a string is returned as an attribute value. So when a string needs to be passed as an `in`, `inout`, or `return` parameter, these methods are used to handle memory management for strings properly.

Depending on the rules of memory ownership, these methods need to be used for allocation and deallocation of memory. When strings are used as `in`, `inout`, or `return type`, use `string_dup` to make a copy of the original variable.

The `CORBA::String_var` Type

CORBA specifies `T_var` types that are helper classes. These classes encapsulate the underlying pointer. When called, the `T_var` class destructor deallocates memory for the pointer. CORBA also specifies a helper class for `CORBA::string` called `CORBA::String_var`. Usage of this type eases memory management. Because memory for the pointer is deallocated when the destructor is called, it helps prevent memory leaks.

Because `CORBA::String_var` is responsible for deallocation of memory, it should be used only in the context of clearly defined ownership of string memory. It should not be used if ownership cannot be ensured. The class defines a copy constructor and `operator=()` that make deep copies.

WARNING

Be careful that you do not initialize a `String_var` with a string literal. The `String_var` cannot gain ownership of the literal; hence it cannot deallocate it. The runtime behavior is undefined. However, given enough time, Murphy's law will kick in and cause a runtime exception.

Server-Side Memory Management for Strings

The three parameters passed into the stringmap operation will help demonstrate the essentials of string memory management:

```
char* stringmap( const char* inString,
  char*& outString,
  char*& inoutString);
```

The first parameter is passed in from the client. The second parameter is an out type, and the third one is an inout parameter. The function also returns a pointer to a char array. The details of how memory management for strings are handled in this context are explained in the next three sections.

Managing an in String

The client retains ownership of the memory allocated for the in string. The server can treat it only as read-only memory. It has access to the memory for the duration of the call, after which the ORB will deallocate it. If local copy is to be maintained, CORBA::String_dup() must be used to keep a copy of the string.

Managing an out String

The String is originally allocated on the server side. On the client side, the memory should be considered as read-only. Because it owns the memory when the call returns, it is the client's responsibility to deallocate this memory. This requirement on the client side can be transparently done by using a CORBA::String_var.

Managing an inout String

Ownership changes hands, albeit only temporarily from the client to the server. On the server side, it can both modify the incoming parameter as is or choose to deallocate the incoming string, allocate a new string, and pass it back to the client. If the latter strategy is used, the server has to deallocate memory for the old string and pass ownership of the new string back to the client.

Listing 6.1 illustrates how a server can manage memory for strings. All four modes of string-passing between client and server are shown.

LISTING 6.1 STRING MEMORY MANAGEMENT ON THE SERVER SIDE

```
char* Mapper::Memory_i::stringmap(const char* inString,
                                  char*& outString,
    char*& inoutString,
CORBA::Environment &IT_env) {
```

continues

LISTING 6.1 CONTINUED

```
    //IN Parameter
    cout<<inString<<endl;
    myCopy = CORBA::string_dup(inString);
    cout<<myCopy<<endl;

    //OUT Parameter
    outString = CORBA::string_dup("Out Parameter");

    //INOUT Parameter
    cout<<inoutString<<endl;
    CORBA::string_free(inoutString);
    inoutString = CORBA::string_dup(
    "inout from the server");

    //Return type
    char* ret_string = CORBA::string_dup("Return String");
    return ret_string;
}
```

Client-Side Memory Management for Strings

When the client has to assume ownership of memory, it ensures that memory is deallocated. This is the case with `out` and `inout` parameters and `return types`. With these types, the server allocates, and the client has to deallocate the memory.

The following code illustrates how this can be accomplished:

```
CORBA::String_var inString = CORBA::string_dup("INString");
    char *return_val, *outString;
    CORBA::String_var inoutString =
CORBA::string_dup("INOUT String From Client");
    try{
        return_val = memoryRef->stringmap(
   inString, outString, inoutString);
        cout<<return_val<<endl;
        cout<<outString<<endl;
        cout<<inoutString<<endl;
    }
```

Memory Management for Sequences

IDL sequences map to a class that essentially behaves like an array. The only difference is that a sequence can be fixed or unbounded. When fixed (or bound), it has an upper

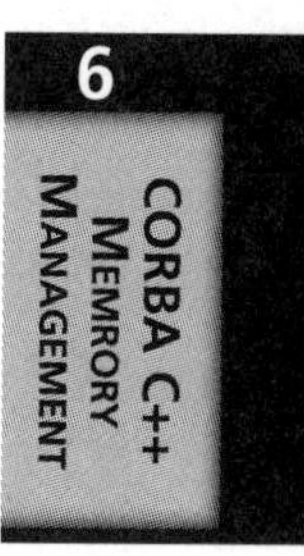

bound and a lower bound. The upper bound is the maximum length a sequence can have, and the lower bound is the actual length an implementation initializes the sequence to. When unbounded, the size of the sequence can be changed.

The way a sequence is constructed has implications on how the memory for the sequence is deallocated. A Boolean flag can be set on one of the overloaded constructors that indicates whether a sequence's buffer space is to be deallocated when the sequence is deleted.

The two constructors in question are

```
class sequence {
    ..
    ..
    ..
    sequence(CORBA::Ulong maximum);
sequence(CORBA::Ulong maximum, CORBA::Ulong
    initial_length, CORBA::Long* datum,
    CORBA::Boolean release = 0);
    ..
    ..
    ..
}
```

The first constructor listed has the `release` flag set to `1` by default. This means that destroying the sequence will release the memory of the sequence buffer.

The second one allows construction of a sequence that should have its data buffers explicitly deallocated. Depending on which constructor is used to create a sequence, memory management issues become slightly different.

This section deals only with memory issues for unbounded sequences, because memory management for unbounded sequences is determined at runtime as opposed to compile-time, the way it is for bounded sequences. The following interface illustrates the principles of sequence memory management:

```
module Mapper{
    interface Memory{
        typedef sequence<long> longsequence;
        longsequence sequencemap(
in longsequence inSeq,
out longsequence outSeq,
inout longsequence inoutSeq);
    };
};
```

The interface will use an unbounded sequence of `long` as parameters and the `return` type.

Managing an `in` Sequence

The client owns the memory that is passed for a sequence from the client to the server. The memory on the server is read-only. The server has access to this memory only for the duration of the call.

As such, there are no major implications for memory management for passing a sequence as an `IN` parameter. The argument is passed as a reference to a C++ object.

Managing an `out` Sequence

As with any `out` parameter, the server is responsible for allocating the memory and passes the pointer back to the client. The ORB that manages the underlying copy of the pointer from the server to the client makes this transparent. The client is responsible for deallocating the memory that the ORB makes available on the client side. This can be made painless if a `T_var` type is used that deallocates the memory when its destructor is called.

With unbounded sequences, things are a little more complex. If the length of the sequence is set to a length larger than the current length, this might cause a reallocation of the sequence data. Reallocation is similar to copying the contents of the old sequence into a new one. With `return types`, the client is responsible for deallocating the sequence returned by the server.

If the release flag is set to `1` when constructing the sequence, the server object receives a pointer to the sequence object. The memory for this pointer must be explicitly deleted when no longer required. This deallocation will cause the buffer to be deleted as well. Using a `T_var` type will make this issue a bit more transparent. `T_vars` are smart pointers that automatically deallocate memory when no longer referenced.

If the release flag is set to `0`, the client is responsible for deallocating the memory for the sequence. However, the server object retains the responsibility for deallocating the buffer explicitly.

Managing an `inout` Sequence

When the release flag is set to `0`, an increase in the length of the buffer holding the sequence will not mean that the old buffer is deallocated when the sequence is assigned to the new buffer. When the client and the server objects are in the same address space, it is the client's responsibility to ensure that the buffer is deallocated after the sequence is deleted.

If the release flag is set to `1`, the server object receives a read/write sequence, which it can change if required. Changing the length of the buffer will implicitly reallocate a new buffer and destroy the old one.

Listings 6.2 and 6.3 show memory management of sequences on the server and the client side, respectively.

LISTING 6.2 SEQUENCE MEMORY MANAGEMENT ON THE SERVER SIDE

```
Mapper::Memory::longsequence* Mapper::Memory_i::sequencemap
(const Mapper::Memory::longsequence& inSeq,
Mapper::Memory::longsequence*& outSeq,
Mapper::Memory::longsequence& inoutSeq,
CORBA::Environment &IT_env) {

  cout<<"IN SEQUENCE"<<endl;
  for(CORBA::ULong i = 0; i < inSeq.length(); i++){
     cout<<inSeq[i]<<endl;
  }

  longsequence* outSequence = new longsequence(10);
  outSequence->length(10);

  for(CORBA::ULong j = 0; j < outSequence->length(); j++){
     outSequence[j] = j;
  }
  outSeq = outSequence;
  delete outSequence;

  cout<<"INOUT SEQ"<<endl;
  for(CORBA::ULong k = 0; k < inoutSeq.length(); k++){
     cout<<inoutSeq[k]<<endl;
    inoutSeq[k] = k +10;
  }

  longsequence* returnSeq = new longsequence(10);
  returnSeq->length(10);
  for(CORBA::ULong l = 0; l < returnSeq->length(); l++){
    returnSeq[l] = l +100;
  }
  return returnSeq;
}
```

LISTING 6.3 SEQUENCE MEMORY MANAGEMENT ON THE CLIENT SIDE

```
try{
    Mapper::Memory::longsequence inSeq(10);
    inSeq.length(10);
    for(CORBA::ULong i = 0; i < inSeq.length(); i++){
        inSeq[i] = i+10;
    }
```

continues

LISTING 6.3 CONTINUED

```
    Mapper::Memory::longsequence* outSeq;
    Mapper::Memory::longsequence inoutSeq(5);
    inSeq.length(5);
    for(CORBA::ULong j=0;j<inoutSeq.length(); j++){
        inoutSeq[j] = i+11;
    }

    Mapper::Memory::longsequence* retSeq;
retSeq = memoryRef->sequencemap
(inSeq,outSeq,inoutSeq);

    for(CORBA::ULong k = 0; k < inoutSeq.length(); k++){
        cout<<inoutSeq[k]<<endl;
    }
    for(CORBA::ULong l = 0; l < retSeq->length(); l++){
        cout<<&retSeq[l]<<endl;
    }

}
```

Memory Management for Arrays

IDL arrays are identical to C++ arrays. As with other IDL types, the pre-compiler also generates an associative `T_var` type to make memory management transparent. If the `T_var` generated for the array is not used, the following methods should be used to allocate and deallocate an array:

Array allocation: `array_name_alloc();`

Array deallocation: `array_name_free(array_name*);`

The pre-compiler also generates an alias for an array that is known as `anArray_slice`. If the IDL defines an array named `anArray`, the pre-compiler will generate an array slice named `anArray_slice`. An array slice differs from the normal array in that the `typedef` enables the declaration of an array without having to specify the first array dimension. This is a handy thing to have when declaring multidimensional arrays.

When an array is specified as a `return type` to an operation, the pre-compiler will generate code that returns `anArray_slice`. The same happens when an unbounded array is specified as an `out` parameter.

Managing an `in` Array

The client retains ownership of this memory for the array. The server can treat the memory only as read-only. It has access to the memory for the duration of the call, after which the ORB will deallocate it. Listing 6.4 shows memory management on the server side, and Listing 6.5 shows memory management on the client side.

LISTING 6.4 ARRAY MEMORY MANAGEMENT ON THE SERVER SIDE

```
Mapper::Memory::anArray_slice* Mapper::Memory_i::
sequencemap (const Mapper::Memory::anArray inArray,
Mapper::Memory::anArray outArray,
Mapper::Memory::anArray inoutArray, CORBA::Environment
&IT_env) {

    cout<<"IN Array"<<endl;
    int i = 0;
    for(i ; i < 5; i++){
        cout<<inArray[i]<<endl;
    }
    i = 0;

    for(i; i < 5; i++){
        outArray[i] = i + 10;
    }
    i = 0;

    cout<<"INOUT Array"<<endl;
    for(i; i < 5; i++){
        cout<<inoutArray[i]<<endl;
        inoutArray[i] = i + 10;
    }
    i = 0;

    anArray_slice* slicedArray = anArray_alloc();
    for(i; i < 5; i++){
        slicedArray[i] = i + 11;
    }
    return slicedArray;
}
```

LISTING 6.5 ARRAY MEMORY MANAGEMENT ON THE CLIENT SIDE

```
    try{
Mapper::Memory::anArray inArray,
    outArray,
    inoutArray;
    Mapper::Memory::anArray_slice* returnArray;

    int i = 0;
        for(i ; i < 5; i++){
            inArray[i] = i + 2;
```

continues

LISTING 6.5 CONTINUED

```
            inoutArray[i] = i + 3;
        }
        i = 0;

returnArray = memoryRef->sequencemap
                    (inArray,outArray,inoutArray);

        for(i; i<5; i++){
            long x = returnArray[i];
            cout<<"INOUT " <<inoutArray[i]<<endl;
            cout<<"RETURN "<<returnArray[i]<<endl;
        }

        Mapper::Memory::anArray_free(returnArray);
    }
    catch (CORBA::SystemException &sysEx) {
        cerr << "Unexpected system exception" << endl;
        cerr << &sysEx;
        exit(1);
    }
```

Summary of C++ Parameter Types

The complete listing for IDL-to-C++ mappings for primitive types are shown in the following table. The mappings are very simple and uninvolved as far as memory management issues are concerned.

Type	in	out	inout	Return
short	short	short&	short&	short
long	long	long &	long &	long
longlong	longlong	longlong &	longlong &	longlong
ULong	ULong	Ulong &	Ulong &	Ulong
ULonglong	Ulonglong	Ulonglong&	Ulonglong&	Ulonglong
Ushort	Ushort	Ushort&	Ushort&	Ushort
float	float	float&	float&	float
double	double	double&	double&	double
Ldouble	Ldouble	Ldouble&	Ldouble&	Ldouble
boolean	boolean	boolean&	boolean&	boolean
char	char	char&	char&	char
wchar	wchar	wchar&	wchar&	wchar

Memory Management Heuristics

The following table lists concisely who is responsible for memory allocation and deallocation. The following abbreviations are used in the table:

C = Client

S = Server

A = Allocation

D = DeAllocation

Type	`in`	`out / return`	`inout`
Fixed Struct Fixed Union	C A C D	C D S A	C A, D
Variable Struct Variable Union	C A C D	C D S A	C A C D
String Wstring	C A C D	C D S A	C/S A C/S D
Sequence	C A C D	C D S A	Release Flag Depended
Fixed Array	C A C D	{C D S A}Rets C A C D	C A C D
Variable Array	C A C D	C D S A	C A C D

The following table lists the types that are generated from IDL, depending on what is specified. Remember that the heuristics apply only to parameters that are passed as a pointer either to a type or to a reference to a pointer to a type.

Type	`in`	`inout`	`out`	`return`
`octet`	`Octet`	`Octet&`	`Octet&`	`Octet`
`enum`	`enum`	`enum&`	`enum&`	`enum`
`object reference`	`objref_ptr&`	`objref_ptr&`	`objref_ptr`	`objref_ptr_ptr`
`Fixed struct`	`const struct&`	`struct&`	`struct&`	`struct`
`variable struct`	`const struct&`	`struct&`	`struct*&`	`struct*`

continues

Type	in	inout	out	return
Fixed union	const union&	union&	union&	union
variable union	const union&	union&	union*&	union*
string	const char*	char*&	char*&	char*
wstring	const WChar*	WChar*&	WChar*&	WChar*
sequence	const sequence&	sequence&	sequence*&	sequence*
Fixed array	const array	array	array	array_slice*
variable array	const array	array	array_slice*	array_slice*

Summary

CORBA does not have any mechanism for distributed memory management. This does impose a certain responsibility on the shoulders of a programmer implementing CORBA applications in C++. In order to make memory agent transparent, CORBA specified a `T_var` type. Using this type frees the developer from explicitly deallocating memory.

The principle of CORBA memory management is based on ownership. It is the responsibility of the owner to deallocate memory. As a consequence of this, implementations involving pointers or references to pointers have the server allocating the memory and the client responsible for deallocating the memory.

Special care needs to be taken when dealing with distributed memory under CORBA. Always ensure that memory allocation errors are trapped and handled gracefully.

Common Services

Part III

In This Part

CHAPTER 7

The Naming Service

IN THIS CHAPTER

One of the most important aspects of CORBA is the fact that the OMG explicitly set out to build a modular architecture. The implicit goal of the OMG is not IIOP and IDL or, for that matter, CORBAServices, but something far more grand. IIOP and IDL can be considered as the plumbing. The true goal of OMG is to have a solid foundation on which to build the Common Object Facilities—or, in the common tongue, a platform for building and deploying Common Business Objects.

We are not there yet. As an old friend once told me, "Let the world wake up to objects; then perhaps we can think about distributing them..." Though my view is not as pessimistic as his, there is some truth to it.

The role of CORBAServices is simple. If IIOP and IDL are the plumbing, CORBAServices is the mortar that will hold the house together—the house OMG wants you to build. These services enable complex distributed systems to be built. The great thing about them is that, for the most part, the services themselves are very simple to understand and use.

This section of the book, beginning with this chapter and concluding with Chapter 11, "The Security Service," concentrates on the services that are commercially available. Although OMG has specified over 20 services, no one has been able to make a commercial argument for building all of them. In time, when all the world is a web of distributed objects, all these services will be available.

The following are services that are currently available with varying level of compliance:

- The Naming Service—It can be considered the White Pages service for distributed CORBA objects. Here is simple advice about the Naming Service: Don't leave home without one. As a service, it enables applications to find objects by name.
- The Trader Service—It can be thought of as the Yellow Pages of CORBA. As yet, there are only a few mature implementations of this service. It is my opinion that, over time, this service is going to be the cornerstone of many CORBA applications. As a Yellow Pages service, the Trader Service enables the classification of similar services.
- The Event Service—This is by far one of the most useful, albeit underutilized, services out there. The Event Service enables an almost complete decoupling of the server from the client.
- The Lifecycle Service—The CORBA Lifecycle Service was one of the first services that was standardized. Unfortunately, there are not that many commercial implementations out there. The service enables the transparent creation and destruction (among other things) of object references. It is extremely handy in applications that use an inordinate number of remote objects.

- The Transaction Service—Transactions are said to be the lifeblood of commerce. Nothing much works without a robust and resilient implementation of this service. CORBA provides an object-oriented interface to XA-based transaction services. XA is a standard protocol defined by the X/Open consortium. XA specifies a mechanism for open distributed transactions.
- The Security Service—In this age of the Internet, security is a hot issue. CORBA security pushes the envelop. This is particularly true when considering the fact that CORBA, in essence, is a peer-to-peer technology. Client/server roles are arbitrary and transient. If you consider a world with a billion objects distributed over the Web, security gets a whole new dimension.

The CORBA Naming Service is a most useful service. It enables an application to locate an object reference by name. This utility is welcome when you consider the fact that any self-respecting application would probably have tens of hundreds of objects spread over a number of hosts.

Why Use the Naming Service?

It is also conceivable that these objects keep moving around virtually. By *virtually,* it is meant that the name of the host could change or move the services from one host to another one and so on. The Naming Service makes the location of the object transparent to the client. As long as the objects are registered with the Naming Service, the client can always find them.

Essentially a server (or a client acting as a proxy for some server) can bind a name to an object. Parties interested in obtaining a reference to objects pointed to by the name can resolve the name to acquire the object reference.

TIP

Ideally, the Naming Service holds the names only for key object references. The rest of the objects are passed around as arguments to operations. This significantly reduces the communications overhead.

What Is in a Name?

In the CORBA standard, the `COSNaming` module identifies a name by using the `NameComponent` structure.

```
struct NameComponent{
        string id;
```

```
    string kind;
};
```

The name of a component is held in the NameComponent.id. This is the name that is used to find a name, for instance. The Namecomponent.id is useful for providing auxiliary information about the component itself. From the struct, it is but a small step to define a name:

```
typedef sequence <NameComponent> Name;
```

This would allow an application to string together a chain of NameComponents to create a name. Consider the following example.

An airline company has a number of hangars spread across the world. For simplicity, let's say that the Naming Service is available only to the hangars in the U.S. In the U.S., the company has four hangars: Los Angeles, New York, Chicago, and Denver. Aircraft are constantly being moved from one hangar to another. This requires the client to acquire multiple Hangar object references and operate on them.

The organization of a Naming hierarchy revolves around something called a NamingContext. A NamingContext enables the organization of names. The NameServer is the root NamingContext. Everything else is attached to this context.

If SOAR is to use the Naming Service, its services have to be organized around NamingContexts. NamingContexts have names attached to them. The first NamingContext is SOAR. The SOAR NamingContext has four subcontexts: Denver, Chicago, Los Angeles, and New York. Under each geographical region are further NamingContexts associated with the various services found in that particular region. For our purposes, only Chicago and New York have an operations service. Therefore, the aforementioned NamingContext has the operations NamingContext. Finally, there are simple names that are attached to the operations NamingContext: NYOperation and ChicagoOperation have NYHangar and ChicagoHangar attached to them.

A pictorial representation of this hierarchy is shown in Figure 7.1.

The Naming Service API

Before looking at some code, consider the Naming Service API. The following discussion introduces all the major components of the Naming Service and the related API to use them.

Creating Contexts

Sane applications will always use the NamingContext to relate names in some ordered structure. There are two APIs for creating the context:

```
NamingContext new_context();
NamingContext bind_new_context(in Name name)..;
```

The first operation enables the creation of a `NamingContext`. The `bind_context` then is called to attach a context to a name. The next operation, `bind_new_context`, enables the creation of the `NamingContext` and binding it to a name.

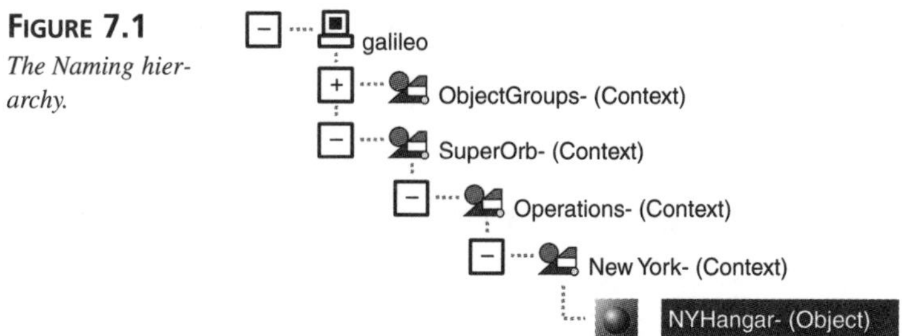

FIGURE 7.1
The Naming hierarchy.

Binding Names

There are two principal APIs for binding names to a Naming Service:

```
void bind(in Name name, in Object object) raises
(NotFound, CannotProceed, InvalidName, AlreadyBound)

void bind_context(in Name name, in NamingContext context)
(NotFound, CannotProceed, InvalidName, AlreadyBound)
```

It is possible to bind everything to a root context, but this would be using the NameServer only by the book and not by its intent. A Naming Service can be used to organize CORBA applications. This is accomplished by allowing applications to create a `NamingContext` first and then bind a name to a particular context. The `bind_context` allows the binding of a name to a `NamingContext`.

The `bind` operation enables the binding of an object reference with a `bind`. It is possible to use a compound name to do this. All but the last element of the sequence corresponds to the name of the component.

WARNING

Names have to be unique to a `NamingContext`. If a name is already in use, the `AlreadyBound` exception is thrown.

The following are two additional APIs provided by the Naming Service:

```
void rebind(in Name name, in Object object) raises
(NotFound, CannotProceed, InvalidName, AlreadyBound)
```

```
void rebind_context(in Name name, in NamingContext context)
(NotFound, CannotProceed, InvalidName, AlreadyBound)
```

These APIs enable the attachment of a new object reference to a name. The `rebind_context` does the same, except the `NamingContext` is changed for the given name. The old bindings are lost if these operations are done.

Deleting Context and Names

If a name has to be removed, the following call can be made on the Naming Service:

```
unbind(in Name name)..
```

A fully qualified compound name will be removed from the Naming context it was attached to. This is the method to invoke on a Naming context if it is to be removed:

```
void destroy()..
```

The operation will raise a `NotEmpty` exception if names are still attached to the context. If so, repeat the call to remove a name.

Resolving Names

The operation `resolve()` should be invoked on the `NameService` if an object reference needs to be acquired. The full API looks like this:

```
    Object resolve(in Name name)
raises (NotFound, CannotProceed, InvalidName);
```

Keep in mind that it is `CORBA::Object` that is being returned. A `narrow()` operation is executed on the returned `CORBA::Object` to cast the object reference to the desired type.

Using the Naming Service

With airplanes, it is sometimes required to move them about from place to place. The `Hangar` interface used in Chapter 3, "The Portable Object Adapter," is modified a bit to allow this to happen. The application will have two servers allowing a client to move an aircraft reference from one server to another server. The modified `Hangar` interface will be used to explain how the Naming Service can be used:

```
interface Hangar{
    struct aircraft{
```

```
        long  id;
    };

    void CheckInAirCraft(in aircraft t_aircraft);
    aircraft retrieveAndDeleteAircraft(in long id_);
};
```

The Naming Service `Hangar` is going to use the following environment:

Server Side ORB:	Orbix 2.3c
Toolkit:	Visual C++ 5.0
Client Side ORB:	Orbix 2.3c
Toolkit:	Visual C++ 5.0

Implementing the `Hangar` Interface

The hangar header file is modified to the extent required by IONA. The hangar itself is a simple array of Aircraft `structs`:

```
#ifndef Hangar_ih
#define Hangar_ih

#include "Hangar.hh"

class IT_DECLSPEC_Hangar Hangar_i:public virtual HangarBOAImpl{
public:
        virtual void CheckInAirCraft (const Hangar::aircraft& t_aircraft,
CORBA::Environment &IT_env=CORBA::default_environment) ;
        virtual Hangar::aircraft retrieveAndDeleteAircraft (CORBA::Long
id_, CORBA::Environment &IT_env=CORBA::default_environment) ;
        Hangar_i();
        ~Hangar_i();
private:
        Hangar::aircraft capacity[10];
        int free;
};
```

Listing 7.1 shows the implementation of this class.

LISTING 7.1 HANGAR INTERFACE IMPLEMENTATION

```
nclude <iostream.h>
#include "Hangar.hpp"


Hangar_i::Hangar_i():free(10){
}

Hangar_i::~Hangar_i(){
}

void Hangar_i::CheckInAirCraft (const Hangar::aircraft& t_aircraft,
CORBA::Environment &IT_env) {

    if(free<10)
        capacity[10 - free].id = t_aircraft.id;
    else
        throw CORBA::SystemException();
}

Hangar::aircraft Hangar_i::retrieveAndDeleteAircraft (CORBA::Long id_,
CORBA::Environment &IT_env) {

    Hangar::aircraft temp_;
    if(id_ < 10)
        temp_.id = this->capacity[id_].id;
          free—;
    else
        throw CORBA::SystemException();
    return temp_;
}
```

The implementation simply assigns an incoming argument to the array if `addNewAircraft` is called. The hangars themselves have a capacity for ten aircraft. This is taken into account.

When `retrieveAndDeleteAircraft()` is called, the appropriate aircraft is returned to the caller, and the capacity variable is decremented.

The Hangar Server Implementation

The main code of the hangar deals with registering the object reference with the `NameServer`. When this is accomplished, the server is ready for business, as shown in Listing 7.2.

LISTING 7.2 HANGAR SERVER IMPLEMENTATION

```
#include <iostream.h>
#include "NamingService.hh"
#include "Hangar.hpp"

#define USE_INIT

void main(int argc, char** argv){

CosNaming::NamingContext_var
     soarContext,regionContext,operationsContext;
    CosNaming::NamingContext_var rootContext;
    CosNaming::Name_var soar;
    CORBA::Object_var object_;

    try{

      CORBA::ORB_var orb = CORBA::ORB_init(argc, argv, "Orbix");
0.      object_ = orb->resolve_initial_references("NS");
    }
    catch(CORBA::SystemException& e){
          cerr<<e<<endl;
    }

    try{
       soar = new CosNaming::Name(1);
      soar->length(1);
        soar[(CORBA::ULong)0].id = CORBA::string_dup("Super Orb");
      soar[(CORBA::ULong)0].kind = CORBA::string_dup("");

      CosNaming::Name_var operations = new CosNaming::Name(1);
      operations->length(1);
      operations[(CORBA::ULong)0].id =
                CORBA::string_dup("Operations");
      operations[(CORBA::ULong)0].kind = CORBA::string_dup("");

      CosNaming::Name_var region = new CosNaming::Name(1);
      region->length(1);
      region[(CORBA::ULong)0].id = CORBA::string_dup("New York");
      region[(CORBA::ULong)0].kind = CORBA::string_dup("");

      CosNaming::Name_var hangar_name = new CosNaming::Name(1);
      hangar_name->length(1);
      hangar_name[(CORBA::ULong)0].id =
CORBA::string_dup("NYHangar");
      hangar_name[(CORBA::ULong)0].kind = CORBA::string_dup("");

      soarContext = rootContext->bind_new_context(soar);
      operationsContext = soarContext->bind_new_context(operations);
```

continues

LISTING 7.2 CONTINUED

```
        regionContext = operationsContext->bind_new_context(region);


        Hangar_var the_hangar = new Hangar_i();
        regionContext->rebind(hangar_name,the_hangar);

        CORBA::Orbix.impl_is_ready("SOAR");
    }

    catch (CosNaming::NamingContext::NotFound &) {
        cerr << "CosNaming::NamingContext::NotFound" << endl;
        exit(1);
    }
    catch (CosNaming::NamingContext::CannotProceed &) {
        cerr << "CosNaming::NamingContext::CannotProceed" << endl;
        exit(1);
    }
    catch (CosNaming::NamingContext::InvalidName &) {
        cerr << "CosNaming::NamingContext::InvalidName" << endl;
        exit(1);
    }
    catch (CosNaming::NamingContext::AlreadyBound &) {
        cerr << "CosNaming::NamingContext::AlreadyBound" << endl;
        exit(1);
    }
    catch (CosNaming::NamingContext::NotEmpty &) {
        cerr << "CosNaming::NamingContext::NotEmpty" << endl;
        exit(1);
    }
    catch (CORBA::SystemException &sysEx) {
        cerr << "Unexpected system exception" << endl;
        cerr << &sysEx;
        exit(1);
    }
    catch (...) {
        cout << "Unexpected exception" << endl;
        exit(1);
    }
}
```

The Naming Service object reference is retrieved from the Orb's interface. This initializes the `rootContext` object. When the `resolve_initial_references()` method is invoked, the `rootContext` object is returned. The `SOAR` context is attached to this context. This is accomplished in the following snippet of code:

```
object_ = orb->resolve_initial_references("NS");
```

A simple name is contructed. The Name's ID is `"Super Orb"`; the kind is left blank. Names are constructed in the following manner:

```
soar->length(1);
soar[(CORBA::ULong)0].id = CORBA::string_dup("Super Orb");
soar[(CORBA::ULong)0].kind = CORBA::string_dup("");
```

From that point, three further names are constructed: `Operations`, `New York`, and `NYHangar`. When all the names are constructed, they are bound to the context to create new contexts. The `soarContext` is bound to the `rootContext`. On the `soarContext`, the `operationsContext` is bound. Finally the last context, the `regionContext`, is bound to the `operationsContext`. The `bind` operations are carried out in the following code:

```
soarContext = rootContext->bind_new_context(soar);
operationsContext = soarContext->bind_new_context(operations);
regionContext = operationsContext->bind_new_context(region);
```

The last step is to bind a name pointing to the appropriate context. This is to be the `Hangar` object reference. Its name, `hangar_name`, is bound to the `regionsContext`. The construction of the object reference and the bind of the object is shown in the following:

```
Hangar_var the_hangar = new Hangar_i();
      regionContext->rebind(hangar_name,the_hangar);
```

This sets up the names for the `SOAR` operations components. When that has been accomplished, the server is ready to receive invocations from the client.

The Hangar Client Implementation

The implementation for the client is very similar to that for the server, except it uses the name to resolve the object reference and make invocations on it (see Listing 7.3).

LISTING 7.3 HANGAR CLIENT IMPLEMENTATION

```
#include <iostream.h>
#include "NamingService.hh"
#include "Hangar.hh"

#define USE_INIT

void main(int argc, char** argv){

    CosNaming::NamingContext_var rootContext;
    CosNaming::Name_var soar;
    Hangar_var theHangar;
    CORBA::Object_var object_;
```

continues

LISTING 7.3 CONTINUED

```
    try{

      CORBA::ORB_var orb = CORBA::ORB_init(argc, argv, "Orbix");
      object_ = orb->resolve_initial_references("NS");
    }
    catch(CORBA::SystemException& e){
      cerr<<e<<endl;
    }

    try{
      soar = new CosNaming::Name(4);
      soar->length(4);
        soar[(CORBA::ULong)0].id = CORBA::string_dup("Super Orb");
      soar[(CORBA::ULong)0].kind = CORBA::string_dup("");
      soar[(CORBA::ULong)1].id = CORBA::string_dup("Operations");
      soar[(CORBA::ULong)1].kind = CORBA::string_dup("");
      soar[(CORBA::ULong)2].id = CORBA::string_dup("New York");
      soar[(CORBA::ULong)2].kind = CORBA::string_dup("");
      soar[(CORBA::ULong)3].id = CORBA::string_dup("NYHangar");
      soar[(CORBA::ULong)3].kind = CORBA::string_dup("");

      object_ = rootContext->resolve(soar);
      theHangar = Hangar::_narrow(object_);

      Hangar::aircraft_var t_aircraft = new  Hangar::aircraft();
      t_aircraft->id = 1001;
      theHangar->CheckInAirCraft(t_aircraft);
      Hangar::aircraft ret_ =
theHangar->retrieveAndDeleteAircraft(1001);



    }
    catch (CosNaming::NamingContext::NotFound &) {
        cerr << "CosNaming::NamingContext::NotFound" << endl;
        exit(1);
    }
    catch (CosNaming::NamingContext::CannotProceed &) {
        cerr << "CosNaming::NamingContext::CannotProceed" << endl;
        exit(1);
    }
    catch (CosNaming::NamingContext::InvalidName &) {
        cerr << "CosNaming::NamingContext::InvalidName" << endl;
        exit(1);
    }
    catch (CosNaming::NamingContext::AlreadyBound &) {
        cerr << "CosNaming::NamingContext::AlreadyBound" << endl;
        exit(1);
    }
```

```
    catch (CosNaming::NamingContext::NotEmpty &) {
        cerr << "CosNaming::NamingContext::NotEmpty" << endl;
        exit(1);
    }
    catch (CORBA::SystemException &sysEx) {
        cerr << "Unexpected system exception" << endl;
        cerr << &sysEx;
        exit(1);
    }
    catch (...) {
        cout << "Unexpected exception" << endl;
        exit(1);
    }
}
```


First, a client has to construct a name for the potential object reference. In this case, the `soar` name is constructed. It is a compound name that has four elements. The last one is the name of the object reference that is required by the client. The construction of the name is shown in the following code:

```
soar = new CosNaming::Name(4);
      soar->length(4);
        soar[(CORBA::ULong)0].id = CORBA::string_dup("Super Orb");
      soar[(CORBA::ULong)0].kind = CORBA::string_dup("");
      soar[(CORBA::ULong)1].id = CORBA::string_dup("Operations");
      soar[(CORBA::ULong)1].kind = CORBA::string_dup("");
      soar[(CORBA::ULong)2].id = CORBA::string_dup("New York");
      soar[(CORBA::ULong)2].kind = CORBA::string_dup("");
      soar[(CORBA::ULong)3].id = CORBA::string_dup("NYHangar");
      soar[(CORBA::ULong)3].kind = CORBA::string_dup("");
```

The name corresponds to `Super Orb/Operations/New York/NYHangar`. This enables the retrieval of the object reference named `NYHangar`.

The `resolve()` method is invoked on the root context to retrieve the object reference. The return type is `CORBA::Object`. This has to be narrowed to obtain the correct type.

The object is narrowed to obtain the correct type. The `resolve()` and `narrow()` operations are shown in the following:

```
object_ = rootContext->resolve(soar);
      theHangar = Hangar::_narrow(object_);
```

With the object reference in hand, it is now possible to make invocations on the object reference.

Summary

The Name Service is a critical CORBA service. It enables objects to be transparently distributed, irrespective of host or location. It is a service that has a very simple API. As such, it is not a very complicated service to use. As a service, it is sort of a White Pages directory. It can be used to locate objects by name.

CHAPTER 8

The Trader Service

In This Chapter

The Trader Service is very similar to the Naming Service. Applications can register their objects with the service, which acts as a locator service for a client requiring some service. For example, a banking application client can require the services of a payment server. In that case, the client can use the Naming Service or the Trader Service to locate this service on the network. However, there is one important distinction between the Trader Service and the Naming Service. Although the Naming Service acts as a simple White Pages service, by which a client can locate an object by name, the Trader Service acts as a Yellow Pages service. A Trader Service could offer many different types of payment objects, all of them classified under the general category "payments." The client needs to figure out the payment object that best suits its requirements.

This enables the client to request the service by a type or by an *offer*. When a request is made, the Trader searches its directory for an object that matches the requirements of the client. When such an object is found, its object reference is returned to the client.

This interaction is very much that like of a trading operation between a merchant and a customer. The customer wants something that the merchant has in the store, and the trade is done on monetary terms. The Trader Service enables such trading to be accomplished using user-defined Quality of Service criteria.

Trader Service Interaction

The Trader Service enables objects to advertise their services. Clients requiring these services can acquire them as the Trader Service Trader matches the requested requirements against the ones that are registered with it.

Registering a service with the Trader Service is known as *exporting* a service. Acquiring a service by searching a trader space is known as *importing* a service. Figure 8.1 shows the general components of a service interaction.

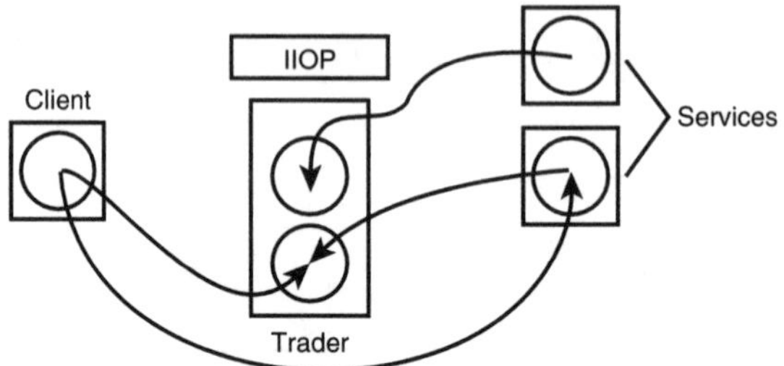

FIGURE 8.1
Trader Service interaction.

Design Rationale for the Trader Service

OMG's primary goal for the Trader Service is the requirement of scalability. *Scalability* means that the Trader server is capable of servicing an arbitrary number of offers that are advertised through it. This is accomplished by the Trader Service's capability of dividing its offers into a number of logically linked trading spaces. One of the side effects of this is the capability of linking up multiple Trader Services into a federated Trader Service Trader. Conceptually, a federated Trader Service could span multiple domains.

A Trader Service Trader that meets this requirement would have to have the capability of supporting an arbitrary number of clients using its services; OMG specifies a concept of policies. It is essentially through a Trader's set of policies that its trading space is searched for an offer that meets the client's requirements.

Main Components of the Trader Service

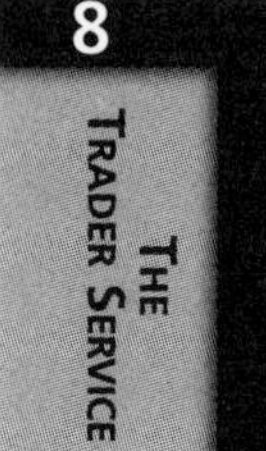

The Trader specification details a gamut of related concepts and data types. For brevity, only the major concepts are described here:

- Exporter—A component that wants to advertise its capability through a Trader.
- Importer—A client that uses the Trader Service to locate an exporter by specifying some criteria.
- Service Types—The primary concept that represents an offer. The service type represents the type that is offering the service. It describes an offer by specifying one or more properties.
- Property—These name-value pairs qualify the offer that is advertised by the exporter. It is essentially on these properties that traders constrain the search for an exporter:

```
typedef Isring PropertyName;
typedef sequence<PropertyName> PropertyNameSeq;
typedef any PropertyValue;

struct Property{
    PropertyName name;
    PropertyValue value;
};

enum HowManyProps {none, some, all};
```

```
union SpecifiedProps switch (HowManyProps) {
    case some: PropertyNameSeq prop_names;
};
```

- Service Offers—The means by which an exporter advertises its capabilities. It contains the following information:

```
struct offer{
    Object reference;
    PropertySeq properties;
};

typedef sequence<Offer> OfferSeq;

struct OfferInfo{
    Object reference;
    ServiceTypeName type;
    PropertySeq properties;
};
```

State of CORBA Trader Implementations

Unfortunately, CORBA Trader implementations are only recently becoming available. This situation will change over the next year or two. The available implementations offer varying degrees of CORBA compliance. It is only a matter of time before a forward-looking company will offer a CORBA Trader over the Web. The implementation that follows will use the Trader implementation from Dais as part of the J^2 implementation.

Let's consider a simple Trader implementation. The example will illustrate the basics of how a Trader should work.

The `CUTrader` interface will demonstrate the *property* concept of the `CosTrading` module. The `CosTrading` module contains the specification for the CORBA Trader Service. In conjunction with this, it will also show an adaptation of the service-offer interface to enable objects to advertise their capabilities. A component may register its capabilities or have its registration withdrawn from the `CUTrader` implementation. Listing 8.1 shows the `CUTrader` interface. The `CUTrader` will help us demonstrate a minimalist Trader Service.

LISTING 8.1 THE `CUTrader` INTERFACE

```
module CUTrader {

typedef string PropertyName;
typedef string PropertyValue;

struct Property{
```

```
        PropertyName      name;
        PropertyValue    value;
};
typedef sequence<Property> PropertySeq;

struct Offer{
        Object reference;
        PropertySeq properties;
};

typedef sequence<Offer> OfferSeq;

interface Register{
        void        add(in Object obj, in string Service_id,
                        in PropertyList list);
        void        remove(in string Service _id);
        Offer          get(in string Service_id,
    in PropertyList criteria);
};

};
```

The core of the CUTrader model is the Register interface. This interface allows the three operations:

```
void        add(in Object obj, in string Service_id,
                        in PropertyList list);
        void        remove(in string Service _id);
        Offer          get(in string Service_id,
    in PropertyList criteria);
```

When a component needs to register its services, it can call the add() operation to add the object reference and the associated property list to the CUTrader repository.

A component may remove a register entry by passing it the Service_id identifier. On doing so, the CUTrader removes all associated information on the component from the CUTrader repository.

An importer has to invoke the get() method on the Trader when it requires a service. When invoking get(), the client has to pass in the name of the service. It also has to pass in a list of properties to aid the search for the appropriate service. The Trader will return an offer with the relative object reference if a match is found in the repository.

The CUTrader Implementation

The CUTrader needs to maintain an internal database to store the offers as they come in. It should also be capable of searching the database by the criteria the client sends in to the Trader.

The CUTrader will use the JGL Hashset to maintain the internal database. Overall, the following environment will be used to implement the Trader:

Server-side Orb:	VisiBroker For Java 3.1
Client-side Orb:	VisiBroker For Java 3.1
Additional Toolkit:	Java Generic Library 3.0

Listing 8.2 shows the implementation of the interface.

LISTING 8.2 IMPLEMENTING THE CUTrader INTERFACE

```
package CUTrader;
import com.objectspace.jgl.*;

public class _example_Register extends CUTrader._RegisterImplBase {

  HashSet repository = new HashSet();
  HashSet Offers = new HashSet();

  public _example_Register(java.lang.String name) {
    super(name);
  }

  public _example_Register() {
    super();
  }

  public void add(
    org.omg.CORBA.Object obj,
    java.lang.String Service_id,
    CUTrader.Property[] list
  ) {
     System.out.println(list);
     Offer temp_ = new Offer();
     temp_.reference = obj;
     temp_.properties = new Property[list.length];

     for(int i = 0; i<list.length; i++){
       temp_.properties[i] = new Property();
       temp_.properties[i].name = list[i].name;
       temp_.properties[i].value = list[i].value;
     }
     RepositoryObject ro = new RepositoryObject(temp_,Service_id);
     repository.add(ro);
  }

  public void remove(
    java.lang.String Service_id
  ) {
```

```
    repository.remove(Service_id);
  }

  public CUTrader.Offer get(
    java.lang.String Service_id,
    CUTrader.Property[] criteria
  ) {
      Offer temp_ = new Offer();
      temp_.properties = new Property[criteria.length];

     for(int i = 0; i<criteria.length; i++){
       temp_.properties[i] = new Property();
       temp_.properties[i].name = criteria[i].name;
       temp_.properties[i].value = criteria[i].value;
     }

     RepositoryObject returnOffer  =
          (RepositoryObject)repository.get(temp_);
     if(returnOffer == null)
        throw new org.omg.CORBA.BAD_TYPECODE();

     return returnOffer.getOffer();
  }
}
```


The implementation uses a class named `RepositoryObject`. It is this object that is stored in the JGL Hashset. When a client invokes an `add()` method, it passes an array of properties and a string identifying the object's capability. The `add()` method also has an an object reference argument of the component that wants to advertise its services. The `Offer` class has the following definition:

```
package CUTrader;

final public class Offer {
  public org.omg.CORBA.Object reference;
  public CUTrader.Property[] properties;
  public Offer() {
  }
  public Offer(
    org.omg.CORBA.Object reference,
    CUTrader.Property[] properties
  ) {
    this.reference = reference;
    this.properties = properties;
  }
  public java.lang.String toString() {
    org.omg.CORBA.Any any = org.omg.CORBA.ORB.init().create_any();
    CUTrader.OfferHelper.insert(any, this);
```

```
    return any.toString();
  }
}
```

The `Offer` class defines two public instance variables: a `CORBA.Object` and an array of properties. The `CORBA.Object` refers to the exporter's reference. The array holds the list of offer constraints that the exporter was to advertise. Both these are initialized with the parameters passed in.

The `Repository` class is necessary for using the JGL Hashset. It has the structure shown in Listing 8.3.

LISTING 8.3 THE Repository CLASS

```
package CUTrader;

public class RepositoryObject {

  private Offer offer = new Offer();
  private String id = null;

  public RepositoryObject(Offer offer, String id) {
    this.offer.reference = offer.reference;
    this.id = id;
    this.offer.properties = new Property[offer.properties.length];
    for(int i = 0; i < offer.properties.length; i++){
      this.offer.properties[i] = new Property();
      this.offer.properties[i].name = offer.properties[i].name;
      this.offer.properties[i].value = offer.properties[i].value;
    }
  }

  public int hashCode(){
     return this.offer.properties.hashCode();
  }

  public boolean equals(String id){
    return (this.id.equals(id));
  }
  public boolean equals(Object object){

    boolean found = false;

    if(object instanceof RepositoryObject){
      RepositoryObject ro = (RepositoryObject)object;
      Offer temp_ = ro.getOffer();
      while(!found){
        for(int i = 0; i < temp_.properties.length; i++){
     if(temp_.properties[i].name.equals
```

```
        (this.offer.properties[i].name)){
          found = true;
        break;
          }
        }
      }
    }
    return found;
  }

  public String toString(){
    return this.offer.reference.toString();
  }

  public Offer getOffer(){
    return this.offer;
  }
}
```

This method:

```
public int hashCode()
```

determines the key to access an element from the Repository. The Repository object will not allow similar objects to be added to the hashset. This is determined in the following line:

```
public boolean equals(Object object)
```

The implementation of this method verifies whether the names are the same. If the names are the same, the object is not added to the Hashset.

With the `Repository` class defined, let's get back to the `Register` interface implementation. After the `Offer` object is constructed, an instance of the `Repository` class is added to the Hashset. The Hashset is named `Repository`. The `Repository` class constructor takes two parameters: the `Offer` object and the `Service_id` string. Adding an object is accomplished by the following line of code:

```
RepositoryObject ro = new RepositoryObject(temp_,Service_id);
repository.add(ro);
```

The `get` method is very simmilar to `add`. First, an `Offer` object is constructed from the parameter that is passed. After this is done, the `get()` method is invoked on the `Repository` Hashset:

```
for(int i = 0; i<criteria.length; i++){
       temp_.properties[i] = new Property();
       temp_.properties[i].name = criteria[i].name;
       temp_.properties[i].value = criteria[i].value;
```

```
    }

    RepositoryObject returnOffer  =
          (RepositoryObject)repository.get(temp_);
..
```

Internally, the Hashset uses a `hashCode` comparison to establish whether an object of the given constraint is located in the `Repository`. If it is found, it is returned. This is the `returnOffer` object in the preceding code.

Of course, if a match is not found, an exception needs to be thrown. Otherwise, the returned object is returned to the client that invokes the operation.

The Trader Server Implementation

The `CUTrader` server is a run-of-the-mill CORBA server. The following code should be self-explanatory:

```
public class Trader {

  public static void main(String[] args) {
    org.omg.CORBA.ORB orb =
    org.omg.CORBA.ORB.init(args,null);
    org.omg.CORBA.BOA boa = orb.BOA_init();
    CUTrader.Register Trader = new _example_Register ("CUTrader");
    boa.obj_is_ready(Trader);
    System.out.println(Traer + " is ready.");
    boa.impl_is_ready();
  }

}
```

The `Register` object reference is initialized with the name `CUTrader`. After this is done, the basic object adapter is notified of its readiness, and the server goes into a blocked state waiting for incoming invocations.

Using the `CUTrader`

With the `CUTrader` up and running, any server should be able to register its services with the Trader. The other side of the coin is that any client can search for a traded object by some criteria. First, a server that exports its services will be built, and then a client that uses the Trader to locate a service will be implemented.

A `CUTrader` Exporter

Essentially, a service that wants to export its capability needs to acquire the Trader's object reference and invoke the `add()` operation on it. It passes the required parameters into add(). These parameters include the name of the service and an array of properties that it would like to advertise using the Trader.

The CUTrader exporter will use the following interface to implement a skeletal service:

```
module SOAR{
    interface Reservations{
        void reserve();
    };
};
```

Run this IDL through the VisiBroker idl2java pre-compiler. The interface need not be implemented. This example shows only how the Reservation uses the server to export its capabilities with the CUTrader. Listing 8.4 shows the server implementation.

LISTING 8.4 USING THE CUTrader SERVICE

```
package SOAR;
import CUTrader.*;

public class ReservationServer {
  org.omg.CORBA.ORB orb = null;
  Register trader = null;
  _example_Reservations reservations = null;

  public ReservationServer(String[] args) {
    orb = org.omg.CORBA.ORB.init(args,null);
    org.omg.CORBA.BOA boa = orb.BOA_init();
    trader = RegisterHelper.bind(orb, "CUTrader");

    reservations = new _example_Reservations("Reservation");
    this.RegisterServer();

    boa.obj_is_ready(reservations);
    System.out.println(reservations + " is ready.");
    boa.impl_is_ready();

  }

  public void RegisterServer(){
    String Service_id = "Reservation";

    Property[] offer = new Property[2];
    for(int j =0; j<offer.length;  j++)
       offer[j] = new Property();

    offer[0].name = "Cost";
    offer[0].value = "$30";
```

continues

LISTING 8.4 CONTINUED

```
    offer[1].name = "Availability";
    offer[1].value = "24 Hours";
    try{
      trader.add(reservations, Service_id, offer);
    }
    catch(org.omg.CORBA.SystemException e){
      System.out.println(e.toString());
    }
  }

  public static void main(String[] args) {
    ReservationServer reservationServer = new ReservationServer(args);
  }

}
```

When an instance of `SOAR.Reservations` is instantiated, the implementation calls the `RegisterServer()` method. The server has to call the `add()` method on the `CUTrader` server. It has to pass three parameters: a `CORBA.Object` object reference, an array of properties, and the name of the service.

The object reference it passes is `Reservations`. The following is a list of properties:

```
Property[] offer = new Property[2];
for(int j =0; j<offer.length;  j++)
   offer[j] = new Property();

offer[0].name = "Cost";
offer[0].value = "$30";
offer[1].name = "Availability";
offer[1].value = "24 Hours";
```

The `Reservations` object exports two properties: "`Cost`" and "`Availability`". The first is a common constraint to use in a trading environment. This instance of the `Reservation` server charges `"$30"` for its services. It further distinguishes itself by specifying its availablity constraint, which is `"24 Hours"`.

This enables a potential client to constrain a search by specifying a particular property. For instance, it can specify that a cost of a service should be less than `"$40"`. This would, in theory, return the `Reservations` object reference from the `CUTrader`.

The CUTrader Importer

Any potential client should be able to log into the Trader Service and request an object reference. To do so, the client invokes the following method:

```
public CUTrader.Offer get(
    java.lang.String Service_id,
    CUTrader.Property[] criteria
  )
```

When a client invokes this method, it passes in the name of the service and an array of properties that it would like the Trader to search the repository for. In Listing 8.5, you see a client using `CUTrader` to locate and use the service for the object that it requires.

LISTING 8.5 CLIENT USING THE CUTrader SERVICE

```
package SOAR;
import CUTrader.*;

public class ReservationClient {

  Reservations ReservationServer = null;

  public ReservationClient(String[] args) {

    org.omg.CORBA.ORB orb = org.omg.CORBA.ORB.init(args,null);
    org.omg.CORBA.BOA boa = orb.BOA_init();
    Register trader = RegisterHelper.bind(orb, "CUTrader");

    String Service_id = "Reservation";

    Property[] criteria = new Property[1];
    Offer bestOffer = null;
    for(int i = 0; i<criteria.length; i++)
      criteria[i] = new Property();

    criteria[0].name = "Cost";
    criteria[0].value = "$30";

    try{
      bestOffer = trader.get(Service_id, criteria);
    }
    catch(org.omg.CORBA.SystemException e){
      System.out.println(e.toString());
    }

    if(bestOffer != null)
      System.out.println("Got it..");
    else
      System.out.println("Haven't Got it..");
  }

  public static void main(String[] args) {
    ReservationClient reservationClient = new ReservationClient(args);

  }
}
```

The client wants to locate a service by a single constraint. It constructs this constraint by initializing an array of properties. The array has only one element. This is shown the following code:

```
Property[] criteria = new Property[1];
    Offer bestOffer = null;
    for(int i = 0; i<criteria.length; i++)
      criteria[i] = new Property();

    criteria[0].name = "Cost";
    criteria[0].value = "$30";
```

When this is done, the `Property` object, along with a string identifying the service, is passed on to the `CUTrader`. If an appropiate service is located, this is returned. Otherwise, the `CUTrader` throws an exception that is handled.

Summary

The Trader Service could prove to be an extremely useful service. It enables a service to export its capabilities through a service analogous to the Naming Service. The difference is that the Trader acts as a Yellow Pages service.

The Trader can maintain a database of properties a service would like to advertise. These properties could then be used by clients to locate a service by a desirable constraint. These could be a variety of constraints, both qualities of service criteria as well as technical qualifications.

CHAPTER 9

The Event Service

IN THIS CHAPTER

Modeling a system on state transitions enables the construction of very flexible and cohesive systems. The system is loosely coupled because it is designed with the fewest possible dependencies. Object-orientation is a paradigm that enables systems with fewer dependencies than those possible with a more procedural approach. Although object-oriented approaches have banished the dependencies based on global variables through encapsulation, they have their own dependencies. In object-oriented approaches, these dependencies are on the interfaces that objects expose.

Nevertheless, after an interface has been designed, it is a contract that should not be violated. This means that these interfaces should not change. Objects, in short, are sensitive to changes in the interface. This is, to a certain extent, manageable with deskbound systems. Under distributed systems, this sensitivity could be problematic.

The Power Nine Problem

A scenario where a client depends on the constancy of an interface will help illuminate the problems. If the server changes the interface, the client does not function correctly. The fact that CORBA is inherently peer-to-peer has the potential for exasperating this problem. This is a problem I call the "power nine" problem. A system comprising a billion objects (possible by 2005 AD) would have enormous sensitivity to changes in the interface. In a sense, the limits of objects are inherent in the technique of encapsulation. I have arbitrarily set the limit at 10^9 objects, or a billion objects with an average of five methods per interface.

In my view, the problem cannot be solved without meta-interfaces. These are interfaces with a mechanism for describing the semantics of the interface. This paradigm will allow not just the representation of interfaces but their semantics as well. Nevertheless, this is an enormously complicated problem. The solution for this problem space lies somewhere between Artificial Intelligence and "smart" components. Smart in my view is possible, but AI is in the I-don't-know-if-that-will-work category.

Reducing Interface Dependencies

Before interfaces become smart or something "more," distributed systems with high overall complexity need to be kept as cohesive as possible. This means that if new elements are introduced, it should not bring down the whole house. The designer can use the Event Service to specify systems where the overall dependency of the system component is not on interfaces but on events. This is a dependency, but one that has a higher cohesion ratio than just a pure object-oriented system.

As long as the client and the server agree on the semantics of what an event means, the CORBA Event Service provides a standard API for producing and consuming events. CORBA provides a standard mechanism for achieving this agreement. Before going into the details of how this can be achieved, let's look at the different event semantics CORBA supports.

The CORBA Event Service enables a near-maximum decoupling of clients and servers by delegating the interdependencies between them to events. There are three main components of the CORBA Event Service: the supplier, the consumer, and the Event Channel. Within the context of these three components, the CosEvents Service supports two types of event delivery: deliveries through push or through pull modes of event access. Events can be delivered through a push mechanism. Events can also be delivered by using pull.

The Supplier-Driven Event Model

The supplier-driven type of event model involves the supplier of events generating the event and *pushing* the event to a registered consumer. In this mode of event delivery, the supplier of the event is the *client* and the consumer of the event is the *server*.

The supplier of the event can communicate with the consumer as it supports the `PushConsumer` interface:

```
interface PushConsumer{
    void push (in any date) raises (Disconnected);
    void disconnect_push_consumer();
};
```

When a supplier has an event to deliver, the supplier invokes the `push` operation on the client. The operation takes `CORBA::Any` as the argument. The `disconnect_push_consumer()` provides an operative mechanism for the server to disconnect the consumer for some reason. Such needs may arise for quality-of-service criteria. A server could offer its services only periodically. When the server needs to be shut down, it could use this method to disconnect all consumers.

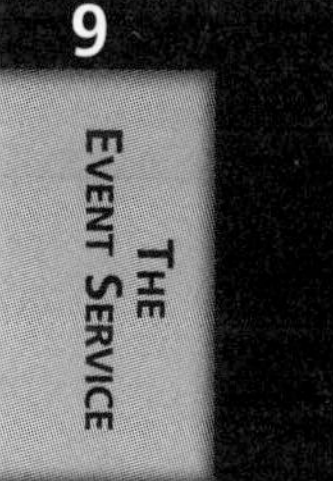

A supplier of `push` events has to support a simple interface:

```
interface PushSupplier{
    void disconnect_push_supplier();
};
```

This API provides the consumer of the pushed events with the capability of informing the event server that it is about to disconnect itself from the interaction.

The Consumer-Driven Event Model

This model enables the consumer of an event to dictate when an event is delivered. This is also known as the *pull* model of event delivery. The model in terms of its API is very similar to the push model, except that the responsibility of retrieving the event rests with the consumer. This results in the reversal of roles, so to speak. The consumer is the client and the producer of the event is the server. When a supplier supports pull as a mechanism for supporting event delivery, it needs to support the following interface:

```
interface PullSupplier{

    any Pull raises (Disconnected);
    any try_Pull(out boolean has_event) raises
(Disconnected)
    void disconnect_pull_supplier();
};
```

The events that the server wants to distribute can be cached in an event queue. The client can then pull an event out of this queue when required. It is conceivable that the supplier does not have any events to supply. In this case, the `pull` operation will be costly for the client. To remove this overhead, the specification provides the `try_pull()` operation. This operation does not block the client when making the invocation using `try_pull`. The `out` argument will indicate whether the server has events to service.

Any server wishing to become a pull supplier has to implement the interface that was defined previously. Using the previous interface, the client can `pull` events it requires, when it requires them.

The client has to support only a simple interface:

```
interface PullConsumer{
    void disconnect_pull_consumer()
};
```

The two `disconnect` APIs provide a clean mechanism for either the client or the server to disconnect themselves from an event contract.

The Delegated Event Model

The Event Channel provides the most flexible model for event delivery. Using an Event Channel–based design enables the incorporation of various quality-of-service criteria to be added to the system. The Event Channel offers the following benefits over a more direct model of event communication:

- The Event Channel offers a much more scalable system than those offered by direct events communictions. Scalability in this context means that the number of suppliers and interested consumers can be arbitrary.
- There is a greater decoupling between client and server. This means that the Event Channel needs to support only certain types of events. A client "subscribing" to these need not bother about the originator of these events. On the other hand, the supplier need not be concerned about what is ultimately consuming the events.
- Events can be made persistent and transactional. This allows clients to play back an event. Another major benefit is the possibility of logging events when they happen. In this fashion, if a failure occurs, the Event Channel can reinitialize its state to recover from the failure.
- Designs can mix and match push and pull models.

Semantics of Delegation-Based Event Models

The Event Channel allows the mixing and matching of push and pull models. This enables the following combinations of event delivery models:

- Push-Push model

  In this model, the supplier pushes an event to the channel, and the channel in turn pushes the event to the client.
- Push-Pull model

  The supplier pushes the event as usual to the channel. At the Event Channel, these events are buffered. The client pulls events from the Event Channel buffer as and when required.
- Pull-Push model

  In this model, the Event Channel pulls events from the supplier, which buffers events. These `pulls` can be thought of as analogous to polling. After an event has been retrieved, the event is pushed to a registered consumer.
- Pull-Pull model

  Using the pull-pull semantics, the supplier of events buffers events as state changes occur in them. The Event Channel polls the supplier during regular intervals to pull events from it when they become available. The Event Channel buffers these events for some client to eventually pull them out from its buffer.

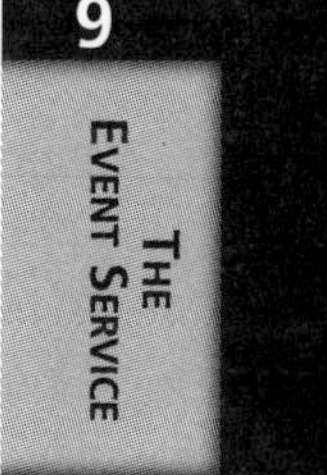

The Event Channel is a proxy for event producers. In that respect, the introduction of channels is irrelevant to a client, because, as far as the client is concerned, the channel is the producer of events.

Event Channels are just like other CORBA servers. As such, a client can obtain its services as it does with any other CORBA servers. This may include the bind call or using the IOR. The preferred means of accessing the channel would be through a Naming Service or a Trader Service.

The Event Channel APIs are mainly for administering the various suppliers and consumers. As mentioned, the Event Channel enables the mixing of event delivery models:

The following example shows how you can use both `push` and pull mechanisms for event delivery:

```
interface ConsumerAdmin{
    ProxyPushSuppler obtain_push_supplier();
    ProxyPullSuppler obtain_pull_supplier();
..
};
```

The supplier and consumer ultimately deal with the proxy object. These two interfaces enable them to retrieve the appropriate proxy object references held by the Event Channel:

```
interface EventChannel{
    ConsumerAdmin for_consumer();
    ConsumerAdmin for_suppliers();
    void destroy();
};
```

When the reference to `EventChannel` is obtained, a client can request the interfaces for the consumer or for the supplier. These interfaces are used to obtain the required proxy references. Using the proxies, the client can connect to the required model for event delivery.

Event Types

CORBA supports two types of events: untyped events and typed events. The interfaces described previously were for untyped events.

Untyped Events

Whether an application is using push or pull models for event delivery, with untyped events, these operations deliver an `Any` type. As you may recall, a `CORBA::Any` type is essentially a void pointer with an associated typecode pointer.

An any type can encapsulate any IDL type. One of the consequences of this feature is the fact that the client must clearly understand the semantics of the encapsulated type. This means that if the client is excepting a `foo` type encapsulated in an `Any`, the server should not deliver a `bar` type.

Typed Events

Typed events enable a supplier to deliver IDL interfaces as events to a consumer. It means that any valid IDL interfaces could be passed as an event using typed events. This is the closest an object reference–based system such as CORBA can come to a Mobile Agent type of architecture. The mechanism for events is different, depending upon what model is used to deliver an event.

If the model used is a push model, the event consumer supplies the interface. If the model used is a pull model, the supplier furnishes an interface. The typed events also enable the construction of typed Event Channels that deliver typed events.

Implementing a `CORBAEvents`-Based Application

The following sections illustrate how to use `CORBAEvents`. The first example develops an untyped push-based application. The second illustrates the typed push model.

The following is the environment:

Servers:	Orbix 2.3c
Clients:	Orbix 2.3c
UnTyped events:	OrbixEvents 1.1c
Typed events:	OrbixEvents 1.1d

Implementing Untyped Push Models

The application builds a push supplier and a push consumer. They share a `push` Event Channel. The model being built is a push-push model.

The Push Supplier

To implement an `OrbixEvents` push supplier, the code should accomplish three things:

1. The supplier retrieves a ProxyPushConsumer from the event channel.
2. After the ProxyPushConsumer is retrieved, it invokes the connect_push_supplier().
3. After the push supplier is connected, the event server can push events into the Event Channel.

The Event Channel can be obtained in one of three ways. The first mechanism is to obtain an Event Channel by using the low-level bind() that is usually provided by ORB implementations. Keep in mind that some of these implementations are not CORBA-compliant. This means that the bind() call does not usually use IIOP to attach to a server by a vendor-specific protocol. The second mechanism is to use the Naming Service or the Trader Service. This is a much more flexible manner of advertising an Event Service channel. The third mechanism is to use the IOR. This mechanism might be used if the design is to enable interoperability of an Event Channel across multiple ORBs.

With the Event Channel retrieved, the server should invoke the for_suppliers() method on it to retrieve the SupplierAdmin object reference. The SupplierAdmin supports the following operations:

```
interface SupplierAdmin{
    ProxyPushSupplier obtain_push_supplier();
    ProxyPullSupplier obtain_pull_supplier();
};
```

Because the application is using the push model, the server invokes the first operation. If the server implements a pull model, it invokes an obtain_pull_supplier to register its services.

With the SupplierAdmin object reference in hand, the server invokes the obtain_push_supplier() to retrieve a reference to a ProxyPushSupplier. The ProxyPushSupplier is the interface that the server uses to connect its supply to the Event Channel:

```
interface ProxyPushSupplier:CosEventComm:PushSupplier{
void connect_push_supplier(in CosEventComm:PushSupplier
  push_supplier) raises (AlreadyConnected);
  };
```

With the administration of the event server out of the way, the server can then proceed to push events into the Event Channel, as events become available.

The server implements the following IDL as the event type to pass to the Event Channel. The file contains a struct that will hold departure details for flights:

```
Departure.idl
struct DepartureDetail{
```

```
        string<5> flighno;
        string<5> time;
        string<1> status;
};
```

The idea is to have an event server that transmits departure data when this information becomes available. Compile the preceding structure with the Orbix IDL pre-compiler:

```
prompt$> IDL -A departure.idl
```

The `-A` flag generates support for `Any`.

The `EventSupplier` must be subclassed from `PushConsumerBOAImpl`. This class is generated by IDL pre-compiling the `EventService.idl` with a `-B` flag with the Orbix IDL pre-compiler.

The following header file lays out the definition on the `Eventsupplier`:

```
flightserver.hpp

class FlightSupplier_i : public CosEventComm::PushSupplierBOAImpl{

private:
  unsigned char m_connected;

public:
  FlightSupplier_i(){
    m_connected = 0;
  }

  virtual void disconnect_push_supplier (CORBA(Environment) &IT_env){
  cout << "Called disconnect_push_supplier";

  }

  unsigned char connected(){
    return m_connected;
  }

  void connected(unsigned char c){
    m_connected = c;
  }

};
```

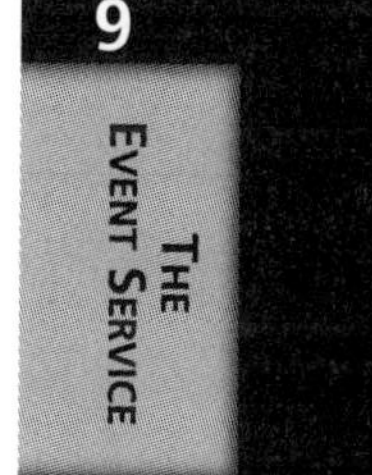

The `disconnect_push_supplier()` is the method that is overridden to support the `PushSupplier` interface. This method enables the client to disconnect from the server when required. Calling this method ends the connection to the channel and releases all associated resources. Listing 9.1 shows the implementation of the untyped event supplier.

LISTING 9.1 THE UNTYPED EVENT SUPPLIER IMPLEMENTATION

```
#include <iostream.h>
#include <stdlib.h>
#include <stdio.h>

#include <EventService.hh>
#include "flightserver.hpp"


void main(int argc, char** argv){

  CORBA::Orbix.bindUsingIIOP(TRUE);

  CORBA(Any)  event_data;
  DepartureDetail departures;
  departures.flighno = CORBA::string_dup("GRN445");
  departures.time = CORBA::string_dup("01:30");;
  departures.status = CORBA::string_dup("D");

 event_data <<= departures;

  CosEventChannelAdmin::EventChannel_var ec;
  try{
    Channel =
CosEventChannelAdmin::EventChannel::_bind("Departures:ES");


    CosEventChannelAdmin::SupplierAdmin_var admin_ =
Channel->for_suppliers();
    CosEventChannelAdmin::ProxyPushConsumer_var proxy_ =
sadmin->obtain_push_consumer();

      FlightSupplier_i DepartureData;
    proxy_->connect_push_supplier(&DepartureData);
      DepartureData.connected(1);

     int count = 1;
     while (DepartureData.connected()){
         proxy_->push(event_data);
     }
   proxy_->disconnect_push_consumer();
  }
  catch (CORBA(SystemException) &sysEx) {
    cerr << ""Unexpected System Exception " << endl;
    cerr << &sysEx;
    exit(1);
  }
  catch(...){
    cerr << "Unexpected Exception" << endl;
    exit(-1);
  }
}
```

Because we are dealing with CORBA::Any type, a user-defined type has to be cast into CORBA::Any. This is accomplished using the overloaded left-shift operator, which inserts a type into an Any. First, a departure structure is constructed, and then it is cast into a CORBA::Any. Here is the relevant code:

```
DepartureDetail departures;
  departures.flighno = CORBA::string_dup("GRN445");
  departures.time = CORBA::string_dup("01:30");;
  departures.status = CORBA::string_dup("D");
 event_data <<= departures;
```

The Naming Service is the preferred mechanism for acquiring the Event Channel, but this implementation uses the Orbix-specific bind() method. The departure server binds to the OrbixEvent server ES:

```
Channel = CosEventChannelAdmin::EventChannel::_bind("Departures:ES");
```

After the object reference to the Event Service is retrieved, the SupplierAdmin object reference has to be retrieved from the Event Channel. The SupplierAdmin enables the retrieval of the proxy object references from the Event Channel:

```
CosEventChannelAdmin::SupplierAdmin_var admin_ =
Channel->for_suppliers();
```

At this point, the ProxyPushConsumer is retrieved from the SupplierAdmin object reference. ProxyPushConsumer enables the delivery of push events. The code snippet to accomplish this is shown in the following:

```
CosEventChannelAdmin::ProxyPushConsumer_var proxy_ =
sadmin->obtain_push_consumer();
```

The connect_push_supplier() connects the event structure with the ProxyPushConsumer.

As long as the PushSupplier is connected to the Event Channel, the event server invokes push on the proxy object reference, pushing the DepartureData structure into the channel.

The application should be linked with ES.lib.

NOTE

The headers required for the Event Service need to be generated by running the IDL pre-compiler on EventService.idl.

The `EventChannel` server is registered with the Orbix implementation repository. When registered, an Event Channel proxy is initialized with the server. This can be done as follows:

```
prompt$> ES Departures -nonames
```

This will start up the `EventChannel` server with a `Departures` channel in it.

push Event Client Implementation

A `PushConsumer` inherits from the `PushConsumer` interface. This interface has two operations to be implemented: The first, the `push()` operation, is the method through which the `EventChannel` communicates with the consumer. The second operation, `disconnect_push_consumer()`, enables a client to disconnect the consumer from the channel. Listing 9.2 shows the implementation of the push event client.

LISTING 9.2 THE push EVENT CLIENT IMPLEMENTATION

```
#include "eventClient.hpp"

class FlightClient : public CosEventComm::PushConsumerBOAImpl{
private:
  unsigned char m_connected;

public:
  FlightClient(){
    m_connected = 0;
  }

 virtual void disconnect_push_consumer (CORBA(Environment) &IT_env){
    m_connected=0;
  }

 virtual void push(const CORBA(Any)& DepartureAny
, CORBA::Environment &IT_env){

    DepartureDetail *departures;
    DepartureAny >>= departures;

    cout << "Flight Number " << departures->flighno << endl;
  }

  unsigned char connected(){
    return m_connected;
  }
```

```
  void connected(unsigned char conn){
    m_connected = conn;
  }
};
```

The whole implementation revolves around the `m_connected` variable. When the `disconnect_push_consumer()` method is called, this variable is set.The `push()` method delivers the event to the consumer. The method uses the Orbix right-shift overloaded operator to extract the `Any` type that is delivered into the consumer.

Listing 9.3 shows how a client could use the push mechanism for event delivery.

LISTING 9.3 THE `FlightConsumer` IMPLEMENTATION

```
#include <iostream.h>
#include <stdlib.h>
#include <stdio.h>

#include <EventService.hh>
#include "Eventclient.hpp"

int main(int argc, char* argv[]){

  CORBA::Orbix.bindUsingIIOP(TRUE);
  CosEventChannelAdmin::EventChannel_var channel_;


try{
    channel_ =
CosEventChannelAdmin::EventChannel::_bind("Departures:ES");
    CosEventChannelAdmin::ConsumerAdmin_var admin_ =
channel_->for_consumers();
    CosEventChannelAdmin::ProxyPushSupplier_var proxy_ =
admin_->obtain_push_supplier();

      FlightClient DepartureChannel;
    proxy_->connect_push_consumer(&DepartureChannel);
      DepartureChannel.connected(1);

    while(DepartureChannel.connected()){
           CORBA::Orbix.processNextEvent();
      }
    proxy_->disconnect_push_supplier();
      delete &DepartureChannel;
  }
  catch (CORBA::SystemException &sysEx) {
    cerr << "Unexpected System Exception " << endl;
```


continues

LISTING 9.3 CONTINUED

```
    cerr << &sysEx;
    exit(1);
  }
  catch(...){
    cout << "Unexpected Exception " << endl;
    exit(-1);
  }
  return 0;
}
```

The client has to retrieve the Event Channel to receive events. The implementation uses the Orbix-specific `bind()` method to acquire the `EventChannel` object reference. The Event Channel is registered as `Departure` with the Event Service. Here is the code:

```
channel_ =
CosEventChannelAdmin::EventChannel::_bind("Departures:ES");
```

The `for_consumer()` method retrieves the `ConsumerAdmin` object reference for connecting the consumer with the `EventChannel`.

The `ConsumerAdmin` object reference enables the client to refer to the `ProxyPushSupplier`, the object reference. This object reference enables the client to establish a connection to the Event Channel.

```
CosEventChannelAdmin::ProxyPushSupplier_var proxy_ =
admin_->obtain_push_supplier();
```

The `ProxyPushSupplier` object reference can be used by the the `Consumer`, which connects to the Event Channel The `PushConsumer` in this implementation is `FlightClient`. Here is the code:

```
FlightClient DepartureChannel;
    proxy_->connect_push_consumer(&DepartureChannel);
```

After the `Consumer` is connected, the instance variable indicating whether the connection is alive is set to true. For the duration of this truth, the implementation loops on this variable, listening for incoming events.

`CORBA::Orbix.processNextEvent()` enables an implementation to be sensitive to three types of events that the ORB interface handles:

- Operations requests
- Connection requests
- Disconnection requests

The event falls into the operations request. Before exiting, the `EventConsumer` disconnects from the `EventChannel`.

Implementing Typed Push Models

The main difference between typed and untyped is that the former enables definition of events via a user-defined interface. This enables the event supplier to `push` events using the interface defined. The application will implement a typed push-push model.

The Typed Event Interface

The Event Consumer application uses the following interface to have events delivered to it:

```
Flight.idl

#include "EventService.idl"

interface Flight:CosTypedEventComm::TypedPushConsumer {

    void getArrival(in string flightNo
  ,in string time
  ,in string status);
};
```

The `Flight` interface inherits from `CosTypedEventComm::TypedPushConsumer`. In a typed push model, the event interfaces are provided for the consumer. If the model being implemented is pull, it should be the `CosTypedEventComm::TypedPullSupplier`. The `Flight` interface needs to be pre-compiled and implemented. Compile the interface by issuing the following command:

```
prompt$>idl -B -S -R flight.idl
```

This implementation must support the operation that needs to be overridden for the `TypedPushConsumer` interface. The implementation will be used by the `EventConsumer` when it is built.

The header file for the `Flight` class is shown in Listing 9.4.

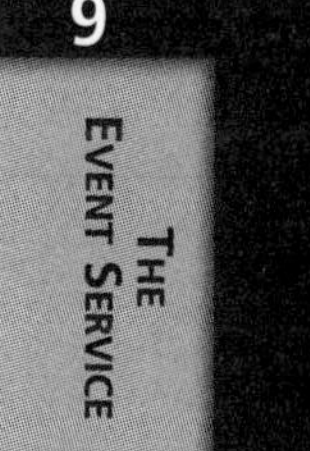

LISTING 9.4 THE `Flight` INTERFACE IMPLEMENTATION

```
#include "arrival.hh"
#include <EventService.hh>


class IT_DECLSPEC_arrival Flight_i: public virtual FlightBOAImpl{

    unsigned char m_disconnected;
```

continues

LISTING 9.4 CONTINUED

```
public:

    Flight_i(){
        m_disconnected = 0;
    }

    void disconnect_push_consumer(CORBA::Environment &) {
        m_disconnected = 1;
    }

    CORBA::Object_ptr get_typed_consumer(CORBA::Environment &) {
        return this;
    }

    virtual void  push(const CORBA::any& data
,CORBA::Environment &IT_pEnv);

    virtual unsigned char disconnected(){
        return m_disconnected;
    }

public:
    virtual void getArrival (const char * flightNo
      ,const char * time
      ,const char * status
      ,CORBA::Environment
        &IT_env=CORBA::default_environment);
};
```

There are two classes that the `Flight_i` subclasses and overrides: the `FlightBOAImpl` and the `PushConsumer` interface defined in the `CosEventComm` module. The class implements the methods defined in the interface. As with the untyped application, the class defines a flag `m_connected`, which indicates whether the object is connected to the Typed Event Channel.

The class should implement the `getArrival()` method:

```
#include <iostream.h>
#include "arrival.hpp"

void Flight_i:: getArrival (const char * flightNo
     ,const char * time
     ,const char * status
     ,CORBA::Environment &IT_env){

     cout<<"Fligh Number: "<<flighNo<<endl;
     cout<<"Arrival Time: "<<time<<endl;
     cout<<"Flight Status: "<<status<<endl;
}
```

The event supplier invokes this method to deliver the event. The implementation is simple enough to demonstrate how it would work. The supplier of the events invoke the `getArrival` method to deliver the event.

Implementing a Typed Push Supplier

Implementing a Typed Push Supplier is very similar to developing an untyped one. The supplier is a simple `PushSupplier`; therefore, it needs to subclass `CosEventComm::PushSupplierBOAImpl` and implement its methods.

The following tasks must be accomplished before it can start delivering typed events:

1. Retrieve a reference to a Typed Event Channel.
2. After the Event Channel is obtained, the application retrieves an instance of the `TypeSupplierAdmin` so that it can connect to the channel.
3. Finally, the code retrieves an instance of the `TypedProxyPushConsumer` by passing the name of the interface to push to one of the following:
   - The Event Channel may be retrieved in any manner that is suitable. The prescribed manner is by using a Trader Service or a Naming Service. But for this exercise, the Orbix `bind()` method is used. If interoperability is desired, use the IOR to the Event Channel to retrieve an object reference to a typed Event Channel.
   - The `CosTypedEventChannelAdmin::TypedSupplierAdmin` can be retrieved from the Typed Event Channel by invoking the `for_suppliers()` method. The `Admin` object reference is required to acquire a `TypedProxyPushConsumer` object reference.
   - The `Proxy` reference, once retrieved, is used to get the typed consumer. This can be accomplished by invoking `get_typed_consumer()` on the `Proxy`. The method returns a generic `CORBA::Object` object reference. This reference points to the interface that the consumer supports to have events delivered to it.
   - The `Type Push` interface can be narrowed to the appropriate object reference. When this is accomplished, the supplier can start invoking methods on it.

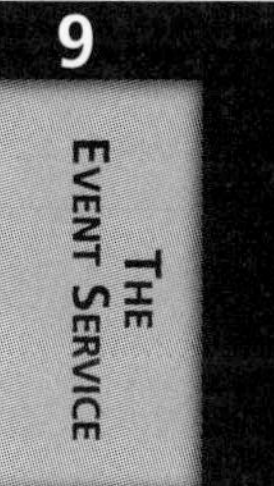

The typed push server is defined in the following class:

```
#include <iostream.h>
#include "arrival.hh"
#include "EventService.hh"
```

```
class ArrivalSupplier_i:public CosEventComm::PushSupplierBOAImpl{

    unsigned char m_disconnected;
public:

    ArrivalSupplier_i(){
        m_disconnected = 0;
    }
    virtual void disconnect_push_supplier(
        CORBA::Environment &IT_env=CORBA::IT_chooseDefaultEnv()){
        m_disconnected = 1;
    }

    char disconnected(){
        return m_disconnected;
    }

};
```

The `disconnect_push_supplier()` is implemented in this code. This enables a client to disconnect the supplier from the Event Channel and have all associate resources deallocated (see Listing 9.5).

LISTING 9.5 THE TYPED SUPPLIER IMPLEMENTATION

```
#include "typedsupplier.hpp"

void main(int argc,char **argv){
   Flight_var arrivalData;

   CosTypedEventChannelAdmin::TypedEventChannel_var channel_;
   CosTypedEventChannelAdmin::TypedSupplierAdmin_var admin_;
   CosTypedEventChannelAdmin::TypedProxyPushConsumer_var proxy_;

   ArrivalSupplier_i Eventsupplier_;
   CORBA::Object_ptr object_;

   try{

    CORBA(Orbix).bindUsingIIOP(TRUE);
    channel_ =
      CosTypedEventChannelAdmin::TypedEventChannel::_bind(
"Arrival:typed_es"
);

    admin_ = channel_->for_suppliers();
    proxy_= admin_->obtain_typed_push_consumer("Flight");
    proxy_->connect_push_supplier(&Eventsupplier_);
    object_ = proxy_->get_typed_consumer();
    arrivalData = Flight::_narrow(object_);
```

```
    }
    catch(CosTypedEventChannelAdmin::InterfaceNotSupported &) {
       cout << "Interface not supported" << endl;
       exit(1);
    }
    catch(CORBA(SystemException& se)){
    cout << "System Exception " << &se << endl;
    exit(1);
    }
    catch(...){
    cout << "Unknown error" << endl;
    exit(1);
    }

    while(!Eventsupplier_.disconnected()){
    try{
        arrivalData->getArrival("RF199","13:50","N");
    }
    catch(CORBA(SystemException& se)){
        cout << "System Exception: " << &se << endl;
        exit(1);
    }
    catch(...){
        cout << "Unknown exception" << endl; exit(1);
    }
   }

  CORBA::release(object_);
  cout << "Disconnecting ..." << endl;
  proxy_->disconnect_push_consumer();
}
```


In this implementation, the Orbix `bind()` method is used to retrieve the `TypedEventChannel` object reference.

With the `TypedEventChannel` object reference resolved, the administration object reference for suppliers has to be retrieved. The `Admin` interface enables the retrieval of the proxy object. This retrieval is accomplished by invoking the following method on the Event Channel:

```
admin_ = channel_->for_suppliers();
```

The next step is to retrieve the proxy object. The proxy object reference for typed push consumers is retrieved by invoking the `obtain_typed_push_consumer()` operation on the `Admin` reference. This operation needs a string name of the interface that the supplier hopes to deliver events. The code snippet for this invocation follows:

```
proxy_= admin_->obtain_typed_push_consumer("Flight");
```

The implementation then has to register the typed event supplier with the proxy. This enables proxies to invoke disconnects on the supplier if necessary. The relevant code follows:

```
proxy_->connect_push_supplier(&Eventsupplier_);
```

With the supplier registered, the application must retrieve an object reference to the interface it uses to deliver events. This is accomplished by invoking `get_typed_consumer()`. The operation returns a `CORBA::Object`:

```
object_ = proxy_->get_typed_consumer();
```

The `CORBA::Object` that is retrieved is narrowed to provide the right type.

The following line:

```
arrivalData->getArrival("RF199","13:50","N");
```

is an infinite loop that invokes the lone operation `getArrival()` on the interface that was retrieved from the proxy.

NOTE

Ensure that the following steps have been taken with the implementation:

- The headers required for the Event Service need to be generated by running the IDL pre-compiler on `EventService.idl`.
- The application needs to be linked with `typed_es.lib`.
- The typed `EventChannel` server needs to be registered with the Orbix implementation repository. It needs to be registered as `typed_es`, because it is the name used in the code.
- The typed Event Service uses the Interface Repository (IR) to retrieve the required interface. In our case, it is the `Flight` interface. Therefore, this interface must be registed with the repository.

  This can be accomplished by running the IDL pre-compiler with the following switches:

  ```
  prompt$> idl -R -N Flight.idl
  ```

  This will populate the IR with the `Flight` interface. The IR needs to be registered with the Orbix Implementation Repository as well so that it can be launched when required.

When registered, an Event Channel proxy is initialized with the server. This can be done as follows:

```
prompt$> TES Flight -nonames
```

This starts up the EventChannel server. The marker Flight indicates the name of the interface to be loaded and used from the Interface Repository.

Typed Push Consumer Implementation

The Typed Push Consumer uses the Flight interface to have the event delivered to it. The architecture of this solution is simple. The consumer defines the interface that it will expose, using the IR to an event supplier. The supplier acquires a reference to this interface through the TypedProxyPushConsumer. When this remote object reference is retrieved, the communication is essentially the event server making an invocation on a remote server. The only difference is that these invocations are delegated to the TypedEventChannel for delivery.

The interface inherits from TypedPushConsumer, which is a subinterface of PushConsumer. For this reason, push() is overridden in the implementation. The implemention of this interface and its associated skeletons must be linked with the Consumer application. The following steps should be taken for the consumer to receive events from the EventChannel:

1. Obtain an object reference to the TypedEvent channel.
2. Obtain the TypedConsumerAdmin from the channel.
3. Obtain the ProxyPushSupplier object reference from the admin object reference.

The implementation is shown in Listing 9.6.

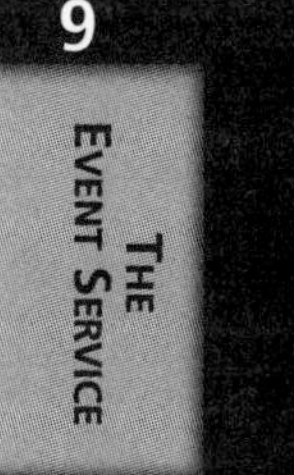

LISTING 9.6 THE TYPED EVENT CLIENT

```
#include "arrival.hpp"
#include "EventService.hh"
#include <iostream.h>

void main(int argc, char** argv){

   Flight_i Listener;

   CosTypedEventChannelAdmin::TypedEventChannel_var channel_;
   CosTypedEventChannelAdmin::TypedConsumerAdmin_var admin_;
   CosEventChannelAdmin::ProxyPushSupplier_var proxy_;

   CORBA(Orbix).bindUsingIIOP(1);
   try{
```

continues

LISTING 9.6 CONTINUED

```
  channel_ =
CosTypedEventChannelAdmin::TypedEventChannel::_bind(
"Arrival:typed_es"
);
  admin_ = channel_->for_consumers();
  proxy_ = admin_->obtain_typed_push_supplier("Flight");
  proxy_->connect_push_consumer(&Listener );

    while(!Listener.disconnected()){
        CORBA(Orbix).processNextEvent();
    }
    proxy_->disconnect_push_supplier();
   }
   catch(CosTypedEventChannelAdmin::NoSuchImplementation &) {
    cout << "No Such Implementation" << endl;
    exit(1);
   }
   catch(CORBA(SystemException& se)){
    cout << "System Exception: " << &se << endl;
    exit(1);
   }
   catch(...){
    cout << "Unknown exception" << endl;
    exit(1);
   }
}
```

The first thing the client has to do is to acquire the Event Channel. Under typical circumstances, it is best to use the Naming Service to achieve this; but in this case, the Event Channel is acquired by using the Orbix `bind() method.`

```
channel_ =
CosTypedEventChannelAdmin::TypedEventChannel::_bind(
"Arrival:typed_es"
```

With the Event Channel retrieved, the client can request the object reference to the `TypedConsumerAdmin` for consumers from the Event Channel:

```
admin_ = channel_->for_consumers();
```

The client in this implementation is interested in receiving events from the `Flight` event implementation. In order to do so, the client has to initialize the `ProxyPushSupplier` object reference. The code for doing that is shown in the following line:

```
proxy_ = admin_->obtain_typed_push_supplier("Flight");
```

The `Typed` interface is registered with the proxy reference to listen for incoming events. The `Typed` interface is the `Flight` interface that was implemented at the beginning of the chapter. Here is the code that does this registration:

```
proxy_->connect_push_consumer(&Listener );
```

As long as the connection is maintained, the consumer listens to the ORB for ORB events. To ensure that the client will listen to incoming events until the disconnect is called, the following code will execute listening to events:

```
while(!Listener.disconnected()){
        CORBA(Orbix).processNextEvent();
    }
```

Summary

The CORBA Event Service is one of the key services specified by the OMG. The primary rationale behind using the Event Service is the possibility of using events to reduce inter-dependencies between clients and servers.

The CORBA Event Service specifies two types of events. `CosEvents` can be either typed or untyped events. Untyped events deliver types encapsulated as `CORBA::Any type`.

In the context of typed and untyped events, the CORBA Event Service specifies three components in its architecture. The Event Supplier generates the events. The Event Consumer acts on the events delivered. Within the specification, the architecture also defines an Event Channel, which enables a delegation-based event model. Between these three components, CORBA supports both push- and pull-based event models.

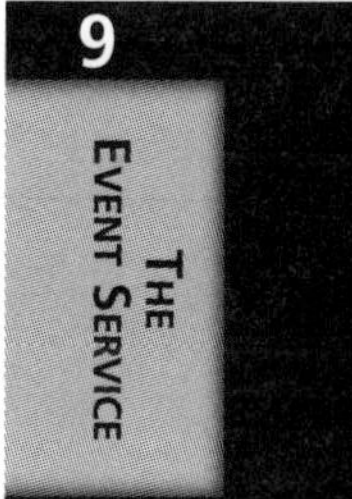

CHAPTER 10

The Transaction Service

IN THIS CHAPTER

The Object Transaction Service (OTS) presents a model for managing transactions. A practical definition of transactions follows, along with how to use transactions in the context of the OTS.

This chapter describes two examples where a distributed transaction is required. The first example is a simple fund transfer for a banking application. The second example is order processing for an online bookstore.

Transactional programming is key to controlling complex software systems in a distributed computing environment. A well-designed transaction is a manageable piece of work, executing in an autonomous fashion. The robustness of a transaction acts as a strong foundation for large software systems.

Distributed systems often have decentralized access to system resources. This separation introduces potentially complex permutations of object interaction. Under this circumstance, you have to have some third agency that coordinates all these complex permutations of object interactions. Under CORBA, the OTS provides a relatively transparent solution to the problem of coordinating changes to distributed objects.

Definition of Transaction

A transaction is a unit of work that is atomic, consistent, isolated, and durable (ACID). These characteristics are defined in the following list:

- Atomic—A transaction is an indivisible set of operations, grouped as an all-or-nothing unit of work. If one of the operations fails or is interrupted, changes made by the other operations are reverted to their state before the start of the transaction.
- Consistent—Invariant properties must be preserved. If they were not broken before the transaction, they should not be broken due to the transaction.
- Isolated—Transactions are unaffected by concurrent transactions. If two transactions make changes to the same resource, it appears as if they access the resource in a serial manner. Additionally, transactions are protected from intermediate states of other transactions that may fail.
- Durable—When the transaction is complete, any changes the transaction makes are permanent and persistent.

Commit and Rollback

When a transaction is finished, the transaction is committed. If an error occurs, the transaction is rolled back. Most DBMSs have API calls for commit and rollback operations. DBMS transactions rarely have the capability of coordinating transactions beyond a single data source.

An OTS can coordinate transactions across many different databases, messaging systems, and other user-defined transactional objects.

Many developers are familiar with accessing a single relational data store. Commit and rollback function APIs provided by the database vendor control the data store's transactional boundaries. A transaction's coordination occurs within a single database.

Transaction Scenario: Funds Transfer

A transaction is a set of operations that can be grouped together in such a way that they will either all succeed or all fail. If a transaction fails in a bank, its customers might get upset if the mistake is not to their advantage.

In this example, there is a transfer of $200 from a $1,000 savings account to a $900 checking account. The bank uses ledgers to keep track of customer accounts. Using ledgers, the bank clerk enters a debit of $200 under the savings account and a credit of $200 under the checking account. This leaves the savings balance of $800, and a checking balance of $1,100.

When the clerk transfers the funds, he or she makes sure that both ledgers are available and changes them at the same time.

If the clerk changed one ledger and only made a note to change the other ledger later, the customer's checks may bounce. You would expect the clerk to group debit and credit operations together so that the accounts balance before other clerks can change the account.

If you matched up the ACID characteristics to this example, you would get the following results:

- Atomic—The clerk makes sure that either both account ledgers are changed or that he or she changes neither ledger.
- Consistent—If the clerk reverses the transaction, both ledgers go back to their original state, and it is as if the partial transaction never took place.
- Isolated—The clerk changes only the accounts in question, not any other accounts at the bank. This also means that transactions to any other accounts do not affect the accounts in question while the clerk completes the transaction.
- Durable—The transaction is not permanent if the clerk merely makes a note to perform a transaction. The change has not truly been made. If the note is lost, the transaction will not even be recorded.

> **NOTE**
>
> When grouped together, sets of operations with ACID characteristics represent a unit of work. Transaction boundaries are defined by the beginning and ending of the unit of work.

The Two-Phase Commit

The two-phase commit protocol is used by distributed transactions for coordinating multiple transactional resources.

When a single resource is involved in a transaction, only one phase of commitment is required. The resource is either committed or, if the transaction fails, rolled back.

Multiple resources require two phases of commitment: prepare and commit. The prepare phase enables each resource to vote on whether it can commit. The OTS rolls back the entire transaction if the resources do not vote unanimously.

If all resources vote to commit, the Transaction Manager continues to the commit phase and instructs the resources to commit.

Transaction Service

The CORBAServices specification for the OTS defines several IDL interfaces for transaction management. These interfaces are essentially the latest incarnation of an API defined by the X/Open Group, the Distributed Transaction Process (DTP).

The three interfaces for DTP are

- XA for data sources
- TX for transaction processing monitors
- RM for other resources

> **NOTE**
>
> An OTS-compliant service is required to support
>
> - XA sources
> - Import/export transaction for the TX interface

Transaction Manager

The Transaction Manager (TM) is the software controlling the transaction behind the scenes. The implementation of the TM is entirely up to the implementor.

The TM can be linked into the client and perform its duties in the process, sharing the same process as the client. Or, the TM can be a standalone service that remotely controls the transaction.

With the OTS interfaces, the TM is flexible, scalable, and extensible. *Flexibility* means the TM can optimize small transactional systems, *scalability* is for large transactional systems, and *extensibility* means the largest systems can delegate transactional processing to external transaction managers.

Transaction Context

The *transaction context* is a shared entity passed between operations associated with a single transaction. All the operations in a unit of work share a single transaction context.

The TM typically maintains the transaction context. The context may be contained in a single thread, multiple threads, or extend to processes across a network.

Implicit/Explicit Propagation

How do you propagate the transactional context? You can do it implicitly or explicitly. *Implicit* propagation is the transparent mechanism for coordinating transactions. *Explicit* propagation involves specification of the transaction context to objects that are intended to participate in the transaction.

When using implicit propagation, the client code begins the transaction and then performs a commit or rollback at some point. This is the simplest way to add transactional capabilities to existing and new applications.

Transactional resources join the transaction as they are called by the client. The transaction context is propagated implicitly to these resources by the TM.

For 95 percent of transactional development, implicit propagation is sufficient for robust transaction management.

There are cases when the client application needs to control the transaction to a finer granularity. The client may wish to determine which operations are included in the transaction.

Developing OTS Clients

In the following sections, we will develop a simple transactional application. Before doing that we need to look into the primary interface that the client will interact with, which is known as `Current`.

The Interface

During implicit transaction propagation, the client application interacts with the `Current` interface. This interface is defined by this IDL:

```
interface Current : CORBA::Current
{
    void begin()    raises( SubtransactionsUnavailable );

    void commit( in boolean report_heuristics )
        raises( NoTransaction, HeuristicMixed, HeuristicHazard );

    void rollback()        raises( NoTransaction );

    void rollback_only()    raises( NoTransaction );

    Status get_status();
    string get_transaction_name();
    void set_timeout( in unsigned long seconds );

    Control get_control();

    Control suspend();
    void resume( in Control which )    raises( InvalidControl );
};
```

`Current` is a pseudo-object provided by the ORB and OTS vendors to implement implicit propagation. The client code may assume that the object always exists and is available.

To start a transaction, call `Current`'s `begin()` method. To delineate each transaction, perform a `commit()`. If you wish to cancel changes since the last `commit()`, call `rollback()`.

Transactional C++ and Java

Database vendors implemented the X/Open DTP XA interface for external TMs to coordinate their transactions. For an OTS to be compliant, it must interface with XA resource interfaces. This enables you to coordinate a transaction over two or more databases at the same time.

With the XA interface, the data source connection must be handled through the XA interface, not the DBMS's transactional API. For C and C++, this isn't a problem; if the

DBMS vendor supports XA, it should have a C library interface for exposing the XA interface to the TM.

Java is more of a challenge for XA access. The JDBC 1.0 specification for database access does not specify a method for the XA connection.

The JDBC 2.0 Extension Specification includes the `javax.sql.XAConnection` and `javax.sql.XADataSource` classes. It is not yet clear whether these classes will allow connection delegation for OTS or are just to support the upcoming JTA-XA interface.

Until the dust settles, vendor-specific extensions seem to be the only way a Java application can extend a transaction across more than one DBMS. The vendor extensions often involve a native interface, which means sacrificing Java's portability.

Data-joining tools can make separate databases appear as if they are a single database. This solves the problem of coordinating transactions across different databases.

Example: Banking

This example is an implementation of the funds transfer scenario described earlier in this chapter. The architecture defines a CORBA interface for the savings account and another interface for the checking account. Each of these interfaces accesses a separate table in the database.

Scenario Description

Figure 10.1 shows the operations participating in the transaction. The client application instructs the OTS to begin the transaction. As the client's operations involve transactional resources, the Transaction Manager includes these resources in the transaction. In this case, the transactional resources are the two databases. The TM also manages the connection to these resources on behalf of the client application.

In step 1, the client application instructs the `Savings` object to debit an account. The `Savings` object performs a query on the Savings table in the database. This query returns the current balance for the specified account. The `Savings` object then subtracts the debit amount and updates the account balance in the database.

If the client application experiences a crash, the changes caused by the table update would be rolled back. The integrity of the data would be maintained.

The client application calls the `Checking` object's credit operation in step 2. The `Checking` object retrieves the balance for the Checking account, calculates the new balance, and updates the account balance.

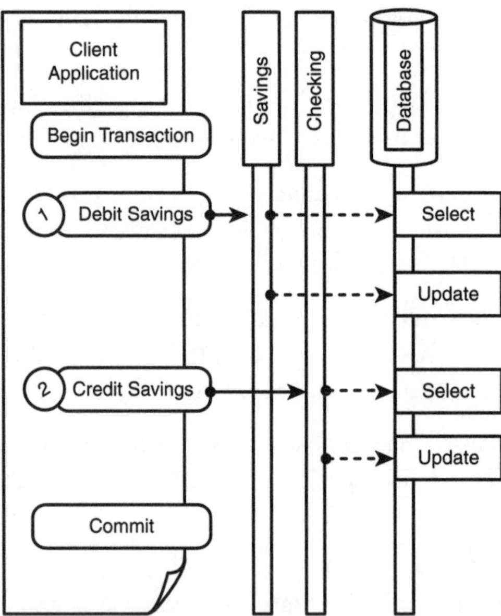

FIGURE 10.1
Interaction diagram for banking example.

LittleBank's Interface IDL

The IDL for `LittleBank` defines the following elements:

- `AccountTransfer` structure
- `SavingsAccount` interface
- `CheckingAccount` interface

The `SavingsAccount` interface has a `debit()` method that returns an `AccountTransfer` structure. The `AccountTransfer` structure contains the account identifier and the transfer amount.

The `CheckingAccount` interface has a `credit()` method that accepts an `AccountTransfer` structure as an argument.

Both of the `SavingsAccount` and `CheckingAccount` interfaces are inherited from `CosTransactions::TransactionalObject`. The `TransactionalObject` will enable the implementations of these interfaces to automatically be included in transactions.

Listing 10.1 will be used to specify an interface to illustrate how to construct a `TransactionalObject`.

LISTING 10.1 LittleBank.IDL

```
#include "cos_ots.idl"
module LittleBank
{

struct AccountTransfer
{
   string accountId;
   string transferId;
   string clerkId;
   double amount;
};

interface SavingsAccount : CosTransactions::TransactionalObject
{
   AccountTransfer debit( in string anAccountId, in double anAmount );
};

interface CheckingAccount : CosTransactions::TransactionalObject
{
   void credit( in AccountTransfer aTransfer );
};

}; // end module LittleBank
```

LittleBank's Interface Header

The header file defining the inherited implementations of the IDL interfaces is shown in Listing 10.2.

LISTING 10.2 LittleBankImpl.CPP

```
#include "littlebank.hh"

namespace LittleBank{

class IT_DECLSPEC_littlebank SavingsAccount_i :
       public virtual SavingsAccountBOAImpl
{
public:
   virtual AccountTransfer debit(
        const char* anAccountId,
        double      anAmount
        CORBA::Environment& IT_env=CORBA::default_environment );
};

class IT_DECLSPEC_littlebank CheckingAccount_i :
```

continues

LISTING 10.2 CONTINUED

```
        public virtual CheckingAccountBOAImpl
{
public:
   virtual void credit(
        const AccountTransfer* aTransfer,
        CORBA::Environment& IT_env=CORBA::default_environment );
};

}; // end namespace LittleBank

#endif
```

LittleBank's Embedded SQL

For database access, let's use PRO*C (Oracle's embedded SQL); we could have used DB2 just as easily.

Four functions are defined: `dbGetSavingsAccountBalance`, `dbGetCheckingAccountBalance`, `dbUpdateSavingsAccountBalance`, and `dbUpdateSavingsAccountBalance`. These functions enable you to query and update the balance of any account.

Listing 10.3 contains the implementation of required embedded SQL that is required to make the actual call the underlying Database engine for the actual transaction.

LISTING 10.3 LittleBank.PC

```
double dbGetSavingsAccountBalance( const char* anAccountId )
{
   EXEC SQL BEGIN DECLARE SECTION;

   varchar  dbAccountId;
   double   dbAmount;

   EXEC SQL END DECLARE SECTION;

   dbAccountId.len = strlen(
        strcpy( (char*)dbAccountId.arr, anAccountId ) );

   EXEC SQL
      SELECT BALANCE
         INTO :dbAmount
      FROM SAVINGSACC
         WHERE ID = :dbAccountId
      FOR FETCH ONLY;
```

```
   return dbAmount;
}

double dbGetCheckingAccountBalance(
       const char* anAccountId )
{
   EXEC SQL BEGIN DECLARE SECTION;

   varchar  dbAccountId;
   double   dbAmount;

   EXEC SQL END DECLARE SECTION;

   dbAccountId.len = strlen(
        strcpy( (char*)dbAccountId.arr, anAccountId ) );

   EXEC SQL
      SELECT BALANCE
         INTO :dbAmount
      FROM CHECNINGACC
         WHERE ID = :dbAccountId
      FOR FETCH ONLY;

   return dbAmount;
}

char* dbUpdateSavingsAccountBalance(
       const char* anAccountId, double anAmount )
{
   EXEC SQL BEGIN DECLARE SECTION;

   varchar  dbAccountId;
   varchar  dbAmount;

   EXEC SQL END DECLARE SECTION;

   dbAccountId.len = strlen(
        strcpy( (char*)dbAccountId.arr, anAccountId ) );

   EXEC SQL
      UPDATE SAVINGSACC
         SET BALANCE = :dbAmount
         WHERE ID = :dbAccountId;

   return NULL;
}

char* dbUpdateCheckingAccountBalance(
       const char* anAccountId, double anAmount )
```

continues

LISTING 10.3 CONTINUED

```
{
   EXEC SQL BEGIN DECLARE SECTION;

   varchar  dbAccountId;
   varchar  dbAmount;

   EXEC SQL END DECLARE SECTION;

   dbAccountId.len = strlen(
        strcpy( (char*)dbAccountId.arr, anAccountId ) );

   EXEC SQL
     UPDATE CHECKINGACC
        SET BALANCE = :dbAmount
        WHERE ID = :dbAccountId;

   return NULL;
}
```

The `LittleBank` Interface Implementation

The interface implementation is composed of straightforward calls to the embedded SQL functions. The `debit()` method retrieves the balance from the SAVINGSACC table, subtracts the amount specified, and then updates the balance in the same table. The balance is packaged into an `AccountTransfer` structure and returned to the client.

The `credit()` method retrieves the balance from the CHECKINACC table, increases the balance by the amount specified in the `AccountTransfer` structure, and then updates the balance in the same table.

With the implementation of the required embedded SQL out of the way (Listing 10.3), we can now implement the interface that was specified for `LittleBank.idl` in Listing 10.1. This is the interface that the client will use to make the call on the server object (see Listing 10.4).

LISTING 10.4 `LittleBank.CPP`

```
#include "littlebank.hpp"

extern 'C'
{
   #include "oracle.h"
```

```
}

LittleBank::AccountTransfer* LittleBank::SavingsAccount_i::debit(
const char* anAccountId,
double      anAmount
CORBA::Environment& IT_env );

{
   double balanace = dbGetSavingsAccountBalance(
                                  anAccountId );

   balance -= anAmount;

   dbUpdateSavingsAccountBalance(
                           anAccountId, balance );

   AccountTransfer* transfer = new AccountTransfer();
   transfer->amount = anAmount;

   return transfer;
}

void LittleBank::CheckingAccount_i::credit(
const AccountTransfer* aTransfer,
CORBA::Environment& IT_env );

{
   double balanace = dbGetCheckingAccountBalance(
                                  anAccountId );

   balance += aTransfer->amount;

   dbUpdateCheckingAccountBalance(
                           anAccountId, balance );
}
```

The LittleBankServer Implementation

This server creates an OTS and then initializes the OTS. Then it registers Oracle's XA interface with the OTS instance. At this point, the OTS will handle database connections for all transactional objects created in the process.

Two implementation objects are created: `SavingsAccount` and `CheckingAccount`. Because these objects inherit from `CosTransactions::TransactionalObject`, they will delegate transactional authority to the OTS.

All that remains for now is to construct a server to host our transactional object. This listing is provided in Listing 10.5.

LISTING 10.5 LittleBankServer.CPP

```
#include <OrbixOTS.hh>
#include <stdio.h>

extern 'C'
{
    #include "oracle.h"
    extern __declspec( dllimport ) struct xa_switch_t xaosw;
}

void main( int argc, char* argv[] )
{
   OrbixOTS::Server_var ots = OrbixOTS::Server::IT_create();

   ots->serverName       ( ":OTS1"  );
   ots->logDevice        ( "ots1.log" );

   ots->restartFile      ( "ots1.r1"  );
   ots->mirrorRestartFile( "ots1.r2"  );

   /* Register XA Resource Managers
   */
   char openString = "Oracle_XA+Acc=P/scott/tiger+SesTm=60+Threads=true";
   CORBA::Long resourceId =
ots->register_xa_rm( &xaosw, openString, "", 1 );

   ots->init();

   /* Implementation Objects
   */
   SavingsAccount_i  savings;
   CheckingAccount_i checking;

   try
   {
      ots->impl_is_ready();
   }
   catch ( const CORBA::SystemException& anException )
   {
      cerr << "Unexpected system exception" << endl;
      cerr << anException << endl;
      ots->exit( 1 );
   }
   catch ( ... )
   {
      cerr << "Exception raised" << endl;
```

```
        ots->exit( 1 );
    }

    ots->exit( 0 );
}
```

The LittleBank Transaction Client

The client first creates and initializes the OTS client interface. Then the client starts the transaction by calling begin on the `Current` pseudo-object.

The client establishes a connection to the `SavingsAccount` and `CheckingAccount` interfaces through the `"OTS1"` interface defined by the `LittleBankServer`.

With the server done, let us now construct a client that will use the services of the LittleBank. In this implementation, the `Current` interface that was introduced earlier comes into play (see Listing 10.6).

LISTING 10.6 `LittleBankClient.CPP`

```
#include <iostream.h>
#include <stdlib.h>
#include <ctype.h>

#include <OrbixOTS.hh>
#include "littlebank.hh"

void main( int argc, char** argv )
{
    OrbixOTS::Client_var ots =
          OrbixOTS::Client::IT_create();
    ots->init();

    CosTransactions::Current_var current =
         CosTransactions::Current::IT_create();
    current->set_timeout( 30 );

    try
    {
        currentContext->begin();

        SavingsAccount_var savingsAccount =
          SavingsAccount::_bind( "OTS1", "localhost" );

        CheckingAccount_var checkingAccount =
          CheckingAccount::_bind( "OTS1", "localhost" );
```

continues

LISTING 10.6 CONTINUED

```
        AccountTransfer* transfer = savingsAccount->debit( 100.00 );

        checkingAccount->credit( transfer );

        currentContext->commit();
    }
    catch ( CORBA::SystemException& anException )
    {
        cerr << "(system exception)" << " "
                         << anException << endl;
        currentContext ->rollback();
    }
    catch ( CORBA::UserException& anException )
    {
        cerr << "(user exception)" << " "
                         << anException << endl;
        currentContext ->rollback();
    }
    catch ( ... )
    {
        cerr << "(unknown exception)" << endl;
        currentContext ->rollback();
    }

    ots->exit( 0 );
}
```

Example: e-commerce

This section shows how you use transactions in a highly distributed environment. The problem domain is an online bookstore, and the example covers the checkout transaction:

1. First, the user selects a book. The inventory interface then holds the book.
2. The user selects another book that is also put on hold by the inventory interface.
3. When the user completes his or her order, the order information goes to the order interface, which creates an order in the order database.
4. The order interface then calls the credit card authorization interface.
5. The order interface tells the inventory interface to decrement the book count for each book in the order.
6. The order interface sends the order information to the shipping interface.

Figure 10.2 shows the propagation of the device context for each operation. The dashed lines represent an interaction with a transactional interface. If any of the operations fail, a rollback occurs. The rollback reverts any changes that were made in either database.

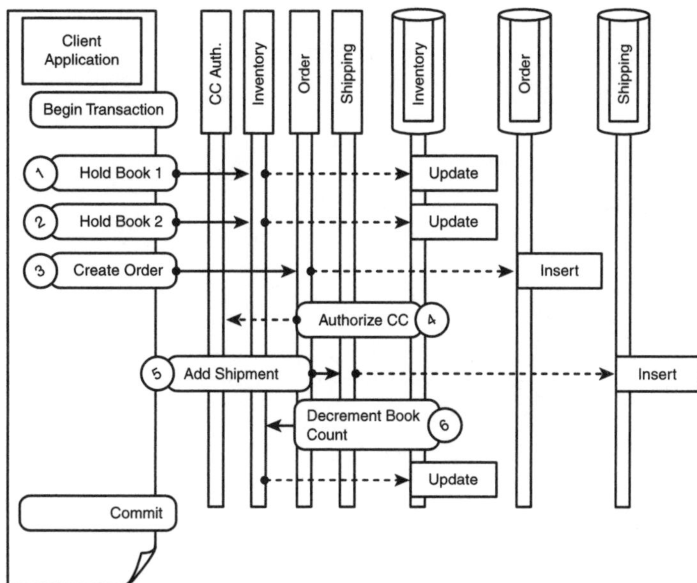

FIGURE 10.2
Interaction diagram for e-commerce application.

If all operations complete without error, the Transaction Manager will query the two databases as to their commit status. When the DBMSs report that they are ready to commit, the TM will then issue a commit against each of them.

Examine the interaction diagram closely. You will see a combination of transactional operations that must be coordinated behind the scenes. The TM does this coordination transparently.

The client finishes the transaction by instructing the TM to commit. The TM tells the DBMSs to prepare; each returns a vote to commit. The TM then has the DBMSs commit their respective transactions.

At the end of the transaction, the data is in a consistent state. During the transaction, other applications are blocked from accessing the uncommitted changes; this insures the data integrity.

OnlineBookStore's Interface IDL

Compared to the `LittleBank` example, the following IDL, as shown in Listing 10.7, is quite extensive. There is an IDL for a `MerchantServices` system and the `OnlineBookShop` itself. The `MerchantServices` defines the `CreditCardAuthorization` interface. This interface is a wrapper to an external application for authorizing credit card transactions.

The `OnlineBookShop` defines several structures and three interfaces. The interfaces are `Inventory`, `Order`, and `Shipping`. Each interface has methods corresponding to those outlined in the scenario description.

LISTING 10.7 `OnlineBookStore.IDL`

```
#include <OrbixOTS.idl>

module MerchantServices
{

struct SaleTransaction
{
    string      number;
    string   expiration;
    double   amount;
};

typedef string AuthorizationCode;

interface CreditCardAuthorization :
               CosTransactions::TransactionalObject
{
    AuthorizationCode authorize(
               in SaleTransaction aSale );
};

}; // end module MerchantServices

module OnlineBookShop
{

typedef string HoldCode;

interface Inventory :
               CosTransactions::TransactionalObject
{
    HoldCode holdBook( in string anIsbn,
                       in unsigned long aQuantity );

    void decreaseBookQuantity( in HoldCode aCode );
    void increaseBookQuantity( in string anIsbn,
                               in unsigned long aQuantity );
};

struct SaleItem
{
      string         isbn;
      unsigned long  quantity;
```

```
        double          price;
        HoldCode        holdCode;
};

struct SaleOrder
{
    ShippingAddress                 address;
    MerchantServices::SaleTransaction creditCardInfo;
    sequence<SaleItem>                 items;
};

typedef string OrderId;

interface Order : CosTransactions::TransactionalObject
{
    OrderId createOrder( in SaleOrder anOrder );
};

interface Shipping : CosTransactions::TransactionalObject
{
    void addShippment( in SaleOrder anOrder );
};

}; // end module OnlineBookStore
```

The OnlineBookStore Transaction Client

For such an involved transaction, the client code, as shown in Listing 10.8, is quite simple. After the transaction context is established, the two books are put on hold. Then an order is built up. In a real application, the data would come from a Web front-end.

The order object is then instructed to create an order based on the gathered data. The implementation of the order interface authorizes the credit card, sends the order to shipping, and removes the books from inventory.

LISTING 10.8 OnlineBookStoreClient.CPP

```
#include <iostream.h>
#include <stdlib.h>
#include <ctype.h>

#include <OrbixOTS.hh>
```

continues

LISTING 10.8 CONTINUED

```
#include "Inventory.hh"
#include "Order.hh"


main( int argc, char* argv[] )
{
   OrbixOTS::Client_var ots = OrbixOTS::Client::IT_create();
   ots->init();

   /* Create and establish the transaction context
   */
   CosTransactions::Current_var currentContext =
CosTransactions::Current::IT_create();
   currentContext->set_timeout( 30 );
   currentContext->begin();

   /* Bind to the Inventory and Order servers
   */
   Inventory_var inventory  = Inventory::_bind( ":Inventory" );
   Order_var     order      = Order::_bind( ":Order" );


   /* Transaction Body
   */
   try
   {
      SaleItem book1;
      SaleItem book2;

      /* Make sure no one else can get our copies of these books
      */
      book1.holdCode = inventory->holdBook( "ISBN-123", 1 ); // STEP 1
      book2.holdCode = inventory->holdBook( "ISBN-456", 1 ); // STEP 2

      /* Credit card info
      */
      SaleTransaction sale;

      sale.number         = "4389-8940-0904-0094";
      sale.expiration     = "09/99";
      sale.amount         = 98.99;

      /* Full order
      */
      SaleOrder bookOrder;

      bookOrder.address.name   = "Jane Doe";
      bookOrder.address.line1  = "2040 Smith Farm Road";
      bookOrder.address.line2  = "North Chittenden, VT";
```

```
        bookOrder.address.zip     = "05763";

        /* Add books
        */
        book1.isbn = "ISBN 123";
        book1.price = 50.00;

        book2.isbn = "ISBN 456";
        book2.price = 40.00;

        bookOrder.items.add( book1 );
        bookOrder.items.add( book2 );

        order.createOrder( bookOrder ); // STEP 3
        /* createOrder does the following:
STEP 4 : Authorize credit card
CreditCardAuthorization::authorize( sale );

STEP 5 : Add shipment
Shipping::addShipment( bookOrder );

STEP 6 : Decrease book quantity
Inventory::decreaseBookQuantity( book1.holdCode );
Inventory::decreaseBookQuantity( book2.holdCode );
        */

        currentContext->commit();
    }
    catch ( CORBA::SystemException& anException )
    {
        cerr << "(system exception)" << " " << anException << endl;
        currentContext ->rollback();
    }
    catch ( CORBA::UserException& anException )
    {
        cerr << "(user exception)" << " " << anException << endl;
        currentContext ->rollback();
    }
    catch ( ... )
    {
        cerr << "(unknown exception)" << endl;
        currentContext ->rollback();
    }

    ots->exit( 0 );
}
```

If any of the steps were to roll back, the three databases would revert the intermediate changes to their original values. The integrity of the data sources would be maintained.

If other transactions attempted to access the records that were updated, they would be blocked until this transaction completed. Thereby, the customer would be assured that the books they ordered were not sold while they were waiting for the transaction to complete.

MOM

Message-oriented middleware (MOM) enables asynchronous transfer of messages between two applications. MOM is helpful when transferring data between systems with conflicting goals.

Legacy systems often have session management and protocols that are difficult or awkward to integrate with distributed systems. Using a MOM layer between the two systems is a functional compromise for each system.

You can use MOM to mediate control issues between different domains. For instance, two divisions of a company integrate some of their ORB services for workflow purposes. Each division may be unwilling to allow the other division to have transactional control over remote resources.

A MOM layer between the two domains enables each domain to share transactional control of remote objects. Of course, this may introduce performance degradation and data integrity issues.

Nested Transactions

The examples presented in this chapter use *flat transactions*: There is a single unit of work that is either committed or rolled back. If any operation in the transaction fails, all other changes are reverted.

For many transactional scenarios, flat transactions are appropriate. There are cases where it would be more efficient to correct the fault that caused the rollback of part of a transaction, thereby creating a committable transaction.

The OTS specification enables an alternative to flat transactions: *nested transactions*. Nested transactions are not required for an OTS to be compliant, so it is up to the implementor. With nested transactions, you can recover and commit transactions when a subtransaction fails.

Transaction Processing Monitors

Transaction Processing (TP) Monitors have many similarities to the CORBA architecture. Although both OTS and TP Monitors coordinate transactions, they have different agendas.

Combining the ORB and OTS provides much of the TP Monitor's transactional functionality.

Summary

In this chapter, you learned about explored simple and complex examples of transactional coordination in a distributed development environment. What is critical to remember is that CORBA transactions allow you to deploy complex distributed transactions using rather simple API to control.

Once again, CORBA implementations provide both the integration and management elements for creating large enterprise systems.

The Security Service

IN THIS CHAPTER

Using the OMG's CORBA Security Specification (CORBASEC), layers of security can be added to a CORBA application. These security layers can be integrated into existing transports and system security. It is also possible to compromise a system's integrity through CORBASEC, either maliciously or accidentally.

The elements of the CORBASEC are heavily based on the Distributed Computing Environment (DCE) security model. CORBASEC provides an object-based model for the DCE's security model.

The CORBA developer encounters many security obstacles when deploying applications. Some of these hurdles include firewalls and the Java security "sandbox." These issues have little to do with CORBASEC, but present security-related challenges to developers.

This chapter presents an overview of security, a description of CORBASEC, a discussion on integrating CORBASEC with existing security mechanisms, and an overview of security products.

Goals of CORBASEC

CORBASEC is a unification framework for different security mechanisms with differing levels of security.

Performing service without changing application code is a common goal for CORBAServices. The security services are designed to slide in and around defined CORBA layers (see Figure 11.1). The ORB accesses standard security interfaces. You can set up a secure data transport at both the sockets layer and above IIOP.

Elements of CORBASEC

You don't need to be a security guru to understand CORBASEC, but it is helpful to be familiar with some of the terms and definitions of security. Developing CORBA applications exposes data in ways that aren't always well understood by system administrators—or even the developers themselves. The terms and definitions in this section give you a point of reference for the discussions that follow.

Figure 11.1 illustrates how elements described in this chapter are related. Use this figure as a model for dependency and interaction for APIs, interfaces, and applications.

Principal

A person or application who tries to gain access to a protected resource is considered a *principal*. You must be able to authenticate a principal's identity. A principal is uniquely identifiable, an entity who is responsible for his or her own actions.

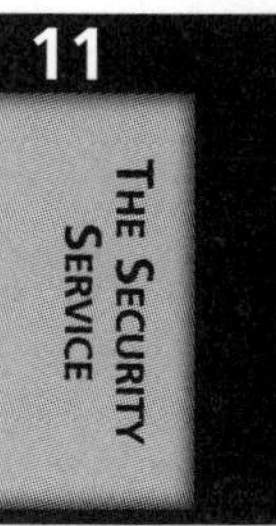

Principals have attributes associated with them. Some of these attributes include the principal's identity, role, group, and access control lists.

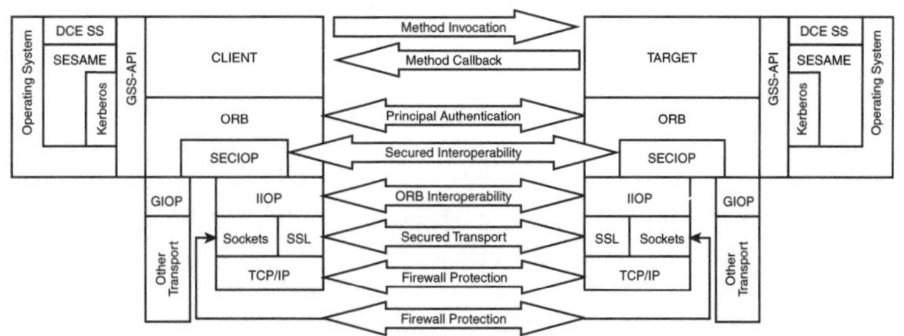

FIGURE 11.1
Layered diagram for CORBASEC elements.

Authentication and Authorization

Principals must provide proof of their identity through *authentication*. The target challenges the principal for a piece of secret information, such as a password or certificate. The target then uses this information to verify the identity of the principal.

If the principal counter-challenges the target's principal, this is considered *mutual authentication*.

Authorization occurs when the principal is assigned rights to access resources controlled by the authorizing entity.

Policy

A *policy* is a high-level rule that limits access control. Usually, you enforce the policies within the scope of a domain.

A system may specify that all users are restricted from accessing a subdomain, this would be an example of a policy. A user could subsequently be granted the privilege to access the subdomain.

Privileges

Privileges authorize or deny access for a principal or groups of principals. A privilege can control access to a host, object, or even an individual method.

While policies provide broad-based access control, privileges provide exception-based resource management. An example of privileges is provided in the policy definition.

Session/Context

A *security session* or *context* refers to an authenticated state between a client and target. A session is managed transparently, and the ORB propagates the context to objects involved in the client's request.

Domain

A *domain* is a geographic or logical scope against which policies are applied. You can use domains as convenient divisions in which to apply access and provide performance-based or protection-based administration.

Figure 11.2 illustrates how a domain is related to policies and privileges, as explained earlier. Figure 11.3 shows how security is handled when objects interact across multiple domains.

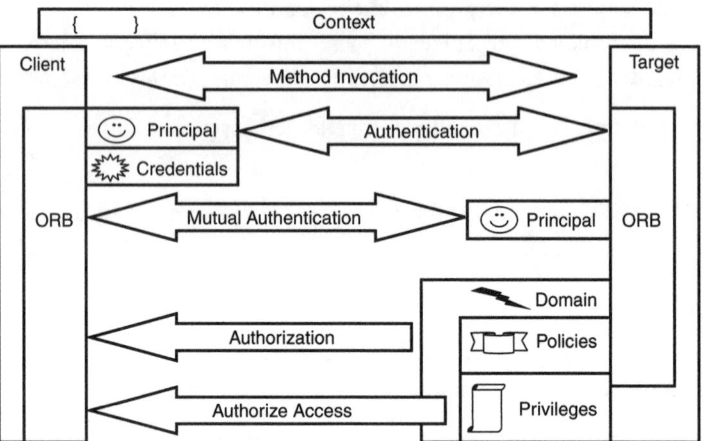

FIGURE 11.2
The relationship of the domain to policies and privileges.

Security Systems: GSS API, Kerberos, SESAME

The Generic Security Services Application Program Interface (GSS API) defines a functional interface that acts as a common interface for security APIs. You can port programs written to the GSS API between different security APIs. GSS is the lowest common denominator for different security services.

Kerberos allows a client and server to authenticate across a connection using secret-key encryption. Built as an extended version of Kerberos, SESAME provides several additional features to simplify distributed system access.

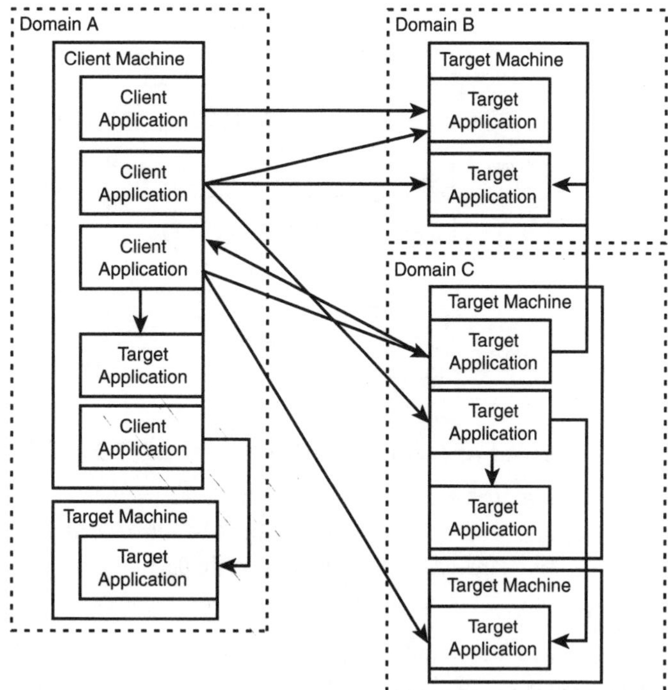

FIGURE 11.3
ORB interaction between different domains.

Distributed Security Issues

Today's CORBA developers and administrators have some new challenges to face when trying to protect distributed systems. Firewalls are the surest sign of inadequate security integration.

When administrators cannot control access, they may resort to unilateral access denial and limit access by using a firewall.

Server Location

Traditional computing models were commonly based on a centralized server that would authorize access to resources. The server controlled access to printers, files, databases, and other resources (see Figure 11.4).

Distributed systems do not necessarily have a centralized server. Each distributed component can be viewed as a server, or resource, with access restrictions on its functionality.

FIGURE 11.4
Client/server architecture.

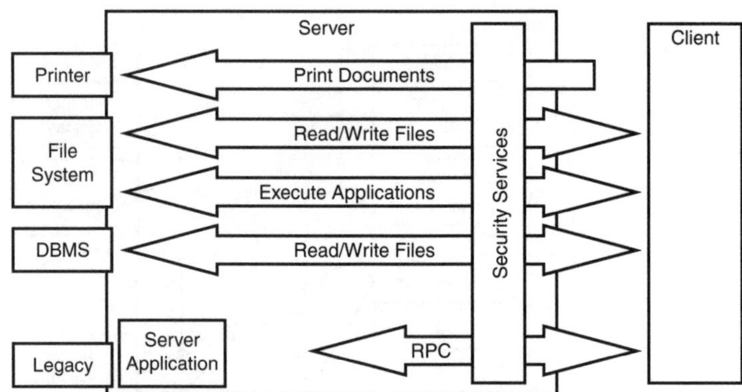

Constantly Changing Implementations

Object interfaces introduce variations in transparent ways, bypassing security features. For instance, using polymorphism, an object could be introduced into a system, overriding some of its parent's interface. The object's methods could make changes, whether intentional or accidental, to compromise the system's integrity.

How can the system administrator keep track of changes on a CORBA object? Access rights may be too liberal or, alternatively, too restrictive. If system administrators don't fully understand what they are doing, they might just give up and insert firewalls between objects.

CORBASEC attempts to provide security attributes that describe types of objects and methods that will help create a better dialog between developers and administrators on security requirements. These attributes include the access restrictions for classes and methods.

Invocation Chaining

A client object's call chain can extend to several target objects. You can reach each target within different security domains (refer to Figure 11.3, which shows invocations chaining across domains). There is the potential for a user to access systems without appropriate authorization.

This is a difficult security model to conceptualize for system administrators. Through delegation control, principal information can travel to the target objects, who can decide whether to authorize the principal.

Secure Transport

As data travels over network connections, it can be intercepted and examined. Not only can the confidentiality be compromised; data can be tampered with. If the data is encrypted and validated through a secure mechanism upon arrival, data integrity is increased dramatically. Applying cryptography to the transport facilitates this protection.

ORB vendors have two ways to add cryptography: Secure Socket Layer (SSL) and Secure Inter-ORB Protocol (SECIOP). SECIOP promises interoperable cryptography, and SSL implementations are implemented through proprietary mechanisms. SSL is proven technology; Web browsers use SSL to secure credit card transactions over the Internet.

Secure Socket Layer (SSL)

SSL provides an encrypted TCP/IP sockets layer. Because SSL is at the transport layer, it is usually transparent to the application programmer. CORBA's IIOP protocol sits on top of SSL, using it as if it were using standard sockets.

The initial connection of an SSL session starts with authentication. The two sides then negotiate which encryption scheme will be used. At this point, the two sides of the connection may use the connection as if it were a standard socket connection.

Anyone eavesdropping on the socket connection is unable to decrypt the data stream without knowing the encryption key. If the encrypted data is altered during transport, data validation will fail, causing the receiver to refuse the data. This is a great solution when you want to transmit data over networks that you don't really trust.

Because IIOP uses sockets as a transport, SSL provides a secure transport for ORB communication. Adding SSL is a transparent application change, usually just changing out runtime libraries and ORB executables.

The cost of SSL's symmetric encryption is in CPU cycles. When a message is received, it is decrypted and verified; then the response is encrypted and sent. This additional processing can vary, based on the encryption algorithm used. In general, the higher the security, the greater the processing.

Other sockets-based protocols can take advantage of SSL as well. This allows proprietary GIOP socket transports to integrate to SSL.

SECIOP and Common Secure Interoperability (CSI)

SSL sits between the IIOP protocol and TCP/IP. SECIOP differs from SSL, in that it is layered between GIOP/IIOP and the ORB. Both provide a means for securing the data transport. SECIOP is the CORBA-specified method for data encryption. The CSI is the interoperable specification for SECIOP, providing three levels of conformance for SECIOP implementations.

Within the scope of SECIOP, the specification deals with various security mechanisms and associated cryptographic algorithms. It also goes on to specify the actual SECIOP protocol message and IOR security tags that are involved when clients and servers interact over SECIOP. CSI specifies three levels of compliance. Each of these levels of compliance goes with its own security mechanism and has its own associated cryptographic mechanism to assure the required level of security.

The following are levels of CSI conformance:

1. ID passes to target, no delegation beyond target—This provides user authentication at the target.
2. ID and delegation to other targets—The ID is passed beyond the target; if operations attempt to access restricted resources, the operation will fail.
3. Controlled delegation and assignment of privileges—The target may dynamically assign privileges and even allow the client to negotiate for access rights. If access fails, the client application would have other access contingencies.

CORBASEC Compliance

Levels of compliance are defined in the CORBASEC specification. These levels are intended to provide logical implementation levels for vendors. A vendor would state a conformance level for their product. The reality is that vendors mix and match functionality across conformance levels.

CORBASEC Compliance Level 1

The first of two compliance levels, Level 1 is meant for applications that are unaware of security. Security is implemented through external mechanisms that interface with the ORB. These external mechanisms could be the underlying security model of the host operating system. Such an access to security would constitute a mechanism for ensuring CSI Level 1 security compliance. Authentication and auditing are handled outside the ORB, and this level of conformance does not affect the applications themselves.

The ORB does need to provide the methods necessary for the `Current` object to access the `Credentials` object of the current principal. The principal object was discussed a little earlier under the elements of the CORBASEC architectural elements.

CORBASEC Compliance Level 2

Along with Level 1 compliance, Level 2 supports security-aware applications. Level 2 conformance is so robust, only partial implementations are available at this time. The application is given access to management interfaces. These interfaces allow the creation and definition of policies, domains, and access rights.

Transport protection can be performed at the ORB level. This allows interoperability between different transport protection schemes.

Access of interface methods can be controlled to a finer granularity than is possible with Level 1 compliance. Types of methods—such as get, set, management, and user methods—can have different access rights. Individual methods may have access rights applied to them.

Selective auditing of methods on objects is supported. This audit capability is much more efficient than logging every method invocation.

Privileges can be changed in credentials to dynamically authorize principals at runtime.

A quality of protection can be required, specifying the minimum security a principal will accept. If the security is too restrictive, the interaction between the client and target will fail.

ORB Integration and the `Current` Interface

The CORBASEC interfaces are accessed through the `Current` interface of the ORB. Depending on the level of compliance, operations against `Current` can reveal information about the current security context.

The target ORB examines incoming message headers. If a security tag is attached, it is passed to the CORBASEC implementation. Depending on the contents of the tag, the target ORB may initiate authorization and/or an encryption protocol.

The reverse is true as well. The client ORB may detect security tags from the target ORB, initiating security protocols.

If neither ORB requires security, tags may be ignored. Otherwise, the client and/or target ORBs may require a certain Quality Of Protection (QOP). Without meeting the minimum security requirements, either connection may refuse the other.

CORBA security, or at least the capability of supporting security, is implemented in the ORB. CORBASEC defines replaceable interfaces that allow a CORBA environment to be retrofitted with security. The ORB is meant to support these replaceable interfaces.

In practice, ORBs often have tight integration with their respective security functionality. As the CORBASEC implementors strive for interoperability, however, replaceablility will become more prevalent.

Using IIOP Proxy Servers and Firewalls

Many intranets protect themselves from the Internet using firewalls and proxy firewalls. Firewalls restrict access to ports on specific machines. This prevents malicious or inadvertent user tampering. Firewalls also can filter connections to those ports, terminating connections when certain criteria violate the access restrictions defined by the administrator.

IIOP connections can be made on any port and often are dynamically generated. Allowing connections to any port defeats the effectiveness of the firewall.

Proxy firewalls translate IP addresses to prevent unauthorized access to protected networks. This translation prevents ORBs from executing callbacks.

An IIOP proxy server can be used to resolve the firewall and proxy firewall conflicts. The proxy server represents a network of ORBs on different ports as a single port connection on one machine.

A firewall can be configured to expose the proxy server's port to the Internet. Now external ORBs can connect to ORBs behind the firewall. The price is the processing and translation of IP addresses in every IIOP message.

Because the only exposed IP address is the proxy server, there is no need for external resources to have direct access to client applications.

HTTP Tunneling

IIOP proxy servers often support wrapping IIOP requests in the HTTP protocol. Wrapped as an HTTP connection, the IIOP requests can pass through highly restrictive firewalls. HTTP tunneling adds another layer of potential inefficiency on top of the proxy translation.

Figure 11.5 illustrates how HTTP tunneling works.

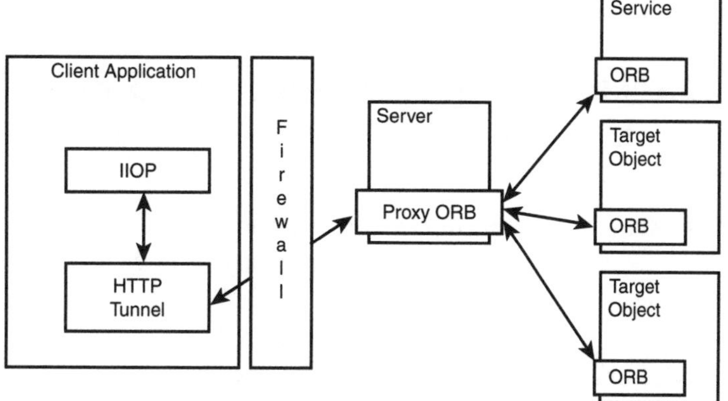

FIGURE 11.5
HTTP tunneling.

Java Security

Built from the ground up with security in mind, Java proves to be quite prohibitive for distributed computing. The Java sandbox security model places prohibitive restrictions on Java applets. The sandbox prevents applets from having network connections to any host other than the one the applet came from.

IIOP proxy servers come to the rescue again. The proxy server allows Java applets to obey their security restrictions while being able to participate completely in a CORBA environment.

Figure 11.6 shows how a proxy server can fit into a CORBA environment.

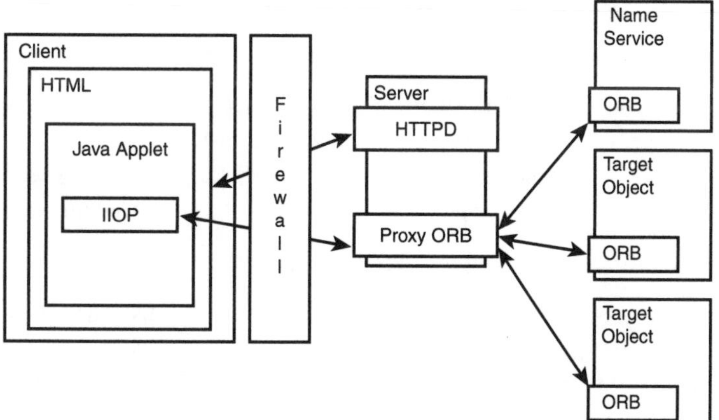

FIGURE 11.6
A proxy server.

Pervasive Security Standards

The following descriptions cover many of the security technologies used in some form throughout most security frameworks, including CORBASEC.

DCE Security Services and the GSS API

X/Open has defined the Distributed Computing Environment Security Services. These are based on the GSS API.

The GSS API is a definition of functions that allow applications to interface to an underlying security mechanism. There is an implementation of the GSS API that interfaces to DCE-compliant Security Services.

Kerberos

Supposedly, Kerberos is a three-headed dog guarding the entrance to hell. MIT developed a single sign-on security system for distributed computing environments called Kerberos. In its current incarnation, Kerberos V5, it provides a mechanism for encrypting the authorization of principals using a secret key. Secure European System for Applications in a Multi-vendor Environment (SESAME) is an extended version of Kerberos V5. SESAME extends the Kerberos name to include attribute information. Packaged and digitally signed, the Privilege Attribute Certificate (PAC) is used to delegate authentication on behalf of the client.

Summary

Software systems are becoming more highly integrated than they have been in the past. Monolithic mainframes are exposing interfaces to their data and applications to intranets and the Internet. CORBA middleware, among other solutions, is being deployed to facilitate this integration.

Enforcing mainframe security in a distributed, heterogeneous workstation/PC environment is a goal that might never be reached. The OMG has defined a security service to help provide the foundation for a solution. The Security Service Specification defines interfaces and facilities for providing security in a CORBA environment.

Both secure access and secure communication are defined by the specification.

It has been contended that the specification has ambiguous elements, preventing implementers from creating standalone Security Services. Proprietary solutions are being created, with tight integration between the ORB and the Security Service.

Vendor Extensions and Implementation Issues

Part IV

In This Part

CORBA Server Activation Modes

In This Chapter

CHAPTER 12

Activation modes determine the scalability of a CORBA server. CORBA servers constitute processes that are launched either automatically or manually. CORBA specifies a number of modes for launching these servers. These different modes help engineers design servers having different scalability and availability constraints.

The capability of a server to have state determines how scalable it is. A pure stateless server is the most scalable. These servers are usually supported by a stateless protocol as well. Web Servers and the HTTP protocol fall into this category. In fact, it can even be argued that the explosive growth of the Internet is owed in part to this aspect of Web technology.

CORBA and IIOP are *stateful*. This has repercussions on design. Although it is true that most implementations do not explicitly leverage this aspect of CORBA, it is being done under the covers. This statefulness is required for server-driven transactions. It is also required for security.

However, sometimes design dictates that this statefulness has different semantics. By this, I mean that sometimes the degree of state needs to be controlled to ensure maximum scalability. This is usually derived from some design constraints. For example, sometimes a design might dictate that the state of the server and the objects contained therein be unique for each client. Or consider a data access server; it is usually designed as a single server that services any number of clients. Both of these requirements can be implemented as a single process with severe dependence on threads.

CORBA does allow the use of threads, explicitly or painlessly, as part of the ORB implementation. When threads are controlled explicitly by the programmer, the programmer has to deal with the underlying Operating System thread API to control threads. Several implementations of the ORB also provide simplified API for using threads. CORBA also allows designers to explicitly control the activation of processes themselves so that many such design issues may be tackled without resorting to multithreading. This is what process activation modes (PAM) enable a programmer to accomplish. Nevertheless, keep in mind that multithreading is never far away from using CORBA effectively. At least in one form of process activation known as *shared activation*, multithreading is used in most design.

Using PAM, a designer could specify that a process be unique for a client or that a process be shared between any number of clients. The activation modes even specify that CORBA servers function essentially like a CGI process. All these modes of CORBA allow a great deal of flexibility in determining the degree of scalability a server has. It should be noted here that throughout this chapter, the words *servers* and *processes* will be used interchangeably. A CORBA server is a process that can contain one or more services encapsulated in objects that a client accesses.

This chapter primarily covers how Orbix C++ 2.3 and OrbixWeb deal with process activation. Simple examples are used to illustrate how PAM can be used.

Process Activation Modes

CORBA specifies three modes of activation, allowing different degrees of scalability:

- Shared activation modes
- Unshared activation modes
- Per-method activation modes

The shared and unshared activation modes also define subactivation modes that enable finer granularity of activation:

- Per-client activation modes
- Per-client process activation modes
- Multiple-client activation modes

NOTE

Please note that the three subactivation modes are found for both the shared activation and the unshared activation modes. This means, for example, that there is a shared per-client activation mode and an unshared per-client activation mode.

Let's first develop a simple application that demonstrates how these can be used in a design. All PAM applications will use the following interface:

```
module pam{
    struct simpleStruct{

          short one;
          long two;
          double three;
    };

    exception activationException {string reason;};

    interface activation{

       void inactivate(in simpleStruct inStruct) raises (
                                     activationException);
       void outactivatate(out simpleStruct outStruct) raises (
                                     activationException);
       void inoutactivate(inout simpleStruct outStruct) raises (
                                     activationException);
       simpleStruct returnStruct() raises (
                                     activationException);
    };
```

```
    interface nactivation{
       void dinactivate(in simpleStruct inStruct) raises (
                                     activationException);
       void doutactivatate(out simpleStruct outStruct) raises (
                                     activationException);
       void dinoutactivate(inout simpleStruct outStruct) raises (
                                     activationException);
       simpleStruct returnnactivation() raises (
                                     activationException);
    };
};
```

The interface is nothing to write home about! Nevertheless, it will show how to use process activation. The implementation itself is extremely simple. The `pam` module specifies two interfaces: `activation` and `nactivation`. Both interfaces perform the same function. There are two identical interfaces to show the differences between various process activation modes. These differences and similarities are explained later in this chapter when I explain the various activation modes in detail.

Compile the `pam` interfaces using the Orbix IDL pre-compiler. We will implement the interface using both C++ (Orbix) and Java (OrbixWeb). First, we will do the implementation using C++ (Orbix), and then we will do the implementation using Java (OrbixWeb).

Orbix C++ Implementation

Compile the interfaces using the Orbix IDL pre-compiler. Run the IDL pre-compiler using the following command:

```
prompt$>idl -B -S pam.idl
```

Listing 12.1 shows how the `pam` module is implemented. In itself, the interfaces do not demonstrate any underlying activation mode that is being planned. Later in the chapter, you will learn how these implementations relate to activation modes.

LISTING 12.1 THE C++ IMPLEMENTATION OF `pam` MODULE

```
#include "pam.hpp"
#include <iostream.h>

void pam::activation_i:: inactivate (
       const pam::simpleStruct& inStruct, CORBA::Environment &IT_env) {

    cout<<"pam::activation_i:: inactivate has been called "<<endl;
    cout<<"The Three values passed are "<<endl;
    cout<<inStruct.one<<endl;
    cout<<inStruct.two<<endl;
    cout<<inStruct.three<<endl;
}
```

```
void pam::activation_i::outactivatate (
        pam::simpleStruct& outStruct, CORBA::Environment &IT_env) {

    cout<<"pam::activation_i::outactivatate has been called "<<endl;
    outStruct.one = 1001;
    outStruct.two = 3455;
    outStruct.three = 6456;
}

void pam::activation_i:: inoutactivate (
        pam::simpleStruct& outStruct, CORBA::Environment &IT_env) {

    cout<<"pam::activation_i:: inoutactivate has been called "<<endl;
    cout<<"The Three values passed are "<<endl;
    cout<<outStruct.one<<endl;
    cout<<outStruct.two<<endl;
    cout<<outStruct.three<<endl;

    outStruct.one = 1001;
    outStruct.two = 3455;
    outStruct.three = 6456;

}
pam::simpleStruct pam::activation_i::returnStruct (
        CORBA::Environment &IT_env) {
    pam::simpleStruct returnpam;
    returnpam.one = 1001;
    returnpam.two = 3455;
    returnpam.three = 6456;
    return returnpam;
}
void pam::nactivation_i:: dinactivate(
        const pam::simpleStruct& inStruct, CORBA::Environment &IT_env) {

    cout<<"pam::activation_i::dinactivate has been called "<<endl;
    cout<<"The Three values passed are "<<endl;
    cout<<inStruct.one<<endl;
    cout<<inStruct.two<<endl;
    cout<<inStruct.three<<endl;
}
void pam::nactivation_i:: doutactivatate (
        pam::simpleStruct& outStruct, CORBA::Environment &IT_env) {

    cout<<"pam::activation_i::doutactivatate has been called "<<endl;
    outStruct.one = 10010;
    outStruct.two = 39920;
    outStruct.three = 4526;

}

void pam::nactivation_i:: dinoutactivate (
        pam::simpleStruct& outStruct, CORBA::Environment &IT_env) {
    cout<<"pam::activation_i::dinoutactivate has been called "<<endl;
    cout<<"The Three values passed from the client are "<<endl;
```

continues

LISTING 12.1 CONTINUED

```
    cout<<outStruct.one<<endl;
    cout<<outStruct.two<<endl;
    cout<<outStruct.three<<endl;

    outStruct.one = 101001;
    outStruct.two = 34455;
    outStruct.three = 69456;
}

pam::simpleStruct pam::nactivation_i:: returnnactivation (
        CORBA::Environment &IT_env) {
    pam::simpleStruct returnpam;
    cout<<"Returning struct back to  the client"<<endl;
    returnpam.one = 10001;
    returnpam.two = 344555;
    returnpam.three = 646756;
    return returnpam;
}
```

This implementation corresponds to the interface that corresponds to the `pam::nactivation` and the `pam::activation` interfaces. The interfaces have four operations each: one that takes a `struct`, `pam::simpleStruct`, as an `in` parameter; a second that takes the `pam::simpleStruct` as an `out` parameter: a third that receives the `pam::simpleStruct` `struct` as an `inout` parameter; and a fourth operation that returns the `pam::simpleStruct` `struct`.

The implementation of these four operations carries the simple modifier/accessor function on the `pam::simpleStruct struct`.

OrbixWeb Implementation

Compile the interfaces using the OrbixWeb IDL pre-compiler. Run the IDL pre-compiler using the following command:

```
prompt$>idl -B -S pam.idl
```

Listing 12.2 shows the corresponding Java implementation of the `pam` module. As with the C++ implementation, the rationale for the code is similar to the Orbix C++ implementation. I use Java code as well as C++ code to show that the amount of work that is required between the two is very similar.

LISTING 12.2 THE JAVA IMPLEMENTATION OF PAM::activation

```
package pam;
public class activation_i extends pam._activationImplBase {
  public activation_i(java.lang.String name) {
```

```
    super(name);
  }
  public activation_i() {
    super();
  }
  public void inactivate(
    pam.simpleStruct inStruct
  ) throws
    pam.activationException {

    System.out.println("IN strcut recieved" );
    System.out.println(new Short(one));
    System.out.println(new Integer(two));
    System.out.println(new Double(three));

  }
  public void outactivatate(
    pam.simpleStructHolder outStruct
  ) throws
    pam.activationException {
    System.out.println("Out strcut requested" );
    simpleStruct sstruct = new simpleStruct(
      10001,
      12356,
      64332
    )
  }
  public void inoutactivate(
    pam.simpleStructHolder outStruct
  ) throws
    pam.activationException {

    System.out.println("INOUT strcut recieved" );
    System.out.println(new Short(one));
    System.out.println(new Integer(two));
    System.out.println(new Double(three));
    Syste.out.println("Out strcut requested" );
    simpleStruct sstruct = new simpleStruct(
      10001,
      12356,
      64332
    )
  }
  public pam.simpleStruct returnStruct(
  ) throws
    pam.activationException {
    System.out.println("Out Return requested" );
    simpleStruct sstruct = new simpleStruct(
      10001,
      12356,
      64332
    )
    return sstruct;
  }
}
```

The code in Listing 12.2 implements the activation interface. Listing 12.3 shows the implementation of the pam::nactivation interface in Java. As with the C++ code, the implementation for pam::nactivation is similar to the implementation of the pam::activation interface.

LISTING 12.3 THE JAVA IMPLEMENTATION OF PAM::nactivation

```
package pam;
public class nactivation_i extends pam._nactivationImplBase {
  public nactivation_i(java.lang.String name) {
    super(name);
  }
  public nactivation_i() {
    super();
  }
  public void dinactivate(
    pam.simpleStruct inStruct
  ) throws
    pam.activationException {

    System.out.println("IN strcut recieved" );
    System.out.println(new Short(one));
    System.out.println(new Integer(two));
    System.out.println(new Double(three));
  }
  public void doutactivatate(
    pam.simpleStructHolder outStruct
  ) throws
    pam.activationException {
    Syste.out.println("Out strcut requested" );
    simpleStruct sstruct = new simpleStruct(
      10001,
      12356,
      64332
    )
  }
  public void dinoutactivate(
    pam.simpleStructHolder outStruct
  ) throws
    pam.activationException {
    System.out.println("INOUT strcut recieved" );
    System.out.println(new Short(one));
    System.out.println(new Integer(two));
    System.out.println(new Double(three));
    Syste.out.println("Out strcut requested" );
    simpleStruct sstruct = new simpleStruct(
      10001,
      12356,
      64332
```

```
    )
  }
  public pam.simpleStruct returnnactivation(
  ) throws
    pam.activationException {
    System.out.println("Out Return requested" );
    simpleStruct sstruct = new simpleStruct(
      10001,
      12356,
      64332
    )
    return sstruct;
  }
}
```


Implementation of both the C++ interfaces and the Java interfaces is similar. The object of this exercise is to demonstrate how to use the activation modes. As mentioned earlier, the code itself doesn't demonstrate activation. The only thing the methods do is output messages to the standard I/O.

The implementation of the server depends on the type of activation that is being used. The server's design controls how process activation can be used to control the scalability of a service. The Basic Object Adapter (BOA) and the way the server that hosts the components is coded control the process of activation. The interfaces that we have used previously in this chapter are essentially stateless by design. This means that they can be used with any process activation modes without modification. This allows us to use a single module as an example with different types of process activation modes. This is not to say that any interface could arbitrarily use any type of process activation. Let's now look at the various PAMs in detail.

The type of solution a component provides essentially drives what type of process activation mode you select. This implies that care should be taken while you design your components. You need to identify how state is to be maintained. Depending on how this is defined, you will have a good handle on what kind of process activation you need for your process.

For example, consider requirements for providing access to databases. Let's further assume that such a system should allow an arbitrary number of clients to use this service. This means that the service should be extremely scalable. Let's further impose a requirement that this service should have fast response times. In short, we are imposing the requirements of scalability and responsiveness on the solution.

You have to decide how a server that hosts the objects implementation will be built. As mentioned earlier in this chapter, CORBA offers three activation modes for designing such a process: shared, unshared, and per-method. These are each discussed in the following sections.

Shared Activation Mode

Shared activation mode is usually the default activation for CORBA implementations. In this mode of activation, all the objects that have the same server name are contained and managed within one server. This means that when the server process is launched, all the objects that are hosted by the server are instantiated.

If you consider the data access server, this is one of the solutions you could propose. Using a shared activation mode would have a number of benefits. The following are several of these benefits:

- Conservation of system resources
- Ability to share state across clients.
- Ability to retain state across sessions.
- The option of using multithreading to improve responsiveness

Processes are expensive in terms of the resources that they could use. Every time a process is launched, it uses resources that are available from the underlying operating environment.

The constraint of resources is mainly in terms of memory. Resources of any kind are always finite. If such resources are used arbitrarily, a process can be starved, and it inevitably affects the availability and responsiveness of the server-to-client request.

A single process enables you to conserve these resources.

If the data server were designed as a shared activation server, certain consequences would flow from that decision. The first would be that a mechanism would have to be found to allow clients to be serviced simultaneously. This would allow a server to respond to more than one client at the same time. It is obvious that a data server would have to be multithreaded.

When the data server is designed to respond using threads, you could choose a number of strategies and patterns to ensure that more than one client is serviced efficiently. You will find more information on multithreading issues in Chapter 14, "CORBA and Threads."

Under Orbix, this type of activation must be registered with the Implementation Repository. A shared server that is registered with Orbix does have one demand: *The name given to the impl_is_ready() must be the same name that is used in registering the server.*

Per-Client Shared Activation

When a per-client shared activation is chosen, a new server is launched for every client. This enables the design of servers with states that are unique for each user. The per-client–activated server corresponds to a user process. This means that if two clients run by the same user are accessing a server, there will be only a single server process for both the user processes.

It is possible to design a data server as a per-client activation server. This would have its benefits as well as its disadvantages. Let us first look at the benefits:

- Easier state management
- Less design overhead because multicomplex, multithreading issues can be avoided

A per-client shared activation server is unique for a client. This means that the objects that are hosted by the server could be designed to have a state that is unique for each client. This could prove extremely useful for data access servers.

I have not mentioned the "dangers" of multithreaded services. The important thing about multithreaded services is that shared resources have to be shielded from attaining inconsistent states. This does impose an additional responsibility on the designers of a shared data server.

A per-client activation server would have state that imposes fewer demands on the expertise of a designer. Because the state of the server is unique, a data server could easily be transformed into a transaction service as well. This would be made possible by the fact that a transaction resource would have to be isolated on a client basis.

Per-Client Process Shared Activation

This type of activation launches a new server process for every client-side process that is launched by a user. This enables designs where a server process is unique for every client process. This can be ideal where a server process cannot have shared resources between clients.

If the constraints on resources are severe, such an activation process is not suitable to "heavyweight" processes. The use of per-client process activation is suitable only for lightweight processes. Ideally, such processes would contain very little state. The per-client process activation modes should ideally be designed and implemented to timeout by themselves.

Data servers are very rarely implemented using per-client process activation modes. These modes could prove useful if the constraint of scalability is not present. Nevertheless, activation of processes is usually heavy. It has been my experience that UNIX operating systems are usually more responsive to process activation than others.

The Server Implementations

The C++ server shown in Listing 12.4 is used for shared activation modes. After we have finished building the C++ server, we will implement the server in Java.

LISTING 12.4 SHARED C++ SERVER

```
#include <iostream.h>
#include <stdlib.h>
#include "pam.hpp"

int main() {
  pam::activation_var activation = new pam::activation_i();
  pam::nactivation_var _nactivation = new pam::nactivation_i();
  try {
    CORBA::Orbix.impl_is_ready("PAM");
  }
    catch (CORBA::SystemException &sysEx) {
    cerr << "Unexpected system exception" << endl;
    cerr << &sysEx;
    exit(1);
  } catch (...) {
    cout << "Unexpected exception" << endl;
    exit(1);
  }
  cout << "server exiting" << endl;
  return 0;

}
```

Listing 12.5 shows how to implement a shared server using Java.

LISTING 12.5 SHARED JAVA SERVER

```
package pam;

import IE.Iona.OrbixWeb._OrbixWeb;
import IE.Iona.OrbixWeb._CORBA;
import org.omg.CORBA.ORB;

public class PamServer {
  public static void main(String args[]) {

    activation activate = null;
    nactivation nactivate = null;
    org.omg.CORBA.ORB orb = org.omg.CORBA.ORB.init(args,null);
    try {
     activate = new activation_i();
```

```
      nactivate = new nactivation_i();
      CORBA.Orbix.impl_is_ready("PAM");
      System.out.println("Shutting down server...");
      orb.disconnect(activate);
    }
    catch(org.omg.CORBA.SystemException se) {
      System.out.println("Exception raised
        during creation of Pam_Implementations" + se.toString());
      System.exit(1);
    }
    System.out.println ("Server exiting....");
  }
}
```


The objects `activation` and `nactivation` are instantiated first. They are declared as instances of `pam::activation_var` in C++. When these objects are constructed, the BOA is notified that the PAM server is active and ready for client invocation. It should be noted that the name that is provided to the BOA in the `impl_is_ready()` is the same name that is used when the server is registered. The server code for both a shared server and the shared per-client server are the same. The difference is made with the process of registration.

The essential distinction between a shared server and a shared per-client server is that with a shared server only one server exists for all clients. When I talk about client, I mean any number of clients that connect from either one physical machine or a client process from any physical machine over the network. For the shared per-client server, the difference is that a new server process is launched when a client connects on a per-client basis. This means that when a client connects to a server from a physical machine, a new server process is launched. Any new connection that is made from the same machine (client) results in the same server being made available for that client. If a new connection is made from a different location, a new server process is launched. Let's now look at how the shared and the shared per-client servers can be registered.

To rephrase, in a shared mode there can be only one server for any number of clients. In a shared per-client, there can be only one server per client (or per-client process identifier). For example, in the former if there are five clients that exist on five different machines, there can be only one server for all of them. In a per-client activation, there would be five servers, one for each client.

Server Registration

The Orbix `putit` utility or the Orbix Server Manager may be used to register the server under Orbix or OrbixWeb. You usually use the former tool if you are running Orbix under UNIX. Because we are using Windows NT for these examples, we will use the

Server Manager. The Server Manager is a graphical tool to register the servers with the Basic Object Adapter.

Registering Shared Per-Client Activation Servers

The server has to be registered with the same name as the one given to `impl_is_ready()`, which is `PAM`. Remember to use the same name for the server that was used to register the server with the Basic Object Adapter.

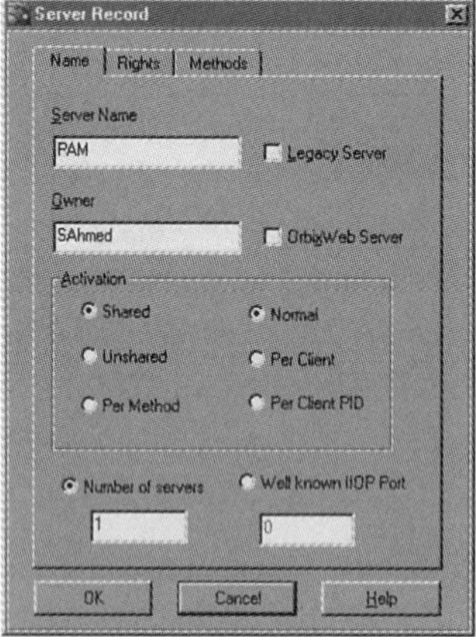

FIGURE 12.1
Orbix registration for per-client servers.

The server is registered as a shared server. The activation is set to `client`. This means that when a client connection comes in, the Basic Object Adapter will automatically activate the Shared Server when a client attempts a connection. This would be especially useful when availability of a server is critical to an application.

Shared Per-Client Process Activation

As with the shared per-client, the server has to be registered with the same name as the one given to `impl_is_ready()`, which is `PAM`. This is similar to how a shared server is registered. The only thing that changes is the action settings. The user interface for shared per-client is shown in Figure 12.2.

The server is registered as a shared server. The action is set to `Per Client PID`. The shared per-client activation is launched automatically for every new client process identifier. A physical node on the network will have a unique process identifier. This means that when a new PID attempts to launch a server, the Basic Object Adapter automatically launches the server, provided that the PID is not registered with a server that is already running.

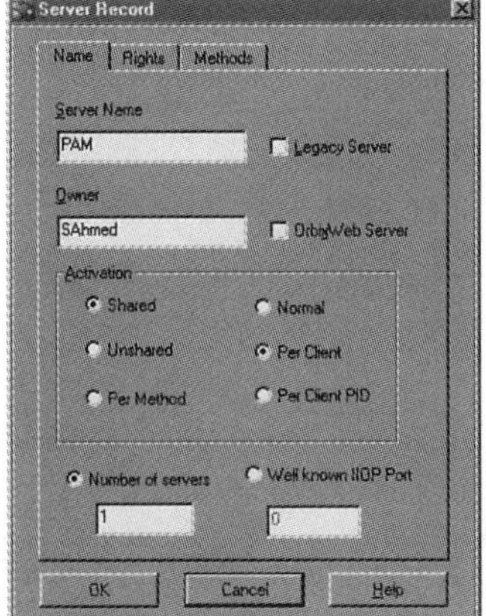

FIGURE 12.2
Orbix registration for per-client PID servers.

Unshared Activation Mode

In the unshared activation mode, each object has to be registered individually. This means that each object is going to run in its own server process. This activation might be useful where individual objects need to be isolated in terms of their state.

The server implementation has to change. Each object that can be invoked using the unshared activation mode has to be given a *marker*. This is illustrated in Listing 12.6. When a client makes a request to a server using this marker, the Basic Object Adapter will launch a server that will host this object. In the context of the examples that have been used, the interfaces specified in the `pam` module contain two interfaces: `activation` and `nactivation`. In Listing 12.6, two objects are instantiated. The `nactivation` object is assigned the marker so that a client can invoke it on a per-object mode.

LISTING 12.6 AN UNSHARED C++ SERVER

```
#include <iostream.h>
#include <stdlib.h>
#include "pam.hpp"

int main() {
  pam::activation_var activation = new pam::activation_i();
  pam::nactivation_var nactivation =  new pam::nactivation_i();
  nactivation._marker("Method");

  try {
    CORBA::Orbix.impl_is_ready("PAM");
  }
```

continues

LISTING 12.6 CONTINUED

```
    catch (CORBA::SystemException &sysEx) {
    cerr << "Unexpected system exception" << endl;
    cerr << &sysEx;
    exit(1);
  } catch (...) {
    cout << "Unexpected exception" << endl;
    exit(1);
  }
  cout << "server exiting" << endl;
  return 0;

}
```

Listing 12.7 shows the implementation of the server in Java.

LISTING 12.7 AN UNSHARED JAVA SERVER

```
public class PamServer {
      public static void main(String args[]) {

        activation activate = null;
        nactivation nactivate = null;
        org.omg.CORBA.ORB orb = org.omg.CORBA.ORB.init(args,null);

        try {
           activate = new activation_i();
          activate.setMarker("Method");
    _    CORBA.Orbix.impl_is_ready("PAM");
         System.out.println("Shutting down server...");
         orb.disconnect(activate);
       }
       catch(org.omg.CORBA.SystemException se) {
       System.out.println("Exception raised
        during creation of PAM_Implementation" + se.toString());
       System.exit(1);
    }
    System.out.println ("Server exiting....");
  }
}
```

As you can see, the server implementation remains the same as other shared servers in the preceding section, except the `nactivation` object is given a marker name, `Method`. A client can use this name to bind to a particular object within the server `PAM`. This implementation contains only one object that is activated on a per-object basis; therefore, only one marker name is used. Under typical circumstances, it is usual for a server such as this to contain more than one object. This would require that each one be given unique names. The marker names cannot be hard-coded in the implementation. The solution under these cases is to use a property file or an initialization file to assign markers to the object. If a client needs to use a "marked" object, the `bind` method on the object reference should be modified slightly. Instead of specifying just the server to bind to, a client should also provide the marker name of the object that needs to be acquired explicitly.

The implementation is shown in Listing 12.8. As with the previous examples, first we will do a client in C++; then a Java client will be built.

LISTING 12.8 A C++ UNSHARED ACTIVATION CLIENT

```
#include "pam.hh"
#include <iostream.h>


void main (int argc, char **argv) {
  pam::activation_var active;
  pam::nactivation_var nactive;
  try {
      active = pam::activation::_bind(":PAM");
    nactive = pam::nactivation::_bind("Method:PAM");
  }
  catch (CORBA::SystemException &sysEx) {
    cerr << "Unexpected system exception" << endl;
    cerr << &sysEx;
    exit(1);
  }
  catch(...){
    cerr << "Bind to object failed" << endl;
    cerr << "Unexpected exception " << endl;
    exit(1);
  }

    pam::simpleStruct inStruct;
    inStruct.one = 10010;
    inStruct.two = 11010;
    inStruct.three = 12110;

  try {
    active->inactivate (inStruct);
    active->outactivatate(inStruct);
    nactive->dinactivate(inStruct);
    nactive-> doutactivatate(inStruct)
    pam::simpleStruct AnStruct active->returnnactivation();
    pam::simpleStruct DnStruct nactive->returnnactivation();
 }
  catch (CORBA::SystemException &sysEx) {
    cerr << "Unexpected system exception" << endl;
      cerr << &sysEx;
      exit(1);
  }
}
```

The key methods in this code are

```
try {
      active = pam::activation::_bind(":PAM");
      nactive = pam::nactivation::_bind("Method:PAM");
  }
```

The `nactive` object reference is retrieved using the marker `"Method"`. This allows the client to retrieve the exact object from the server. When the objects are retrieved successfully, the client can invoke methods on the service as usual.

The implementation for a Java client is shown in Listing 12.9. The ORB is OrbixWeb 3.0. The process of activating a server is the same as with the VisiBroker ORB.

LISTING 12.9 A JAVA SHARED ACTIVATION CLIENT

```
package pam;

public class PamClient {
  public PamClient() {
    org.omg.CORBA.ORB orb = org.omg.CORBA.ORB.init();
    org.omg.CORBA.BOA boa = orb.BOA_init();
    pam.nactivation nactive;
    pam.activation active;
    try{
      nactive = new pam.nactivation_i("Method");
      active = new pam.activation_i();
      _CORBA.Orbix.impl_is_ready("PAM");
      orb.disconnect(nactive);
      orb.disconnect(active);
    }
    catch (SystemException se) {
      System.out.println("Exception in new PamServer: ");
      System.out.println(se.toString());
      System.exit(1);
    }
  }

  public static void main(String[] args) {
    PamClient pamClient = new PamClient();
  }
}
```

When the server has been constructed, the servers have to be registered with the Implementation Repository. Both OrbixWeb and Orbix include the Server Manager tool to assist in the registration process, which is depicted in Figure 12.3.

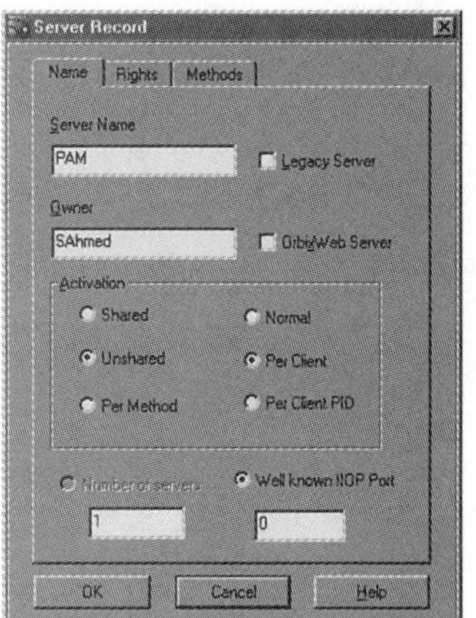

FIGURE 12.3
Unshared server registration.

The server is registered with an unshared mode. The activation is per-client. The marker has to be identified so that when an invocation comes in for a `Method` marker, the BOA looks for the marker in the Implementation Repository, and if found, it returns the object reference to the client.

Per-Method Activation

The per-method activation mode is closest to a CGI process. This activation model enables a process to be registered by a method or an attribute operation. When an invocation comes into the method, a new process can be instantiated and executed.

The per-method activation mode can be used as you would use a CGI process. Extremely long calculations or other computational processes can be designed to be encapsulated in a per-method activation server. This ought to be designed as a stateless server, existing only for the duration of the computation.

Keep in mind that processes are expensive to construct. This means that you would have to design your per-method servers to be as light as possible, so as to utilize as little of the underlying resources as possible. The code used for the per-method registration is the same as the code that we used for the unshared per-client activation model.

Figure 12.4 depicts the registration with the server manager. The method has to be registered as well; this is shown in Figure 12.5.

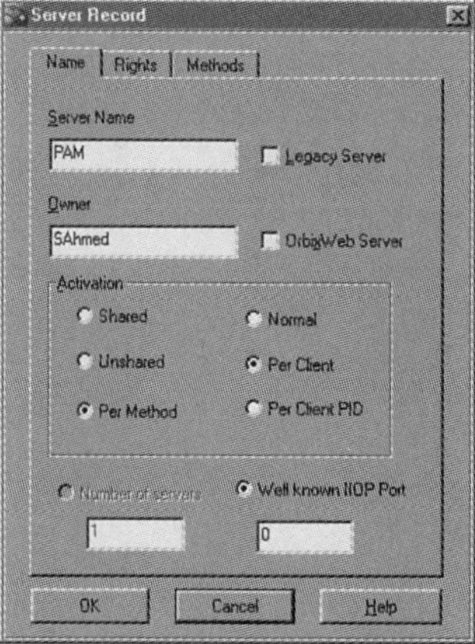

FIGURE 12.4
Registering per-method servers property one.

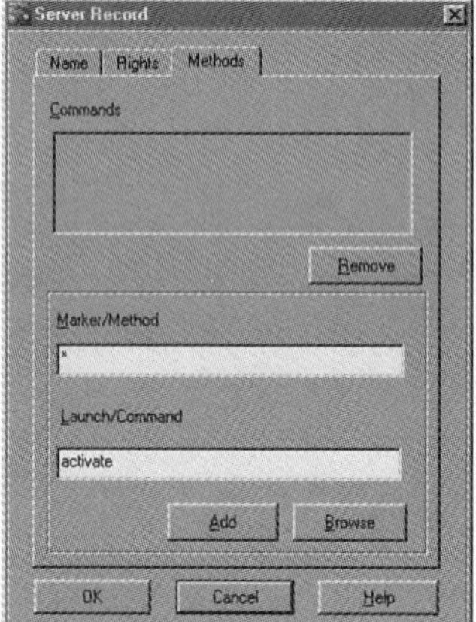

FIGURE 12.5
Registering per-method server property two.

Persistent Server Activation

We have one more process activation model to consider. This is the persistent activation model. This mode of activation involves the servers being launched manually by an operator. Further, the server names do not have to be registered with the Implementation Repository.

Persistent servers have to be manually managed by an administrator. One of the ways this server model can be used is for servers that manage other server processes. This would enable, for example, the construction of servers that offer architectural services to be constructed as persistent servers that are launched manually by the user before the clients connect to them.

Persistent servers are useful whenever you have a server that takes an inordinate amount of time to be fully initialized. In terms of the code, the only changes are with the notification to the Basic Object Adapter. You do not have to explicitly provide a name to the server when you use this type of server activation.

The following line shows the Java code:

```
_CORBA.Orbix.impl_is_ready();
```

This line shows the C++ Code:

```
CORBA::Orbix.impl_is_ready();
```

The server is coded as usual except that no name is provided in the `impl_is_ready()` method. Persistent servers do not have to be registered with the Implementation Repository.

Summary

Process activation is the mechanism by which a server is launched by the Basic Object Adapter when a client requests a service. There are a number of modes that are possible under various implementations of CORBA.

Process activation is a design issue. It is primarily a function of how much state a designer wants a server to maintain. CORBA allows a server to be a static process serving any number of clients. CORBA also allows servers that are unique to every client, in essence the ability to have a single server for each client that needs a service.

CHAPTER 13

Orbix Filters

IN THIS CHAPTER

Filters are a useful functionality provided by Orbix. They enable an application to execute some code either before or after an invocation comes into a normal operation on the server side. This functionality could prove to be vital in many designs. For instance, Orbix pre-filters could be used to authenticate a client's requests or for redirection, whereas post-filters can be used for logging or caching requests. Another vital area of using filters is for designing a thread-shared server. VisiBroker provides a similar mechanism called Interceptor. This is covered in detail in Chapter 20, "VisiBroker Interceptors."

Orbix specifies two types of filters: per-process filters and per-object filters. A per-process filter has the capability of monitoring the entire application space. This is irrespective of the number of objects contained in a process. These per-process filters are for the entire application.

The per-object filter is responsible for only a given object. This could be used to shield sensitive objects in an application. For instance, if an invocation comes in for a security-sensitive object, a per-object *pre*-filter could intercept the request before it arrives at the object. It could then perform a request authentication to ensure that the client has the right credentials to make the request. A per-object *post*-filter could log when a service has been rendered to a client request. With such logging, the client might not be able to repudiate a service being rendered by the server. Nonrepudiation is extremely important in a distributed environment. Essentially, it means that a client cannot deny that it requested and received some service from the server. For instance, a client could request a remote object to make a transfer of money from one account to another. After the service has been rendered, the client should not have the option of ever denying this fact.

Filter Monitor Points

Orbix specifies a number of points where a filter might intervene before a certain marshaling operation takes place. There are two types of marshaling: *out request marshal* and *in request marshal,* and *out reply marshal* and *in reply marshal*. A request is something a client makes; a reply is something that a server responds with. At both these points, either a pre- or a post-filter may be attached.

Marshaling is the process by which a language-specific request is converted to IIOP. With an out request pre-marshal, before the request is marshaled by the stub on the the client side, you could install a pre-filter that would take some action. Just as the server needs to have the capability of denying the client the chance to repudiate a request, the client has the same rights. It should have the capability of proving that the client did make a request to a server. Pre-filters would allow this. For instance, a server could provide a tax auditing object, but it would be catastrophic if the numbers such an object came up with were imaginary. Under these circumstances, the client should have the right to prove that it did make the request. The distinctions between the various filters are explained later in this chapter.

Filters may be attached for reply failures as well. Failures, though unpleasant, are a fact of circumstances. When the server ends in some inconsitent state, good designers would always throw exceptions. A failure can occur in many contexts; it could happen because the client did not do everything that was required or perhaps because the server is not functioning. A filter could be built to handle such failures. For instance, a filter could be built to handle a server not functioning. Such a filter could locate a functioning server and reissue the invocation to that server.

Per-Process Filters

To define a per-process filter, derive a class from the `CORBA::Filter` abstract class. This class defines ten methods that may be overridden to implement per-process filters. The derivation is shown in Listing 13.1. No matter what type of filter you want to build, the `CORBA::Filter` class encapsulates all the functions necessary. If you want to implement the `inReplyPreMarshal()` function for the client, you subclass the `CORBA::Filter` class and implement this function. The following list describes each of these ten methods:

- `outRequestPreMarshal()`

  A monitor point to execute a filter before an outgoing request. This occurs before the actual marshaling is done. Before a client invocation is marshaled, this filter monitor will execute.

- `outRequestPostMarshal()`

  A monitor point that executes after the marshaling of a request. This monitor is triggered before the process responds to a request.

- `inRequestPreMarshal()`

  When a server process receives an invocation, this monitor point is triggered. The filter executes before the actual marshaling takes place.

- `inRequestPostMarshal()`

  This monitor triggers at the receiver's end after the invocation has been marshaled.

- `outReplyPreMarshal()`

  This filter point executes on the server's end before responses to invocations are sent out, meaning before they are marshaled.

- `outReplyPostMarshal()`

  After the server has marshaled the response, a filter that has overridden this method will execute.

- `inReplyPreMarshal()`

  A client filter that executes before a server's response has been marshaled.

- `inReplyPostMarshal()`

  After the server's response has been marshaled, this trigger will kick in and execute.

- `outReplyFailure()`

  If the server or one of the preceding trigger points raises some exception, a filter can take appropriate action. For instance, it could log the exception or enable recovery strategies.

- `inReplyFailure()`

  This is the same as `outReplyFailure()`, but one that triggers in the caller's address space. As with `outReplyFailure()`, this monitor point will allow the addition of error correction, logging, or auditing to take place.

CORBA design is never simple. As the power and flexibility of the architecure becomes apparent, the design invariably changes. But more often than not, a number of auxiliary but critical design constraints are usually considered last. Such issues as security and fault tolerance are considered when the design is in an advanced stage. At that point, it is usually difficult to modify the design. Monitor points are a good mechanism to alter the design of a system. The auxiliary design constraints mentioned earlier can be added with as little disruption to the overall design as possible.

Implementing a Per-Process Filter

The per-process filter methods take two essential parameters: the usual `CORBA::Environment` and the `CORBA::Request` object. By far, the `Request` object is very interesting. For instance, its API (discussed in Appendix A, "CORBA API Reference" enables you to discover useful information, such as which user is making the invocation, which object is the target object the invocation is meant for, and so forth.

Listing 13.1 shows a simple object that traps all ten triggers. It does not do much except retrieve the principal that is making the request. The principal corresponds to the user that is making the request.

LISTING 13.1 CONSTRUCTING A FILTER

```
#define EXCEPTIONS
#include <CORBA.h>
#include <iostream.h>

class ProcessFilter : public CORBA::Filter {

public:

     virtual int inRequestPreMarshal (CORBA::Request& r,
                                CORBA::Environment&) {
     const char* callee;
     callee = r.principal();
       cout <<"Inside inRequestPreMarshal Before executing "
      << r.operation ()
      << " For "
      << callee << endl;
     return 1;
    }


    virtual unsigned char outReplyPostMarshal (CORBA::Request&
r,CORBA::Environment&) {
      const char* callee;
      callee = r.principal();
    cout << "Inside outReplyPostMarshal After executing "
      << r.operation ()
      << " For "
      << callee
      << endl;
    return 1;
    }


    virtual unsigned char outRequestPreMarshal (CORBA::Request& r,
                                CORBA::Environment&) {
     const char* callee;
     callee = r.principal();
     cout << "Inside outRequestPreMarshal After executing "
          << r.operation ()
          << " For "
          << callee
          << endl;
     return 1;
    }

    virtual unsigned char inReplyPreMarshal (CORBA::Request& r,
CORBA::Environment&) {
```

continues

LISTING 13.1 CONTINUED

```
     const char* callee;
     callee = r.principal();
     cout << "Inside inReplyPreMarshal After executing "
          << r.operation ()
          << " For "
          << callee
          << endl;
     return 1;
    }


    virtual void outReplyFailure(CORBA::Request& r
,CORBA::Environment& env){
    const char* callee;
    callee = r.principal();
    cout << "Inside outRequestPreMarshal After executing "
   << r.operation ()
   << " For "
   << callee
   << endl;
   }

   virtual void inReplyFailure(CORBA::Request& r
                              ,CORBA::Environment& env){
   const char* callee;
   callee = r.principal();
   cout << "Inside inReplyFailure After executing "
        << r.operation ()<< " For "<< callee << endl;
   }
};
```

The `ProcessFilter` class is derived from the `CORBA::Filter` class. It implements all ten methods specified as virtual functions in the super class. As mentioned earler, it is possible to extract all sorts of useful information from the request object.

The code extracts two pieces of information from the request object: It discovers the principal that is making the invocation and what method is part of the request that is being made. The acquisition of the principal is accomplished through invoking

```
request.principal();
```

The code returns a constant character array indicating the user. This information may be used to implement a simple Access Control Filter.

The operation is discovered by using `r.operation ()`. It returns a character array telling the name of the operation. A combination of principal and the requested operation would allow the design of profile-based access to an interface. For instance, the filter could maintain a list of users and a list of associated authorization to an interface. If an unauthorized invocation is attempted, the filter could throw an exception.

Installing a Per-Process Filter

Installation of per-process filters is easy: Just instantiate an instance of the filter in the appropriate process. For instance, consider the following interface:

```
module sentry{
        interface filters{

           void inn(in short a_value);
           void outt(out short b_value);
           short response();
    };

};
```

This interface will illustrate how to use a filter. The interface itself is rather trivial. The idea is to show how filters can be used.

A per-process filter can be installed to both the client and the server processes. Listing 13.2 illustrates installing a filter on the server.

LISTING 13.2 INSTALLING THE SERVER FILTER

```
#include "filter.hpp"
#include "processf.h"

ProcessFilter ServerFilter;

int main() {
  sentry::filters_var Filters_ = new sentry::filters_i();
  try {
    CORBA::Orbix.impl_is_ready("Filters");
  }
    catch (CORBA::SystemException &sysEx) {
    cerr << "Unexpected system exception" << endl;
    cerr << &sysEx;
    exit(1);
  } catch (...) {
    cout << "Unexpected exception" << endl;
    exit(1);
  }
  cout << "server exiting" << endl;
  return 0;
}
```

In the preceding code, the per-process filter is installed as a global object. This filter will trigger two methods: the `inRequestPreMarshal()` and the `outReplyPostMarshal()`. Listing 13.3 shows intalling a filter on the client.

LISTING 13.3 INSTALLING THE CLIENT FILTER

```
#include "filter.hh"
#include <iostream.h>
#include "processf.h"

ProcessFilter Filter_instance;

void main (int argc, char **argv) {
  sentry::filters_var Filters_;
  try {
    Filters_ =  sentry::filters::_bind(":Filters");
  }
  catch (CORBA::SystemException &sysEx) {
    cerr << "Unexpected system exception" << endl;
    cerr << &sysEx;
    exit(1);
  }
  catch(...){
    cerr << "Bind to object failed" << endl;
    cerr << "Unexpected exception " << endl;
    exit(1);
  }

  try {
        Filters_->inn(200);
        CORBA::Short out_val;
        Filters_->outt(out_val);
        cout<<out_val<<endl;
        cout<<Filters_->response()<<endl;
  }
  catch (CORBA::SystemException &sysEx) {
    cerr << "Unexpected system exception" << endl;
    cerr << &sysEx;
    exit(1);
  }
}
```

As in the server, the filter is instantiated as a global object. The filter will trigger two methods: `outRequestPreMarshal()` and `inReplyPreMarshal()`.

Per-Object Filters

Unlike the per-process filters, the per-object filter is attached to individual objects. There are a couple of details that you have to follow when using the per-object filtering technique:

- The implementation must use TIE to facilitate per-object filtering.
- The `-F` switch must be toggled on the Orbix IDL pre-compiler to generate per-object filtering on the object.

The mechanism of defining a per-object filter involves creating two classes that intercept the invocation of operations specified in an interface. Let us consider such an interface:

```
interface objectFilter{

short objFilter(in short a_val, out short b_val);
};
```

The `objectFilter` interface has a single operation that can be intercepted. Run the Orbix IDL pre-compiler with the following switches:

```
prompt$> idl -S -F objectfilter.idl
```

The `-F` switch will generate support for per-object filters. The generated class has to be implemented with the definitions of the filters. You could define and implement the filter as shown in Listing 13.4.

LISTING 13.4 DEFINING AND IMPLEMENTING A PER-OBJECT FILTER

```
#ifndef objfil_ih
#define objfil_ih

#include "objfil.hh"
#include <iostream.h>

class IT_DECLSPEC_objfil objectFilter_i{
public:
      virtual CORBA::Short objFilter (CORBA::Short a_val,
CORBA::Short& b_val, CORBA::Environment
&IT_env=CORBA::default_environment) ;
};

class PreObjectFilter{
public:
virtual CORBA::Short objFilter (CORBA::Short a_val,
   CORBA::Short& b_val, CORBA::Environment
   &IT_env=CORBA::default_environment) {
```

continues

LISTING 13.4 CONTINUED

```
        cout<<"Pre Filter Called.."<<endl;
        cout<<a_val<<endl;
        b_val = 0;
        return 0;
    }
};

class PostObjectFilter{
public:
    virtual CORBA::Short objFilter (CORBA::Short a_val,
CORBA::Short& b_val, CORBA::Environment
&IT_env=CORBA::default_environment) {
            cout<<"Post Filter Called.."<<endl;
            cout<<a_val<<endl;
            cout<<b_val<<endl;
      return 0;
    }
};

DEF_TIE_objectFilter(objectFilter_i);
DEF_TIE_objectFilter(PreObjectFilter);
DEF_TIE_objectFilter(PostObjectFilter);

#endif
```

Along with the modification to the `objectFilter` class, two additional classes are defined: `PreObjectFilter` and `PosObjecttFilter`.

The second thing is the definition of three macros. These macros will generate TIE support. (Refer to Appendix B, "TIE and BOA," for more information.) Orbix's implementation of the filters mandates TIE support as compulsory for using per-object filters.

The implementation of the `objectFilter` class itself is trivial. Nevertheless, it is shown for clarity:

```
#include "objfil.hpp"
#include <iostream.h>

CORBA::Short objectFilter_i:: objFilter (CORBA::Short a_val,
  CORBA::Short& b_val, CORBA::Environment &IT_env) {

    cout<<a_val<<endl;
    b_val = 1001;
    return 1002;

}
```

Keep in mind that the parameters that are passed into the per-object filter cannot be modified. Any modification will be lost. This is all that remains to building per-object filters. The next step is to create a server to host the TIE object and to attach the filters to this object.

The Per-Object Filter Server

The code for the server is given in Listing 13.5. If you are not familiar with the TIE approach, please refer to Appendix B.

LISTING 13.5 CONSTRUCTING A PER-OBJECT FILTER SERVER

```
#include "objfil.hpp"
#include <iostream.h>

int main(int , char *argv[]){

   objectFilter_ptr objFilter = new
     TIE_objectFilter(objectFilter_i) (new objectFilter_i());
   objectFilter_ptr PreFilterPtr = new
     TIE_objectFilter(PreObjectFilter) (new PreObjectFilter());
   objectFilter_ptr PostFilterPtr = new
     TIE_objectFilter(PostObjectFilter) (new PostObjectFilter());

   objectFilter_ptr temp_PrePtr = PreFilterPtr;
   objFilter->_attachPre (temp_PrePtr);
   objectFilter_ptr temp_PostPtr = PostFilterPtr;
   objFilter->_attachPost (temp_PostPtr);

   try {

    CORBA::Orbix.impl_is_ready("ObjectFilter");

   }
   catch (CORBA::SystemException &sysEx) {
    cerr << "Unexpected system exception" << endl;
    cerr << &sysEx;
    exit(1);
   }
   catch (...) {
     cerr << "Unexpected exception : impl_is_ready" << endl;
     exit(0);
   }
   CORBA::release(objFilter);
   CORBA::release(PreFilterPtr);
   CORBA::release(PostFilterPtr);

    return 0;
}
```

The first three lines of code essentially instantiate the three TIE objects. After these objects are successfully instantiated, the filters have to be attached to the object that requires pre- and post-filtering.

Here are the lines that accomplish this:

```
objectFilter_ptr temp_PrePtr = PreFilterPtr;
objFilter->_attachPre (temp_PrePtr);
objectFilter_ptr temp_PostPtr = PostFilterPtr;
objFilter->_attachPost (temp_PostPtr);
```

The two methods that accomplish the attachments are `_attachPre()` and `_attachPost()`. If any filters (pre- or post-) are attached to the objects, these are removed and returned from the call. It is possible to chain these filters by recursively calling the `_attach..()` method on successive filters.

Register the server with the Orbix implementation repository, using either the `putit` utility or the Orbix Server Manager. Ensure that the right name is given to the server.

To summarize, the following steps have to be taken to implement per-object filters on an object:

1. Implement the interface as usual, except the class has to support TIE instead of the BOA approach.
2. Derive a class from the interface that needs to have filter support. Every operation and attribute operation needs to have a corresponding member function in the filter class.
3. Inside the server, attach these filter classes either as a pre-filter or a post-filter.

The Per-Object Filter Client

The client implementation is straightforward, as usual. If the client does not have any process filter support, it does not even know that the server objects have filter support. The code is given in Listing 13.6.

LISTING 13.6 CONSTRUCTING A PER-OBJECT FILTER CLIENT

```
#include "objfil.hh"
#include <iostream.h>
#include <stdlib.h>

int main (int argc, char **argv) {

    objectFilter_var objecfilter;

    try{
```

```
        objecfilter = objectFilter::_bind (":ObjectFilter");
    }
    catch (CORBA::SystemException &sysEx) {
        cerr << &sysEx;
        cerr << "Bind failed" << endl;
        exit(1);
    }

    try{
        CORBA::Short out_val;
        CORBA::Short x = objecfilter->objFilter(1002,out_val);
        cout<<x<<endl;
        cout<<out_val<<endl;
    }
    catch (CORBA::SystemException &sysEx) {
        cerr << &sysEx;
        cerr << "Bind failed" << endl;
        exit(1);
    }
    return 0;
}
```

The code is typical for any "normal" CORBA client. It binds to the appropriate object reference and make its invocations as usual. The client is oblivious to the fact that there are filters between it and the server objects.

Summary

Orbix filters are a versatile mechanism for controlling client/server interactions to a very fine granularity. These filters have the capability of intercepting incoming and outgoing method invocations.

Through this interception, a number of auxiliary design constraints may be imposed on an implementation. These could be issues relating to security or auditing requirements. There are two types of Orbix filters. The first type is a global filtering mechanism known as a per-process filter. It is attached to the process as a whole. The second type of filter is a per-object filter. It allows the filtering of invocations on individual objects. Between the two, a certain granularity of interceptions can be achieved.

CHAPTER

CORBA and Threads

In This Chapter

One of the consequences of a shared activation server is the fact that, in terms of scalability, its potential is rather limited. For simple objects, this might not be a problem. On the other hand, if a server process has an arbitrarily large number of objects, each of them complex, the ensuing design will be full of bottlenecks that will degrade performance.

Threads provide a clean and consistent mechanism for introducing parallelism into a design. Just as there are different modes of process activation, there are also different strategies for managing threads.

Any complex CORBA application design will use threads. Some ORB implementations have built-in multithread support that can be leveraged by just changing the link libraries. Some ORBs, on the other hand, require server design to explicitly use threads. This chapter will look at some of the issues involved.

CORBA Thread Strategies

There are three strategies that could be adopted for managing threads in a CORBA implementation:

- Thread per session
- Thread per object
- Thread pool

Thread Per Session

A thread-per-session strategy, as shown in Figure 14.1, involves the allocation of a thread for every client that connects to the server. These are called *worker threads*. When the connection is lost, these worker threads are discarded. All the objects in the server execute in this one thread.

FIGURE 14.1
Thread per session.

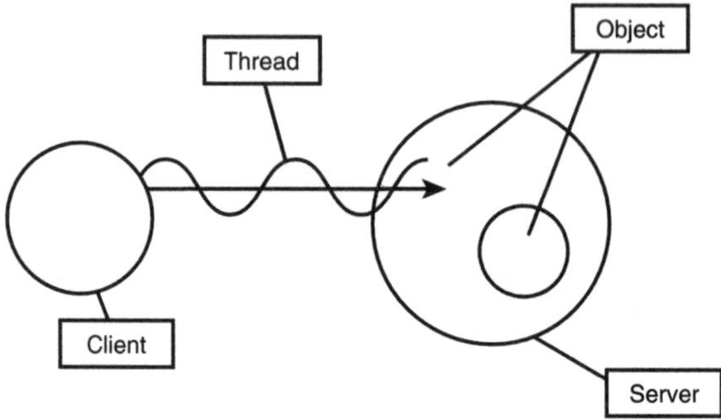

Thread Per Object

In a thread-per-object strategy, as shown in Figure 14.2, a worker thread is created for each object that is hosted by a server. This strategy could be ideal where a design has to have certain objects having priority over other objects.

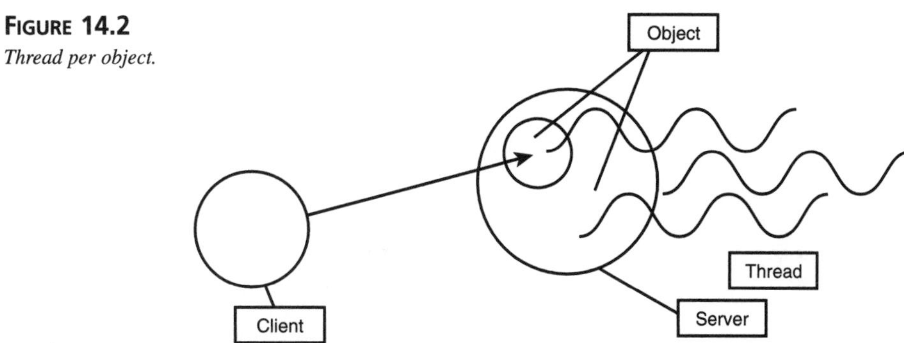

FIGURE 14.2
Thread per object.

Thread Pools

This is the most efficient strategy in terms of resource allocations. A fixed set of threads is created during server initialization. When a request comes in, this request is assigned to a thread. If all the threads are busy, the request could be buffered in a queue until a thread becomes free. The thread pool is shown in Figure 14.3.

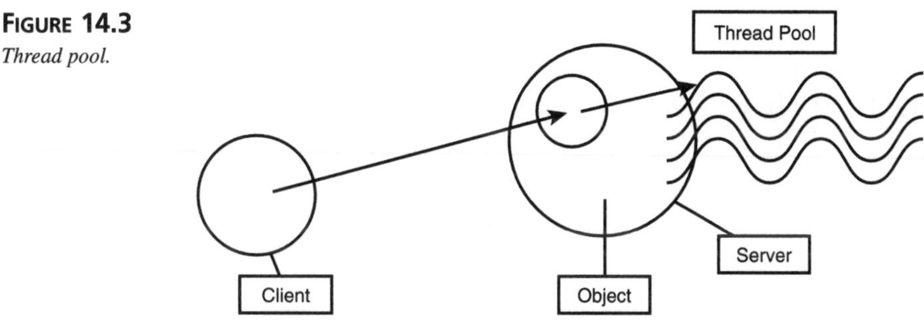

FIGURE 14.3
Thread pool.

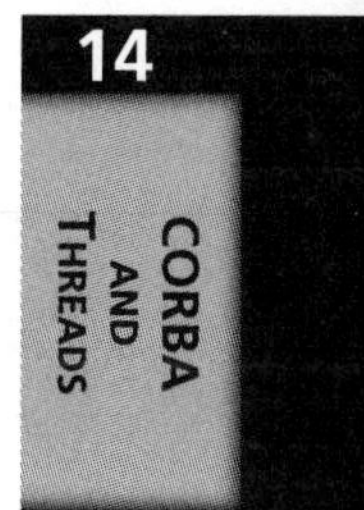

Implementing Threads

Threads are implemented using variations of waiting on shared semaphores. A *semaphore* is a mechanism that prevents two or more threads from accessing a shared resource simultaneously. In conjunction with interceptors or Orbix filters, a thread could be designed to wait on this shared resource in an `inRequestPreMarshal()` filter.

When the filter is triggered, the synchronization mutex could be signaled so that the waiting thread could do its job on a thread.

Thread-Per-Client

A thread-per-client strategy could be implemented in the following manner. The implementation will use Orbix and its filter capability. Before getting on with the task of implementing the thread-per-client strategy, consider the following interface:

```
interface tpc {
  void read(out short a_value);
    void write(in short b_value);
};
```

The goal is to have a client call these two operations asynchronously. The example will not attempt to show how to efficiently synchronize the invocations so that reads and writes happen in one step.

A number of factors affect the functioning of threads. Thread priority is determined by the underlying operating system. But it is possible to change the priority setting by invoking the appropriate API.

The client will invoke the two methods on two separate threads, while the server, on the other hand, should be able to service the request on a thread. This means that each incoming request will have the server launch a thread to handle the request.

The implementation uses Orbix and Orbix filters. Compile tpc.idl with the following switches:

```
prompt$>idl -S tpc.idl
```

Implementing Thread-Per-Client

Modify the generated header file, as shown in Listing 14.1.

LISTING 14.1 THREAD-PER-CLIENT HEADER FILE

```
#ifndef tpc_ih
#define tpc_ih

#include "tpc.hh"
#include <windows.h>
#include <process.h>

class IT_DECLSPEC_tpc tpc_i{
    HANDLE mutex_;
    CORBA::Short readWriteVariable;
public:
```

```
    tpc_i();
    ~tpc_i();
    virtual void read (CORBA::Short& a_value,
CORBA::Environment &IT_env=CORBA::default_environment) ;
    virtual void write (CORBA::Short b_value,
CORBA::Environment &IT_env=CORBA::default_environment) ;
};


class tpcFilter:public CORBA::ThreadFilter{
    virtual int inRequestPreMarshal(
CORBA::Request& request, CORBA::Environment& env);
};

DEF_TIE_tpc(tpc_i)

#endif
```

Support for WIN32 threads are defined in `<process.h>`. This chapter assumes familiarity with WIN32 threads. The `tcp` class has to use the TIE mechanism because it is using Orbix filters to implement threads.

The variable `mutex_` is the shared synchronized variable that will maintain a synchronization lock on a shared resource. In this case, it is `CORBA::Short ReadWriteVariable`. A constructor and destructor are also defined for the class.

The implementation will use an Orbix filter to control the threading requirements. This can be accomplished by subclassing the `CORBA::ThreadFilter` class. This is a per-process filter. As with any per-process filter, the 10 monitor points described in Chapter 13, "Orbix Filters," may be handled on a thread. For this exercise only, the `inRequestPreMarshal()` monitor point is attached to the filter. This means that when a request comes in, the filter will intercept the request before marshaling the code.

Finally, the TIE macro `DEF_TIE_tpc(tpc_i)` is defined so that TIE support is generated for the `tpc_i` class.

The Per-Client Thread Implementation

With the header files defined, the associated classes can be implemented, as shown in Listing 14.2.

LISTING 14.2 THREAD-PER-CLIENT IMPLEMENTATION FILE

```
#include <iostream.h>
#include "tpc.hpp"
```

continues

LISTING 14.2 CONTINUED

```
tpc_i::tpc_i(){
    readWriteVariable = 0;
    mutex_ = CreateMutex(0,FALSE,0);
}

tpc_i::~tpc_i(){
    CloseHandle(mutex_);
}

void tpc_i::read (CORBA::Short& a_value, CORBA::Environment &IT_env) {
    WaitForSingleObject(mutex_,INFINITE);
        cout<<"Read Called.."<<endl;
        a_value = readWriteVariable;
    ReleaseMutex(mutex_);
}

void tpc_i::write (CORBA::Short b_value, CORBA::Environment &IT_env) {
    WaitForSingleObject(mutex_,INFINITE);
        cout<<"Write Called.."<<endl;
        readWriteVariable = b_value;
    ReleaseMutex(mutex_);

}

static void* startThread(void *voidptr)
{
    CORBA::Orbix.continueThreadDispatch(*(CORBA::Request *)voidptr);
    return NULL;
}

int tpcFilter::inRequestPreMarshal(
       CORBA::Request& request, CORBA::Environment& env){

int    threadid;
threadid =
       (int)_beginthread((void(*)(void*))startThread,0,(void *)&request);
    return -1;
}

tpcFilter threadDispatcher;
```

The constructor creates an unnamed `mutex` object. Any thread of the calling process can specify the `mutex` object handle in a call to one of the wait functions. The single-object wait functions return when the state of the specified object is signaled. The destructor of the class releases the `mutex` handle.

The heart of the threading strategy is the implementation of the `inRequestPreMarshal` method:

```
int tpcFilter::inRequestPreMarshal(
        CORBA::Request& request, CORBA::Environment& env){

int    threadid;
threadid =
        (int)_beginthread((void(*)(void*))startThread,0,(void *)&request);
    return -1;
}
```

This method will be invoked when a request comes in. The implementation creates a thread using the `_beginThread()` function that is defined in `<process.h>`. The function takes three parameters. The first parameter is a pointer to the starting address of the routine that begins execution of the new thread. The second is the stack size that has to be allocated for the thread. The third is any argument that needs to be passed into the thread.

The starting address of the routine that begins execution of the new thread is defined in the function `startThread()`:

```
static void* startThread(void *voidptr)
{
    CORBA::Orbix.continueThreadDispatch(*
(CORBA::Request *)voidptr);
    return NULL;
}
```

The `startThread()` function is a static function and takes a `void` pointer. Internally, it calls a static `Rrbix` function named `continueThreadDispatch()`. This function notifies Orbix that the request needs to be dispatched to a new thread. This means that, for example, if the `read()` method is encapsulated in the request, it is handled on the thread.

The read and write functions essentially wait for the state of the `mutex` object to change. This is accomplished when the request comes into the function. At that point, the function executes because it owns the `mutex`. A `mutex` can be owned by only one thread at a time. This enables threads to control mutually exclusive access to a shared resource. The `mutex` is for the class as a whole. Because this is a per-client thread, each client would have to wait its turn to have access to the shared resource.

The Per-Client Thread Server Implementation

The server, as shown in Listing 14.3, is nothing special. The only difference is that it is dealing with a TIE object.

LISTING 14.3 PER-CLIENT THREAD SERVER IMPLEMENTATION

```
#include <string.h>
#include "tpc.hpp"
#include <iostream.h>
#include <stdlib.h>

int main()
{
  tpc_ptr ThreadForAClient;
  ThreadForAClient = new TIE_tpc(tpc_i) (new tpc_i());


  try {
      CORBA::Orbix.impl_is_ready("TPC");
  }
  catch (CORBA::SystemException &sysEx) {
      cerr << "Unexpected system exception" << endl;
      cerr << &sysEx;
      cerr << "Exception in impl_is_ready" << endl;
      exit(1);
  }
  catch (...) {
      cerr << "Exception in impl_is_ready" << endl;
      exit(1);
  }

  CORBA::release(ThreadForAClient);

  return 0;
}
```

Register the server as a shared activation process "TPC".

The Per-Client Thread Client Implementation

The client implementation, shown in Listing 14.4, is a little involved. It uses two threads: one to invoke the write operation and another to invoke the read operation.

LISTING 14.4 PER-CLIENT THREAD CLIENT IMPLEMENTATION

```
#include "tpc.hh"

#include <stdlib.h>
#include <iostream.h>
#include <process.h>

int main (int argc, char *argv[]){
```

```
    tpc_ptr    object_one;
    tpc_ptr    object_two;
    unsigned long thread_one, thread_two;

    try {
        object_one = tpc::_bind (":TPC");
        object_two = object_one;
    }
    catch (CORBA::SystemException &sysEx) {
    cerr << "Unexpected system exception" << endl;
    cerr << &sysEx;
    }
    catch (...) {
        cerr << "Unexpected exception" << endl;
    }

    if ((thread_one = (unsigned long)CreateThread(
       NULL, 0, (LPTHREAD_START_ROUTINE)thread_read,
       (void *)object_one, 0, &thread_one)) == NULL){
        cerr << "thread: creation failed" << endl;
        exit(-1);
    }

    if ((thread_two = (unsigned long)CreateThread(
       NULL, 0, (LPTHREAD_START_ROUTINE)thread_write,
       (void *)object_two, 0, &thread_two)) == NULL){
        cerr << "thread: creation failed" << endl;
        exit(-1);
    }

    if(WaitForSingleObject
       ((HANDLE)thread_one, INFINITE) == WAIT_FAILED){
        cerr << "thread:" << thread_one << " wait failed " << endl;
    }

    if(WaitForSingleObject
       ((HANDLE)thread_two, INFINITE) == WAIT_FAILED){
        cerr << "thread:" << thread_two << " wait failed " << endl;
    }
    CORBA::release(object_one);
    return 0;
}

void * thread_write(void *ptr_){
    tpc_ptr tpc_ = (tpc_ptr)ptr_;
    for (CORBA::Short j = 0; j < 5; j++){
        try {
             tpc_->write(j+1);
        }
        catch (CORBA::SystemException &sysEx) {
```


continues

LISTING 14.4 CONTINUED

```
            cerr << "Unexpected system exception" << endl;
            cerr << &sysEx;
        }
        catch (...) {
            cerr << "Unexpected exception" << endl;
        }

    }

    return ptr_;
}


void * thread_read(void *ptr_){
    register tpc_ptr tpc_ = (tpc_ptr)ptr_;
    register int i;

    for (i = 0; i < 5; i++)
    {
    try {
        CORBA::Short out_var;
        tpc_->read(out_var);
        cout<<"Called Read on thread "<<"Read Variable is:
"<<out_var<<endl;
    }
    catch (CORBA::SystemException &sysEx) {
        cerr << "Unexpected system exception" << endl;
        cerr << &sysEx;
    }
    catch (...) {
        cerr << "Unexpected exception" << endl;
    }

    }

    return ptr_;
}
```

The application defines two instances of the `tpc` interface. The first one is acquired by calling Orbix `bind()`. The second one essentially points to the same object reference. This means that `object_one` and `object_two` point to the same object reference.

The implementation defines two functions: `thread_read()` and `thread_write()`. These functions are executed on the threads created by the following functions:

```
if ((thread_one =
       (unsigned long)CreateThread(NULL, 0,
       (LPTHREAD_START_ROUTINE)thread_write,
```

```
            (void *)object_one, 0, &thread_one)) == NULL){
            cerr << "thread: creation failed" << endl;
            exit(-1);
    }

    if ((thread_two =
            (unsigned long)CreateThread(NULL, 0,
            (LPTHREAD_START_ROUTINE)thread_read, (void *)object_two,
            0, &thread_two)) == NULL){
            cerr << "thread: creation failed" << endl;
            exit(-1);
    }
```

The `CreateThread()` function is a WIN32 API function to create threads within the application. On these threads, the two functions execute `thread_read()` and `thread_write()`.

The `thread_read()` and `thread_write()` functions are essentially normal CORBA code. The only distinction is the fact that they execute on two separate threads.

The execution of two clients and the server is shown in Figure 14.4.

FIGURE 14.4
Thread-per-client execution.

Thread Pools

This section demonstrates how thread pools can be used to control requests on a server. Typically, *thread pools* are configured to handle a maximum number of simultaneous threads, where numerous requests are made on the server. Thread pooling is the default thread model for VisiBroker 3.3, which will be used to demonstrate this example. The following interface will be used to demonstrate the thread pool model. Compile the IDL using VisiBroker's idl2java pre-compiler:

```
module Pool {
        interface Request{
               void stopThread(in long stime);
        };
};
```

The implementation of the interface, `Request`, is shown in Listing 14.5.

LISTING 14.5 REQUEST IMPLEMENTATION

```
package Pool;
import java.io.*;

public class RequestImpl extends Pool._RequestImplBase {

  public RequestImpl(java.lang.String name) {
     super(name);
  }

  public RequestImpl() {
     super();
  }

  public void stopThread(int stime) {
       Thread thisThread = Thread.currentThread();
         try{
             thisThread.sleep((long)stime);
         } catch (Exception e){
         System.out.println("Sleep Exception");
         }

  }
}
```

The argument to the `stopThread()` method is an integer representing the time (in milliseconds) that is used to put the object to sleep:

```
Thread thisThread = Thread.currentThread();
        try{
            thisThread.sleep((long)stime);
        } catch (Exception e){
        System.out.println("Sleep Exception");
        }
```

The `Thread.currentThread()` method obtains a reference to the thread on which the object is running. The thread is then put to sleep using the time, `stime`, passed to the `stopThread()` method.

The request server implementation, which will instantiate the `Request` objects, is shown in Listing 14.6.

LISTING 14.6 REQUEST SERVER IMPLEMENTATION

```
package Pool;

import java.util.*;

public class RequestServer {
  org.omg.CORBA.ORB orb_ = null;
  org.omg.CORBA.BOA boa_  = null;

  public RequestServer(String[] args) {
    orb_ = org.omg.CORBA.ORB.init(args,null);

    Properties props = new Properties();
    props.put("OAthreadMax","2");

    boa_ = orb_.BOA_init("TPool", props);

    RequestImpl request1 = new RequestImpl("Request1");
    RequestImpl request2 = new RequestImpl("Request2");
    RequestImpl request3 = new RequestImpl("Request3");
    try{
      boa_.obj_is_ready(request1);
      System.out.println(request1 + " is ready.");
      boa_.obj_is_ready(request2);
      System.out.println(request2 + " is ready.");
      boa_.obj_is_ready(request3);
      System.out.println(request3 + " is ready.");

    }
    catch(org.omg.CORBA.SystemException ex){
      System.out.println(ex.toString());
    }

     boa_.impl_is_ready();

  }

  public static void main(String[] args) {
    RequestServer reqestServer = new RequestServer(args);
  }
}
```

In order to demonstrate how a thread pool can be modified, the server class is going to set the maximum number of threads running to two. This is accomplished by using a Java `Properties` class to set the parameter `"OAthreadMax"` to two. The object adapter uses "OAthreadMax", a VisiBroker-specific parameter, to set the thread pool size during the adapter's initialization:

```
Properties props = new Properties();
    props.put("OAthreadMax","2");

    boa_ = orb_.BOA_init("TPool", props);
```

The adapter can also use other parameters to modify threading characteristics, such as thread model, minimum thread size, and thread idle time. These can be found in the VisiBroker reference documentation.

When the server is instantiated, it creates three different request objects: Request1, Request2, and Request3:

```
RequestImpl request1 = new RequestImpl("Request1");
RequestImpl request2 = new RequestImpl("Request2");
RequestImpl request3 = new RequestImpl("Request3");
```

These three objects are instantiated to simulate multiple server objects to handle requests.

The client implementation, as shown in Listing 14.7, is a simple program that will invoke the stopThread() method on the request server.

LISTING 14.7 REQUEST CLIENT IMPLEMENTATION

```
package Pool;


public class RequestClient {

   public static void main(String[] args) {

    String sRequest = args[0];
    System.out.println(sRequest);

    org.omg.CORBA.ORB orb = org.omg.CORBA.ORB.init(args,null);

    Request request = RequestHelper.bind(orb, sRequest);

     System.out.println("Invoking request on "+sRequest);
     request.stopThread(30000);
     System.out.println("Finished request on "+sRequest);

   }
}
```

The request client uses a String argument, sRequest, to determine which request object to bind to. The stopThread() method on the request object is invoked using a time of

30,000 milliseconds, or 30 seconds. This invocation puts the request object's thread to sleep, thus keeping the thread busy for a while.

Now it is time to run the example. Start the request server:

```
>start vbj Pool.RequestServer Request1
```

This will start three request server objects, as shown in Figure 14.5.

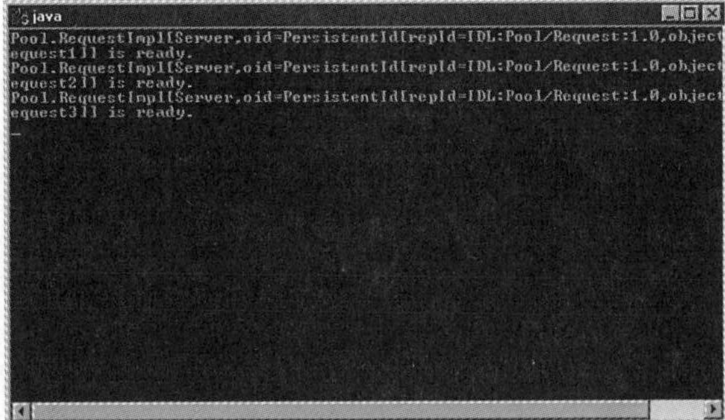

FIGURE 14.5
Request server objects.

Now, start three request client executions, using `Request1`, `Request2`, and `Request3` as arguments:

```
>start vbj Pool.RequestClient Request1
>start vbj Pool.RequestClient Request2
>start vbj Pool.RequestClient Request3
```

This will start three request client requests, as shown in Figure 14.6.

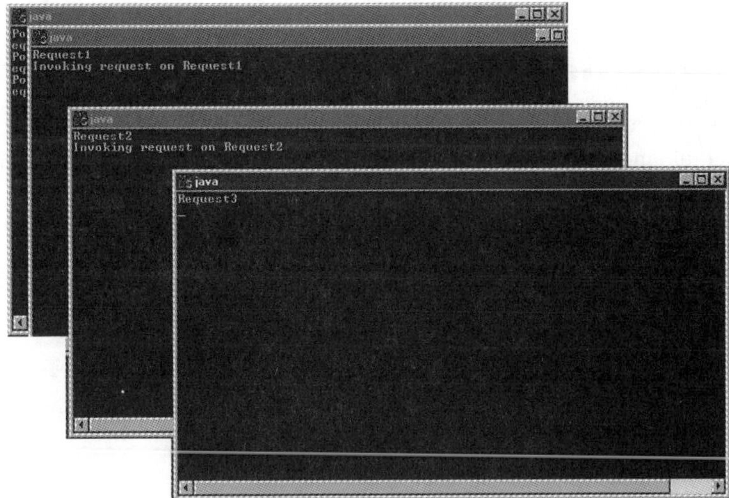

FIGURE 14.6
Three request clients.

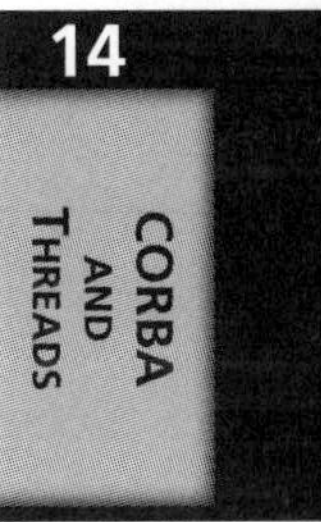

The `Request1` and `Request2` client programs invoke the `stopThread()` method on their respective request server objects, as shown by the entry `"Invoking request on RequestX"`. Because the maximum thread pool size is set to two, the `Request3` client must wait until a thread is returned to the thread pool. After 30 seconds, `Request1` is finished, and its thread is returned to the thread pool. `Request3` now has a thread available to process its request, which it obtains to start its invocation (see Figure 14.7).

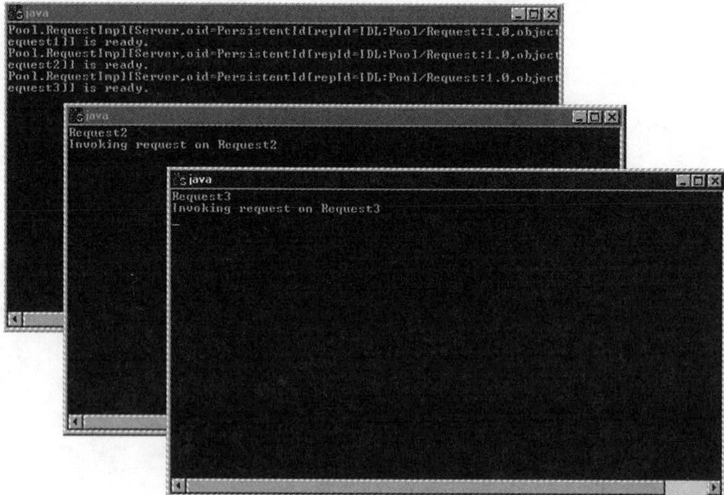

FIGURE 14.7
`Request3` *client invocation.*

Of course, it is doubtful that a thread pool would be set to two for an actual system implementation. However, for high-volume server transactions, consider the size of the thread pool in order to manage throughput and performance.

Summary

Threads are an integral part of any serious CORBA solution. Designing programs with multiple independent threads provides concurrency within an application and improves performance. Threads enable the design of applications to service multiple requests simultaneously.

This is required especially when multiple clients connect to a shared server and request an arbitrary number of services at the same time. Threads enable writing apps that asynchronously manage incoming requests.

There are three types are threading strategies: thread per session, where every client is allocated a thread to service its requirements; thread per object, which involves every object executing in its own thread; and thread pooling, which enables allocation of a fixed number of threads to service any request that comes in.

Ultimately, threads improve performance and increase the efficiency of an implementation's utilization of host resources. However, care must be taken when using threads, because implementations that do not take the underlying complexity of threaded architectures into account tend to create unmaintainable and unreliable applications.

CHAPTER

Orbix Dynamic Loaders

IN THIS CHAPTER

Orbix Loaders enable a server to load objects during runtime. The loaders can provide this service under two situations. The loaders can instantiate an object when a client dispatches a request for an object reference through `string_to_object()` or `bind()` and when a request comes into the server's address space for an object that isn't initialized. Under the latter scenario, the ORB responds with an exception if an object is not found. If, however, a loader is installed, the server will request it to load the object when an invocation comes in.

Loaders are implemented by subclassing the `CORBA::LoaderClass`. When a loader is defined and implemented, it has to be installed with the Orbix ORB. A loader can be associated with an object when it is created. This is accomplished by passing a pointer to the loader as a parameter into either the TIE constructor or the BOAImpl constructor with Orbix.

Why Write Loaders?

A loader has the capability of dynamically loading objects during runtime. This could provide a designer with interesting design options. For one, depending on which object is being requested, a loader could initialize the object to a predefined state. This feature is also ideal if you have multiple implementations of the same interface. Depending on the type that is requested by a client, a loader could initialize different implementations of the same interface.

All loaders should be subclassed from the `CORBA::LoaderClass`. This class specifies a number of methods that need to be overridden to create a loader:

- `load()`—This method is invoked when an invocation arrives at the server for an object that hasn't been loaded into memory. The `load()` method is passed the marker identifying the object that is required to handle the invocation.

  The `load()` request could be the place to implement load audit information. For instance, every time an object reference is requested, you could write information to an audit file regarding when the object reference was requested.
- `save()`—This method is called when the process that hosts the loader is terminated. This enables a loader to save an object. This method is also called when the object managed by a loader is destroyed. For example, you could save an object by storing it in an object-oriented database. It is also possible to write audit information about an object reference when the `save()` method is called.
- `record()` and `rename()`—These are essential functions that enable a loader to control the naming of an object that it manages.

Using a Loader

The process of implementing an interface that uses a loader is not any different from what we have done before. In fact, Orbix uses a default loader if you do not provide one. To illustrate the implementation of a loader, let's consider a simple interface to illustrate the essentials of coding an Orbix loader.

We will implement loaders in both C++ and Java. The differences between them are not that great. Both implementations use the following interface. It is only in the server implementation that changes occur. That is primarily because it is easier to construct user interfaces in Java Swing than in MFC:

Here is the Hangar interface:

```
module Soar{
    interface Aircraft{
        attribute long identifier;
    };

    interface Hangar{
        Soar::Aircraft CheckOutAircraft(in long identifier);
       void CheckInAircraft(in Soar::Aircraft anAircraft);
    };
};
```

The preceding module is very simple. It specifies two interfaces, one named `Aircraft` and the other named `Hangar`. The object is to pass an instance of an `Aircraft` to and from the `Hangar`. It is rather simple. The interface is not under scrutiny here. Rather, at issue is how we could write a loader to intervene between the object that implements the interface and the client that requests the interface. The interface can be implemented in the following manner.

The first thing that you have to provide for an interface implementation is to overload its constructor so that it can use a user-defined constructor. If this is not done, the default Orbix loader is used. Listing 15.1 is the C++ `Soar::Aircraft` implementation, Listing 15.2 is the Java `AirCraft` implementation, and Listing 15.3 is the Java `Hangar` Implementation.

LISTING 15.1 C++ `Soar::Aircraft` IMPLEMENTATION

```
#ifndef hangar_ih
#define hangar_ih
#include "hangar.hh"
```

continues

LISTING 15.1 CONTINUED

```
namespace Soar{

    class IT_DECLSPEC_hangar Aircraft_i:public virtual AircraftBOAImpl{
    public:
        Aircraft_i(const char* marker, CORBA::LoaderClass* loader);
        virtual void identifier (
          CORBA::Long identifier,
          CORBA::Environment &IT_env=CORBA::default_environment);
        virtual CORBA::Long identifier (
          CORBA::Environment &IT_env=CORBA::default_environment) ;
    private:
        CORBA::Long id;
    };

    class IT_DECLSPEC_hangar Hangar_i:public virtual HangarBOAImpl{
    public:
        Hangar_i(const char* marker, CORBA::LoaderClass* loader);
        ~Hangar_i();
        virtual Soar::Aircraft_ptr CheckOutAircraft (
               CORBA::Long identifier,
               CORBA::Environment &IT_env=CORBA::default_environment) ;
        virtual void CheckInAircraft (
               Soar::Aircraft_ptr anAircraft,
               CORBA::Environment &IT_env=CORBA::default_environment) ;
    private:
        Soar::Aircraft_ptr aircraft;
        CORBA::LoaderClass *t_loader;
    };

};

#endif
#endif
```

LISTING 15.2 JAVA AirCraft IMPLEMENTATION

```
package Loader;
import IE.Iona.OrbixWeb.Features.LoaderClass;
import Soar.*;

public class Aircraft_i extends _AircraftImplBase{
  private int id = 0;

  public Aircraft_i(String marker, LoaderClass loader){
    super(marker,loader);
  }

  public int identifier(){
```

```
    return id;
  }

  public void identifier(int value){
    id = value;
  }
}
```

LISTING 15.3 JAVA Hangar IMPLEMENTATION

```
package Loader;
import Soar.*;
import IE.Iona.OrbixWeb.Features.LoaderClass;

public class Hangar_i extends _HangarImplBase{
  private int aircraftID;
  private Soar.Aircraft aircraft;

  public Hangar_i(String marker, LoaderClass loader){
    super(marker,loader);
    aircraft = new Aircraft_i("AircraftOne",loader);
  }

  public Soar.Aircraft CheckOutAircraft(int identifier){
    return aircraft;
  }

  public void CheckInAircraft(Soar.Aircraft anAircraft){
    this.aircraft = anAircraft;
  }
}
```

We have provided the `Aircraft` and the `Hangar` classes with overloaded constructors for both C++ and Java implementations.

These are the constructors for the C++ implementation of `Hangar` and `Aircraft`:

```
Hangar_i(const char* marker, CORBA::LoaderClass* loader);
Aircraft_i(const char* marker, CORBA::LoaderClass* loader);
```

These are the constructors for the Java versions of these classes:

```
public Hangar_i(String marker, LoaderClass loader)
public Aircraft_i(String marker, LoaderClass loader)
```

The methods take two parameters: a marker to identify the interface instance itself and a parameter pointing to the loader instance that is to load the object. If a `Loader` object is not specified, Orbix uses the default loader to instantiate a class. But in this case, a `LoaderClass` is specified. The first parameter in both the constructors is the marker name for the object. A marker is a way to enable an implementation to differentiate different objects of the same type in a server.

Besides this small change, the implementation is as normal as for any other implementation. Listing 15.4 shows the implementation of the C++ classes. Because Java classes contain the definition and the implementation in one place, you need to show only the C++ code here. The Java equivalent for this code was provided in Listing 15.2 and 15.3.

LISTING 15.4 C++ IMPLEMENTATION

```
include "hangar.hpp"
#include <iostream.h>

void Soar::Aircraft_i:: identifier (
        CORBA::Long identifier, CORBA::Environment &IT_env){
        id = identifier;
}

CORBA::Long Soar::Aircraft_i::identifier(
        CORBA::Environment &IT_env){
         return id;
}

Soar::Hangar_i::Hangar_i(
        const char* marker, CORBA::LoaderClass* loader){
         aircraft = new Soar::Aircraft_i("AirCraftOne",t_loader);
}

Soar::Hangar_i::~Hangar_i(){
    CORBA::release(aircraft);
}

Soar::Aircraft_ptr Soar::Hangar_i::CheckOutAircraft (
        CORBA::Long identifier, CORBA::Environment &IT_env) {
        return Soar::Aircraft::_duplicate(aircraft);
}

void Soar::Hangar_i:: CheckInAircraft (
        Soar::Aircraft_ptr anAircraft, CORBA::Environment &IT_env) {
        aircraft =  Soar::Aircraft::_duplicate(anAircraft);
}
```

The `Hangar` class constructor instantiates the `Aircraft` object. To the `aircraft` constructor, it passes a marker `AirCraftOne` and the loader that was passed to it by the server. This means that the Orbix loader is used at two different places: One is at the server that instantiates the `Hangar`, and the other is when the `Hangar` has to instantiate the `Aircraft`. The `Hangar` constructor needs to be elaborated a bit, as shown in the following code:

```
Soar::Hangar_i::Hangar_i(const char* marker, CORBA::LoaderClass*
loader):HangarBOAImpl(marker,loader),t_loader(loader){
```

```
    aircraft = new Soar::Aircraft_i("AirCraftOne",t_loader);
}
```

The `Hangar_i` constructor attaches the marker and the loader to its superclass `HangarBOAImpl`. It then proceeds to instantiate an instance of the `Soar::Aircraft_i`, to which it passes the marker and the loader that was passed into the `Soar::Hangar_i` constructor. Because the BOA-related classes are closest to the ORB, it is there that the loader interfaces with your classes.

For brevity, I have not shown any Java code here. But it should be obvious from the preceding discussion that the implications for the Java code are the same as for the C++ code. This takes care of the SOAR module implementation. In terms of the requirements, the Java code does the same as the C++ code. The constructor instantiates the `Aircraft` object and so forth. We can now proceed to construct a loader to interface between these implementations and the client.

Implementing a Loader

As mentioned earlier, the loader has to be a subclass of `CORBA::LoaderClass` (or `Corba.LoaderClass` in Java). Further, it needs to override the necessary methods. This means that if you need to specialize any of the methods that are specified in the `CORBA::LoaderClass` (or `Corba.LoaderClass`), it can be done in the subclass. Listing 15.5 is a simple loader interface.

LISTING 15.5 A SIMPLE LOADER INTERFACE

```
#include <CORBA.h>
#include <string.h>
#include "hangar.hpp"

class loader : public CORBA::LoaderClass{

public:
      loader ();
      virtual ~loader ();
      virtual CORBA::ObjectRef load (const char* interfce,
const char* marker, CORBA::Boolean isBind, CORBA::Environment& env);
      virtual void save (CORBA::Object*, CORBA::saveReason reason,
CORBA::Environment& );
};
```

The `loader` overrides the `load()` and `save()` methods. The `load()` method is called when an object needs to be loaded. The `save()` method is called when the object is deleted or if the process is deleted. Later in this chapter, you learn how persistence could be provided to these classes as well.

Listing 15.6 shows only the implementation of the loader class.

LISTING 15.6 A SIMPLE LOADER IMPLEMENTATION

```
#include "loader.hpp"
#include <iostream.h>
#include <string.h>

loader::loader ():CORBA::LoaderClass(1){}
loader::~loader () {}

CORBA::ObjectRef loader::load (const char *interfce, const char
*marker,CORBA::Boolean, CORBA::Environment&  env){

    CORBA::ObjectRef retValue;

    if(strcmp(marker,"")){
        Soar::Aircraft_ptr aircraft = new Soar::Aircraft_i(marker, this);
        cout << "[LOADER]: "<<marker<< " Loaded"<< endl;
        retValue = Soar::Aircraft::_duplicate(aircraft);
    }
    if(strcmp(marker,"Hangar51")){
        Soar::Hangar_ptr hangar = new Soar::Hangar_i(marker, this);
        cout << "[LOADER]: "<<marker<< " Loaded"<< endl;
        retValue = Soar::Hangar::_duplicate(hangar);
    }
    else{
        cout << "[LOADER]: "<<marker<< " Not Loaded"<< endl;
    }
    return retValue;
}

void loader::save (CORBA::Object* obj, CORBA::saveReason reason,
CORBA::Environment&) {

    cout<<"[LOADER]: unloaded"<< endl;
    if(reason == CORBA::objectDeletion){
        const char *marker = obj->_marker ();
        cout<<"[LOADER]: Save called for "<< marker << endl;
        CORBA::release(obj);
    }
    if(reason == CORBA::processTermination){
        const char *marker = obj->_marker ();
        cout<<"[LOADER]: Save called for "<< marker << endl;
        CORBA::release(obj);
    }
}
```

The `load()` method determines which object to load by the marker that is passed into the constructor for the object required. This construction can take place when a `bind()` is called or an object is passed as a parameter. In any case, the code checks whether the marker is null. If so, it constructs an instance of the `Aircraft` interface. Otherwise, a `Hangar` is constructed and returned.

The `save()` method is called when the object is released or the process is terminated. The `save()` method can also be explicitly called on the loader. The implementation checks for both. The code does not do anything interesting other than deallocating the object reference that was loaded.

ADDING A `cleanOut()` OPERATION

More interesting things could be done on the instance if the object reference is cast back to the type it is. In the previous code, all the methods are invoked on an instance of `CORBA::object`. But this object can be cast into its subtype. For instance, if the `Hangar` interface had defined an operation named `cleanOut()`, the code could be modified to do the following:

```
if(reason == CORBA::processTermination){
        const char *marker = obj->_marker ();
        if(strcmp(marker,"Hangar51"){
         Soar::Hangar *hangar = (Soar::Hangar*)obj
         hangar->cleanOut();
        }
        cout<<"[LOADER]:Save called for "<< marker << endl;
        CORBA::release(obj);
}
```

The `cleanOut()` operation could be implemented to accomplish any number of things. This could do things such as logging or persistence of state data. If persistence is accomplished, this data could be read back when the `load()` method is called so that the state of an object could be initialized to a state that was saved before the object was deactivated.

Logging can be accomplished through a simple text log. A more sophisticated log could use a database to capture the log information. Persistence can be accomplished by using either serialization or through the use of an object-oriented database.

Implementing a loader in Java is reasonably similar to C++. The only major distinction between them is that Java does memory management differently. As far as Orbix and OrbixWeb is concerned, the Application Programming Interfaces are fairly similar. The superclass that has to be subclassed to construct a loader is defined in `IE.Iona.OrbixWeb.Features.LoaderClass`. This class has to be subclassed and the relevant methods overridden.

The first thing about the loader itself is that just as in C++, the Java loader has to be subclassed from `IE.Iona.OrbixWeb.CORBA.LoaderClass`. In terms of the actual implementation, you then need to determine which methods need to be overridden. In Listing 15.7, you will find an implementation of a loader that closely mirrors the loader that was implemented earlier in C++.

LISTING 15.7 JAVA LOADER IMPLEMENTATION

```
package Loader;
import org.omg.CORBA.SystemException;
import org.omg.CORBA.Object;
import IE.Iona.OrbixWeb.Features.LoaderClass;
import IE.Iona.OrbixWeb._CORBA;
import IE.Iona.OrbixWeb._OrbixWeb;
import org.omg.CORBA.StringHolder;
import java.io.*;

class Loader extends LoaderClass {
  private PrintWriter log = null;

  public Loader() {
    super (true);
    try{
     FileWriter file = new FileWriter("loader.log");
     log = new PrintWriter(file,true);
    }
    catch(IOException e){
      System.out.println(e.toString());
      System.exit(-1);
    }
  }

  public org.omg.CORBA.Object load (String interface,String marker,
boolean isBind){

    org.omg.CORBA.Object returnobject = null;

    if(marker.equals("")){
     Soar.Aircraft returnAircraft = new Loader.Aircraft_i(marker,this);
     String message = "[LOADER] " + marker + " Loaded.";
     System.out.println(message);
     log.println(message);
     returnobject = returnAircraft;
    }

    if(marker.equals("Hangar51")){
      Soar.Hangar returnHangar = new Loader.Hangar_i(marker,this);
      String message = "[LOADER] " + marker + " Loaded.";
      System.out.println(message);
```

```
      log.println(message);
      returnobject = returnHangar;
    }
    return returnobject;
  }

  public void save (org.omg.CORBA.Object obj, int reason){

    String message = "[LOADER] Saving";
    System.out.println(message);
    log.println(message);

    String marker = _OrbixWeb.Object(obj)._marker();
    message = "[LOADER] " + marker + " Loaded.";
    System.out.println(message);
    log.println(message);

    if (reason == _CORBA.processTermination){
      message = "Save Called because reason = _CORBA.processTermination";
      System.out.println(message);
      log.println(message);
    }
    else if (reason == _CORBA.explicitCall){
      message = "Save Called because reason = _CORBA.explicitCall";
      System.out.println(message);
      log.println(message);
    }
    else if (reason == _CORBA.objectDeletion){
      message = "Save Called because reason = _CORBA.objectDeletion";
      System.out.println(message);
      log.println(message);
    }
  }

public boolean rename (Object obj, StringHolder marker)
  {
    String message = "Renaming marker = "  + marker.value;
    System.out.println(message);
    log.println(message);
    marker.value = new String("DummyMarker");
    return true;
  }

  public void record (Object obj, StringHolder marker){
    String message = "Recording Marker "  + marker.value;
    System.out.println(message);
    log.println(message);
    if (marker.value.equals("DummyMarjer"))
      marker.value = new String ("Hangar51");
  }
}
```

The Java loader overrides all the methods in the `IE.Iona.OrbixWeb.CORBA.LoaderClass`. These are the `load()`, `save()`, `record()`, and `rename()` methods. Before you look at the nature of implementing these methods, let's see how the constructor has changed in a subtle manner.

The `super` constructor of `LoaderClass` takes a parameter. This boolean parameter is used by the superclass to indicate whether the current loader that is being constructed is added to a list of loaders that are invoked when an object fault occurs. Such faults can occur when a client invokes a service and the object is not discovered by the ORB, forcing it to return an object-not-found exception. When a client needs a loader, the orb looks up a list of loaders that are installed. A loader can be installed with the ORB by controlling the boolean parameter. The default behavior is always false. In Listing 15.7, passing a `true` indicates that instances of the current loader should be added to this list.

The server that hosts the service that a client requests usually constructs the instance of the loader. When installed, the requests that come in from the client will be passed on to the loader for action. Further on, the `loader` class also specifies an instance of a `PrintWriter`. An instance of this class is used to create a log file. Whenever an invocation is received by the loader, an entry is written to the log file. The log file itself is not very sophisticated, but it could easily be extended to contain other information, such as the date and time and information about the client.

In the preceding implementation, all the methods of the `LoaderClass` are specialized in the loader implementation. The `load()` method is called when a client requires an object reference. At that point, the loader can instantiate and return the object reference to the client. In Listing 15.7, the object reference is returned in the context of the marker provided from the client. If the client requests an object without providing any marker, an instance of the `Aircraft` object reference is returned to the client. On the other hand, if the client explicitly requests a hangar named `Hangar51`, the loader creates an instance of the `Hangar` object reference and returns that to the client.

The `save()` method can be called under three different circumstances:

- `processTermination` A process termination is triggered when a server exits. At that point, the `save()` method on the loader instance will be called. This point can be useful for general "cleaning up" of a system. For instance, in Listing 15.7, the log file is closed when the `save()` is called because of process termination.
- `explicitCall` An explicit call is made when a process or an object explicitly invokes the `save()` method on the loader instance.
- `objectDeletion` When an object that is controlled by the loader is deleted, the `save()` method is called. As mentioned earlier, this would be a good place to provide persistence for the objects that are controlled by the loader process.

NOTE

Another, perhaps more important, action that can be taken on all three types of reasons for the `save()` method being called is to enable the objects that are being controlled by the loader to save their state to some medium such as a database of a file system. Of course, the benefit of the loader is to enable these objects to also internalize their state when the `load()` method is called.

Providing Persistence Using Loaders

Both the `load()` and `save()` methods are provided with two pieces of information that can be used to provide persistence to the objects. The first piece of information is the name of the interface. This enables the loader to load an instance of a class that implements the required interface. If the object is persistent, the marker can be used as a key to locate the object and internalize the object into memory. This would entail that each object be uniquely identified by a marker to enable the loader to save and/or load the appropriate object into memory.

There are a number of ways persistence could be achieved. The following are three of these ways:

- A relational database—Using such a storage enables you to externalize the state of an object when the `save()` is called and to internalize it when `load()` is called.
- An object-oriented database—Such a database enables entire sets of objects to be saved efficiently. Because object-oriented databases are single-level storage engines, you need not work with intermediate languages, such as SQL.
- A file system—This is the easiest and the least expensive. Under this strategy, the state of the object can be written to a record table as text. When required, this information can then read in by the `load()` method.

The Loader Server Implementation

It is the server's responsibility to instantiate the loader class. The loader is just a normal class like any class, which means that there is no special application programming interface to use a loader. First, let's implement a C++ server, then a Java server.

With the `LoaderServer` class, as with the interface, implementation is kept simple to show only the aspects of the simple loader. Listing 15.8 shows the C++ server, and Listing 15.9 shows the Java server.

LISTING 15.8 C++ SERVER

```
#include <iostream.h>
#include "loader.hpp"

void main(int argc, char** argv)  {

    loader *a_loader = new loader();

    try {
      CORBA::Orbix.impl_is_ready("Area51");
    }
    catch (CORBA::SystemException &sysEx) {
        cerr << "Unexpected system exception" << endl;
        cerr << &sysEx;
    }
    catch(...) {
        cerr << "Unexpected exception" << endl;
    }
}
```

LISTING 15.9 JAVA SERVER

```
package Loader;
import com.sun.java.swing.*;
import IE.Iona.OrbixWeb._CORBA;
import IE.Iona.OrbixWeb._OrbixWeb;

import org.omg.CORBA.ORB;
import org.omg.CORBA.SystemException;

import java.util.*;
import java.awt.*;
import java.awt.event.*;

public class LoaderServer extends JFrame{
  JTextArea DisplayArea = new JTextArea();
  JButton StartButton = new JButton();
  JButton StopButton = new JButton();
  LoaderThread lthread = null;
  Thread thread = null;


  public static void main(String args[]) {
    new LoaderServer();
```

```
}


public LoaderServer() {
  try  {
    jbInit();
  }
  catch (Exception e) {
    e.printStackTrace();
  }
}

private void jbInit() throws Exception {
  this.addWindowListener(new java.awt.event.WindowAdapter() {
    public void windowClosing(WindowEvent e) {
      this_windowClosing(e);
    }
  });
  DisplayArea.setBounds(new Rectangle(8, 8, 375, 213));
  StartButton.setText("Start");
  StartButton.setBounds(new Rectangle(302, 235, 80, 23));
  StartButton.addMouseListener(new java.awt.event.MouseAdapter() {
    public void mouseClicked(MouseEvent e) {
      StartButton_mouseClicked(e);
    }
  });
  StopButton.setText("Stop");
  StopButton.setBounds(new Rectangle(220, 236, 80, 23));
  StopButton.addMouseListener(new java.awt.event.MouseAdapter() {
    public void mouseClicked(MouseEvent e) {
      StopButton_mouseClicked(e);
    }
  });
  StopButton.enable(false);
  this.getContentPane().setLayout(null);
  this.getContentPane().add(DisplayArea, null);
  this.getContentPane().add(StartButton, null);
  this.getContentPane().add(StopButton, null);
}

void StopButton_mouseClicked(MouseEvent e) {
  lthread.stop();
  StartButton.enable(true);
  StopButton.enable(false);
}

void StartButton_mouseClicked(MouseEvent e) {
   lthread = new LoaderThread();
   thread = new Thread(lthread);
```

continues

LISTING 15.9 CONTINUED

```
      thread.start();
      StartButton.enable(false);
      StopButton.enable(true);
  }

  void this_windowClosing(WindowEvent e) {
    System.exit(0);
  }
}

class LoaderThread implements Runnable{

  public void run() {
      ORB.init();
      Loader loader = new Loader();

      try {
        _CORBA.Orbix.impl_is_ready("Area51");
      }
      catch(SystemException se) {
        System.out.println(
         "Exception during creation of construction of Area51: "
         + se.toString());
        return;
      }
      System.out.println(" Server Exiting ...");
    _CORBA.Orbix.finalize();
  }

  public void stop(){
  }
}
```

Note that in the code, neither the `Hangar` nor the `Aircraft` is instantiated. The loader will construct them when an invocation comes in from a client. In Listings 15.8 and 15.9, besides the instantiation of the loader, no other object is constructed. When a request for a particular object does come in, the loader will dynamically construct and return the object through the `load()` method.

Implementation of the client is just as simple as implementation of the server. Listings 15.10 and 15.11 illustrate this implementation.

LISTING 15.10 C++ CLIENT

```
#include <iostream.h>
#include "hangar.hh"
```

```
void main(int argc, char** argv){

    Soar::Hangar_ptr hangar;
    try {
        hangar = Soar::Hangar::_bind ("Hangar51:Area51");
    }
    catch (CORBA::SystemException &sysEx) {
        cerr << "Unexpected system exception" << endl;
        cerr << &sysEx;
    }
    catch(...) {
        cerr << "Unexpected exception" << endl;
    }
    try{
        Soar::Aircraft_ptr aircraft = hangar->ChecOutAircraft(1554);
        CORBA::release(aircraft);
    }
    catch (CORBA::SystemException &sysEx) {
        cerr << "Unexpected system exception" << endl;
        cerr << &sysEx;
    }
    CORBA::release(hangar);
}
```

LISTING 15.11 JAVA CLIENT

```
package Loader;
import IE.Iona.OrbixWeb._OrbixWeb;
import IE.Iona.OrbixWeb._CORBA;

import org.omg.CORBA.ORB;
import org.omg.CORBA.SystemException;
import org.omg.CORBA.IntHolder;

public class LoaderClient {
  private Soar.Hangar hangar = null;
  private Soar.Aircraft aircraft = null;

  public LoaderClient() {
    try{
      hangar = Soar.HangarHelper.bind("Hangar51:Area51");
      aircraft = Soar.AircraftHelper.bind(":Area51");
    }
    catch(SystemException se) {
       System.out.println(
        "Exception during retrieval of the Hangar object reference"
        + se.toString());
       return;
```

continues

LISTING 15.11 CONTINUED

```
    }

    try{
      aircraft.identifier(5001);
      hangar.CheckInAircraft(aircraft);
      Soar.Aircraft temp = hangar.CheckOutAircraft(5001);
    }
    catch(SystemException se) {
       System.out.println(
        "Exception during retrieval of the Hangar object reference"
        + se.toString());
       return;
    }
  }

  public static void main(String[] args) {
    LoaderClient loaderClient = new LoaderClient();
    loaderClient.invokedStandalone = true;
  }
  private boolean invokedStandalone = false;
}
```

When the client invokes `Soar::Hangar::_bind ("Hangar51:Area51")` on the server, the loader dynamically loads the hangar object into memory. The marker determines which loader is loaded into memory; in the previous example, the marker is `Hangar51`. The loader looks for this marker if it is to load the `Hangar` object into memory. If on the other hand only the name of the server is provided, the aircraft is loaded into memory. The default marker is an empty string, and the loader considers this a request to load an instance of the `Aircraft` object into memory.

At any point during the execution of the client (or for that matter the server), the two objects can be "unloaded" if the `save()` method is invoked. As mentioned earlier, this can be accomplished in one of three ways. The most common point when the `save()` is called is when the object reference is removed from memory or when the server process terminates. The loader handles all these cases.

Summary

Orbix loaders enable the dynamic loading of classes. This could be a benefit in designing flexible systems that could intercept an incoming request for objects. Depending on the name of the object that is requested to be loaded, the loader can load the object. If can also load different implementations of the same interface.

This can be used in security features if required. The other benefit of the loader is that it also gets called when an object is deactivated or if the process is naturally terminated. The `save()` method enables an object to save data that needs to be persistent. It can also log important data. The object can use the state that is made persistent when it is loaded again so that the state of the object can be long-lived.

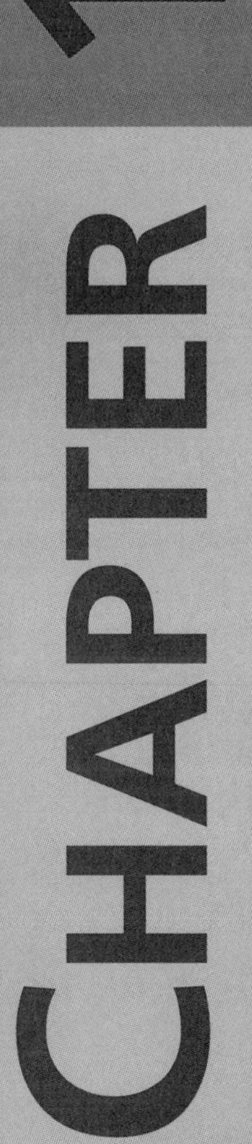

Distributed Callbacks

In This Chapter

Callbacks are a mechanism of coupling components. The use of the word *components* is intentional. It is meant to denote a system where the subcomponents are essentially "black box" elements. In such a system, designers try to ensure as little coupling as possible. This leads to systems that are inherently more flexible and scalable.

One of the ways of achieving this is by designing systems that do callbacks. Using this technique, a client registers with a server for notification of a state change or something similar through callbacks. The callback registration interface needs to be kept as simple as possible so that the dependency introduced between client and server is minimized. Another approach is to standardize the callback interfaces through standard coding conventions so that the server will always know what operation to invoke on the client. This is the approach taken by the JavaBeans event notification design. This standardization should be two-sided. The client interfaces for notification and the server interfaces for registration should be standard.

Callbacks allow the design of systems that are driven by the server. If asynchronicity is introduced using `oneway` calls from the client to the server, callbacks will enable a mechanism for the server to notify the client if the operation succeeded. Another possibility is to use callbacks as a simpler and lighter alternative to the CORBA Event Services that implement the push mechanism. Using callbacks, especially in a peer-to-peer CORBA application, interdependencies can be managed by using callback interfaces that enable the various peers to notify each other when conditions are met.

Callbacks in themselves are rather simple to implement. However, care should be taken to use the callback mechanism judiciously. If used, the interfaces need to be defined to be consistent across the entire architecture. This would allow the callback interfaces to be reused across the architecture.

Areas where callbacks can be used include simple push architectures. They are also an ideal pattern when a different component of the architecture needs to be synchronized to a consistent state. In this chapter, we will build the latter to demonstrate callbacks.

Defining Callback Interfaces

Callback interfaces have to be defined for both registration and notification. This can best be demonstrated through the construction of a simple chat application. The interfaces to be defined are

- Server interface for registration
- Client interface for notification

Defining the Chat Server

The chat server needs to do two things. Its primary function is to act as a gateway for chat clients. Its other function is to enable clients to register themselves for callbacks so that chat messages can be passed on to the appropriate client. Any number of clients can be logged into the server. The intricacies of concurrency are beyond the scope of the chapter. However, one constraint that can be imposed on the implementation is that authors of messages should not be notified of their own messages.

The following interface is simple enough to demonstate how a chat server can be built:

```
module callback{

    interface ChatParty{
      attribute string name;
  void chatListener(in string message);
    };


    interface chatServer{
        void registerParty( in ChatParty party);
        void deregister(in ChatParty party);
    void chat(in ChatParty party, in string message);
};
};
```

`chat.idl` specifies two interfaces. One will be implemented as a `chatServer`, and the other as a `chatClient`. Both these are to be implemented as servers. Depending on the roles the interfaces are playing, one of them will always be a client while the other is the server.

The primary operations for allowing a client to be registered for notifications or deregistration are the `registerParty()` and `deregister()` operations. For registration or deregistration, the `chatServer` is treated as a server. After it is registered, a `chatParty` can send messages to others by invoking the `chat()` operation. When the `chatServer` receives the invocation through this operation, the server then chooses the client role and invokes the `chatListener()` method to notify the client of what other clients have sent to the `chatServer`. Listing 16.1 shows the implementation of the `chatParty` interface.

LISTING 16.1 IMPLEMENTING THE `chatParty` INTERFACE

```
package callback;
import com.sun.java.swing.*;

public class ChatPty extends callback._ChatPartyImplBase {
```

continues

LISTING 16.1 CONTINUED

```
  private String name = null;
  private JTextArea RemoteWindow = null;

  public ChatPty(String name,JTextArea RemoteWindow) {
    super(name);
    this.RemoteWindow = RemoteWindow;
  }

  public void chatListener(
    java.lang.String message
  ) {
    RemoteWindow.append("message");
  }
  public void name(java.lang.String name) {
    this.name = name;
  }
  public java.lang.String name() {
    return this.name;
  }
}
```

The only important method is `chatListener()`. It is at this point that `chatServer` notifies the client with a message that has been sent by others. The implementation appends the incoming message into a Swing `TextWindow`.

Implementing the `chatParty` Client/Server

The client code presented in Listing 16.2 is, for most part, GUI-related. All the server-related code is in the `chatClientServer` class.

LISTING 16.2 THE CHAT CLIENT

```
package callback;

import java.awt.*;
import com.sun.java.swing.*;
import java.awt.event.*;

public class ChatClient extends JFrame {
  JTextField LoginName = new JTextField();
  JLabel jLabel1 = new JLabel();
  JButton LoginButton = new JButton();
  JScrollPane jScrollPane1 = new JScrollPane();
  JScrollPane jScrollPane2 = new JScrollPane();
  JTextArea LocalWindow = new JTextArea();
  JButton ChatButton = new JButton();
  JButton Logoutbutton = new JButton();
```

```
chatClientServer party = null;
Thread thread = null;
JTextArea RemoteWindow = new JTextArea();
callback.chatServer chatSrv = null;

public ChatClient(String[] args) {
  party = new chatClientServer(RemoteWindow);
  try  {
    jbInit();
  }
  catch (Exception e) {
    e.printStackTrace();
  }
}

public static void main(String[] args) {
  ChatClient chatClient = new ChatClient(args);
}

public ChatClient() {
  try  {
    jbInit();
  }
  catch (Exception e) {
    e.printStackTrace();
  }
}

private void jbInit() throws Exception {
  this.getContentPane().setLayout(null);
  this.setDefaultCloseOperation(WindowConstants.DISPOSE_ON_CLOSE);
  LoginName.setBounds(new Rectangle(4, 23, 153, 19));
  jLabel1.setText("Login Name");
  jLabel1.setBounds(new Rectangle(4, 6, 97, 15));
  LoginButton.setText("Login");
  LoginButton.setBounds(new Rectangle(165, 21, 71, 23));
  LoginButton.addMouseListener(new java.awt.event.MouseAdapter() {
    public void mouseClicked(MouseEvent e) {
      LoginButton_mouseClicked(e);
    }
  });
  jScrollPane1.setBounds(new Rectangle(3, 50, 447, 111));
  jScrollPane2.setBounds(new Rectangle(4, 167, 446, 108));
  ChatButton.setText("Chat");
  ChatButton.setBounds(new Rectangle(377, 282, 71, 23));
  ChatButton.addMouseListener(new java.awt.event.MouseAdapter() {
    public void mouseClicked(MouseEvent e) {
      ChatButton_mouseClicked(e);
    }
  });
```

continues

LISTING 16.2 CONTINUED

```
    Logoutbutton.setText("Logout");
    Logoutbutton.setBounds(new Rectangle(239, 21, 71, 23));
    Logoutbutton.addMouseListener(new java.awt.event.MouseAdapter() {
      public void mouseClicked(MouseEvent e) {
        Logoutbutton_mouseClicked(e);
      }
    });
    this.getContentPane().add(LoginName, null);
    this.getContentPane().add(jLabel1, null);
    this.getContentPane().add(LoginButton, null);
    this.getContentPane().add(jScrollPane1, null);
    jScrollPane1.getViewport().add(RemoteWindow, null);
    this.getContentPane().add(jScrollPane2, null);
    jScrollPane2.getViewport().add(LocalWindow, null);
    this.getContentPane().add(ChatButton, null);
    this.getContentPane().add(Logoutbutton, null);
    jScrollPane1.getViewport().add(RemoteWindow, null);
    this.getContentPane().add(RemoteWindow, null);
    this.setVisible(true);
  }

  void LoginButton_mouseClicked(MouseEvent e) {
     party.register(LoginName.getText());
     chatSrv = party.getChatServer();
     thread = new Thread(party);
     thread.start();
  }

  void Logoutbutton_mouseClicked(MouseEvent e) {
     party.deregister();
     thread.stop();
  }

  void ChatButton_mouseClicked(MouseEvent e) {
    String msg = LocalWindow.getText();
    try{
      chatSrv.chat(LoginName.getText(),msg);
    }
    catch(org.omg.CORBA.SystemException e){
      System.out.println(e.toString());
    }
  }
}
//The Server Implementation
class chatClientServer implements Runnable{
  private org.omg.CORBA.ORB orb;
  private org.omg.CORBA.BOA boa;
  private callback.ChatPty party;
  private com.visigenic.vbroker.URLNaming.Resolver resolver = null;
  private callback.chatServer chatSrv = null;
```

```
  chatClientServer(JTextArea RemoteWindow){
   orb = org.omg.CORBA.ORB.init();
   boa = orb.BOA_init();
   party = new callback.ChatPty("Party", RemoteWindow);
   try{
      resolver =
        com.visigenic.vbroker.URLNaming.ResolverHelper.narrow(
               orb.resolve_initial_references("URLNamingResolver"));
      org.omg.CORBA.Object obj = resolver.locate(
               "http://localhost:15000/chatserver.ior");
      chatSrv = callback.chatServerHelper.narrow(obj);
    }
    catch(org.omg.CORBA.SystemException e){
      e.printStackTrace();
    }
    catch(org.omg.CORBA.ORBPackage.InvalidName ivn){
      ivn.printStackTrace();
    }
    catch(com.visigenic.vbroker.URLNaming.ReqFailure rf){
      rf.printStackTrace();
    }
    catch(com.visigenic.vbroker.URLNaming.CommFailure cf){
      cf.printStackTrace();
    }
    catch(com.visigenic.vbroker.URLNaming.InvalidURL ivu){
      ivu.printStackTrace();
    }
  }

  public void run(){
    try{
      boa.impl_is_ready();
    }
    catch(org.omg.CORBA.SystemException e){
      e.printStackTrace();
    }
  }

  public void register(String name){
     party.name(name);
     chatSrv.registerParty(party);
  }
  public void deregister(){
     chatSrv.deregister(party);
  }

  callback.chatServer getChatServer(){
    return chatSrv;
  }
}
```

An instance of chatClientServer is created. This is accomplished in the line

```
party = new chatClientServer(RemoteWindow);
```

An instance of RemoteWindow is passed into the implementation. This will be as shown in the implementation so that callback.ChatPty can output messages back to the GUI.

All the CORBA-related aspects are implemented in the chatClientServer. The code uses VisiBroker URL naming to acquire the object reference to the chatServer. This instance is passed back to the GUI so that it can respond to user events (button clicks). When the required ORB initializations are finished, the chatClientServer then calls the impl_is_ready() waiting for incoming events from the chatServer.

The logic of the implementation is in the user-generated events. When the user clicks login, the chatParty is registered with the chatServer. The reverse occurs when deregister is called on the chatServer. When the chat button is clicked, the message that was typed in the LocalWindow is sent to the chatServer.

The chatClientServer is implemented as a thread so that the user interface can be operated upon, independent of the chatClientServer. This is required because the impl_is_ready() blocks until the server exists. When implemented, the server can be launched just as any other CORBA server.

Implementing the chatServer

The chatServer will use a JGL stack to keep a list of chatPartys in memory. When a request comes in, the implementation will iterate over the stack and invoke the chatListener() operation on the chatClient. Listing 16.3 shows the implementation of chatServer.

LISTING 16.3 THE CHAT SERVER

```
package callback;
import com.objectspace.jgl.*;
import java.util.*;

public class ChatSrv extends callback._chatServerImplBase {
  private com.objectspace.jgl.Stack listeners =
new com.objectspace.jgl.Stack();
  public ChatSrv(String name) {
    super(name);
  }

  public void registerParty(
    callback.ChatParty party
  ) {
```

```
     System.out.println(party.name());
     listeners.push(party);
  }

  public void deregister(
    callback.ChatParty party
  ) {
   System.out.println(party.name());
   for (Enumeration e = listeners.elements() ; e.hasMoreElements() ;) {
      callback.ChatParty temp_ = (callback.ChatParty)e.nextElement();
      if(temp_.name() == party.name()){
        listeners.remove(e);
      }
    }
  }
  public void chat(
    java.lang.String id,
    java.lang.String message
  ) {
    System.out.println(message);
    for (Enumeration e = listeners.elements() ; e.hasMoreElements() ;) {
      callback.ChatParty temp_ = (callback.ChatParty)e.nextElement();
      if(temp_.name() != id){
        temp_.chatListener(message);
      }
    }
  }
}
```

The `registerParty` and the `deregister` operations essentially add and remove a party from the stack that is maintained by the implementation. When a client invokes the `chat()` method, the server iterates over the stack and invokes the notification operation on the client. At this point, the client should receive the callback from the server.

The `chatServer` Runtime Implementation

The runtime to host the `chatServer` implementation is typical of most of the servers we have constructed. It uses the VisiBroker URL naming to register the IOR so that a client can easily bind to the server, as shown in Listing 16.4.

LISTING 16.4 THE CHAT SERVER RUNTIME

```
package callback;

public class ChatServerImpl{
  private org.omg.CORBA.ORB orb;
  private org.omg.CORBA.BOA boa;
```

continues

LISTING 16.4 CONTINUED

```
  private com.visigenic.vbroker.URLNaming.Resolver resolver = null;
  private callback.ChatSrv chatserver = null;

  public ChatServerImpl() {
    try{
      orb = org.omg.CORBA.ORB.init();
      boa = orb.BOA_init();
      chatserver = new callback.ChatSrv("ChatServer");
      resolver =
        com.visigenic.vbroker.URLNaming.ResolverHelper.narrow(
        orb.resolve_initial_references("URLNamingResolver"));
      resolver.force_register_url(
        "http://localhost:15000/chatserver.ior",chatserver);
    }
    catch(org.omg.CORBA.SystemException e){
      e.printStackTrace();
    }
    catch(org.omg.CORBA.ORBPackage.InvalidName ivn){
      ivn.printStackTrace();
    }
    catch(com.visigenic.vbroker.URLNaming.ReqFailure rf){
      rf.printStackTrace();
    }
    catch(com.visigenic.vbroker.URLNaming.CommFailure cf){
      cf.printStackTrace();
    }
    catch(com.visigenic.vbroker.URLNaming.InvalidURL ivu){
      ivu.printStackTrace();
    }

  try{
      boa.impl_is_ready();
  }
  catch(org.omg.CORBA.SystemException e){
      e.printStackTrace();
  }
  }

  public static void main(String[] args) {
    ChatServerImpl chatServerImpl = new ChatServerImpl();
  }
}
```

The entire applicaton is shown running in Figure 16.1. This application is a simple demonstration of the essential feature of CORBA: peer-to-peer technology. Client/server roles are just that—*roles* that a designer assigns to a component of an architecture.

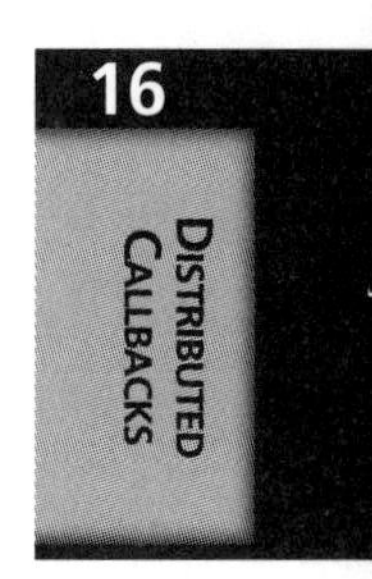

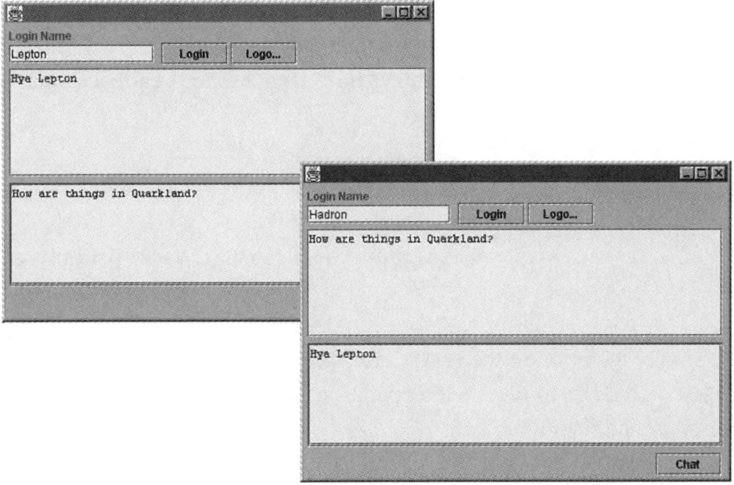

FIGURE 16.1
The chat application.

Let's implement another callback application, this time using OrbixWeb. The use of some ORB application programming interfaces to enable callbacks will differentiate the OrbixWeb implementation from the VisiBroker. A further distinction is the use of asynchronous callbacks in the OrbixWeb application.

Asynchronous Callbacks

The default invocation semantics that CORBA enables is a blocking call from the client to a service. This means that for the duration of the invocation, the client blocks until the service returns from the invocation. Callbacks are one requirement where this type of invocation might be undesirable.

An asynchronous invocation by the client means that the invocation immediately returns from the call, enabling the client to continue with autonomous processing. This is accomplished if operations on the interface are specified as `oneway`. When an operation is specified as being `oneway`, a client that makes the invocation is immediately returned control from the call. The `oneway` calls do have some constraints placed on them. For one, the operations that are specified as being `oneway` cannot return anything to the client. This means that the only type that can be returned is a void. The other restriction is that an `oneway` invocation cannot throw any exception. A service that implements a `oneway` operation is not required to notify the client if the operation succeeds or not.

A simple interface will illustrate how callbacks are accomplished asynchronously. The basic principles are the same as that for the VisiBroker Java implementation. In the VisiBroker application, we leveraged the peer-to-peer nature of CORBA. This enabled us to reverse the roles of clients and servers as and when it suited us. The OrbixWeb application will be a little more "traditional": There will be clearly defined client and server roles. The following interface shows how asynchronous callbacks can be constructed:

```
module Callback{
    interface client{
        void notify(in string message);
    };
    interface server{
        oneway void registerReference(in Callback::client aClient);
    };
};
```

The single operation in the server interface is specified as `oneway`. This enables the `Callback.client` to invoke the operation asynchronously. The next sections implement the server and then the client.

The Interface Implementation

Every client that is interested in having the `CallbackService` object asychronously callback on the registered interface is kept in an instance of `Java.util.Vector`. The `CallbackService` implements the `Callback.server` interface. It also implements the Java `Runnable` interface so that you can execute the service in a thread.

The callback is made in the `run()` method. Every client that is registered with the server object is retrieved and the `notify()` method is invoked on it. This callback from the server does not go through the ORB. The consequence of this aspect is that the `CallbackService` object does not have to retrieve the `Callback.client` interface through a `bind()` or other mechanism. The server can directly invoke the method on the client. The invocation is made in the `run()` method so that it does not interfere with the normal running of the server that host the `CallbackService` object. Listing 16.5 shows the implementation of the asynchronous server.

LISTING 16.5 THE ASYNCHRONOUS SERVER IMPLEMENTATION

```
package Callbacks;
import Callback.*;
import java.util.Vector;
import com.sun.java.swing.*;

public class CallbackService extends
       Callback._serverImplBase implements Runnable{
  private Vector clients;
  private JTextArea DisplayWindow;

  public CallbackService(String name,JTextArea DisplayWindow){
```

```
    super(name);
    clients = new Vector();
    this.DisplayWindow = DisplayWindow;
  }

  public synchronized void registerReference(Callback.client aClient){
    clients.addElement(aClient);
    DisplayWindow.append(aClient.toString() + " registered.");
  }

  public synchronized void run(){
    while(true){
      if(clients.size() > 0){
        for(int i = 0; i <clients.size(); i++){
           Callback.client temp = (Callback.client)clients.elementAt(i);
           temp._notify("Server Notification " + new Integer(i));
        }
      }
    }
  }
}
```

The Server Implementation

The implementation shown in Listing 16.6 is very similar to the other servers that we have implemented using OrbixWeb. The constructor `CallbackServer()` initializes the `CallbackService` object, passing it an instance of the GUI object. `CallbackService` is then executed in an instance of a `Thread` object so that the implementation can execute the callback routines without interfering with the server's execution.

LISTING 16.6 THE CALLBACK SERVER

```
package Callbacks;
import java.util.*;
import IE.Iona.OrbixWeb._OrbixWeb;
import IE.Iona.OrbixWeb._CORBA;
import org.omg.CORBA.ORB;
import com.sun.java.swing.*;

public class CallbackServer implements Runnable{

  CallbackService cs = null;
  JTextArea DisplayWindow = null;

  public void run(){
    org.omg.CORBA.ORB orb = org.omg.CORBA.ORB.init();
```

continues

LISTING 16.6 CONTINUED

```
    try{
       _CORBA.Orbix.impl_is_ready("Callback");
       orb.disconnect(cs);
       System.out.println("Shutting down server...");
    }
    catch(org.omg.CORBA.SystemException se) {
      System.out.println(
        "Exception raised during creation of Callback Server" +
        se.toString());
      System.exit(1);
    }
  }

  public CallbackServer(JTextArea DisplayWindow) {
    this.DisplayWindow = DisplayWindow;
    cs = new CallbackService("Callback",DisplayWindow);
    Thread serviceThread = new Thread(cs);
    serviceThread.start();
    DisplayWindow.append("Server Is Ready \n");
  }
}
```

The final piece of constructing of the callback back-end is to construct a user interface to hold the server objects.

The Callback Server User Interface

The user interface, as shown in Listing 16.7, is a simple `JText` object to display any messages that the service or the server object wants to display. The `CallbackServer` is constructed when the user clicks the Start button. When this event occurs, the `CallbackServer` is constructed and launched in a thread. When the server is up and running, it just waits for a `Callback` client to register its object reference for callback.

LISTING 16.7 THE CALLBACK SERVER USER INTERFACE

```
package Callbacks;

import java.awt.*;
import com.sun.java.swing.*;
import java.awt.event.*;

public class CallbackServerWindow extends JFrame {
  JScrollPane jScrollPane1 = new JScrollPane();
  JTextArea DisplayWindow = new JTextArea();
  JButton StartButton = new JButton();
  CallbackServer cs = null;
```

```
  Thread thread = null;

  public CallbackServerWindow() {
    try  {
      jbInit();
    }
    catch (Exception e) {
      e.printStackTrace();
    }
  }

  public static void main(String[] args) {
    CallbackServerWindow callbackServerWindow1 =
    new CallbackServerWindow();
  }

  private void jbInit() throws Exception {
    this.setTitle("Callback Server Window");
    jScrollPane1.setBounds(new Rectangle(8, 7, 444, 214));
    StartButton.setText("Start");
    StartButton.setBounds(new Rectangle(376, 229, 71, 23));
    StartButton.addMouseListener(new java.awt.event.MouseAdapter() {
      public void mouseClicked(MouseEvent e) {
        StartButton_mouseClicked(e);
      }
    });
    this.getContentPane().setLayout(null);
    this.getContentPane().add(jScrollPane1, null);
    jScrollPane1.getViewport().add(DisplayWindow, null);
    this.getContentPane().add(StartButton, null);
    this.setVisible(true);
  }

  void StartButton_mouseClicked(MouseEvent e) {
    cs = new CallbackServer(DisplayWindow);
    thread = new Thread(cs);
    thread.start();
  }
}
```

We can now construct a client to make the callback on the `CallbackServer`.

The Client Interface Implementation

The client interface has to be implemented as shown in Listing 16.8. This enables the server to make a callback on that interface. It is this interface that is registered with the server.

LISTING 16.8 THE CALLBACK CLIENT

```
package Callbacks;

import com.sun.java.swing.*;
import java.awt.*;
import java.awt.event.*;
import IE.Iona.OrbixWeb._CORBA;
import org.omg.CORBA.SystemException;
class CallbackClient extends Callback._clientImplBase implements Runnable{
   private JTextArea DisplayWindow;

   public CallbackClient(JTextArea DisplayWindow){
    this.DisplayWindow = DisplayWindow;
    this.DisplayWindow.append("Waiting For Callback \n");

    try{
      Callback.server srv = Callback.serverHelper.bind(":Callback");
      srv.registerReference(this);
    }
    catch (SystemException se) {
      System.out.println("Unexpected exception:\n"+ se.toString());
    }
   }

   public void run(){
      try {
        _CORBA.Orbix.processEvents();
      }
      catch (SystemException se) {
        System.out.println("Unexpected exception:\n" + se.toString());
        return;
      }
   }

   public void _notify(String message){
    DisplayWindow.append(message + "\n");
   }
}
```

The first thing that the client object does is acquire the object reference to a `Callback.server`. This is accomplished with the following line of code:

```
Callback.server srv = Callback.serverHelper.bind(":Callback");
```

When this is accomplished, the client registers its own object reference with the server object reference:

```
srv.registerReference(this);
```

When the registration is completed, the core of the client code will be executed. This occurs in the following lines of code, which are executed in the `run()` method of the client code:

```
try {
        _CORBA.Orbix.processEvents();
      }
      catch (SystemException se) {
        System.out.println("Unexpected exception:\n" + se.toString());
        return;
      }
```

`_CORBA.Orbix.processEvents()` waits for incoming events from the `Callback` server. When this occurs, methods on the callback interface on the client side are invoked to notify the client that an event arrived from the server.

Next, we implement a user interface to host the `Callback.client` object.

The Callback Client GUI

The callback client GUI, as shown in Listing 16.9, is very simple. The user interface is very similar to the server user interface. A window is created to display the server callback messages. The user interface button enables a user to click on it to launch the `Client` object on a thread. When that occurs, the client connects to the server and registers its interface to enable the server to make a callback.

LISTING 16.9 THE CALLBACK CLIENT USER INTERFACE

```
package Callbacks;
import com.sun.java.swing.*;
import java.awt.*;
import java.awt.event.*;
import IE.Iona.OrbixWeb._CORBA;
import org.omg.CORBA.SystemException;

public class CallbackClientWindow extends JFrame {
  private CallbackClient cc;
  private Thread thread;

  public CallbackClientWindow() {
    try  {
      jbInit();
    }
    catch (Exception e) {
      e.printStackTrace();
    }
  }

  public static void main(String[] args) {
```

continues

LISTING 16.9 CONTINUED

```
    CallbackClientWindow callbackClientWindow =
                         new CallbackClientWindow();
    callbackClientWindow.invokedStandalone = true;
  }
  private boolean invokedStandalone = false;
  JScrollPane jScrollPane1 = new JScrollPane();
  JTextArea DisplayWindow = new JTextArea();
  JButton ListenButton = new JButton();

  private void jbInit() throws Exception {
    this.getContentPane().setLayout(null);
    this.setTitle("Callback Client Window");
    jScrollPane1.setBounds(new Rectangle(11, 10, 379, 209));
    ListenButton.setText("Listen");
    ListenButton.setBounds(new Rectangle(304, 227, 80, 23));
    ListenButton.addMouseListener(new java.awt.event.MouseAdapter() {
      public void mouseClicked(MouseEvent e) {
        ListenButton_mouseClicked(e);
      }
    });
    this.getContentPane().add(jScrollPane1, null);
    jScrollPane1.getViewport().add(DisplayWindow, null);
    this.getContentPane().add(ListenButton, null);
    this.setVisible(true);
  }

  void ListenButton_mouseClicked(MouseEvent e) {
    cc = new CallbackClient(DisplayWindow);
    thread = new Thread(cc);
    thread.start();
  }
}
```

As you can see, the VisiBroker and OrbixWeb callback strategies are similar.

Summary

Callback is a mechanism that enables coupling of clients and servers in a bidirectional manner. This enables architectures that are driven by both tiers of a client/server relationship. One of the pitfalls of this type of design is that it introduces all sorts of dependencies between the client and server. This can be mitigated to a large extent if the design adheres to a standardized interface throughout the architecture.

Callbacks can be designed as either synchronous or asynchronous callbacks. Both can be used to benefit an architecture. Asynchronous callbacks can be useful when a client needs to autonomously process while it makes an invocation on the server. Asynchronous callbacks, on the other hand, enable a client to wait for a server while the server completes some processing on its end.

CHAPTER 17

VisiBroker Caffeine

In This Chapter

The Caffeine extensions from Visigenic are extensions of the standard CORBA specification. As a product, it is in the forefront of CORBA—Java integration. Application level development is rather cumbersome in C++. In this type of environment, the emphasis is most likely to be on the generation of user interfaces. C++ is my language of choice for general-purpose systems level programming. By this, I mean programming general architectural services. Java, on the other hand, is ideally suited for more general level programming, because it enables you to test your assumptions and show it off to the user.

Just as Caffeine extends CORBA, Caffeine is also an attempt to extend this usefulness of Java to distributed computing. Using Caffeine, you can design and implement CORBA components in Java. The development process using Caffeine works largely like Java RMI. It enables a developer to work with the constructs that Java provides. At any point, if the design requires these components to be distributed, they can use the tools provided with Caffeine.

The Caffeine enhancements come with three components:

- The Java2iiop compiler
- The Java2idl compiler
- The URL Naming facility

Java2iiop

Java2iiop enables an application to work with IIOP-compliant stubs and skeletons. It is ideal for a Java-only implementation. Using Java2iiop, you could pass a Java interface and the compiler would generate IIOP-compliant stubs, skeletons, and support files.

Java2idl

The Java2idl compiler turns normal Java interfaces to idl. If certain constraints are adhered to, the compiler generates OMG IDL. If usage of Java is pushed to constructions that may not have support in IDL, VisiBroker IDL is generated. This idl cannot be used outside the VisiBroker for Java environment.

URL Naming

URL Naming is a nifty feature that enables a Java-based application to refer to an object with an URL.

Java to IIOP

The starting point of Java2iiop is a Java interface. Within this Java interface, you can define a distributable public interface for which you can generate the CORBA support code. The benefit of such a scheme is that an applications developer is working only with Java interfaces, no IDL. As long as you understand one of the major reasons for having OMG IDL, you can use this feature. The OMG IDL is used to provide language independence to CORBA. If there is no IDL, there is no language independence on the fly. Therefore, if Java is the only platform in your distributed application, Java2iiop may not be such a bad thing.

It is possible to generate OMG-compliant IDL using Java2iiop and Java2IDL. Then it stands to reason that it is a lot easier to start with OMG IDL in the first place! I would use Caffeine when OMG IDL is no longer enough to implement all my requirements without undue heartache. Caffeine is an extension to CORBA. As such, it should be used only when standard CORBA is not enough.

For instance, it would be useful to pass objects such as `Vectors` or `Hashtables` between clients and servers. IDL enables you to pass a sequence or an array. For example, a data access server that provides access to databases could find it useful to pass `Hashtables` between server and client.

All Java interfaces must be subclasses of `org.omg.CORBA.Object`. Only such interfaces can be used with Java2iiop. This marker enables the Java2iiop tool to recognize whether an interface is a Caffeine interface. On finding the marker, the compiler generates all the marshaling and demarshaling code. The rest of the development process is mostly typical to CORBA.

This brings up the question: When could I use Caffeine?. Use Caffeine if requirements dictate that the full power and flexibility of Java as a language be utilized for a solution. Such a solution would be an all-Java affair, because the solution would be using IDL that the rest of CORBA would not be able to understand. The following example demonstrates one such use. Before getting into the details of development, let's define a Caffeine interface in Java:

The First step in the Caffeine development process is to define a Java interface that subclasses from org.omg.CORBA.Object:

```
package Java2iiop;

public interface RuntimeInterface extends org.omg.CORBA.Object{

    Object getTableModel();
    Object getJGLContainter();
    Object getGuiObject();
}
```

Note that the interface extends the `org.omg.CORBA.Object`. The interface helps demonstrate a number of things. The first aspect is that all three methods return objects of the type `java.lang.Object`. These will be passed back by value. The three methods are `getTableModel()`, `getJGLContainer()`, and `getGUIObject()`. This means that the states of the objects are transferred back to the client.

The first method, `getTableModel()`, is coded to pass back an instance of `com.sun.java.swing.table.DefaultTableModel`. This object allows an application to set up the data model for a `JTable`. The second method, `getJGLContainer()`, passes back an instance of a `com.objectspace.jgl.Stack`, and the third method, `getGUIObject()` passes an instance of a GUI widget.

NOTE

Keep in mind the semantics of pass-by-value: A copy is passed back, not an object reference. This means that an action on the copy is local and not transferred back to the original.

Implementing a Java2iiop Application

Take the following steps to construct a Java2iiop application:

1. Define a Java interface subclassed from `org.omg.CORBA.Object`.
2. Compile the interface produced in step one using the javac compiler.
3. On the Java bytecode produced by step two, run the Java2iiop compiler. The Java2iiop compiler produces the CORBA stubs and skeletons source files.

   At this point, implementation of the interface can be done as with any other CORBA implementation.
4. Implement the Server.
5. Compile all the source files using the Javac bytecode pre-compiler.
6. Deploy the server.
7. Implement the client to use the server interface.
8. Compile and run the client.

The development process is depicted in Figure 17.1.

The `RuntimeInterface` is designed to enable you to demonstrate a number of things. It enables you to show any type of Java object as a CORBA object. The interface passes three different objects back to the client: a user interface element (through getGUIObject()), a model object that drives a user interface object (through getTableModel()), and a collection object (through getJGLContainer()). The example does not show passing of any business object between client and server, because that feature has been demonstrated adequately using just IDL.

The implementation is shown in Listing 17.1.

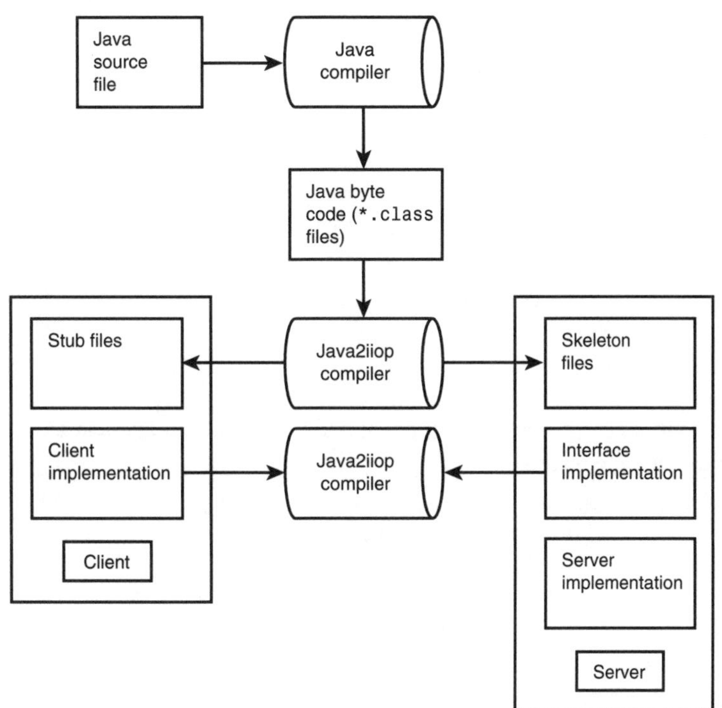

FIGURE 17.1
Implementing the generated interface.

LISTING 17.1 JAVA2IIOP COMPONENT

```
package Java2iiop;
import  com.sun.java.swing.*;

public class DistributedJava extends
       Java2iiop._RuntimeInterfaceImplBase {

  com.objectspace.jgl.Stack stack = null;
  DistributedModel model = null;
  JTextArea gui = null;

public DistributedJava(java.lang.String
```

continues

LISTING 17.1 CONTINUED

```
  name,com.objectspace.jgl.Stack stack,DistributedModel
  model,JTextArea gui) {
      super(name);
      this.stack = stack;
      this.model = model;
      this.gui = gui;
  }

public DistributedJava() {
    super();
  }
  public java.lang.Object getTableModel() {
    return model;
  }
  public java.lang.Object getJGLContainter() {
    return stack;
  }
  public java.lang.Object getGuiObject() {
    return gui;
  }
}
```

The coupling between the component and the rest of the application is implemented with the following constructor:

```
public DistributedJava(java.lang.String name,
        com.objectspace.jgl.Stack stack,
        DistributedModel model,
        JTextArea gui) {

    super(name);
    this.stack = stack;
    this.model = model;
    this.gui = gui;
}
```

The Server class using the component passes the three objects when it instantiates the `DistributedJava` class. These objects are then are passed to a distributed client when it invokes the three methods specified in the `RuntimeInterface` interface. A word on the design of this class: The preceding class has an unpardonable fault. At the end of the day, the class that uses the preceding implementation will have tight coupling as a result of the way the constructor is designed. Consider this question; What would you do if the three objects that are passed to the constructor change their interface? If such issues are a concern of yours, read any good book on design patterns and perhaps some good tomes on OO software metrics.

The rest of the implementation simply passes back the objects that were passed to the component. The three objects will be constructed in the server runtime.

Constructing the Server

For the most part, the server, which is shown in Listing 17.2, is just JFC Swing code. The source file defines two classes: the `orbRuntime` class and the `DistributedModel` class. The former encapsulates the code required for setting up and running the CORBA component. The latter class defines a Datamodel for a `Jtable` that is defined in the runtime. This is the component that is passed back to the client. This enables a client to use the same Datamodel that is being used by the client.

NOTE

Swing uses the Smalltalk-inspired Model View Controller pattern to couple user interfaces to data. Almost all the user interfaces that make up a Swing have an associated `Model` object that encapsulates data. In the previous case, `Jtable` objects have a corresponding `Model` object that is derived from the the `DefaultTableModel` class. In the previous discussion, this object is referred to as the `Datamodel`.

LISTING 17.2 JAVA2IIOP SERVER

```
package Java2iiop;

import java.awt.*;
import java.util.*;
import com.sun.java.swing.table.*;
import com.sun.java.swing.event.TableModelListener;
import com.sun.java.swing.event.TableModelEvent;
import com.sun.java.swing.*;
import com.objectspace.jgl.*;
import java.awt.event.*;

public class DJavaServer extends JFrame {

  JScrollPane jScrollPane1 = new JScrollPane();
  JTextArea GuiObject = new JTextArea();
  JScrollPane jScrollPane2 = new JScrollPane();
  DistributedModel t_tabelModel = new DistributedModel();
  JTable TableObject = new JTable(t_tabelModel);
```

continues

LISTING 17.2 CONTINUED

```
JButton StartButton = new JButton();
JButton StopButton = new JButton();
orbRuntime orb_ = null;
com.objectspace.jgl.Stack t_stackObject = new com.objectspace.jgl.Stack();
String[] arg = null;

public DJavaServer(String[] args) {
  this.addWindowListener(new WindowAdapter() {
  public void windowClosing(WindowEvent e) {System.exit(0);}});

  for(int i=0; i<args.length;i++){
    arg[i] = args[i];
  }

  try  {
    jbInit();
  }
  catch (Exception e) {
    e.printStackTrace();
  }
}

public static void main(String[] args) {
  DJavaServer RuntimeApp = new DJavaServer(args);
}

private void jbInit() throws Exception {
  this.setDefaultCloseOperation(WindowConstants.DISPOSE_ON_CLOSE);
  this.setTitle("Pass By Value Monitor");
  jScrollPane1.setBounds(new Rectangle(6, 127, 415, 112));
  jScrollPane2.setBounds(new Rectangle(7, 5, 413, 120));
  StartButton.setText("jButton1");
  StartButton.setLabel("Start");
  StartButton.setBounds(new Rectangle(274, 246, 71, 23));
  StartButton.addMouseListener(new java.awt.event.MouseAdapter() {
    public void mouseClicked(MouseEvent e) {
      StartButton_mouseClicked;
    }
  });
  StopButton.setText("jButton2");
  StopButton.setLabel("Stop");
  StopButton.setBounds(new Rectangle(349, 246, 71, 23));
  StopButton.addMouseListener(new java.awt.event.MouseAdapter() {
    public void mouseClicked(MouseEvent e) {
      StopButton_mouseClicked;
    }
  });
  this.getContentPane().setLayout(null);
```

```
    this.getContentPane().add(jScrollPane1, null);
    jScrollPane1.getViewport().add(GuiObject, null);
    this.getContentPane().add(jScrollPane2, null);
    jScrollPane2.getViewport().add(TableObject, null);
    this.getContentPane().add(StartButton, null);
    this.getContentPane().add(StopButton, null);

    DistributedModel _model = (DistributedModel)TableObject.getModel();
    java.util.Vector rows = new java.util.Vector();
    String[] temp_ = new String[2];
    temp_[0] = "This Airline";
    temp_[1] = "001992K";
    rows.addElement(temp_);
    _model.addRow(temp_);
    TableObject.setModel(_model);
    TableObject.tableChanged(new TableModelEvent
(_model,t_tabelModel.getRowCount()));
    TableObject.repaint();

    t_stackObject.push(temp_[0]);
    t_stackObject.push(temp_[1]);
        GuiObject.setText("This text is from the remote object");
    this.setVisible(true);
  }

  void StartButton_mouseClicked(MouseEvent e) {
    orb_ = new orbRuntime(arg, t_stackObject, t_tabelModel, GuiObject);
    Thread thread = new Thread(orb_);
    thread.start();
  }

  void StopButton_mouseClicked(MouseEvent e) {
    this.dispose();
  }
}

class DistributedModel extends DefaultTableModel{

  String columns[] =  {"Airline", "FlightNumber"};
  String[] row = new String[0];
  Vector rows = new Vector();

  public DistributedModel(){
  }

  public int getColumnCount(){
    return columns.length;
  }
```

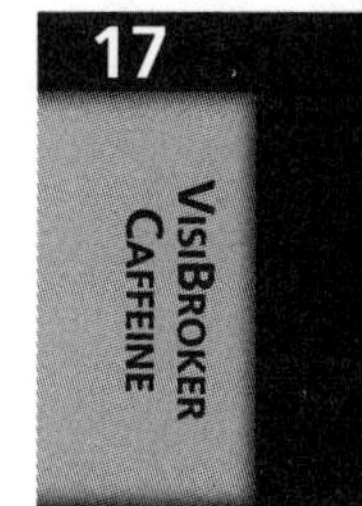

continues

LISTING 17.2 CONTINUED

```
  public int getRowCount(){
    return rows.size();
  }

  public java.lang.Object getValueAt(int row,int column){
    java.lang.Object temp_[] = (String[])rows.elementAt(row);
    return   temp_[column];
  }

  public boolean isCellEditable(int row, int col) {return false;}

  public void setValueAt(java.lang.Object aValue, int row, int column){
    java.lang.Object temp[] = (String[])rows.elementAt(row);
    temp[column] = aValue;
    rows.setElementAt(temp,row);
    fireTableChanged (new TableModelEvent(this,row));
  }

  public String getColumnName(int columnIndex){
    return columns[columnIndex];
  }

  public void addRow(String row[]){
    rows.addElement(row);
  }

  public void removeRow(int index){
    rows.removeElementAt(index);
  }
}

class orbRuntime implements Runnable{

   org.omg.CORBA.BOA boa = null;

   orbRuntime(String[] args,com.objectspace.jgl.Stack
stack,DistributedModel model,JTextArea gui){
    org.omg.CORBA.ORB orb = org.omg.CORBA.ORB.init(args,null);
    boa = orb.BOA_init();
    RuntimeInterface impl = new DistributedJava("Server",stack,model,gui);
    boa.obj_is_ready(impl);
    System.out.println(impl + " is ready.");
   }

   public void run(){

     try{
       boa.impl_is_ready();
     }
```

```
      catch(org.omg.CORBA.SystemException e){
        e.toString();
      }
    }
}
```

The CORBA component is initialized in the constructor for the `orbRuntime`:

```
RuntimeInterface impl = new DistributedJava("Server",stack,model,gui);
```

The three objects initialized by the server are passed in the CORBA component. Because Java2iiop passes objects around by value, the object state as the server initialized them is passed to the client. The Datamodel is initialized with just one row. The stack object contains only one object. The `GuiObject` is initialized with a line of text, `"This text is from the remote object"`. The establishes the state of the `GuiObject`, which is an instance of `JText`.

This ends the implementation of the server object. All that remains is to implement a client that uses the Java2iiop interface.

Implementing a Java2iiop Client

The `Java2iiop` client is like any other CORBA client (see Listing 17.3). The exception is that the objects the client retrieves from the server are used to construct the client-side user interface objects.

LISTING 17.3 JAVA2IIOP CLIENT

```
package Java2iiop;
import java.awt.*;
import java.util.*;
import java.awt.event.*;
import com.sun.java.swing.*;

public class DJClien extends JFrame{

  JScrollPane jScrollPane1 = new JScrollPane();
  JTextArea GuiObject = null;
  DistributedModel t_tabelModel = null;
  JScrollPane jScrollPane2 = new JScrollPane();
  JTable TableObject = new JTable();
  com.objectspace.jgl.Stack t_stackObject = new
com.objectspace.jgl.Stack();

  public DJClien(String[] args) {
```

continues

LISTING 17.3 CONTINUED

```
    this.addWindowListener(new WindowAdapter() {
    public void windowClosing(WindowEvent e) {System.exit(0);}});

    org.omg.CORBA.ORB orb = org.omg.CORBA.ORB.init(args,null);
    Java2iiop.RuntimeInterface remoteObject =
Java2iiop.RuntimeInterfaceHelper.bind(orb);

    try{
      t_tabelModel = (DistributedModel)
 remoteObject.getTableModel();
      TableObject.setModel(t_tabelModel);
      GuiObject = (JTextArea)remoteObject.getGuiObject();
      t_stackObject = (com.objectspace.jgl.Stack)
  remoteObject.getJGLContainter();
       GuiObject.append("\n" + t_stackObject.toString());
    }
    catch(org.omg.CORBA.SystemException e){
      e.toString();
    }
    catch(Exception ex){
      ex.toString();
    }

   try  {
      jbInit();
    }
    catch (Exception e) {
      e.printStackTrace();
    }
   }
   private void jbInit() throws Exception {
     this.setTitle("Pass By Value Client");
     jScrollPane1.setBounds(new Rectangle(6, 127, 415, 112));
     jScrollPane2.setBounds(new Rectangle(7, 5, 413, 120));
     this.getContentPane().setLayout(null);
     this.getContentPane().add(jScrollPane1, null);
     jScrollPane1.getViewport().add(GuiObject, null);
     this.getContentPane().add(jScrollPane2, null);
     jScrollPane2.getViewport().add(TableObject, null);
     this.setVisible(true);
   }

  public static void main(String[] args) {
    DJClien dJClien = new DJClien(args);
  }
```

The client also defines three objects: a `JText` object, a `DistributedModel`, and a JGL stack object. These objects are not constructed by the class itself, but they are constructed by the server object and retrieved by the client:

```
t_tabelModel = (DistributedModel)remoteObject.getTableModel();
   TableObject.setModel(t_tabelModel);
   GuiObject = (JTextArea)remoteObject.getGuiObject();
   t_stackObject = (com.objectspace.jgl.Stack)
   remoteObject.getJGLContainter();
   GuiObject.append("\n" + t_stackObject.toString());
```

All the methods defined by the Java2iiop are specified to return `java.lang.Object`. Therefore, the implementation has to explicitly cast into the desired object. The state of the objects is the same as it was when we initialized the objects on the server side. This means that the state of the object is copied by value over to the client side. This does not mean, however, that modifying the state of the object is transparently transmitted back to the server.

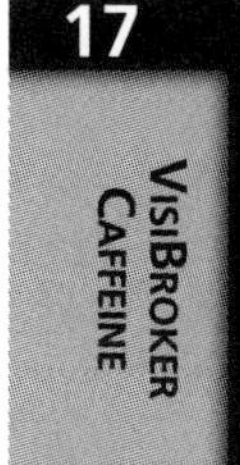

The finished application is shown executing in Figure 17.2.

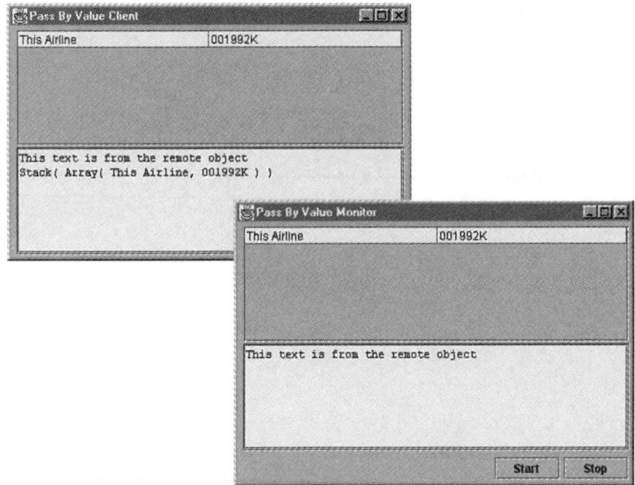

FIGURE 17.2
Java2iiop in action.

If a change of state has to be transmitted back to the server, the design of the implementation has to modified. Such bidirectional communication could be accomplished by callbacks or by implementing a peer-to-peer client/server relationship between the components.

How could an application benefit from Caffeine? Pass-by-value is a very powerful technique. It can be the basis of replicated workflow where document objects are shipped from place to place to alter its state.

Summary

The Caffeine extensions from Visigenic are a powerful extension over the OMG-defined standard for CORBA. If a CORBA application uses only Java, it is a technology that enables CORBA to have pass-by-value semantics. Using pass-by-value, a client can retrieve a server component by value. This enables the state of a component to be distributed as well.

The Caffeine product enables a developer to work entirely in Java. The Java2iiop technology enables a developer to generate iiop compliant from Java interfaces. When this is done, any Java Language construction can be passed between client and server. Care must be taken with such design on two levels: First, it is quite easy to build implementations that can work only with Visigenic. The second, more important pitfall is that a designer might inadvertently introduce multidimensional dependencies between distributed components. An indication of this habit was briefly touched on when an unnecessary coupling was introduced between client and server in the previous implementation.

CHAPTER

VisiBroker SmartStubs

In This Chapter

Interactions between clients and servers are rather simple in their mechanisms. Architecturally, a server is coupled to a skeleton, and a client is connected to a stub. Invocations in either direction are marshaled and demarshaled by these components.

An invocation going in from the client side is marshaled by the stubs and passed to the ORB. A server receiving an invocation receives the invocation after it has been demarshaled by a skeleton. The reverse of this process is done when the server responds to the invocation. VisiBroker enables you to modify the proxy on the client side. SmartStubs are a mechanism by which the stubs on the client side can be modified to interpose between the client and the server.

SmartStubs can intercept the messages before they are marshaled or demarshaled on the client side. The SmartStub, in turn, can invoke the methods on the actual stub that the VisiBroker idl2java pre-compiler generates to make the invocation on the server. The difference is shown in Figures 18.1 and 18.2.

FIGURE 18.1
Application before marshaling.

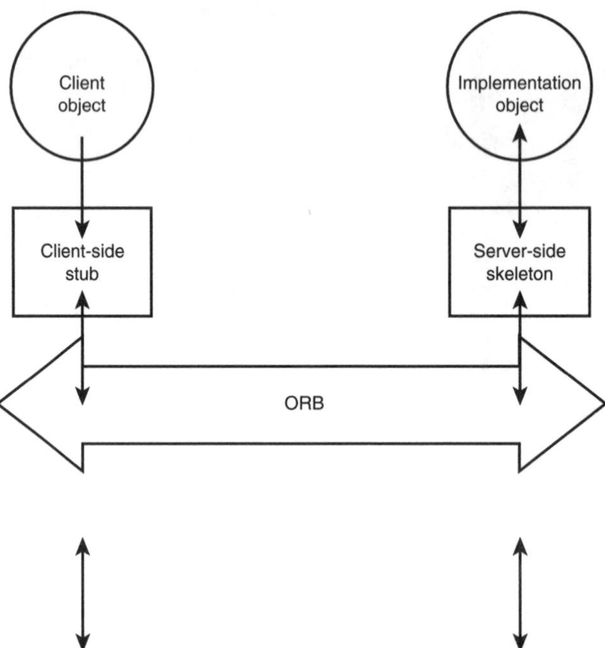

Functionally, SmartStubs and Interceptors seem similar. However, they are different in fundamental respects. VisiBroker Interceptors are more general and low-level than SmartStubs. Interceptors are installed with the ORB. As such, they can be used on the client side or the server side. Interceptors can redirect invocations at a very low level.

FIGURE 18.2
Application after marshaling.

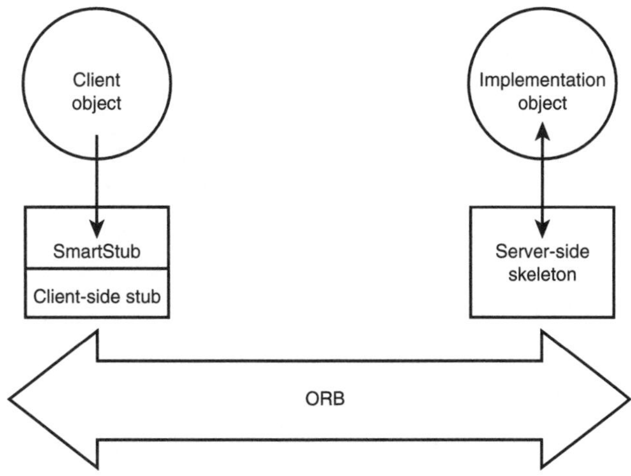

SmartStubs are specific for each interface, whereas Interceptors can be generalized to be useful with any client. As a result, the general areas of using SmartStubs are rather limited. Among the areas where you could use SmartStubs are the following:

- Logging—Potentially any methods you specify in an interface could be designed to be invoked through a SmartStub. This feature can be used to transparently log the client invocations and server responses. This means that when a client invokes a method on an interface, the SmartStub could be designed to intercept the invocation and log information to some form of persistent log. Such logging could be used as a trace log, or perhaps you could establish nonrepudiation parameters on a client requesting a service from a server.
- Network invocations—No matter how efficient the protocol is, it is still slower than a local method call. Proxies, whether normal stubs or SmartStubs are statically bound to a client. If a SmartStub is implemented to cache state information that a server responds with, the next time the client makes a repeat invocation on the server it could have the SmartStub return the cached information. This means that repeated invocations on the server object would be reduced. When an invocation is made by the client, the SmartStub could respond with a cached result. The parameters for what information is cached are, of course, dependent on the fact that the information the server provides is more-or-less invariant in time. If this invariance cannot be established, an expiration time on the state of the cached information would have to be determined to get rid of state information.

  Such a mechanism could be used in a variety of applications. Consider an application that uses real-time data—for example, a weather-monitoring application. This application usually uses polling to retrieve data from the monitoring station.

Polling is usually inefficient because it tends to repeat over a predetermined interval of time. This application can be modified to use SmartStubs to reduce the network communication by providing the client with cached information.

Internals of a SmartStub

Extending a normal stub generated by the VisiBroker idl2java pre-compiler creates SmartStubs. The pre-compiler specifies a switch that generates SmartStub support. Running the following command:

```
prompt$> idl2java -smart_stub file.idl
```

generates SmartStub support with the normal stub class. With this example, you can create a SmartStub by extending the `_st_file` class that the idl2java pre-compiler generates on the interface file. When you extend the normal stub, you can override a method specified in the interface to add value-added support. The methods that are not handled are still handled by the normal stub.

The following interface illustrates how SmartStubs can be used:

```
module smartStub{

    interface proxy{

        void newConnection(in string name);
        string getConnectionName();
        void getParameters(inout string status, out string params);

    };
};
```

This interface needs to be pre-compiled with the idl2Java pre-compiler that VisiBroker provides. Run this interface through the pre-compiler using the following command:

```
prompt$>idl2Java no_tie no_comments smart_stub smartstub.idl
```

The pre-compiler will have generated all the files that are necessary to support CORBA. You subclass and extend the `st_proxy` class. The `st_proxy` class will have support for SmartStubs. Some or all of the operations can be handled by the SmartStub. The mechanism by which SmartStubs are actually constructed is shown later in the chapter.

After the stub has been defined and implemented, it should be installed with a client. VisiBroker provides a set of simple APIs that enables installing SmartStubs with the client:

- `setStubClass()` enables you to install a specific SmartStub with the client. It is possible to have more than one subclass of a stub class. This means that you can have multiple SmartStubs for a given interface. The `setStubClass()` enables you to install a specific SmartStub. For instance, you could design SmartStubs for user profiles so that when a user with a specific user profile uses an application, a SmartStub that corresponds to that profile could be installed on the client side.

NOTE

You can create any number of specific SmartStubs and, depending on the context of the client, you can specify that one or the other is loaded.

- `getStubClass()` enables you to access the current stub that is being used. Perhaps you could run the Java operator `instanceof` to figure out what stub is being used.
- `resetStub()` method releases the SmartStub and relinquishes control to the normal default stub.

These methods are defined on the helper class for the interface. The next code snippet illustrates how SmartStubs can be used with the previous API.

The interface that was specified previously is named `proxy`. The IDL pre-compiler generates a `holder` class for this interface, which is named `proxyholder`. The previously mentioned methods are specified in this class. So if you want to invoke these methods, you could do the following:

```
proxyholder.setStubClass(..);
proxyholder.getStubClass();
proxyholder.resetStub(..)
```

Constructing a SmartStub

Developing a SmartStub is reasonably simple. In terms of this development, the effect on the rest of your normal development is almost zero. You still build your servers the way you always do. The client has a minor change; you use the `setStubClass()` to install the SmartStub with the client.

The interface that was defined previously will now be developed in full to show how SmartStubs can be used. More specifically, you create a simple SmartStub to do logging:

```
module smartStub{

    interface proxy{

        void newConnection(in string name);
        string getConnectionName();
```

```
        void getParameters(inout string status, out string params);

    };
};
```

The interface specifies three methods. The first one passes a string object to the server. For performance reasons it is possible that if the same string is sent to the server, the invocation need not be made. Instead, the proxy could be programmed to do nothing. The second method returns a string. Here, there is a clear case for the invocation not being made at all after the string has been retrieved. The third method is a little trickier. There is one `inout` parameter and an `out` parameter. It can be argued that the server might choose to send over whatever it likes. This means that the SmartStub really cannot cache anything locally, just in case it gets it wrong. On top of all this, the logging bit has to be implemented as well.

You could use the SmartStub to override the `newConnection()` and the `getConnectionName()` methods and not the `getParameters()` method. But for clarity, we will implement support for all the methods.

Run the idl2java pre-compiler on the interface. Here is the exact command:

```
prompt$>idl2java -smart_stub -no_tie -no_comments proxy.idl
```

Implementing the Server

The implementation of the server and client is extremely straightforward:

1. Implement the interface (see Listing 18.1).
2. Implement a server runtime (see Listing 18.2).
3. Construct a SmartStub (see Listing 18.3).
4. Construct a client (see Listing 18.4).

As discussed in the preceding paragraph, you can decide what methods the SmartStub could support. Listing 18.1 shows how you can construct a SmartStub.

LISTING 18.1 THE PROXY INTERFACE IMPLEMENTATION

```
public class Smart extends smartStub._proxyImplBase {

  String connection = null;

  public Smart(java.lang.String name) {
    super(name);
  }
  public Smart() {
    super();
```

```
  }
  public void newConnection(
    java.lang.String name
  ) {
    connection = name;
  }
  public java.lang.String getConnectionNAme() {
    return connection;
  }
  public void getParameters(
    org.omg.CORBA.StringHolder status,
    org.omg.CORBA.StringHolder params
  ) {
      System.out.println(status.value);
      if(status.value.equals("Open")){
        params.value = "Rift:Valley";
      }
      if(status.value.equals("Closed")){
        params.value = "Open:Seseme";
        status.value = "Open";
      }
       System.out.println(params.value);
  }
}
```


The implementation of the interface is standard as advertised. For instance, the `getParameters()` method is passed two `StringHolder` classes. As mentioned in Chapter 5, "Java/IDL Mapping," when complex types are passed as `out` or `inout`, the types map to a holder class. All the implementation does is check out the `inout` parameter, set its state, and then set the state of the `out` parameter.

The server is also standard. It advertises to the VisiBroker ORB that it is ready for business, as shown in Listing 18.2.

LISTING 18.2 THE SMARTSTUB SERVER IMPLEMENTATION

```
package smartStub;

public class StubServer {

  public StubServer(String[] args) {

    org.omg.CORBA.ORB orb = org.omg.CORBA.ORB.init(args,null);
    org.omg.CORBA.BOA boa = orb.BOA_init();
    proxy object = new Smart("StubServer");
    try{
      boa.obj_is_ready(object);
```

continues

LISTING 18.2 CONTINUED

```
      System.out.println(object + " is ready.");
      boa.impl_is_ready();
      boa.deactivate_obj(object);
      orb.shutdown();
    }
    catch(org.omg.CORBA.SystemException e){
      System.out.println(e.toString());
    }
  }

  public static void main(String[] args) {
    StubServer stubServer = new StubServer(args);
  }
}
```

Implementing the SmartStub

You implement the SmartStub by subclassing a normal stub and providing value added support. In this case, the idl2java pre-compiler would generate a class called `_st_proxy`. This class can be extended to create a SmartStub. The implementation is shown in the next section (see Listing 18.3). As discussed earlier, we will support all the operations that we specified in the proxy interface definition. In order to build a SmartStub, you do the following:

1. Create a class that subclasses the appropriate stub class. In this case, you subclass the `st_proxy` class.
2. Override all the methods that you want to handle in the SmartStub from the superclass. In this example, we want to support the entire proxy interface in the SmartStub. This means that we need to override all the methods.

Implementation of the Proxy SmartStub Client

The SmartStub serves two purposes in this case. In the first instance, it logs every invocation. The second purpose is to cache information so that unnecessary invocations to the server are not made. A sample implementation is shown in Listing 18.3.

LISTING 18.3 IMPLEMENTATION OF THE PROXY SMARTSTUB

```
package smartStub;
import org.omg.CORBA.StringHolder;
import java.io.*;
import java.util.*;
```

```
public class SmartProxy extends _st_proxy{
  String ConnectionName = null;
  FileOutputStream logFile = null;
  PrintWriter ios = null;
  Date now = new Date();

  public SmartProxy() {
    try{
      logFile = new FileOutputStream("Log.dat",true);
      ios = new PrintWriter(logFile,true);
    }
    catch(IOException e){
      System.out.println(e.toString());
    }
    ios.println(new String("[Logfile]: Started " + now.toString()));
  }

public void newConnection(String parm1) {
    if(ConnectionName == null){
      super.newConnection( parm1);
      ios.println(now + " [Remote newConnection Called]");
      ConnectionName = parm1;
    }
    else{
      if(parm1.equals(ConnectionName)){
        ios.println(now + " [Local newConnection Called]");
      }
      else{
        ios.println(now + " [Remote newConnection Called]");
        super.newConnection( parm1);
        ConnectionName = parm1;
      }
    }
  }

  public String getConnectionName() {
    if(ConnectionName == null){
      ConnectionName = super.getConnectionName();
      ios.println(now + " [ Remote getConnectionName Called]");
    }
    else{
      ios.println(now + " [ Local getConnectionName Called]");
    }
    return ConnectionName;
  }

  public void getParameters(StringHolder parm1, StringHolder parm2) {
    ios.println(now + " [Remote getParameters Called]");
    super.getParameters( parm1,  parm2);
  }
```

continues

LISTING 18.3 CONTINUED

```
  public void finalize(){
   try{
     ios.close();
     logFile.close();
   }
   catch(IOException e){
     System.out.println(e.toString());
   }
  }
}
```

As you can see, the SmartStub class is a subclass of `_st_proxy`. I have chosen to override every method in the superclass for logging purposes.

Logging is accomplished using the `PrinterWriter` class from the `java.io` package. This is a neat little class that can easily accomplish character output to a file that is opened using the `FileOutputStream` class. One of the reasons why I used this class is that flushing is automatic, which enables new log information to be appended to the end of the file. The logs are initialized in the proxy constructor.

The class maintains a state variable named `ConnectionName`. The client passes this variable to the server in two requests. It first initializes the server with a connection string. The server maintains this string. When the client requests this string, the server returns the same string the client registered with the server. This is a contrived but simple example that seeks to illustrate when to use caching.

Caching is always a useful technique in CORBA. There are a number of areas where caching can be used productively. The ideal place to think about caching is in relationship to the number of network connections a client has to use to get a service. When repeated connections are required, you can cache the information so that the overhead of a network call is minimized.

Let us look at the code a little closer for the `newConnection()` method:

```
public void newConnection(String parm1) {
    if(ConnectionName == null){
      super.newConnection( parm1);
      ios.println(now + " [Remote newConnection Called]");
      ConnectionName = parm1;
    }
    else{
      if(parm1.equals(ConnectionName)){
        ios.println(now + " [Local newConnection Called]");
      }
      else{
```

```
            ios.println(now + " [Remote newConnection Called]");
            super.newConnection( parm1);
            ConnectionName = parm1;
        }
    }
}
```

The first thing the SmartStub checks for is whether its own state variable is initialized. If it is not, it invokes the `newConnection()` method on the server. It logs the invocation and then initializes its own state variable with the one the client has passed to the server. This is essentially what the server is doing. So the state of the server object is mirrored by the SmartStub. On the other hand, if the local state variable is initialized, the stub checks whether the new string that is passed to the server is the same as before. Only if it is a new string does the stub pass the invocation to the normal stub. Otherwise, it does nothing. Whenever an invocation is made on the server, the stub always resets its own local variable to the string that is being passed to the server.

The `getConnectionName()` on the server is essentially the connection string the client passes to the server when it invokes `newConnection` on the server. Because this state is mirrored in the stub, the implementation calls `getConnectionName()` only if the stub's state does not mirror that of the server object.

The `getParameters()` is not cached, because the state of the server cannot be mirrored on the SmartStub. This essentially means that the server's state, as far as this method is concerned, cannot be mirrored. Therefore, this method is always passed on to the normal stub. The only thing the SmartStub does here is log the invocation.

That completes the implementation of the SmartStub. Now let us look at the implementation of the client.

The only difference between normal clients and a client that uses a SmartStub is that a SmartStub has to be installed, as shown in Listing 18.4.

LISTING 18.4 IMPLEMENTATION OF THE PROXY SMART CLIENT

```
package smartStub;

public class ProxyClient {

  public ProxyClient(String[] args) {
    proxy remoteObject = null;
    try{
      proxyHelper.setStubClass(SmartProxy.class);
      org.omg.CORBA.ORB orb = org.omg.CORBA.ORB.init(args,null);
      remoteObject = proxyHelper.bind(orb,"StubServer");
```

continues

LISTING 18.4 CONTINUED

```
    }
     catch(org.omg.CORBA.SystemException e){
      System.out.println(e.toString());
    }
    try{
      remoteObject.newConnection("scot:tiger");
      String connection = remoteObject.getConnectionNAme();
      for(int i = 0; i<3; i++){
        remoteObject.newConnection("scot:tiger");
      }
    }
    catch(org.omg.CORBA.SystemException e){
      System.out.println(e.toString());
    }

    try{
      org.omg.CORBA.StringHolder status = new
org.omg.CORBA.StringHolder();
      status.value = new String("Open");
      org.omg.CORBA.StringHolder params = new
org.omg.CORBA.StringHolder();

      remoteObject.getParameters(status,params);
      System.out.println(status.value);
      System.out.println(params.value);
    }
     catch(org.omg.CORBA.SystemException e){
      System.out.println("Holder " + e.toString());
    }

  }

  public static void main(String[] args) {
    ProxyClient proxyClient = new ProxyClient(args);
  }
}
```

The following is the crucial line in Listing 18.4:

```
proxyHelper.setStubClass(SmartProxy.class)
```

This is executed before the normal initialization of the client. Once this has been done, the client can be implemented as usual. The implementation invokes `newConnection()` with the same parameter, `scot:tiger`, three times. The first time, the SmartStub makes a remote call. Additional times, the calls won't be made on the server object. This should be evident from this log, which is shown for a sample run:

```
[Logfile]: Started Wed Sep 02 20:29:25 GMT+00:00 1998
Wed Sep 02 20:29:25 GMT+00:00 1998 [Remote newConnection Called]
Wed Sep 02 20:29:25 GMT+00:00 1998 [Local getConnectionName Called]
Wed Sep 02 20:29:25 GMT+00:00 1998 [Local newConnection Called]
Wed Sep 02 20:29:25 GMT+00:00 1998 [Local newConnection Called]
Wed Sep 02 20:29:25 GMT+00:00 1998 [Local newConnection Called]
Wed Sep 02 20:29:25 GMT+00:00 1998 [Remote getParameters Called]
```

As you can see, the `newConnection()` is made on the remote object only once. When the SmartStub is installed on the client side, all invocations the client makes go through the stub. In the context of this implementation, all the methods that the service-side component exposes are intercepted by the SmartStub and "value" is added to the implementation. In the implementation, value-added service is twofold. The first is in logging of invocations into a file. The second is that network connections are minimized. The latter enables a more responsive performance for the client.

Summary

SmartStubs are a VisiBroker feature that enables a developer to add value to the client side of a CORBA client/server interaction. Unlike VisiBroker Interceptor or Orbix filters, SmartStubs are used only on the client side. SmartStubs enable a developer to extend the default stub that is statically linked to a client. These extensions can take a number of forms. They can be used for caching state information that is long-lived. Caching minimizes the quantum of network traffic. Logging is another feature that is enabled using SmartStubs. Logging on the client side enables a developer to record various information that could prove useful for fault recovery or security audit.

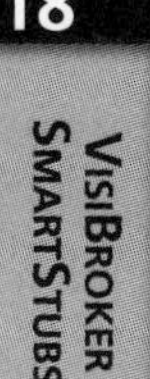

CHAPTER 19

Handling Distributed Events

IN THIS CHAPTER

VisiBroker provides an elegant event-handling mechanism that will notify clients and server objects when a system event occurs. The event-handling mechanism is similar to the concept of VisiBroker Interceptors except for the nature of events that are handled.

VisiBroker specifies two types of event handlers: one for the client side and one for the server side. In the context of these events, the client can handle certain types of events, and the server is capable of handling different kinds of events. The process of creating a handler is the same for both the server and the client.

Specify and implement a communications event handler class. Within this class, you can override any of the allowed methods, depending on where you intend to install the event handler. Either the server side or the client side handler can handle the events shown in Table 19.1.

TABLE 19.1 EVENT TYPES

Client-Side Events	*Server-Side Events*
Successful Bind	Bind Requested
Bind Unsuccessful	Remove Bind Requested
Server Abort	Client Abort
Successful Rebind	Pre-Method Invocation
Unsuccessful Rebind Attempt	Post-Method

Client-Side Event Handler

A client-side event handler can be constructed by implementing a class that is derived from the `ClientEventHandler` interface. After the implementation is completed, the handler has to be registered with the underlying ORB so that notifications can be forwarded to the handler host for further action. A `ClientEventHandler` has to be registered for a specific ORB object. When an event is triggered, the ORB will invoke the handler to handle the event.

The client interface corresponds to the left column of Table 19.1. The methods that are specified for the client do seem rather limiting. But for all intents and purposes, that is all the client really needs in terms of how this situation can be handled.

The event handler is primarily intended to provide connection information to the client. This provides a mechanism to enable logging and auditing functions on the client side. The methods that have to be overriden correspond to the list of events shown in Table 19.1. The methods that the `ClientEventHandler` has to override provide the following as a parameter:

```
struct ConnectionInfo{
    string hostname;
    long port;
};
```

This structure is passed as a parameter into the methods on the client side. It can be used to figure out rudimentary information about the requested connection. Listing 19.1 illustrates how a `ClientEventHandler` can be built.

LISTING 19.1 CLIENT EVENT HANDLER

```
import com.visigenic.vbroker.interceptor.*;

class SimpleClientEventHandler implements ClientEventHandler {

  private String Handler_name;

  MyClientEventHandler(String name) {
 Handler_name = name;
  }

  public void bind_succeeded(org.omg.CORBA.Object obj,
        ConnectionInfo info) {
    System.out.println(_name + ": bind_succeeded: " +
        obj + " info: " + toString(info));
  }

  public void bind_failed(org.omg.CORBA.Object obj) {
    System.out.println(_name + ": bind_failed: " + obj);
  }

  public void server_aborted(org.omg.CORBA.Object obj) {
    System.out.println(_name + ": server_aborted: " + obj);
  }

  public void rebind_succeeded(org.omg.CORBA.Object obj,
        ConnectionInfo info) {
    System.out.println(_name + ": rebind_succeeded: " +
        obj + " info: " + toString(info));
  }

  public void rebind_failed(org.omg.CORBA.Object obj) {
    System.out.println(_name + ": rebind_failed: " + obj);
  }

  private String toString(ConnectionInfo info) {
    return "ConnectionInfo[hostname=" + info.hostname +
      ",port=" + info.port + "]";
  }

}
```

In Listing 19.1, all the methods of the `ClientEventHandler` are overridden. The implementation just outputs the connection information to the standard I/O terminal. The `org.omg.CORBA.Object` that is passed as a parameter into some of the methods is the target object on which some operation was attempted.

The Registration Interface

With the `ClientEventHandler` built, it is necessary to register the handler. This is accomplished by using the services of the `HandlerRegistry` interface. It provides a number of operations that can be used to register a `Handler`. The interface is given in full in Listing 19.2.

LISTING 19.2 REGISTRATION INTERFACE

```
interface HandlerRegistry {
void reg_obj_client_handler(
in Object obj,
in  interceptor ClientEventHandler handler
)
raises(
 interceptor HandlerExists,
 interceptor InvalidObject
);
void reg_glob_client_handler(
in  interceptor ClientEventHandler handler
)
raises(
 interceptor HandlerExists
);
void reg_obj_impl_handler(
in Object obj,
in  interceptor ImplEventHandler handler
)
raises(
 interceptor HandlerExists,
 interceptor InvalidObject
);
void reg_glob_impl_handler(
in  interceptor ImplEventHandler handler
)
raises(
 interceptor HandlerExists
);
void unreg_obj_client_handler(
in Object obj
)
raises(
 interceptor NoHandler,
```

```
 interceptor InvalidObject
);
void unreg_glob_client_handler(
)
raises(
 interceptor NoHandler
);
void unreg_obj_impl_handler(
in Object obj
)
raises(
 interceptor NoHandler,
 interceptor InvalidObject
);
void unreg_glob_impl_handler(
)
raises(
 interceptor NoHandler
);
 interceptor ConnectionInfo get_client_info(
in Object obj
);
};
```

The interface in Listing 19.2 is used by both the client and the server objects for handler administration. Four of the methods correspond to the client-side requirements, and the other four provide support for the server side. The client-side operations are the ones with the word `client` in the names of the operations. Server-side handler operations have the word `impl` in their names.

A client can register the handlers two ways. It can add handler support for one object that is a `ClientEventHandler` for a single object. VisiBroker also enables a client to have a single handler registered for all the objects that it chooses to communicate with.

If the client needs to have support for monitoring events for just one object reference, it can use the `reg_obj_client_handler()` operation. When using this method, the client has to pass the instance of the handler and the reference to the remote object. Only a single handler can be registered for the object at any given time.

On the other end, an implementation can register a single handler for all the objects the client communicates with. Such a handler is called a *global handler*. This type of handler is registered using the `reg_glob_client_handler()` operation. Just like the per-object event handler, only one global event handler can exist at any given time.

After the objects are registered, they need to be unregistered. This is accomplished by using the following API:

`unreg_obj_client_handler()` and `unreg_glob_client_handler()`.

The former unregisters an object event handler, and the latter unregisters a global event handler.

Installing a Handler

The following client implementation is taken from Chapter 20, "VisiBroker Interceptors." Because, technically, `EventHandlers` are the same as `Interceptors`, it would be nice to show both `Interceptors` and the `ClientEventHandler` side by side.

The client has to be modified. The difference between `Interceptors` and `EventHandlers` is highlighted in bold in Listing 19.3.

LISTING 19.3 CLIENT `Handler` IMPLEMENTATION

```
package Interceptor;

public class FilterClient {

   public static void main(String[] args) {
    org.omg.CORBA.ORB orb = org.omg.CORBA.ORB.init(args,null);

    HandlerRegistry registry = HandlerRegistryHelper.narrow(o
        rb.resolve_initial_references("HandlerRegistry"));
SimpleClientEventHandler handler =
        new SimpleClientEventHandler("GlobalClientHandler");
registry.reg_glob_client_handler(handler);

    Filter Global_filter = FilterHelper.bind(orb, "Filter");
Global_filter.foo((short)1002);

SimpleClientEventHandler("ObjectClientHandler");
registry.reg_glob_client_handler(handler);
    Filter Object_filter = FilterHelper.bind(orb, "Filter");
 Object_filter.foo((short)1002);
   }
}
```

The handler instance is retrieved by invoking `orb.resolve_initial_references()`. When the instance of the `HandlerRegistry` is retrieved, the appropriate API methods, which were discussed earlier in the chapter, can be used to administer the client-side handler.

Server-Side Handlers

On the server side, as on the client side, an object reference can register server-side handlers with the ORB. The administration process is on the same object as for the client, on the `HandlerRegistry` object.

The handler on the server side has to be subclassed from `ImplEventHandler`. The following methods are provided for the subclasses to override:

```
interface ImplEventHandler {

  public void bind(ConnectionInfo info,
org.omg.CORBA.Principal princ, org.omg.CORBA.Object obj) ;
  public void unbind(ConnectionInfo info,
        org.omg.CORBA.Principal princ, org.omg.CORBA.Object obj);


  public void client_aborted(ConnectionInfo info,
        org.omg.CORBA.Object obj);

  public void pre_method(ConnectionInfo info,
        org.omg.CORBA.Principal princ,
        String  operation_name, org.omg.CORBA.Object obj) ;

  public void post_method(ConnectionInfo info,
        org.omg.CORBA.Principal princ,
        String  operation_name, org.omg.CORBA.Object obj) ;

  public void post_method_exception(ConnectionInfo info,
        org.omg.CORBA.Principal princ,
        String  operation_name, String exception_rep_id,
        org.omg.CORBA.Object obj);
}
```

The most interesting operations are `pre_method()` and `post_method()`. The `pre_method()` operation is the handler that is invoked by the ORB when a client makes an invocation on the implementation. This handler invocation occurs before the action object reference is called.

The `post_method()` is called after the invocation of the server by a client. The most important parameter in both the methods is the `Principal`. This object encapsulates the information like the method name and a reference of the object are all passed to this method. This enables the server handler to determine what method is being invoked by the client. Along with the name of the method, any parameter that is passed into the method can also be determined. Listing 19.4 implements the server object.

LISTING 19.4 IMPLEMENTING THE SERVER OBJECT

```
class MyImplEventHandler implements ImplEventHandler {

  private String _name;

  MyImplEventHandler(String name) {
```

continues

LISTING 19.4 CONTINUED

```
    _name = name;
  }

  public void bind(ConnectionInfo info,
        org.omg.CORBA.Principal princ, org.omg.CORBA.Object obj) {
    System.out.println(_name + ": bind: " +
               "\n\tinfo=" + toString(info) +
               "\n\tprincipal=" + princ +
               "\n\tobject=" + obj._repository_id());
  }

  public void unbind(ConnectionInfo info,
        org.omg.CORBA.Principal princ, org.omg.CORBA.Object obj) {
    System.out.println(_name + ": unbind: " +
               "\n\tinfo=" + toString(info) +
               "\n\tprincipal=" + princ +
               "\n\tobject=" + obj._repository_id());
  }

  public void client_aborted(ConnectionInfo info,
        org.omg.CORBA.Object obj) {
    System.out.println(_name + ": client_aborted: " +
               "\n\tinfo=" + toString(info) +
               "\n\tobject=" + obj._repository_id());
  }

  public void pre_method(ConnectionInfo info,
        org.omg.CORBA.Principal princ, String  operation_name,
        org.omg.CORBA.Object obj) {
    System.out.println(_name + ": pre_method: " +
               "\n\tinfo=" + toString(info) +
               "\n\tprincipal=" + princ +
               "\n\toperation=" + operation_name +
               "\n\tobject=" + obj._repository_id());
  }

  public void post_method(ConnectionInfo info,
        org.omg.CORBA.Principal princ,
        String  operation_name, org.omg.CORBA.Object obj) {
    System.out.println(_name + ": post_method: " +
               "\n\tinfo=" + toString(info) +
               "\n\tprincipal=" + princ +
               "\n\toperation=" + operation_name +
               "\n\tobject=" + obj._repository_id());
  }

  public void post_method_exception(ConnectionInfo info,
        org.omg.CORBA.Principal princ,
        String  operation_name, String exception_rep_id,
```

```
        org.omg.CORBA.Object obj) {
    System.out.println(_name + ": post_method_exception: " +
                "\n\tinfo=" + toString(info) +
                "\n\tprincipal=" + princ +
                "\n\toperation=" + operation_name +
                "\n\texception=" + exception_rep_id +
                "\n\tobject=" + obj._repository_id());
  }

  private String toString(ConnectionInfo info) {
    return "ConnectionInfo[hostname=" + info.hostname +
      ",port=" + info.port + "]";
  }
}
```

Just as with the client, the object of Listing 19.4 is to show the API of the handler. As with the client, the code for the server only outputs to the standard I/O.

As with the client object, the handler has to be registered with the ORB. The registration is shown in Listing 19.5.

LISTING 19.5 FILTER SERVER IMPLEMENTATION

```
package Interceptor;

public class FilterServer {
  org.omg.CORBA.ORB orb_ = null;
  org.omg.CORBA.BOA boa_  = null;

  public FilterServer(String[] args) {
    orb_ = org.omg.CORBA.ORB.init(args,null);
    Init i = new Init();
    i.install(orb_,null);
    boa_ = orb_.BOA_init();
    Filter filter = new FilterObject("Filter");
    try{
      boa_.obj_is_ready(filter);
      System.out.println(filter + " is ready.");
      boa_.impl_is_ready();
      boa_.deactivate_obj(filter);
    }
    catch(org.omg.CORBA.SystemException ex){
      System.out.println(ex.toString());
    }
  }

  public static void main(String[] args) {
```

continues

LISTING 19.5 CONTINUED

```
    FilterServer filterServer = new FilterServer(args);
  }
}
```

In this listing, most of the code is typical for a CORBA server. The only distinction is shown in the following two lines of code:

```
        Init i = new Init();
i.install(orb_,null);
```

In the first line, an instance of the `Init` class is instantiated. This class is responsible for installing the server-side handler with the ORB. Its functions are similar to that of the `Handler` listed in Listing 19.6.

LISTING 19.6 SERVER `Handler` IMPLEMENTATION

```
package Interceptor;
import com.visigenic.vbroker.interceptor.*;
import com.visigenic.vbroker.orb.*;
import java.util.*;

public class Init {

  public void init(org.omg.CORBA.ORB orb, Properties properties){
      System.out.println("Installing Interceptors");
      ChainServerInterceptorFactory serverFactory = null;
      try{
        org.omg.CORBA.Object obj =
       orb.resolve_initial_references("ChainServerInterceptorFactory");
        serverFactory = ChainServerInterceptorFactoryHelper.narrow(obj);

        serverFactory.add(new Interceptor.ServerFilterFactory());
      }
      catch(org.omg.CORBA.ORBPackage.InvalidName e){
        System.out.println(e.toString());
     }
  }
}
```

The installation of the handler is given in the following line of code:

```
serverFactory.add(new Interceptor.ServerFilterFactory());
```

The code in Listing 19.6 initializes the server object as in Listing 19.3, with the slight complication of initializing the `Handler` object and registering them with the ORB.

Summary

The VisiBroker distributed events are a mechanism that enables clients and servers to respond to various predefined events that take place on the client side and the server side. These events mainly indicate when an ORB-level event takes place. These events are the request to bind or remove a bind. These events can also give indications as to the state of the server process or the client process.

These event handlers can be attached either on the client side or the server side. The main purpose of these events is to allow preprocessing before and/or after these predefined events take place. This would enable the implementations to perform routines such as logging and security audits.

VisiBroker Interceptors

IN THIS CHAPTER

VisiBroker interceptors are filter objects that, when deployed, act as sieves through which invocations to clients or servers pass. These messages may be viewed or altered as they pass through the interceptor. The benefit of an interceptor is that it enables your applications to view how an ORB processes a request. This feature might be of benefit in the following ways:

- Security measures, in terms of access privileges, could be controlled through an interceptor. This could enable the design of a message-based Access Control List implementation strategy.
- Low-level load balancing could be implemented using interceptors. Depending on load constraints imposed on a server, invocations could be forwarded to alternate instances of a CORBA server running in a cluster.

NOTE

Designing an interceptor for load balancing can be effective only in proportion to its statelessness. If an interceptor has to manage its state as well, design would probably dictate a load balance agent for an interceptor. The more stateless an interceptor is, the more scalable it will be in terms of handling client requests.

- Availability and fault tolerance issues could be designed into an interceptor. For designs where these quality-of-service issues are important, an interceptor could redirect requests for a server that is unavailable to one that is available.
- Performance could be monitored to control the constraints of load balancing. An interceptor can be implemented to log invocations to servers and from clients. Load balancing schemes can be devised based on the analysis results of the logs.
- An interceptor could modify the message. This capability can be useful in low-level encryption of the messages. This methodology can be used over and above the facilities provided by secure socket layers.

The most important aspect of an interceptor is the fact that it is essentially a very low-level component. This means that servers and clients are oblivious to its presence. The most powerful feature of the interceptor is that it can can be used to modify the very essence of client/server interactions at a basic semantic level. Power is only one side of the coin. With power comes responsibility.

Client/server programming, especially the CORBA kind, is about *programming by contract*, which means that a server is contractually bound to provide services that it advertises through its interfaces. An interceptor can be juxtaposed on the server to modify this contract—hence its semantics. A careless interceptor can render a contract useless.

Types of Interceptors

There are essentially three basic types of interceptor that a developer can inherit and/or extend:

- Server interceptor

  A *server interceptor* is an interceptor that works on the server side. Invocations coming in from a client to a server can be intercepted to perform functions that you want the interceptor to do. These could be any one of the areas where an interceptor can be used.
- Client interceptor

  A *client interceptor* is analogous to the server interceptor except it is installed on the client side. This interceptor can filter both outgoing invocations as well as incoming messages on the client side.
- Bind interceptor

  Whenever a bind or associated method is called, the *bind interceptor* intercedes on behalf of the invocation. At this point, an interceptor can be used to design a low-level access control list–based service for your applications.

Interceptor APIs are mostly defined to take `in` parameters. These parameters are passed to the interceptors from the ORB. Interceptor APIs are also provided with `inout` parameters that allow bidirectional communication between the ORB and the interceptors. These are especially powerful because they provide a mechanism for directly interacting with the ORB messages themselves.

Interceptor APIs

Let us now look at some of the important APIs for each of the interceptor classes. The APIs can be extended from the default interceptor classes to enable the developer to implement specific interceptor behavior.

`ServerInterceptor` Class

The `ServerInterceptor` methods are invoked on the server by the ORB when client requests are made:

```
public abstract IOR locate(int req_id, byte object_key[],
                                        Closure closure)
```

The `locate()` method in the interceptor is called whenever the client uses an API such as `bind()` to locate and bind to the object. This is a useful method to use for load balancing by forwarding the request to another object and returning the IOR:

```
public abstract InputStream receive_request(
RequestHeader hdr,
ObjectHolder target,
InputStream buf,
```

```
Closure closure
)
```

When a client sends a message to the server, the ORB will invoke this method in the interceptor. Among other things, the method contains all the objects required to make sense of the invocations. The `RequestHeader` encapsulates the GIOP message header and the `InputStream` encapsulates the IIOP message stream. The `ObjectHolder` hides the `out` and `inout` parameters that are passed by the client to the server. Using these parameters, the interceptor can determine the nature of the invocation:

```
public abstract void prepare_reply(RequestHeader hdr,
                                   ReplyHeaderHolder reply,
                                   Object target,
                                   Closure closure)
```

Just as the `receive_request()` in invoked by the ORB on the interceptor when a client makes an invocation, the `prepare_reply()` is invoked on the interceptor before the response from the server is marshaled back to the client. Nonrepudiation, in the context of security, is very important to CORBA. This means that neither the client nor a server should be able to deny services rendered or received. As far as the server is concerned, an interceptor can be designed to log that a server did respond as advertised back to the client:

```
public abstract OutputStream send_reply(RequestHeader
                                  reqHdr,
                                        ReplyHeader hdr,
                                        Object target,
                                        OutputStream buf,
                                        Environment env,
                                        Closure closure)
```

This method is analogous to `receive_request()` in the number of parameters. The `send_reply()` contains parameters referring to the marshaled messages going back to the client. It also contains information about the intended target and the environment object that contains exception information:

```
public void request_completed(RequestHeader hdr,
                              Object target,
                               Closure closure)
```

The `request_completed()` method is invoked upon successful execution of the `send_reply()` method:

```
public abstract void shutdown(ShutdownReason reason)
```

The ORB will invoke this method on the interceptor when a server shuts down.

ClientInterceptor Class

The `ClientInterceptor` methods are invoked by the ORB on the client side when requests are made to the server:

```
public abstract void prepare_request( inout
    RequestHeader hdr,
        Closure closure );
```

This method is invoked by the ORB during the preparation of the request. This method can be used to modify the request header before the request is received by the server:

```
public abstract OutputStream send_request(RequestHeader hdr,
                                          OutputStream buf,
                                          Closure closure );
```

The `send_request method()` is invoked by the ORB before the request is sent. This method can be used to initiate such actions as logging, or be used to make modifications to the `InputStream`:

```
public abstract void receive_reply(ReplyHeader hdr,
                                   InputStream buf,
                                   Environment env,
                                   Closure closure);
```

This `receive_reply` method is invoked when the request is received by the ORB. This method can also be used to modify the contents of the `InputStream` before it is passed on to the server.

BindInterceptor Class

The `BindInterceptor` methods are invoked by the ORB whenever a `bind()` or `rebind()` request is made by the client to the server:

```
public abstract boolean bind(IOR ior,
                             Object object,
                             Closure closure);
```

This method is invoked just prior to the binding of a server object. This method can use the IOR to determine which server object to bind to. A developer can also use this method to monitor binding time to resolve potential bottlenecks in the system.

The `bind_succeeded()` method:

```
public abstract void bind_succeeded(IOR ior,
                                    Object object,
                                    Closure closure)
```

is invoked by the ORB whenever the client successfully binds to the server. This method does not return anything, and it is typically used for notification.

The `bind_failed()` method:

```
public abstract boolean boolean bind_failed(    IOR ior,
                                           Object object,
                                           Closure closure);
```

is invoked by the ORB whenever the client fails to bind to the server. This method can be used to modify the binding request so that the client can bind to an alternate object.

The `rebind()` method:

```
public abstract boolean rebind(IOR ior,
                               Object object,
                               Closure closure);
```

is invoked just prior to rebinding to an object. It can be used when a developer wants to modify the standard `rebind()` done by the ORB.

Constructing a ServerInterceptor

This section will construct a server-side interceptor. The implementation of client-side and bind interceptors is similar in methodology, differing only in the semantics of the classes that are used.

The `ServerInterceptor` interface is an abstract interface that must be implemented to create an interceptor. We will attempt to override only the methods that I have elaborated for the `ServerInterceptor` class. Visigenic provides default interceptor classes that may be reused through extension rather that using the interface. This would enable you to override only the methods that I elaborated previously.

The interceptor demonstration is going to use a very simple interface to demonstrate how it is going to work:

```
module Interceptor
    interface Filter{
        void foo(in short in_value);
    };
};
```

The interface is extremely trivial. Run the interface through the VisiBroker IDL pre-compiler to generate all the support files. The implementation of the Filter interface is equally simple. This is shown in Listing 20.1.

LISTING 20.1 `FilterObject` **IMPLEMENTATION**

```
package Interceptor;
public class FilterObject extends Interceptor._FilterImplBase {
  private short mine = 0;
  public FilterObject(java.lang.String name) {
    super(name);
  }
  public FilterObject() {
    super();
  }
  public void foo(
```

```
    short in_value
  ) {
    mine = in_value;
  }
}
```

The `foo()` method does not do anything except set its own instance variable, `mine`, to the value passed to it.

Critical about interceptors is the fact that they can be used with minimal changes to the server implementation. Before doing that, let's implement the `ServerInterceptor` and install it with the ORB.

First, you implement the interceptor and name it `ServerFilter`. This can be easily accomplished by subclassing the `DefaultServerInterceptor` class provided by Visigenic. The benefit of doing this rather than implementing the `ServerInterceptor` interface is that you don't need to implement all the methods specified in the `DefaultServerInterceptor` class—just the ones you are interested in. The implementation of the interceptor is shown in Listing 20.2.

LISTING 20.2 `ServerFilter` **IMPLEMENTATION**

```
package Interceptor;

import com.visigenic.vbroker.interceptor.*;
import com.visigenic.vbroker.IOP.IOR;
import
com.visigenic.vbroker.interceptor.ServerInterceptorPackage.ShutdownReason;
import org.omg.CORBA.portable.*;
import com.visigenic.vbroker.GIOP.*;
import org.omg.CORBA.Principal;

public class ServerFilter extends DefaultServerInterceptor {

  public ServerFilter(){
    System.out.println("Filter Instantiated");
  }

  public IOR locate(int parm1, byte[] parm2, Closure parm3) {
    System.out.println("[FILTER] locate Invoked: ");
    return null;
  }

  public void shutdown(ShutdownReason parm1) {
    System.out.println(
        "[FILTER] shutdown invoked: " + "Reason is " + parm1.toString());
  }
```

continues

LISTING 20.2 CONTINUED

```
  public InputStream receive_request(
        RequestHeader hdr,
        org.omg.CORBA.ObjectHolder target,
        InputStream buf, Closure closure){

     System.out.println("[FILTER] receive_request invoked");
     System.out.println("[FILTER] Operation " +
        hdr.operation + "'s services requested");
     System.out.println("[FILTER] receive_request invoked on "
        + target.value.toString());
     System.out.println("[FILTER] " + hdr.operation +
        " passed " + new Short(buf.read_short()).toString());
     return null;
  }

  public void prepare_reply(
        RequestHeader hdr,
        ReplyHeaderHolder reply,
        org.omg.CORBA.Object target,
        Closure closure){

    System.out.println("[FILTER] Preparing to return Invocation ");
  }

  public org.omg.CORBA.portable.OutputStream send_reply(
        RequestHeader reqHdr,
        ReplyHeader hdr,
        org.omg.CORBA.Object target,
        OutputStream buf,
        org.omg.CORBA.Environment env,
        Closure closure){

     System.out.println("[FILTER] Return Marshal Of Invocation Complete
");
    return null;
  }

  public void request_completed(
        RequestHeader reqHdr,
        org.omg.CORBA.Object target,
        Closure closure){

    System.out.println("[FILTER] Service Of Invocation Complete ");
  }
}
```

The `locate()` method will be called when a client tries to attach itself to the server object's object reference or IOR. The method can be used to forward the IOR of a different object reference than the one intended by the client.

The `shutdown()` method will be notified when a client terminates the connection and disposes of any object references it might have had.

The `receive_request()` method is key, because this method is invoked by the server when a client sends over an invocation on some interface operation. As mentioned earlier, the implementation of this method uses a number of APIs to determine what the client is trying to do. To this extent, the code even extracts the value of the parameter from the marshaled buffer coming in from the client. This is accomplished by invoking the appropriate method on the `InputStream` object that the ORB passed to the interceptor. At this juncture, it must be pointed out that using the right call on the `InputStream`, `get_short()` is possible because you knew what was being passed to the `foo()` method.

The `prepare_reply()` is called by the ORB just before the return message is converted to an IIOP stream. Just as you introspected the internals of an incoming invocation from the client, it is possible to use a similar API to do the same with the parameters of `prepare_reply()`.

When the return message has been marshaled, it is sent back to the client. In this case, there isn't much to send over because the return type is `void` and the `foo()` method defined only one `in` parameter. At this point, the ORB will inform the interceptor that `send_reply()` is under way.

When the message has been safely returned to the client, the ORB informs the interceptor through the `request_completed()` that the invocation cycle is completed.

That concludes the implementation of the interceptor itself. The next step is to install the interceptor with the ORB. VisiBroker provides the facilities of factories to instantiate an interceptor when the ORB requires one. VisiBroker defines interfaces for all three types of interceptors. In this case, you need to construct a `ServerInterceptorFactory` to create a server interceptor when the ORB requires one. This is accomplished in the code shown in Listing 20.3.

LISTING 20.3 `ServerFilterFactory` **IMPLEMENTATION**

```
package Interceptor;
import com.visigenic.vbroker.interceptor.*;
import com.visigenic.vbroker.IOP.*;

public class ServerFilterFactory implements ServerInterceptorFactory {

   private ServerFilter filter = null;

   public ServerInterceptor create(TaggedProfile client_profile){
      if(filter == null){
          filter = new ServerFilter();
```

continues

LISTING 20.3 CONTINUED

```
        }
        return filter;
    }
}
```

The factory class is created by implementing the `ServerInterceptorFactory` interface. This interface specifies only one method, `create()`. The only thing that it does is instantiate a server interceptor (`ServerFilter`) when the factory is requested to create one. This particular implementation creates only one interceptor. When the interceptor is created, the object that requested the factory's service is returned to the client.

At this point we have two classes that deal with the interceptor and a factory class that will initialize the interceptor when it is needed by the ORB. In order for the ORB to request the interceptor, the interceptor object must be installed with the ORB. It is standard practice to create a simple installer that will install the interceptor with the ORB. The benefit of such an `install` is the fact that it can be used with other interceptors as well. The custom installer is shown in Listing 20.4.

LISTING 20.4 `InterceptorInstaller` IMPLEMENTATION

```
package Interceptor;
import com.visigenic.vbroker.interceptor.*;
import com.visigenic.vbroker.orb.*;
import java.util.*;

public class InterceptorInstaller {

  public void install(org.omg.CORBA.ORB orb, Properties properties){
      System.out.println("Installing Server Interceptors");
      ChainServerInterceptorFactory serverFactory = null;
      try{
        org.omg.CORBA.Object obj =
          orb.resolve_initial_references("ChainServerInterceptorFactory");
        serverFactory = ChainServerInterceptorFactoryHelper.narrow(obj);

        serverFactory.add(new Interceptor.ServerFilterFactory());
      }
      catch(org.omg.CORBA.ORBPackage.InvalidName e){
        System.out.println(e.toString());
      }
  }
}
```

The installer object essentially retrieves an object reference to the already installed chain of `ServerInterceptorFactory` interfaces. This implies that there can be more than one interceptor installed on the server. When the object reference is resolved, the factory class that was implemented previously is registered to the chain of interceptor factories. This does not, however, mean that the interceptor itself is initialized. That can occur only when a client makes an invocation on a server that is attached to an interceptor. The server code is shown in Listing 20.5.

LISTING 20.5 FilterServer IMPLEMENTATION FOR SERVER INTERCEPTOR

```
package Interceptor;

public class FilterServer {
  org.omg.CORBA.ORB orb_ = null;
  org.omg.CORBA.BOA boa_  = null;

  public FilterServer(String[] args) {
    orb_ = org.omg.CORBA.ORB.init(args,null);
    InterceptorInstaller inst = new InterceptorInstaller ();
    inst.install(orb_,null);
    boa_ = orb_.BOA_init();
    Filter filter = new FilterObject("Filter");
    try{
      boa_.obj_is_ready(filter);
      System.out.println(filter + " is ready.");
      boa_.impl_is_ready();
      boa_.deactivate_obj(filter);
    }
    catch(org.omg.CORBA.SystemException ex){
      System.out.println(ex.toString());
    }
  }

  public static void main(String[] args) {
    FilterServer filterServer = new FilterServer(args);
  }
}
```

The only code that is different in this server—that sets it apart from normal CORBA servers—is shown in the following two lines:

```
InterceptorInstaller inst = new InterceptorInstaller ();
inst.install(orb_,null);
```

Essentially, the code instantiates an instance of the `InterceptorInstaller` class and invokes the `install()` method on it. This will have the interceptor installed with the ORB, waiting for invocations from the client side.

The server is now ready to be run. All that remains is to construct a client to use the server to test whether the interceptors are working (see Listing 20.6). The client implementation does not do anything except invoke the `foo()` method on the server.

LISTING 20.6 FilterClient IMPLEMENTATION FOR SERVER INTERCEPTOR

```
package Interceptor;

public class FilterClient {
   public static void main(String[] args) {
    org.omg.CORBA.ORB orb = org.omg.CORBA.ORB.init(args,null);
    Filter filter = FilterHelper.bind(orb, "Filter");
    filter.foo((short)1002);
   }
}
```

When the `foo()` method is invoked, the method passes `1002` to the server side. The application is now ready to be run. The client doesn't do any thing spectacular, so we can skip the mug shots for that screen. The server screen shot (see Figure 20.1), on the other hand, clearly shows that the server interceptor works as advertised.

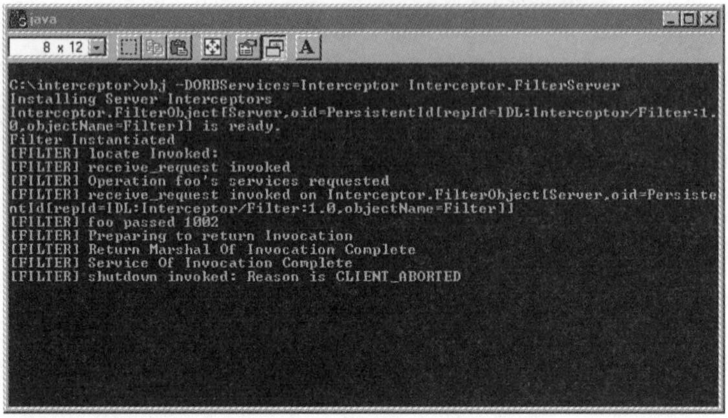

FIGURE 20.1
Filter client.

Constructing a BindInterceptor

This section constructs a bind interceptor. The example is similar to `ServerInterceptor`, except that the interceptor is invoked by the ORB when the `bind()` occurs.

For this example, the bind interceptor is implemented by extending the `DefaultBindInterceptor` class. The code for the bind interceptor is shown in Listing 20.7.

LISTING 20.7 BindFilter IMPLEMENTATION

```
package BindInterceptor;
import com.visigenic.vbroker.interceptor.*;
import com.visigenic.vbroker.IOP.IOR;
public class BindFilter extends DefaultBindInterceptor {
```

```
        public BindFilter(){
        System.out.println("Bind Filter Instantiated");
    }
   public boolean bind(IOR ior,
                     org.omg.CORBA.Object object,
                     Closure closure){
        return false;
   }
    public void bind_succeeded(IOR ior,
       org.omg.CORBA.Object object,
       Closure closure)    {

        System.out.println("Bind succeeded");
}
```

This interceptor is very trivial. The only method that will be invoked in this interceptor is `bind_succeeded()` to notify that the bind was successful.

For the bind interceptor example, an initialization class will be used to install the bind interceptor, rather than the `InterceptorInstaller` class that was used in the `ServerInterceptor` example. The initialization class is subclassed from VisiBroker's `ServiceInit` class, and it will be executed during the ORB's initialization. The initialization is done by the ORB at runtime by using the ORB services option at startup, `-Dorbservices=`*xxxxx*, where *xxxxx* is the name of the package that contains the initialization class. The code for this class is shown in Listing 20.8.

LISTING 20.8 INITIALIZATION CLASS FOR `BindInterceptor`

```
package BindInterceptor;
import com.visigenic.vbroker.interceptor.*;
import com.visigenic.vbroker.orb.*;
import  java.util.*;

public class Init extends com.visigenic.vbroker.orb.ServiceInit
{
    public void init(org.omg.CORBA.ORB orb, Properties properties)
    {
        System.out.println("Installing Bind Interceptors");
        // install bind interceptor
        try
        {
            ChainBindInterceptor bind =
               com.visigenic.vbroker.interceptor.ChainBindInterceptorHelper
       .narrow(
               orb.resolve_initial_references("ChainBindInterceptor"));
            bind.add(new BindFilter());
        }
```

continues

LISTING 20.8 CONTINUED

```
        catch(org.omg.CORBA.ORBPackage.InvalidName e)
        {
            System.out.println(e.toString());
        }
    }
}
```

Basically, when this object executes, it retrieves a reference to the chain of `BindInterceptors` that are already installed and simply adds the `BindFilter` object to the chain:

```
ChainBindInterceptor bind =
        com.visigenic.vbroker.interceptor.ChainBindInterceptorHelper.narrow
(
        orb.resolve_initial_references("ChainBindInterceptor"));
         bind.add(new BindFilter());
```

Because, in this example, the bind interceptor is not installed by the server, the server code is like standard CORBA servers, as shown in Listing 20.9.

LISTING 20.9 `FilterServer` IMPLEMENTATION FOR `BindInterceptor`

```
package BindInterceptor;

public class FilterServer {
  org.omg.CORBA.ORB orb_ = null;
  org.omg.CORBA.BOA boa_  = null;

  public FilterServer(String[] args) {
    orb_ = org.omg.CORBA.ORB.init(args,null);
    boa_ = orb_.BOA_init();
    Filter filter = new FilterObject("Filter");
    try{
      boa_.obj_is_ready(filter);
      System.out.println(filter + " is ready.");
      boa_.impl_is_ready();
     boa_.deactivate_obj(filter);
    }
    catch(org.omg.CORBA.SystemException ex){
      System.out.println(ex.toString());
    }
  }

  public static void main(String[] args) {
    FilterServer filterServer = new FilterServer(args);
  }
}
```

The client is not impacted by the introduction of the bind interceptor class, as shown in Listing 20.10, which is identical to the client implementation used by the server interceptor example.

LISTING 20.10 `FilterClient` **IMPLEMENTATION FOR** `BindInterceptor`

```
package BindInterceptor;

public class FilterClient {
   public static void main(String[] args) {
    org.omg.CORBA.ORB orb = org.omg.CORBA.ORB.init(args,null);
    Filter filter = FilterHelper.bind(orb, "Filter");
    System.out.println(filter);
    filter.foo((short)1002);
   }
}
```

When the `FilterClient` is executed, the ORB invokes the `bind()` and `bind_succeeded()` methods on the interceptor. When executed successfully, the filter object executes its `foo()` method to assign the object's internal value to `1002`. Figure 20.2 depicts the execution of the `FilterClient`. The `bind_succeeded()` methods indicate that the bind was successful and that the ORB intercepted the bind.

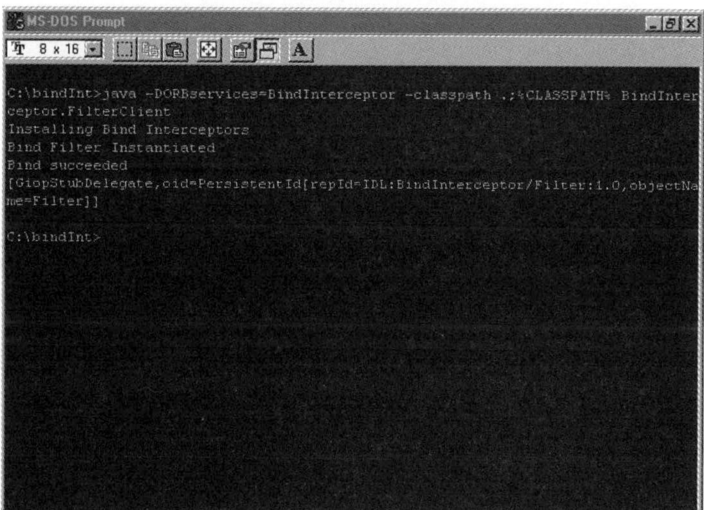

FIGURE 20.2
`BindInterceptor` *execution.*

Summary

VisiBroker interceptor technology enables the creation of a filter to intervene before, after, and during client/server interactions. This can be leveraged in all sorts of ways. It can be used for tracing interactions and logging states of the server objects. Creation of load balancing and enforcing security are important areas where interceptors can be used effectively.

VisiBroker defines three types of interceptors: server interceptors, client interceptors, and bind interceptors. These three interceptors enable a designer to completely control client/server interactions.

CORBA Integration and Interfaces

PART V

IN THIS PART

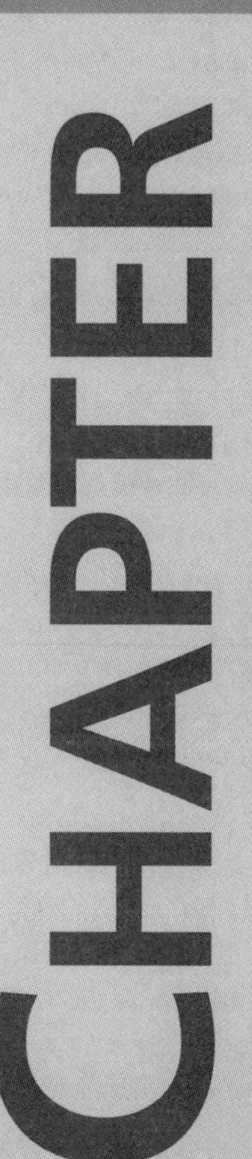

CORBA and Java Servlets

In This Chapter

Java servlets provide a simple but effective mechanism for extending Web servers. There are a number of problems currently evident with server-side extensions on the World Wide Web, because the great majority of server-side extensions are Common Gateway Interface (CGI)–based applications. It should be noted that Perl-derived CGI have been evolving to answer some of the problems that will be enumerated here. First, let's define CGIs and examine their problems.

CGI enables a developer to build applications on the server side that are executed when an invocation arrives from the client side. As such, CGI-based applications are a mechanism to extend a Web server. As it is conceived, the World Wide Web (WWW) is a pure two-tier client/server application. The user interface is "dumb"—just a veneer of presentation written in HTML. For a simple document, hyperlinking this is sufficient. The server is also rather dumb. Its only function is to serve out HTML pages. It contains no logic other than this.

Very early in the evolution of the WWW, developers needed a mechanism to add some "smarts" to the server side. These smarts were CGI. They are per-request executables that are executed on the server side. For every request that came in from the client, a new CGI instance was created and executed. After the execution was completed, the CGI was unloaded from memory.

As a technology, CGI has all the hallmarks of brilliance. For one, it was simple to implement; the vast majority of CGI scripts were written in Perl (I wonder if Perl could be mapped to OMG IDL). It is a technology that is pervasive. In the meantime, the WWW became insanely pervasive! With this pervasiveness, the drawbacks of CGI became obvious. The biggest problem was scalability. As more and more developers got online, CGI was being extended into oblivion! The powers that be decided to "fix" the problem with their own ways of extending CGI, but without its problems. Some of them are MS Active Server Pages; Netscape has Server Side JavaScript. JavaSoft put out its own Web server, the Java Web Server (JWS), and through it JavaSoft introduced Java servlets as a mechanism of extending JWS. The servlets are written entirely in Java, and as a technology, they have been adopted widely as a "Cross Web Server extension" technology.

As a technology, the servlets sit on the server side, persistently loaded into memory of the server for providing immediate response to a client request. After they are loaded into memory, servlets continue to reside in memory until they are explicitly unloaded. They are thus much faster than the classical forms of CGI. Servlets as a technology also follow the rules of the JavaSoft specification process, so they are as open a standard as the circumstances allow. Because they use Java as the language for extending the server, everything that is available in Java can be used within a servlet, including Java implementations of CORBA.

Why Use Servlets with CORBA?

CORBA over the Internet would be of enormous benefit to second-generation Internet applications. Before you can understand what these second-generation applications will look like, let's briefly survey the current state of Web-based applications.

The majority of the Web is purely textual. It is primarily composed of HTML pages that are hyperlinked together to provide a Web of information. Nascent e-commerce applications are also coming online. Most of these applications are CGI protocol–based or use server-side extensions that the Web server vendors provide, such as ASP, server-side JavaScript, or even Java servlets.

With second-generation Internet applications, the WWW will be fundamentally different. A Web page will contain not only hyperlinked pages rich in multimedia and dynamic HTML, XML, and Java, but also will contain hyperlinked objects. For instance, consider a potential e-commerce application such as `http://www.cbooks.com`. This is an electronic shopping center for buying books on the Web. When you put in an order, it forwards the order to a distributor who ships the book to cbooks, and they in turn forward it to you.

There are a number of areas where the service that is offered by cbooks can be automated using CORBA. All the various parties that interact in order to enable me to buy books could build CORBA components that offer their services on the Web. This would mean that publishers could offer their inventory to distributors such as cbooks. Shipping companies could offer their services, and so forth. A firm sych as cbooks could tie up all these various services into a coherent whole and offer it to me. In short, you would have a Web of objects that are hyperlinked to offer you a service.

The problem in the meantime is bandwidth. The Internet right now is, at its peak hours, more like a one-way street with no traffic rules or cops!

Java user interfaces are easy to build, and as most of this book has shown, doing CORBA in Java is relatively painless. Unfortunately, unless the logjams on the electronic "superhighway" are solved, extensive and complex applications using Java on the client side over the Internet is not really an option (on the other hand, an intranet poses no serious problems). HTML, and perhaps DHTML, is by far still the smartest and lightest way to make an application on the Internet. Java servlets enable you to use Java on the server side while still continuing to use HTML on the client side. This option enables you to use the gamut of features and options that Java provides as both a platform and a language. With the integration of CORBA, you could also integrate legacy solutions over the Internet.

HTML as a Presentation Layer

N-tier client/server applications are fast becoming the norm for building applications. They are useful because of the level of decoupling they bring to bear on the solution. Figure 21.1 illustrates what I am talking about.

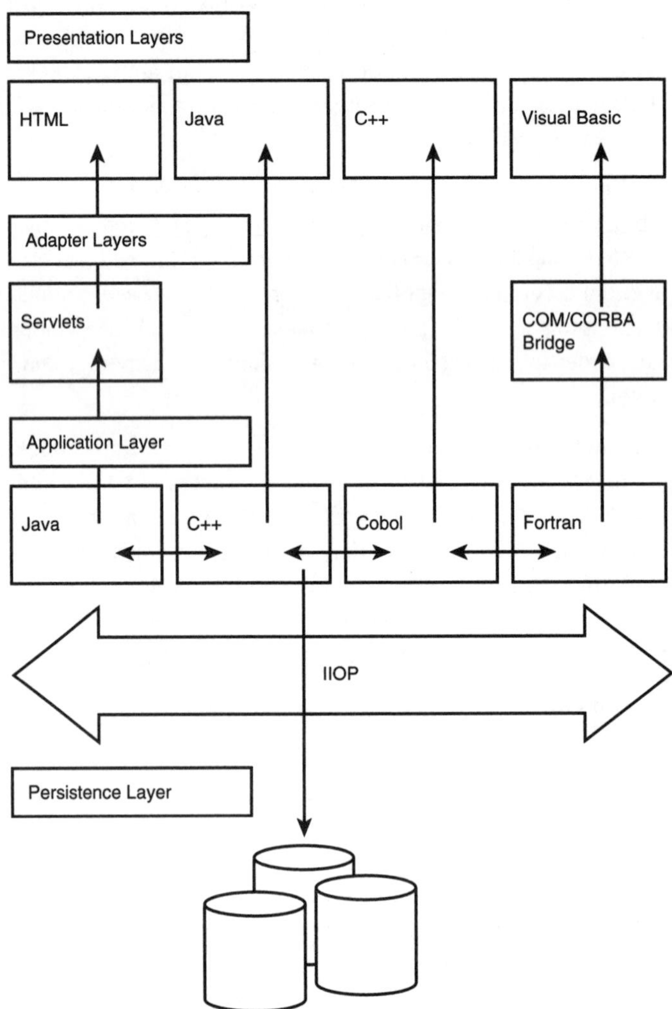

FIGURE 21.1
An enterprise architecture.

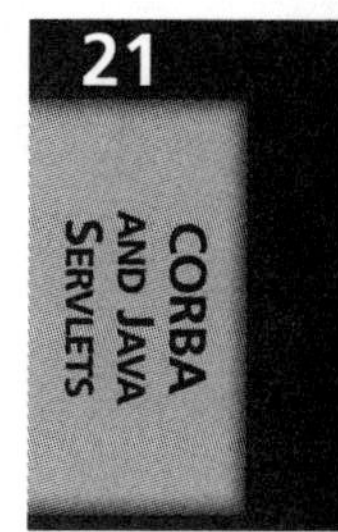

In any large enterprise, it is natural that a variety of heterogeneous solutions must coexist. In a large organization, solutions exist, side by side, that use different languages, different platforms, and even different operating systems. This makes them interesting and also a bother to maintain. CORBA provides the capability of supporting all these variations by breaking up architectures into three tiers.

Three-tier client/server architecture enables you to isolate the dynamics of user interface requirements from the underlying application requirements. In most architecture, the business logic and the process logic can usually be separated.

This enables the same application layer to support many user interface requirements. HTML, in my view, is another presentation layer. As such, if it could somehow support CORBA-based applications, existing business logic (also known as legacy applications) and processes can be adapted to the Internet or HTML-based intranet solutions.

The Java servlet is one such technology. Servlets can be used to add a new presentation layer over existing solutions. For example, you could have a contact application that you would like to extend over the Internet or an intranet. You could use CORBA to wrap these legacy applications and then deploy them over the Internet or intranet using Java servlets. The converse is also true: Newer applications can be built using CORBA, and servlet-based extensions can be used to add Internet support to them. When the necessary bandwidth becomes available, the big-gun applications can be seamlessly deployed over the Internet as well.

Building with Servlets

The example assumes that you are reasonably familiar with servlets and how they can be used in the context of the Internet. I also assume that you have installed either the Java Web server or the Java Servlet Development Kit. The example also assumes that you are adept at administering the Web server.

Servlets at their basic level are extremely simple to use. The simplest way to write a servlet is to subclass the javax.servlet.GenericServlet class. At that point, you only have to override the service(ServletRequest, ServletResponse) method. If you want to code an HTTP-based servlet, you can subclass the javax.servlet.http.HttpServlet class and override the doGet(HttpServletRequest, HttpServletResponse) and doPost(HttpServletRequest, HttpServletResponse) methods. `HttpServlet` is an extension of `GenericServlet`. `GenericServlet` also implements the `javax.servlet.Servlet` and `javax.servlet.ServletConfig` interfaces. The servlet interface contains the lifecycle methods that can be overridden and implemented by your servlets.

In Listing 21.1, a simple servlet is built. This servlet will subclass the `HttpServlet`. When this servlet is invoked, it displays `Hello World` on the client side.

LISTING 21.1 A `Hello World` SERVLET

```
import java.io.*;

import javax.servlet.*;
import javax.servlet.http.*;


public
class HelloWorldServlet extends HttpServlet {

    public void doGet (HttpServletRequest req, HttpServletResponse res)
        throws ServletException, IOException
    {
        res.setContentType("text/html");
        ServletOutputStream out = res.getOutputStream();
        out.println("<html>");
        out.println("<head><title>Hello World</title></head>");
        out.println("<body>");
        out.println("<h1>Hello World</h1>");
        out.println("</body></html>");
    }

    public String getServletInfo() {
        return "Create a page that says <i>Hello World</i> and send it
back";
    }
}
```

A Short Introduction to the Servlet API

The next sections use the `HTTPServlet` to demonstrate how CORBA clients can be wrapped as servlets. At the core of how this class works are the `doPost()` and the `doGet()` methods. Both these methods have two parameters: the `HttpServletRequest` parameter and the `HTTPServletResponse` parameter.

The `HttpServletRequest` object that is passed as a parameter represents the request coming in from an HTTP client. As a class, `HttpServletRequest` contains all the details of an HTTP request protocol. Various parameters, such as parameters being passed from the client and the client connection itself, can be accessed through an instance of `HttpServletRequest`.

The `HTTPServletResponse` class provides a clean set of APIs for interacting with the HTTP response API. The crucial method in this class is the `getOutputStream()`, which returns a stream object representing the output buffer that you want to write a response to. For detailed information on these classes, please refer to the Java servlets API documentation.

A Simple CORBA Servlet

This example uses the application for Dynamic Invocation Interfaces that is demonstrated in Chapter 25, "Using Dynamic Invocation Interfaces." Turn to that chapter for the full details of how this application is built. Using an already existing application helps keep application details not relevant to this chapter in the background. All that remains is to create a servlet.

NOTE

Reusing and extending an already existing application is the usually prescribed strategy for dealing with CORBA applications.

CORBA applications' architectures have always encouraged reuse. This essentially means that if you construct a CORBA service, its potential power is evident only when it is reused in new contexts. For instance, consider applications that do human resource management. It is useful if you can provide a solution to this problem using classical client/server strategies. But if you were asked to extend the solution so that the same solution could be used over the Internet/intranet, you would probably end up constructing a new application.

Using CORBA, you would first create a Common Object Model that is general to both the internal network application and the intended Internet solution. On this foundation, you extend the solution to meet the requirements of the internal solution. Further, if an Internet solution is required, you extend the Common Object Model to provide that solution.

Critical to this solution is the Common Object Model, which can be reused. This essentially means that the Internet/intranet should really be considered as an extension of the work that has already been done. You design the components of the solution that can be reused either on the Internet or on the intranet without having to recode or redesign existing solutions.

Creating a CORBA Client Servlets

The servlet will subclass the `HTTPServlet` class. It will override the `getPost()` method, because the client is going to use a `POST` to send a request to the servlet, as shown in Listing 21.2.

LISTING 21.2 CORBA SERVLETS IMPLEMENTATION

```
package idlservlet;

import javax.servlet.*;
import javax.servlet.http.*;
import java.io.*;
import java.util.*;
import org.omg.CORBA.*;

public class GetInterface extends HttpServlet {
  static org.omg.CORBA.Object DynamicObject;
  static org.omg.CORBA.ORB orb;
  PrintWriter out;


  public void init(ServletConfig config) throws ServletException {
  }

  public void doPost(HttpServletRequest request,
 HttpServletResponse response) throws ServletException,
 IOException {

    response.setContentType("text/html");
    out = new PrintWriter (response.getOutputStream());

    out.println("<html>");
    out.println("<head><title>GetInterface</title></head>");
    out.println("<body>");
    out.println("<p>");
    try{
      makeStructCall();
      out.println("<p>");
      getStructCall();
      out.println("<p>");
      makeSequenceCall();
      out.println("<p>");
      getSequenceCall();
      out.println("<p>");
      makeNumberCall();
      out.println("<p>");
      getNumberCall();
      out.println("<p>");
      makeStringCall();
```

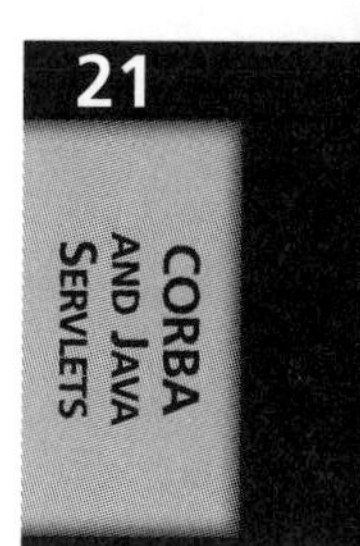


```
      out.println("<p>");
      getStringCall();
      out.println("<p>");
      makeReferenceCall();
      out.println("<p>");
      getReferenceCall();
    }
    catch(Exception e){
      System.out.println(e.toString());
      out.println("Tempad" + e.toString());
      out.println("<p>");
    }
    out.println("<p>");

    out.println("</body>");
    out.println("</body></html>");
    out.close();
  }

  public String getServletInfo() {
    return "idlservlet.GetInterface Information";
  }

private void makeStructCall(){
    orb = org.omg.CORBA.ORB.init();
    DynamicObject = orb.bind("IDL:Dynamic/dii:1.0", "DynamicServer", null,
null);

    Request request = DynamicObject._request("takestruct");
    Dynamic.diiPackage.DyStructHolder outStruct = new
Dynamic.diiPackage.DyStructHolder();
    Dynamic.diiPackage.DyStructHolder inOutStruct = new
Dynamic.diiPackage.DyStructHolder();
    Dynamic.diiPackage.DyStruct inStruct = new
Dynamic.diiPackage.DyStruct();

    inStruct.age = 22;
    inStruct.name = "Koolaire";

    inOutStruct.value = new Dynamic.diiPackage.DyStruct();
    inOutStruct.value.age = 55;
    inOutStruct.value.name = "INOUT VALUE";

    outStruct.value = new Dynamic.diiPackage.DyStruct();
    outStruct.value.age = 0;
    outStruct.value.name = "";

    Any In = request.add_in_arg();
    Any Out = request.add_out_arg();
    Any Inout = request.add_inout_arg();
```

continues

LISTING 21.2 CONTINUED

```
    Out.type(Dynamic.diiPackage.DyStructHelper.type());

    Dynamic.diiPackage.DyStructHelper.insert(In,inStruct);
    Dynamic.diiPackage.DyStructHelper.insert(Out,outStruct.value);
    Dynamic.diiPackage.DyStructHelper.insert(Inout,inOutStruct.value);

    request.invoke();
    outStruct.value = Dynamic.diiPackage.DyStructHelper.extract(Out);
    inOutStruct.value = Dynamic.diiPackage.DyStructHelper.extract(Inout);
    out.println(outStruct.value.name + "\n");
    out.println(inOutStruct.value.name + "\n");
   }

   private void makeSequenceCall(){
    Request request = DynamicObject._request("takesequence");
    java.lang.String[] inSequence;
    Dynamic.diiPackage.stringsHolder outSequence;
    Dynamic.diiPackage.stringsHolder inoutSequence;

    inSequence = new String[2];
    outSequence = new Dynamic.diiPackage.stringsHolder();
    inoutSequence = new Dynamic.diiPackage.stringsHolder();
    outSequence.value = new String[2];
    inoutSequence.value = new String[2];

    for(int i = 0; i < inSequence.length; i++){
       inSequence[i] = "INSEQUENCE STRING " + new Integer(i).toString();
       outSequence.value[i] = "OUTSEQUENCE STRING " + new
Integer(i).toString();
       inoutSequence.value[i] = "";
    }

    Any In = request.add_in_arg();
    Any Out = request.add_out_arg();
    Any Inout = request.add_inout_arg();

    Out.type(Dynamic.diiPackage.stringsHelper.type());
    Inout.type(Dynamic.diiPackage.stringsHelper.type());

    Dynamic.diiPackage.stringsHelper.insert(In,inSequence);
    Dynamic.diiPackage.stringsHelper.insert(Out,outSequence.value);
    Dynamic.diiPackage.stringsHelper.insert(Inout,inoutSequence.value);

    request.invoke();

    outSequence.value = Dynamic.diiPackage.stringsHelper.extract(Out);
    inoutSequence.value = Dynamic.diiPackage.stringsHelper.extract(Inout);

    for(int i = 0; i <  outSequence.value.length; i++)
```

```
        out.println(outSequence.value[i] + "\n");

    for(int i = 0; i <  inoutSequence.value.length; i++)
        out.println(inoutSequence.value[i] + "\n");
  }

  private void getStructCall(){
    Request request = DynamicObject._request("getstuct");
    request.set_return_type(Dynamic.diiPackage.DyStructHelper.type());
    request.invoke();
    Dynamic.diiPackage.DyStruct result;
    result =
Dynamic.diiPackage.DyStructHelper.extract(request.return_value());

    out.println("RETURN STRUCT: AGE " + new Integer(result.age) + "\n");
    out.println("RETURN STRUCT: NAME " + result.name + "\n");

  }

  private void getSequenceCall(){
     Request request = DynamicObject._request("getsequence");
     request.set_return_type(orb.create_sequence_tc(0,
orb.get_primitive_tc(org.omg.CORBA.TCKind.tk_string)));
     request.invoke();
     String[] result;
     result =
Dynamic.diiPackage.stringsHelper.extract(request.return_value());

     for(int i = 0; i < result.length; i++)
       out.println("RETURN SEQUENCE: " + result[i] + "\n");
  }

  public void makeNumberCall(){

    int inNumber = 1001;
    IntHolder outNumber = new IntHolder();
    IntHolder inoutNumber = new IntHolder();
    inoutNumber.value = 1002;
    inoutNumber.value = 0;

    org.omg.CORBA.Request request = DynamicObject._request("takenumber");
    Any ins = request.add_in_arg();
    Any outs = request.add_out_arg();
    Any inouts = request.add_inout_arg();

    ins.insert_long(inNumber);
    inouts.insert_long(inoutNumber.value);
    outs.insert_long(outNumber.value);
    request.invoke();
```

continues

LISTING 21.2 CONTINUED

```
    outNumber.value = outs.extract_long();
    inoutNumber.value = inouts.extract_long();
    out.println("INOUT PRIMITIVE: " + new Integer(inoutNumber.value) +
"\n");
    out.println("OUT PRIMITIVE: " + new Integer(outNumber.value) + "\n");
  }

  public void getNumberCall(){
    Request request = DynamicObject._request("getnumber");

request.set_return_type(orb.get_primitive_tc(org.omg.CORBA.TCKind.tk_long)
);
    request.invoke();
    int ReturnPrimitive = 0;
    ReturnPrimitive = request.return_value().extract_long();
    out.println("RETURN PRIMITIVE: " + new
Integer(ReturnPrimitive) + "\n");
  }

  public void makeStringCall(){

    String inString = new String("IN STRING");
    StringHolder outString = new StringHolder();
    StringHolder inoutString = new StringHolder();
    outString.value = "";
    inoutString.value = "INOUT STRING";

    Request request = DynamicObject._request("takestring");

    org.omg.CORBA.Any ins = request.add_in_arg();
    org.omg.CORBA.Any outs = request.add_out_arg();
    org.omg.CORBA.Any inouts = request.add_inout_arg();
ins.insert_string(inString);
outs.type(orb.get_primitive_tc(org.omg.CORBA.TCKind.tk_string));
    outs.insert_string(outString.value);
    inouts.insert_string(inoutString.value);
    request.invoke();
    outString.value = outs.extract_string();
    inoutString.value = inouts.extract_string();
    out.println("INOUT STRING : " + inoutString.value + "\n");
    out.println("OUT STRING: " + outString.value + "\n");
  }

  public void getStringCall(){
     Request request = DynamicObject._request("getstring");
request.set_return_type(orb.get_primitive_tc
(org.omg.CORBA.TCKind.tk_string));
     request.invoke();
     String returnString;
```

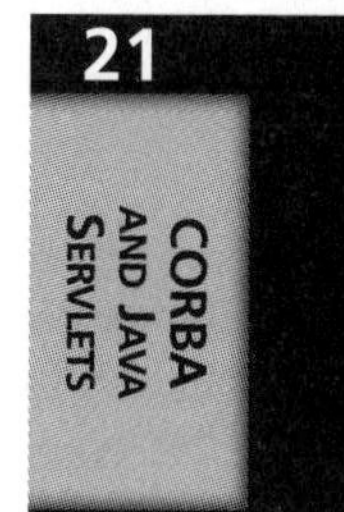


```
      returnString = request.return_value().extract_string();
      out.println("RETRURN STRING : " + returnString + "\n");
   }

   public void makeReferenceCall(){

      Dynamic.dii inReference = new Dynamic.dynamic();
      Dynamic.diiHolder outReference = new
Dynamic.diiHolder();
      Dynamic.diiHolder inoutReference = new
Dynamic.diiHolder();

      Request request =
DynamicObject._request("takereference");
      Any ins = request.add_in_arg();
      Any outs = request.add_out_arg();
      Any inouts = request.add_inout_arg();
      outs.type(Dynamic.diiHelper.type());
      Dynamic.diiHelper.insert(ins, inReference);
      Dynamic.diiHelper.insert(outs, outReference.value);
      Dynamic.diiHelper.insert(inouts, inoutReference.value);
      request.invoke();

      outReference.value = Dynamic.diiHelper.extract(outs);
      inoutReference.value =
Dynamic.diiHelper.extract(inouts);
      out.println("OUT REFERENCE : " +
outReference.value.toString() + "\n");
      out.println("<p>");
      out.println("INOUT REFERENCE : " +
inoutReference.value.toString() + "\n");
   }

   public void getReferenceCall(){
     Request request =
DynamicObject._request("getreference");
     request.set_return_type(Dynamic.diiHelper.type());
     request.invoke();
     Dynamic.dii returnReference;
     returnReference =
Dynamic.diiHelper.extract(request.return_value());
     out.println("RETURN REFERENCE : " +
returnReference.toString() + "\n");
   }
}
```

This servlet is very simple in the way it works. It essentially does exactly the same as the DII. The only difference is that the output is now redirected to a `HttpServletResponse` stream. The client code is just the same as before. The only slight changes have been the insertion of an HTML tag `<p>` to make the output a little more presentable.

To use the servlet, you must also construct an HTML client to invoke it. Here is the code for the HTML page:

```
<HTML>
<HEAD>
<META HTTP-EQUIV="Content-Type"
CONTENT="text/html;
charset=iso-8859-1">
<TITLE>
Corba Servlet
</TITLE>
</HEAD>
<BODY>

<FORM  action=http://galileo.oa.nl:8080/servlet/idlservlet.GetInterface
method=POST>
<BR><BR> Press Submit to Invoke the CORBA Servlet GetInterface
<BR><BR><input type=submit><input type=reset></form>
</BODY>
</HTML>
```

The rendering of the page as output is shown in Figure 21.2.

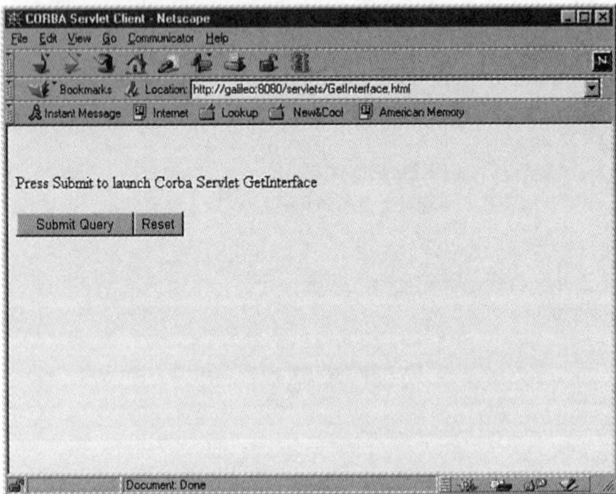

FIGURE 21.2
HTTP servlet client in action.

On pressing the submit button, a `POST` request is sent to the servlets. The `POST` is then handled by the following public void method:

```
doPost(HttpServletRequest request, HttpServletResponse response)
```

The logic of this statement is very simple. The `inputstream` to the response object is retrieved, and a `PrintWriter` object is created from it. The benefit of using `PrintWriter` is that flushing is automatic in this case.

The `doPost()` method then serially invokes the various methods on the DII interface that is hosted on the Dynamic Server. The salient aspect about this servlet is that it uses Dynamic Invocation Interfaces to interact with a remote object. This means that the various client-side stubs are not linked with the servlet. In terms of scalability, this might have some drawbacks, because it usually takes a certain amount of overhead to make the invocation marshaling. Dynamic Invocation enables you to easily integrate diverse CORBA applications. If the overhead of DII is unacceptable in an application, you could design your application to use the default static invocations interfaces with CORBA.

The output from the servlets is shown in Figure 21.3.

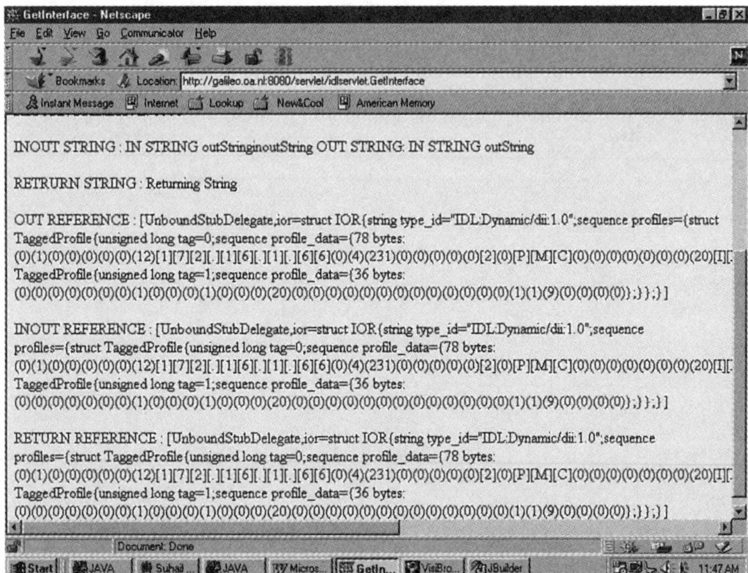

FIGURE 21.3
The servlet output in Netscape.

Summary

Currently, the bandwidth problems on the Internet mean that, for the majority of CORBA applications, using Java would have extremely long download times. This also means that fully fledged GUI applications on the client side using Java are not the best options if the chances are that the user has low bandwidth. HTML under these circumstances is still the best solution.

HTTP and the underlying infrastructure of the Internet are not really equipped to build the kinds of solutions we are trying to build now, especially in the e-commerce space. The ideal architecture for such a solution is a three-tier client/server architecture.

CORBA is ideal for building highly scalable multitier architectures. On top of all this, CORBA is cross-platform and multilingual. Servlets enable a clean solution for painlessly integrating such diverse solution spaces into a coherent Internet/intranet package.

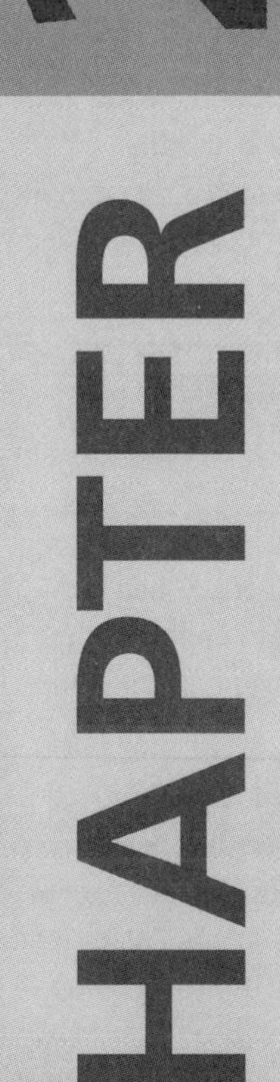

CORBA and Mobile Agents

In This Chapter

The concept of mobile agents is an emerging paradigm shift. As a technology, it perhaps stands at the extreme of distributed computing. Over the last twenty years, information technology has been shifting to greater decentralized systems. Perhaps this shift mirrors and is a consequence of the great decentralization process that is taking place in society.

The first thing that struck me when using mobile agents was a strange sense of dislocation. Danny Lange, one of the preeminent practitioners of agent technology soon put it right for me. In an email to me, he wrote, "The norms of client server relations are no longer valid with mobile agents." Mobile agents are pieces of logic that have the capability of transferring over the network from one node to another. After it arrives at the target site, an agent executes its program. Theoretically, this logic can be anything; after the agent finishes its execution, most implementations enable the retraction or deactivation of the agent at the host.

Mobile agents are best modeled on peer-to-peer schemas. That means that there are essentially no servers or clients. Every agent is a quantum of logic that is usually ascribed a single task. Applications are built using an "ecology" of agents cooperating to get a task done. The ecology can be spread over any number of hosts, both spatially and temporally.

Let's look at a typical scenario. Suppose you want to buy an airplane ticket. The process of doing so involves first dispatching a search agent to a directory server. There, the search agent could interact with other agents to locate an appropriate agent that is willing to sell airplane tickets at the right price (for instance). When this is accomplished, the search agent could invoke the services of a purchase agent to buy the actual ticket. It does so by interfacing with a product agent—in our case, a ticketing agent. When the sale is complete, the purchasing agent could dispatch a payment agent to conclude the sale by paying for the ticket. When all this is accomplished, the purchasing agent comes home with the ticket.

Currently, the problem facing agent technology is not the mechanism of mobility. That part has largely been solved using Java as a platform. Java in that respect has been a great boon to implementers; the Java virtual machine guarantees a homogeneous execution environment that shields an agent from the underlying host environment. Agents can also be considered as an alien piece of code that executes in the host. The world being the world, it is probable that at one time or another some of that code will be akin to a malignant tumor, a network-borne virus. Java's built-in security provides a good immune system in preventing most of these potential attacks.

The threat from virus aside, mobile agents have the potential for radically changing the way in which distributed systems are designed. First, there are no clients and servers. An agent is dispatched to the remote host and it executes when it arrives there. If a more classical approach to client/server is required, an agent is dispatched to the remote host, where it will try to interact with "resident" agents to acquire some service.

At any rate, the fundamental problem that mobile agent technology faces is interagent communications. There is yet no standard lingua franca for agent communications. It is consequently one of the most intensely researched areas of agent technology. OMG has realized the potential of agents. It is currently under the process of standardizing The Mobile Agent Facility specification. After the standard is formally accepted, all current implementations of agents are expected to comply.

Currently, there are a number of agent implementations in the market. As far as I have been able to ascertain, none of them conforms to MAF yet. Nevertheless, a careful look at these technologies could be worthwhile. I have worked with a number of agent technologies. Some of the more interesting ones are IBM Aglets, Oddessey, and Concordia. These can be downloaded from the URLs given at the end of the chapter. I must confess that my favorite is the Aglets because it is an implementation that is closest to the mobile agent spirit.

This book will not demonstrate how agents can be used in their natural domain. That is best left to books specializing in agent technology. Because this is a book on CORBA, it will demonstrate how agents can be integrated with CORBA applications. One of the ways in which agents can be used in the context of CORBA is that a CORBA client can be constructed as an agent. This agent can then be dispatched to a host. On arriving at the host, the agent can then accomplish a normal bind to a server object at the host. After the connection is made, it can then communicate using the normal CORBA distribution mechanism. One of the reasons you might choose to use such a technique is to minimize IIOP traffic over the network.

Voyager—An Agent Orb for Java

Voyager is a fine implementation of mobile agent technology, from among a fine crop of mobile agent technologies. I use a number of agent technologies, and I could have used any one of the agent technologies out there—for example, IBM Japan's Aglet Technology or General Magic's Odyssey. I chose Voyager for this book because it also contains a tidy implementation of CORBA.

Voyager is used to illustrate how mobility can be used in conjunction with classical object reference base communication. Let's look at the steps for using Voyager with CORBA:

1. Define and implement a CORBA component.

   The following interface demonstrates how Voyager can be used:

   ```
   module Agents{
       interface Hangar{
   ```

```
        struct aircraft{
                long  id;
              string name;
        };
        void CheckInAirCraft(in aircraft t_aircraft);
        void CheckOutAirCraft(in long id);
};
};
```

The application will use VisiBroker for the CORBA part and Voyager for the mobility. Compile the interface using the following syntax:

```
prompt$> idl2java -no_tie -no_comment Agents.idl
```

Here is the implementation of the interface:

```
package Agents;

public class AgentCorba extends Agents._HangarImplBase
implements java.io.Serializable{
  Agents.HangarPackage.aircraft craft;

  public AgentCorba(java.lang.String name) {
    super(name);
  }

  public AgentCorba() {
    super();
  }

  public void CheckInAirCraft(
    Agents.HangarPackage.aircraft t_aircraft
  ) {
    System.out.println(new Integer(t_aircraft.id));
    System.out.println(t_aircraft.name);
    craft = t_aircraft;
  }
  public void CheckOutAirCraft(
    int id
  ) {
    if(craft.id == id)
      System.out.println("Checking out aircraft.");
  }

}
```

The implementation is in a class named `AgentCorb.java`. The `CheckInAirCraft()` method just assigns the `in` parameter to a local instance of the `Agents.HangarPackage.aircraft`, and the `CheckOutAirCraft()` method prints a simple message to the standard output if the `in` parameter ID matches that of the local variable.

2. Implement a CORBA server. After the interface has been implemented, the next step is to construct a normal CORBA server to host the component. The CORBA server in our case is not an executable. It will be contained within the actual agent host. For this reason, the server needs to be threaded so that the agent host can construct it and run it on a thread:

```
package Agents;

public class CorbaServer implements Runnable{
  org.omg.CORBA.BOA boa = null;
  public CorbaServer() {
    org.omg.CORBA.ORB orb = org.omg.CORBA.ORB.init();
    boa = orb.BOA_init();
    AgentCorba ac = new AgentCorba("AgentServer");
    boa.obj_is_ready(ac);
    System.out.println(ac + " is ready.");
  }

   public void run(){
     try{
       boa.impl_is_ready();
     }
     catch(org.omg.CORBA.SystemException e){
       e.toString();
     }
   }
}
```

The server is named `AgentServer`. Other than that, this implementation is no different than the other servers that we have built. After the server is built, you need to build a agent host server that will serve as a target for a remotely dispatched agent. Take the following steps to accomplish this:

- Define a Java class named `Store` that represents a store and generate a virtual version of `Store` so it can be constructed remotely.
- Choose a class for the registry and generate a virtual version of this class.
- Compile the Server programs.
- Start the Voyager Server to hold the persistent remote objects.

The class that is built in the last step is given in Listing 22.1.

LISTING 22.1 AGENT SERVER IMPLEMENTATION

```
package Agents;
import com.objectspace.voyager.*;
```

continues

LISTING 22.1 CONTINUED

```
public class AgentServer {

  public AgentServer() {
    try {
      Voyager.setExtendedStackTrace( true );
      VCorbaServer corba = new VCorbaServer("galileo.oa.nl:2001/Hangar");
      Thread corbathread = new Thread(corba);
 corbathread.start();
      System.out.println("AgentServer is " + corba );
      Voyager.shutdown();
    }
    catch( VoyagerException exception ){
      System.err.println( exception );
    }
  }

  public static void main(String[] args) {
    AgentServer agentServer = new AgentServer();
  }
}
```

Voyager works with virtual versions of classes. These classes can be generated using the pre-compiler provided with Voyager called `vcc.exe`. The server that is instantiated in the following line is the `CorbaServer`:

```
VCorbaServer corba = new
VCorbaServer("localhost:2001/Hangar");
```

The server is named `Hangar`. It runs on a specific port, `2001`. Because the `CorbaServer` implements a `java.util.Runnable` interface, a thread object is created and the object executes in that thread. After this has been accomplished, the implementation shuts down. It should be noted that any object that is used by a visiting object needs to be "virtualized." This is accomplished by running the `vcc.exe` on the required classes. When an agent is dispatched to a server, it essentially communicates with the virtual versions of the actual classes. These virtual versions of a class can be thought of as a proxy standing in for the real class. The thread in the preceding instance is not used remotely, so it does not need to be made virtual.

You run the `vcc.exe` on the classes that are to be made virtual. For the purpose of this example, a number of classes need to be made virtual:

```
org.omg.CORBA.ObjectImpl

org.omg.CORBA.Skeleton
Agents._HangarImplBase
Agents.AgentCorba
Agents.CorbaServer
```

Execute the vcc.exe using the following command:

```
prompt$> vcc.exe Agents.AirCraft
```

Repeat the command for these files. After this has been done, you will see that the virtualized classes have been created in the current directory. Move these to the appropriate package subdirectory. After this has been done, run the Java compiler on the files to create the bytecode. The application is now ready to be deployed. To execute the application, two things have to be done: Voyager has to be started and then the AgentServer can be executed. The two applications are shown in Figure 22.1.

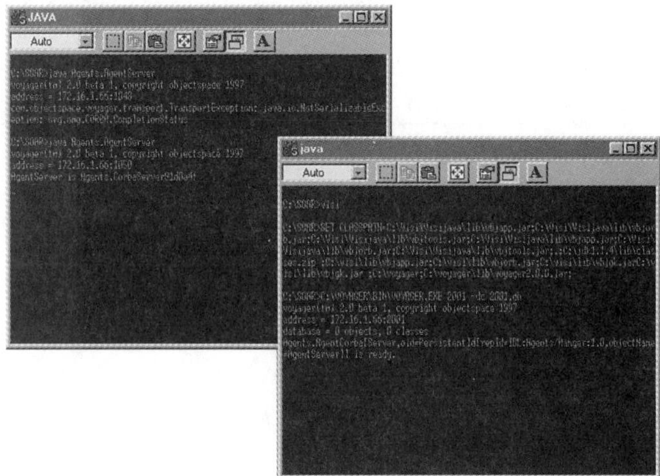

FIGURE 22.1
AgentServer *and* Voyager.

The server side is thus implemented. There are two servers and one component. One is a Voyager server that hosts a CORBA server that acts as a host for incoming clients. The component is a pure CORBA client and is hosted by the CORBA server that runs inside the Voyager server. Now you have to implement an agent that can be dispatched to this server.

Implementing an Agent

You use the following steps to build an agent in this chapter:

1. Define and implement a class named Aircraft that represents an Aircraft agent that is to be moved from one hangar to another.
2. Implement a class named Airport to instantiate and launch an instance of Aircraft.

3. Create a virtual version of `Aircraft`.
4. Compile all the files created earlier in this chapter.
5. Restart the Voyager servers.
6. Run `Agents.Airport` to launch the `Aircraft`.

Step One: The Aircraft Implementation

This class has to be a subclass of agent. The agent specifies a number of methods that, among other things, define the method defining mobility, as shown in Listing 22.2.

LISTING 22.2 AIRCRAFT AGENT

```
package Agents;
import com.objectspace.voyager.*;
import com.objectspace.voyager.agent.*;

public class Aircraft extends Agent{

  public void Depart(VCorbaServer Hangar){
   try{
      moveTo(Hangar,"Arrived");
    }
    catch( VoyagerException exception ){
      System.err.println( exception );
    }
  }
  public void Arrived(CorbaServer Hangar){
     org.omg.CORBA.ORB orb = org.omg.CORBA.ORB.init();
     Agents.Hangar hangar = Agents.HangarHelper.bind(orb);
     Agents.HangarPackage.aircraft airc =
               new Agents.HangarPackage.aircraft();
     airc.id = 2001;
     airc.name = "Agent Air";
     hangar.CheckInAirCraft(airc);
     hangar.CheckOutAirCraft(2001);
  }
}
```

The class implements two methods: `Depart()` and `Arrived()`. The latter is a callback method that is called when the `agent` arrives at its designated server that is passed as a parameter into `depart()`. The method that executes the mobility is the following:

```
moveTo(String address,String callback)
```

This method moves the agent to the specified address and executes the callback function that is provided in the second parameter. When the agent arrives at the server, it executes the callback function `Arrived()`. It is within the callback function that the agent implements the normal CORBA functions. The code in the `Arrived()` method is a similar to typical CORBA method implementations. The only difference is that as opposed to being a remote call, the agent executes the method in the host where the CORBA server runs.

The next step is to virtualize the `Aircraft` class. Execute the following at the command line:

```
prompt$> vcc Agents.Aircraft
```

This will create `Agents.Vaircraft.java`.

Step Two: The Agents.Airport Implementation

The `Airport` class lauches the `Aircraft` agent to the target server, as shown in Listing 22.3.

LISTING 22.3 AIRCRAFT SERVER

```
package Agents;
import com.objectspace.voyager.*;

public class Airport {

  public HangarClient() {
    try{
       VCorbaServer Hangar =
        (VCorbaServer)VObject.forObjectAt("galileo.oa.nl:2001/Hangar");
       Aircraft aircraft = new Aircraft();
       aircraft.Depart(Hangar);

    }
    catch( VoyagerException exception ){
      System.err.println( exception );
    }
  }

  public static void main(String[] args) {
    Airport airport = new Airport();
  }
}
```

The key to the implementation is in the following lines of code:

```
VCorbaServer Hangar =
        (VCorbaServer)VObject.forObjectAt("galileo.oa.nl:2001/Hangar");
       Aircraft aircraft = new Aircraft();
       aircraft.Depart(Hangar);
```

The first line of code creates the remote object that is running at port 2001. In this case, this is the virtual `CorbaServer`. The `Aircraft` is then instantiated and the `Depart()` method is then invoked on the `Aircraft` object. This causes the `Aircraft` to move to the remote server and execute the callback function after it arrives there. The execution of the three runtimes is shown in Figure 22.2.

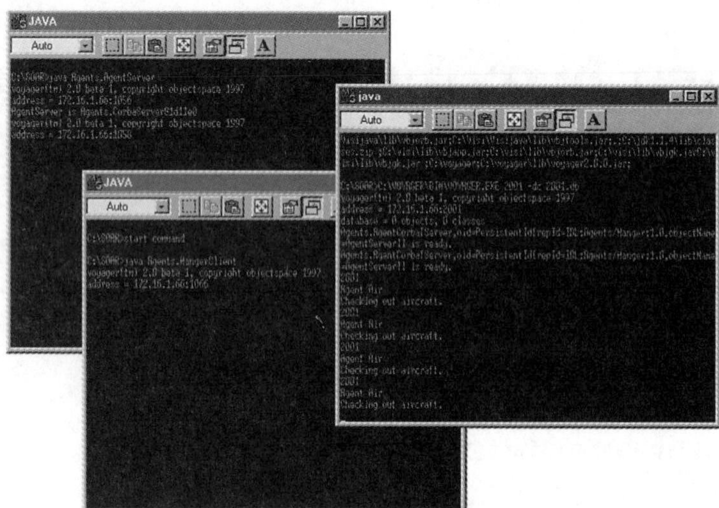

FIGURE 22.2
The three runtimes.

As you can see from the illustration, the `gent` did move to the remote server and execute the callback function. As was shown before, the callback function executes the CORBA code. The aircraft get checked into the hangar, and then the aircraft gets checked out.

Summary

Mobile agents perhaps constitute a radical departure from current technology for enabling distributed computing. A technology enables a piece of code to be dispatched physically to a remote site where, on its arrival, it continues to function autonomously. As technology goes, mobility can be the foundation of many interesting and innovative solutions. Extremely dynamic and responsive workflow environments can be built.

Components with mobility over the next few years will give rise to solutions suites being built on demand—just in time.

More importantly, many outstanding issues at the heart of AI, such as natural language processing and complex adaptive systems, should once again take the forefront of redoubled research. Whatever directions agents take, information technology will perhaps never be the same again.

CHAPTER 23

CORBA and Design Patterns

IN THIS CHAPTER

The preface to *Design Patterns, Elements Of Reusable Object-Oriented* by Erich Gamma, Richard Helm, Ralph Johnson, and John Vlissides, hereafter referred to as the *Gang Of Four* (GoF), defines patterns as "...simple and elegant solutions to specific problems in object oriented software design." Since the publication of the above-mentioned book by the GoF, there has been an explosive growth in both the interest in design patterns and their application to the problems of design. The designs of technologies such as CORBA and Java can be best understood if studied from the application of design patterns.

The problems of design are fundamental to the "quality" of the result of software engineering projects or products. These can be defined as processes that take place along the lines of an industrial process; massive amounts of resources are allocated to see it through. It has been well documented that one of the main problems with object-oriented software engineering is the process of requirements acquisitions. All popular methodologies accept this drawback and devote considerable intelligence to this problem. During the phase in which a product of analysis moves to design, I have found certain vagueness.

Engineering is about trade-offs; it is also a pragmatic science, because it accepts the fact that resources are always finite—hence the ideal product can never be built. So if you accept that engineering is about trade-offs, design is a process where you make those trade-offs. However, a methodology can never tell you what trade-offs to make. I am not faulting any method here; the problem space for design is much too large for any one method to anticipate all requirements.

It has been "discovered" in the context of design patterns that there is a recurrent nature inherent in problems of software design. Corresponding to these recurring problems are associated solutions that, once mastered, can be applied to the problem almost without thought. Design patterns therefore constitute a template that can be applied to many areas to solve many problems.

Design patterns do not teach you how to make a design trade-off, however. Trade-offs are usually made in terms of the relative cost of implementing various alternatives. For instance, in the context of using CORBA, despite the fact that IIOP is comparatively an efficient protocol, there is nevertheless a finite overhead when a client makes a remote invocation. Because the network bandwidth is also finite, it is probable that at some point a bottleneck can occur. How can system design anticipate this?

For example, in CORBA applications a recurrent solution to design systems involves a client making an arbitrary number of calls to transform one object into another. Between each of these transformations, the client makes an invocation on the transformed object. Each such transformation and the subsequent invocation on the transformed object might prove costly under certain circumstances.

There are other situations when an existing application should be modified. Complete reengineering is not an option with most of these problems. Under these circumstances, your only option is to wrap the "legacy" solution.

There are many such situations. Opting between these options means the difference between just a solution and *the* solution. In his groundbreaking book *Object-Oriented Design Measurements,* Whitmore proposed to call design a *hypothesis*. Ultimately, a hypothesis would need to be proved by experiment. Because software construction is so expensive, such experiments can only be simulated. Such a simulation will involve analyzing many variants of a solution to choose the optimal solution. This problem is tackled in the process known as *design metrics*.

You will find that applying the right design pattern to the right problem will constitute a better design. The trick is to know where to apply what and why. There are, unfortunately, no hard and fast rules except a set of idioms and heuristics for those who are not mathematically adept.

In this chapter, you look at only three design patterns. Although this might seem unfair, given the body of knowledge on design patterns and the sheer number of patterns out there, this is a book on CORBA programming and not one on designing CORBA solutions.

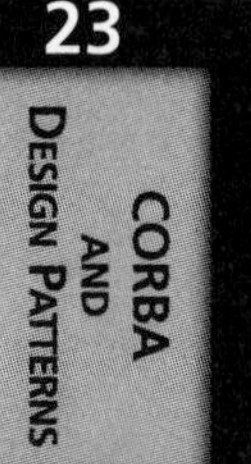

The patterns you will look at—*command*, *proxy*, and *abstract factory*—are taken from the GoF book.

The command pattern is extremely useful in reducing the number of calls made over the network. It does not not eliminate them, but it does reduce them when compared to some alternative designs. In my view, the application of this pattern to the problem keeps with the spirit of the intention of this pattern, which was stated in the book. Essentially, a command pattern can be used to transform a request into an object. Each of these requests can encapsulate a certain implementation of a command. The request objects can then be passed as parameters into a server where they can be executed.

This is sometimes handy when the execution needs to take place at the server; but from a design perspective, it would be unwise for the server to know anything about the operation itself. Consider an operation on the database. Under "normal" circumstances, the server implements an object wrapper over the underlying database API behind a standard interface. The client then makes the appropriate invocation on the server. Such a solution, though adequately satisfying the requirements, introduces undue interdependence between the client and server. The client has to know the various interface operations to make on the server that are specific to the operation that the client would like to perform on the server.

The Command Pattern

The command pattern could be used to encapsulate such operations requested as command objects. The benefit of such a design is that interdependence between the client and the server is at the level of the command interface and nothing more. The client could construct the command object and pass the object to the server. Because the server knows the interface to the command object, all it needs to do is invoke the appropriate method on the command object to cause its execution.

I have found the command object to be extremely useful to design a related set of operations within a single interface as a set of command objects that are passed to the server. The server then makes the invocation on the command interface to execute the operations. These have proved extremely useful in cutting down the number of invocations to the server, as well as reducing the dependencies between client and server.

Consider the interface shown in Listing 23.1.

LISTING 23.1 A COMMAND INTERFACE

```
module Patterns{

    interface Command{
        void execute();
    };

    struct db{
      string user;
      string pwd;
    };

    interface OpenConnection : Command{
         void OpenConnection(in db database);
    };

    interface OperateOnDatabse: Command{
         void sql (in string sqlCommand);
    };

    interface CloseConnection: Command{
    };

    interface DataOperations: Command{
        void Add(in Command aCommand);
        void Remove(in Command aCommand);
    };
};
```

In this module, `Patterns`, there are five interfaces. At the highest level, there is the `Command` interface. It specifies only one operation, `execute()`. Further on, four more interfaces are specified; each is a subclass of the `Command` interface.

Because the four interfaces are subclasses of `Command`, they all have access to the `execute` method. Each of these in turn is going to override and implement the `execute` method.

The last interface specified, `DataOperations`, acts as a container for other command objects. A client could add a series of command objects using the `add(in Command aCommand)` method. The reverse can be accomplished using the `remove()` method. The benefit of the `DataOperations` interface is that when its `execute()` is called, it can execute the command method `execute()` on all the command objects that it holds. This way, the client can save on a couple of network calls.

The implementations of these interfaces are given in the following sections. The `Command` interface does not have any implementation; it just serves as an abstract interface for classes that are derived from it.

Run the VisiBroker Java IDL pre-compiler on the interface file to generate the required files:

```
prompt$> idl2java patterns.idl
```


The Command Interface

The implementation of the `Patterns::Command` interface is shown in Listing 23.2. As mentioned, it does not contain any implementation.

LISTING 23.2 THE COMMAND PATTERN IMPLEMENTATION

```
package Patterns;
public class iCommand extends Patterns._CommandImplBase {
  public iCommand(java.lang.String name) {
    super(name);
  }
  public iCommand() {
    super();
  }
  public void execute() {
    // IMPLEMENT: Operation
  }
}
```

All the implementation is done with the subclasses of the `Command` interface. Let us take a look at them, one at a time.

The OpenConnection Interface Implementation

The implementation of the interface, as shown in Listing 23.3, contains an instance variable, database, which we will use to simulate a database connection.

LISTING 23.3 THE OpenConnection CLASS

```
package Patterns;
public class iOpenConnection extends Patterns._OpenConnectionImplBase {
  Patterns.db databse;

  public iOpenConnection(java.lang.String name) {
    super(name);
  }
  public iOpenConnection() {
    super();
  }
  public void OpenConnection(
    Patterns.db database
  ) {
     this.databse = database;
  }
  public void execute() {
    System.out.println("Opening Connection to Databse for user: " +
databse.user);
  }
}
```

When the object reference of the iOpenConnection is acquired, the client will invoke the OpenConnection() method, passing it a Patterns.db object. When a client invokes the execute() method, the implementation in this case just prints out a string to the standard I/O. In a concrete real-life implementation of this class, you could use JDBC to connect to the database.

The client is not expected to directly invoke the execute method.

The OperateOnDatabse Interface Implementation

The intent of this interface is to allow a client to pass any valid SQL statement as a string. When that has been accomplished, a client could then call the execute method on the concrete implementation of the OperateOnDatabse interface. In this case, it is implemented along the lines shown in Listing 23.4.

LISTING 23.4 THE `OperateOnDatabase` CLASS

```
package Patterns;
public class iOperateOnDatabse extends Patterns._OperateOnDatabseImplBase
{

  String SQLCommand;

  public iOperateOnDatabse(java.lang.String name) {
    super(name);
  }
  public iOperateOnDatabse() {
    super();
  }
  public void sql(
    java.lang.String sqlCommand
  ) {
     this.SQLCommand = sqlCommand;
  }
  public void execute() {
    System.out.println("Executing SQL command: " + SQLCommand);
  }
}
```


Again, the `execute` could act on a real database. In the context of the preceding design, that is not very realistic, because the `iOperateOnDatabse` does not contain any information about any database. As with the implementation of the other interfaces, the `execute()` method just outputs to the standard I/O.

The `CloseConnection` Interface Implementation

As with `iOperateOnDatabse`, the code shown in Listing 23.5 is also not very realistic, because `iCloseConnection` does not contain any information about the database that was opened. When a client calls the `execute()` method, a realistic implementation would close the active data connection.

LISTING 23.5 THE `CloseConnect` CLASS

```
package Patterns;
public class iCloseConnection extends Patterns._CloseConnectionImplBase {
  public iCloseConnection(java.lang.String name) {
    super(name);
  }
  public iCloseConnection() {
    super();
  }
  public void execute() {
```

continues

LISTING 23.5 CONTINUED

```
    System.out.println("Closing Connection to the Databse.");
  }
}
```

Thus we have the implementation of the three command classes that together could be used to act on a database. All that remains is to implement the `DataOperations` interface.

The `DataOperations` Interface Implementation

As mentioned before, `DataOperations` acts as a container for related sets of command objects that act on databases. A client constructs a command object and calls the `add()` method on the interface. When all the command objects are added, a client could call the `execute()` on this object. On doing so, the `DataOperations` implementation will iterate over all the command objects that it is holding and invoke the `execute()` method on each of them in turn. Listing 23.6 shows the implementation of the interface.

LISTING 23.6 THE `DataOperations` CLASS

```
package Patterns;
import java.util.*;

public class iDataOperations extends Patterns._DataOperationsImplBase {
  Vector Commands = new Vector();

  public iDataOperations(java.lang.String name) {
    super(name);
  }

  public iDataOperations() {
    super();
  }

  public void Add(
    Patterns.Command aCommand
  ) {
      Commands.addElement(aCommand);
  }

  public void Remove(
    Patterns.Command aCommand
  ) {
    Enumeration e = Commands.elements();
    while(e.hasMoreElements()){
      System.out.println("removeing Elements.");
      e.nextElement();
    }
```

```
  }

  public void execute() {
    Enumeration e = Commands.elements();
    while(e.hasMoreElements()){
      Patterns.Command cmd =
(Patterns.Command)e.nextElement();
 cmd.execute();
    }
  }
}
```

Internally, the `iDataOperations` class uses a `Vector` to hold the command object. Inside the `execute()` method, when it is invoked, the `iDataOperations` iterates over all the members of the `Vector` object and invokes `execute` on each of them in turn.

In terms of overall design, things could have been done differently. It is possible to have a similar outcome using other designs. The benefit of this design is that when the `execute()` method is called on the `iDataOperatations` object, the `execute()` method decides what the sequence of the command object's execution would be.

The Command Server

The command server that hosts the three command objects is, as shown in Listing 23.7, similar to the many other CORBA servers that we have built.

LISTING 23.7 THE COMMAND PATTERN SERVER

```
package Patterns;

public class CommandServer {

  public CommandServer() {
    org.omg.CORBA.ORB orb = org.omg.CORBA.ORB.init();
    org.omg.CORBA.BOA boa = orb.BOA_init();

    iOpenConnection oops = new iOpenConnection("OpenDB");
    iOperateOnDatabse sql = new iOperateOnDatabse("SQL");
    iCloseConnection cops = new iCloseConnection("CloseDB");
    iDataOperations dops = iDataOperations("Ops");

    boa.obj_is_ready(oops);
    boa.obj_is_ready(sql);
    boa.obj_is_ready(cops);
    boa.obj_is_ready(dops);

    System.out.println(oops + " is ready.");
```

continues

LISTING 23.7 CONTINUED

```
    System.out.println(sql + " is ready.");
    System.out.println(cops + " is ready.");
    System.out.println(dops + " is ready.");
    boa.impl_is_ready();
  }

  public static void main(String[] args) {
    CommandServer commandServer = new CommandServer();
  }
}
```

The server instantiates the four command objects. These are the objects that the client will talk to. The client, as shown in Listing 23.8, is just slightly different from the usual. This difference is explained after the listing.

LISTING 23.8 THE COMMAND PATTERN CLIENT

```
package Patterns;

public class CommandClient {

  public CommandClient() {
     org.omg.CORBA.ORB orb = org.omg.CORBA.ORB.init();
     org.omg.CORBA.BOA boa = orb.BOA_init();

     DataOperations cmd = DataOperationsHelper.bind(orb, "Ops");
     OpenConnection open = OpenConnectionHelper.bind(orb,"OpenDB");
     OperateOnDatabse sql = OperateOnDatabseHelper.bind(orb,"SQL");
     CloseConnection close = CloseConnectionHelper.bind(orb,"CloseDB");

     db database = new db();
     database.user = "Remrandt";
     database.pwd = "******";

     open.OpenConnection(database);

     cmd.Add(open);

     sql.sql("SELECT * FROM PAINTERS");
     cmd.Add(sql);
     cmd.Add(close);

     cmd.execute();
  }

  public static void main(String[] args) {
    CommandClient commandClient = new CommandClient();
  }
}
```

The key object reference is the `cmd` object. When the other three object references are initialized, the three data command objects are added to the `cmd` object. When the `cmd` object is properly set up, the `execute` method is called on it.

The Proxy Pattern

The proxy pattern is a structural pattern. In the GoF book, it is defined as a placeholder for another object to control access to it. Proxy patterns are especially useful when you need to wrap non–object-oriented code in an object-oriented wrapper. Such a strategy is especially useful when you are dealing with legacy systems or data access systems.

In fact, CORBA uses the proxy pattern. On the client side, the stubs that are generated by the IDL pre-compiler are acually a proxy implementation. As a proxy, the intention is to act as a placeholder for a remote object reference. This enables a number of benefits; for one, it shields the underlying complexity of the IIOP protocol marshaling and demarshaling.

The `for_var` variables are also proxies in a sense. They encapsulate the underlying `foo_ptr` as smart pointers to automatically manage reference counting. Most of the interceptor/filter technology discussed in earlier chapters also serve as proxies. However, as proxies, they are very transparent to both the client and the server.

The following code illustrates how proxies can be used to augment an existing implementation—in this case, wrapping:

```
#include "command.idl"

module Patterns {

    interface proxy:DataOperations{
        exception proxyException{string reason;};
    };
};
```

The preceding interface inherits from the `DataOperations` interface that was defined in `command.idl`. The object of this exercise is to implement the proxy interface to act as a go-between for the client and the component. The implementation is shown in the following section. Compile the interface using the following command:

```
prompt$> idl2java -no_tie -no_comments proxy.idl
```

The Proxy Interface Implementation

The proxy implementation, as shown in Listing 23.9, holds an `iDataOperations` as an instance variable. When an invocation to the `iDataOperations` is made by the client, the proxy masquerading as the `iDataOperations` delegates the service to the real `iDataOperations`. All the methods intended for the `iDataOperations` instance are passed on the instance—all except the `execute()` method. The proxy checks to see whether the number of command objects held by `iDataOperations` is three, the number to execute the `iDataOperations` command object. Within these modifications, the proxy does not do anything other than output the standard I/O.

LISTING 23.9 THE PROXY CLASS

```
package Patterns;
public class iproxy extends Patterns._proxyImplBase {

  iDataOperations cmds = new iDataOperations();

  public iproxy(java.lang.String name) {
    super(name);
  }
  public iproxy() {
    super();
  }
  public void Add (
    Patterns.Command aCommand
  ) {
    cmds.Add(aCommand);
  }
  public void Remove(
    Patterns.Command aCommand
  ) {
    cmds.Remove(aCommand);
  }
  public void execute(){
   if(cmds.Commands.size() == 3)
      cmds.execute();
   else
      System.out.println("Inconsistent Command Object");
  }
}
```

The Proxy Server Implementation

The proxy server, as shown in Listing 23.10, contains only a minor modification to the one implemented for the command objects. Instead of the `iDataOperations` object, an instance of the proxy object is initialized.

LISTING 23.10 THE COMMAND SERVER WITH PROXY

```
package Patterns;

public class CommandServer {

  public CommandServer() {
    org.omg.CORBA.ORB orb = org.omg.CORBA.ORB.init();
    org.omg.CORBA.BOA boa = orb.BOA_init();

    iOpenConnection oops = new iOpenConnection("OpenDB");

    iOperateOnDatabse sql = new iOperateOnDatabse("SQL");
    iCloseConnection cops = new iCloseConnection("CloseDB");
    iproxy proxy = new iproxy("Ops");

    boa.obj_is_ready(oops);
    boa.obj_is_ready(sql);
    boa.obj_is_ready(cops);
    boa.obj_is_ready(proxy);

    System.out.println(oops + " is ready.");
    System.out.println(sql + " is ready.");
    System.out.println(cops + " is ready.");
    System.out.println(proxy + " is ready.");
    boa.impl_is_ready();
  }

  public static void main(String[] args) {
    CommandServer commandServer = new CommandServer();
  }
}
```


The Proxy Client Implementation

The client does not require any modifications; it will function as before without any change. The code is given in Listing 23.11.

LISTING 23.11 THE `CommandClient` CLASS

```
package Patterns;

public class CommandClient {

  public CommandClient() {
     org.omg.CORBA.ORB orb = org.omg.CORBA.ORB.init();
     org.omg.CORBA.BOA boa = orb.BOA_init();
```

continues

LISTING 23.11 CONTINUED

```
    DataOperations cmd = DataOperationsHelper.bind(orb, "Ops");
    OpenConnection open = OpenConnectionHelper.bind(orb,"OpenDB");
    OperateOnDatabse sql = OperateOnDatabseHelper.bind(orb,"SQL");
    CloseConnection close = CloseConnectionHelper.bind(orb,"CloseDB");

    db database = new db();
    database.user = "Remrandt";
    database.pwd = "******";

    open.OpenConnection(database);

    cmd.Add(open);

    sql.sql("SELECT * FROM PAINTERS");
    cmd.Add(sql);

    cmd.execute();
  }

  public static void main(String[] args) {
    CommandClient commandClient = new CommandClient();
  }
}
```

The code is modified to illustrate the presence of the proxy on the server. The client has not been modified at all. The `cmd` object is populated with only two command objects. This means that when the `execute()` is called on the `cmd` object, it will not complete the execution.

The Abstract Factory Pattern

The abstract factory pattern is one of my favorite patterns. One of the main consequences of using this pattern is that you can almost totally decouple the construction of complex objects from the client. When designing CORBA applications, it is inevitable that a client would require the services of a reasonable number of object references to get the job done. Under normal circumstances, it is also usual that the client is given responsibility for constructing each one of these object references in some server and invoking the required interface protocols on them.

The abstract factory pattern enables a designer to hide a lot of this behind a `Factory` interface. This enables you to give a rather simple picture to the client while the implementation of the `abstractFactory` does all the hard work.

The abstract factory pattern can be extremely useful if used in conjunction with Orbix filters or VisiBroker interceptors. Under these mechanisms, when a client request comes in, the filter or interceptor could construct the appropriate object reference and pass it back to the client. This enables the fullfillment of one of the areas that the GoF book lists in which the pattern can be used. The specific area is the design of a system that is independent of how the objects on the server side are "created, composed and represented."

Let's use the abstract factory pattern in a similar fashion. Primarily, let's use VisiBroker to implement a factory to mediate between a client and the server to construct an object reference and return to the client. The example uses the following interface:

```
module patterns {
    interface abstractFactory{

        Object create();
        void destroy();
    };

    interface concreteFactory:abstractFactory{
        struct Struct{
                   short number;
                };
                readonly attribute long identifier;
                Struct getStruct();
    };
};
```

The `patterns` module specifies two interfaces. The `abstractFactory` interface serves as an abstraction for subinterfaces. This enables you to pass back subclasses to the client by utilizing polymorphism.

The `concreteFactory:abstractFactory` interface specifies two operations: one to create an object reference and the other to destroy it. The implementations of these interfaces are shown in the next sections.

The first thing we have to do is implement the `Factory` service.

Implementing the Interface

You implement only the `concreteFactory` interface. Because it is a subclass of the `abstractFactory`, the underlying plug into the Basic Object Adapter (BOA) will ensure that, if required, the client can treat it as an `abstractFactory`. The implementation is shown in Listing 23.12.

LISTING 23.12 THE `ConcreteFactory` CLASS

```
package Patterns;
public class concreteFactory_i extends Patterns._concreteFactoryImplBase {
```

continues

LISTING 23.12 CONTINUED

```
  private Patterns.concreteFactoryPackage.Struct a_struct = new
Patterns.concreteFactoryPackage.Struct();
  private org.omg.CORBA.BOA boa_ = null;

  public concreteFactory_i(java.lang.String name, org.omg.CORBA.BOA boa) {
    super(name);
    a_struct.number = 10010;
    boa_ = boa;
  }

  public concreteFactory_i(org.omg.CORBA.BOA boa) {
    super();
    a_struct.number = 10010;
    boa_ = boa;
  }

  public Patterns.concreteFactoryPackage.Struct getStruct() {
    return a_struct;
  }

  public org.omg.CORBA.Object create() {
    return this;
  }

  public void destroy() {
   boa_.deactivate_obj(this);
  }

  public int identifier() {
    return a_struct.number;
  }
}
```

The `create()` method returns an instance of the current object. The example could be extended so that other objects that extend the `Factory` interface can be returned. In this case, only the current object reference is returned. When the `destroy()` method is invoked by the client, the instance of the BOA is a request to deregister the object reference.

When this has been implemented, you need to construct a server to host this factory instance, of course. This is shown in Listing 23.13.

LISTING 23.13 THE `FactoryServer` IMPLEMENTATION

```
package Patterns;

public class FactoryServer {
```

```
  org.omg.CORBA.ORB orb_ = null;
  org.omg.CORBA.BOA boa_  = null;

  public FactoryServer() {
   orb_ = org.omg.CORBA.ORB.init();
   boa_ = orb_.BOA_init();
   Patterns.concreteFactory cf = new
Patterns.concreteFactory_i("Factory",boa_);

   try{
      boa_.obj_is_ready(cf);
      System.out.println(cf + " is ready.");
      boa_.impl_is_ready();
      boa_.deactivate_obj(cf);
    }
    catch(org.omg.CORBA.SystemException ex){
      System.out.println(ex.toString());
    }
  }

  public static void main(String[] args) {
    FactoryServer factoryServer = new FactoryServer();
    factoryServer.invokedStandalone = true;
  }
  private boolean invokedStandalone = false;
}
```


The key statement in this implementation is the actual construction of the object that implements the `Factory` interface. This is accomplished in the following line of code:

```
Patterns.concreteFactory cf = new
Patterns.concreteFactory_i("Factory",boa_);
```

When the `concreteFactory` instance is created, the BOA goes into a blocked mode awaiting requests from the client. The implementation of the client is shown in Listing 23.14.

LISTING 23.14 THE FACTORYCLIENT CLASS

```
 package Patterns;
public class FactoryClient {

  public FactoryClient() {
    try{
     org.omg.CORBA.ORB orb = org.omg.CORBA.ORB.init();
     Patterns.concreteFactory cf =
Patterns.concreteFactoryHelper.bind(orb, "Factory");
     org.omg.CORBA.Object obj = cf.create();
```

continues

LISTING 23.14 CONTINUED

```
      Patterns.concreteFactory factory =
Patterns.concreteFactoryHelper.narrow(obj);
      Patterns.concreteFactoryPackage.Struct struct = factory.getStruct();
      System.out.println(new Integer(struct.number));
     }
     catch(org.omg.CORBA.SystemException ex){
       System.out.println(ex.toString());
     }
   }

   public static void main(String[] args) {
     FactoryClient factoryClient = new FactoryClient();
   }
}
```

The code in Listing 23.14 shows two mechanisms in which an object reference can be constructed by a client. The first method is to use the `bind()` method:

```
Patterns.concreteFactory cf = Patterns.concreteFactoryHelper.bind(orb,
"Factory");
```

When the instance of the factory is returned, it can then be used to create objects. A fully blown implementation of the `Factory` service would use the Naming Service to register itself so that the client could use a standard CORBA service to acquire the `Factory` object reference.

When the `Factory` object reference is acquired, it can be used to construct the object references that are required by the client to function. When the reference is acquired, it is used to demonstrate how a `Factory` interface can be used to construct an object reference:

```
org.omg.CORBA.Object obj = cf.create();
```

This is the second mechanism that can be used to construct an object reference. This time, let's use the method on the `concreteFactory`. Invoking the `create()` method returns an instance of `CORBA.Object`. This reference has to be narrowed to get hold of the reference to the `concreteFactory` interface. This is accomplished by narrowing the general object reference `CORBA.Object` to a more specific one:

```
Patterns.concreteFactory factory =
Patterns.concreteFactoryHelper.narrow(obj);
```

This enables you to retrieve the interface. When this has been done successfully, you can invoke methods on the interface as you normally do.

The abstract factory pattern can be a powerful tool to decouple the creation of an object from the use of it. This can be helpful when you have to isolate complex routines for creating an object from the client. This might be necessary when the client need not have the knowledge of how to construct the object.

Summary

Design patterns are a fundamental shift in transforming software development to software engineering. Patterns encapsulate the best practices that characterize good software. When you are developing distributed systems, design, more than anything else, is the most critical aspect. The onus on analysis is, to an extent, the same for distributed systems as it has been for classical systems. But the design of distributed systems is different.

Many issues that are nonessential to standalone applications are important when considering distributed applications. Issues of network bandwidth, availability, fault tolerance, and perhaps the aspect of CORBA being essentially a peer-to-peer technology place a strong emphasis on good design.

Design patterns help focus these principles of good design and bring them to bear on CORBA applications. Three-tier client/server applications promise better maintainability and efficient adaptation to changing requirements. With design patterns, that promise can be redeemed.

CHAPTER 24

CORBA Interface Repository

In This Chapter

The Interface Repository (IR) is a runtime database that holds a component's interface definition in a machine-readable format. The IR potentially has many uses. Because it essentially holds a component's IDL information, this information can be used to make a dynamic invocation on the component. Remember that the IR contains only interface information; it does not contain information about the runtime parameters of the component itself. That information is held in the Implementation Repository.

The interface definitions are at the heart of what makes CORBA tick. A client communicates with a server component through a "published" interface. In recent years, there has been a growth of complex architectures being built using CORBA. These can consist of tens of thousands of components. At some point, the management of these interfaces could pose a problem. It is at that point that the IR can become truly useful. A client could introspect the IR to find the right interface definitions. If the client is designed to use dynamic invocations, the various parameters of an interface could be introspected to assist in the invocation of an operation. If, on the other hand, static invocations are being used, the IDL pre-compiler could be modified to directly generate all the required files directly from the IR.

As more visual builders become available for developing CORBA applications (ComponentBroker, IBM VisualAge, VisiBroker, C++ Builder, and so forth), the IR will be at the center of the visual toolkit. The application builder's toolkit will allow the import of component interfaces directly from the IR. This enables a developer to use drag and drop to construct applications. Nevertheless, we have some way to go before the IR becomes pervasive.

The Structure of the Interface Repository

The IR, in a nutshell, contains all the information pertaining to an interface. It can contain modules, interfaces, attributes, operations, exceptions, and so forth. In short, it can contain any valid piece of the IDL. It can be extended to value-added information as well. Such value-added information could enable a repository administrator to have version control information, and so forth. For instance, the SOM/DSOM implementation from IBM that was used for OpenDoc (now sadly put to death by the powers that be. . .sigh) used a repository called Bento that could essentially store anything. But for the most part, the existing repository is fairly simple. Some of them use a binary format to store interface information while others store the information as ASCII stores this information.

OMG has defined a standard API for describing the IR. This enables an application or an application builder to easily access the IR. The benefit of this scheme is that no matter what type of repository is being used, as long as it supports a standard interface, any IIOP client could use the IR to discover interfaces.

From a structural perspective, the IR API defines a number of definitions (DEFS). Refer to the interface used to illustrate dynamic invocations in Chapter 25, "Using Dynamic Invocation Interfaces"; it explains what I am talking about. Listing 24.1 shows the interface.

LISTING 24.1 `Dynamic.idl` FOR THE INTERFACE REPOSITORY

```
module Dynamic {
  interface dii {
    struct DyStruct {
      string name;
      short age;
    };

    void takestruct(in DyStruct ins, out DyStruct outs,
inout DyStruct inouts);

    dii::DyStruct getstuct();

    typedef sequence<string> strings;

    void takesequence(
      in strings ins,
      out strings outs,
      inout strings inouts
    );

    strings getsequence();

    void takenumber(
      in long ins,
      out long outs,
      inout long inouts
    );
    long getnumber();
    void takestring(
      in string ins,
      out string outs,
      inout string inouts
    );

    void takestring(
```

continues

LISTING 24.1 CONTINUED

```
        in string ins,
           out string outs,
        inout string inouts
    )

    string getstring();

    void takereference(
      in Dynamic::dii ins,
      out Dynamic::dii outs,
      inout Dynamic::dii inouts
    );
    Dynamic::dii getreference();
  };
};
```

There are a number of logical divisions in the preceding module. These are shown in Figure 24.1.

The Interface Repository API is structured as definitions. Every element in IDL has its corresponding definition. You might think that it would have been simple just to leave IDL undefined in a repository. But Defs, as I call them, serve a higher purpose: They isolate the semantics of the IDL structure. That way, you don't have to construct a parser to figure out what the IDL file contains. Every aspect of IDL is defined—all the way from modules to exceptions. They all have Defs.

If you consider the previous example, the `Dynamic.idl` contains five Defs: the `ModuleDef`, the `InterfaceDef`, the `StructDef`, the `SequenceDef`, and the `OperationDef`. At the root of all the Defs stands the Repository.

Further still, if you take an operation, the IR API also defines methods to figure out an operation's parameters, the direction in which a parameter is passed, and its type. It also specifies how to look up the details of a return type. Furthermore, if an operation raises any exception, you can use the `ExceptionDef` to gain knowledge of that as well.

All these Defs are fine, but they are pretty much useless unless you have a mechanism of navigating a repository. That is where the next set of abstract entities comes in: `IRObject`, `Contained` objects, and `Container` objects. The relationship is depicted in Figure 24.2.

The following is a brief description of these entities:

- `IRObject`—The `IROBject` is essentially everything in the Repository, including the Repository itself.

- `Container`—These are `IRObjects` that can contain other `IRObjects`. The figure shows three types of containers: the Repository itself, the `ModuleDef` (because it can contain pretty much everything), and the `InterfaceDef`.
- `Contained`—These are the contents of a container. If we are talking about a module, the `Contained` can be `InterfaceDefs`, `ConstantDefs`, `ExceptionDefs`, and so on. The full list is shown in the figure. As you can see, all `IRObjects` can be a `Contained` object.

FIGURE 24.1
The Interface Repository module.

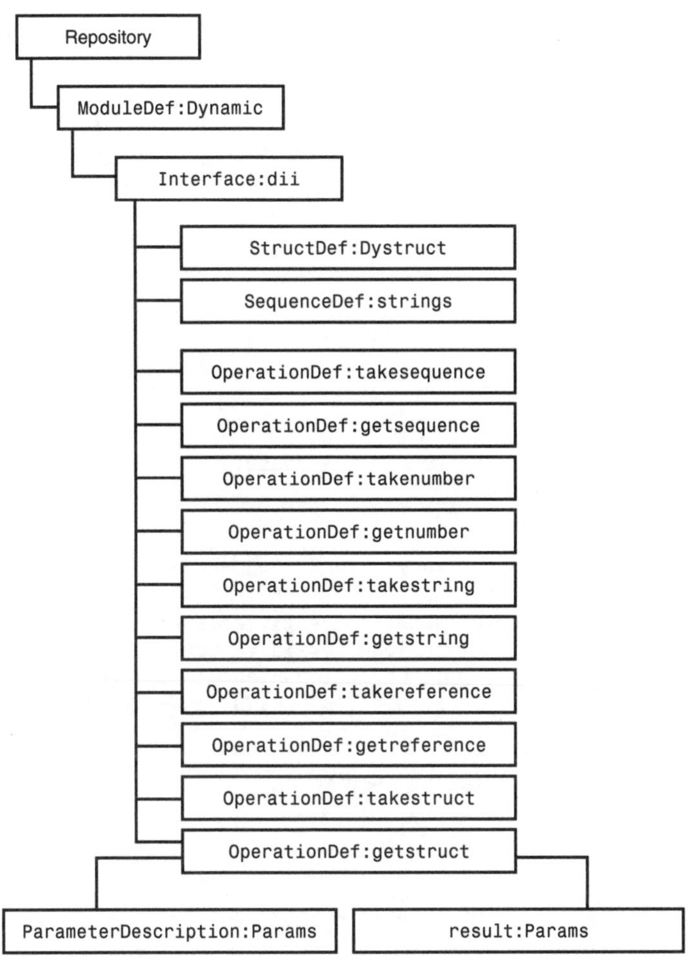

All three concepts are abstract. But it helps to be familiar with their protocol if you intend to use the Interface Repository. The following code shows the internals of `IRObject` and the interface describing the container.

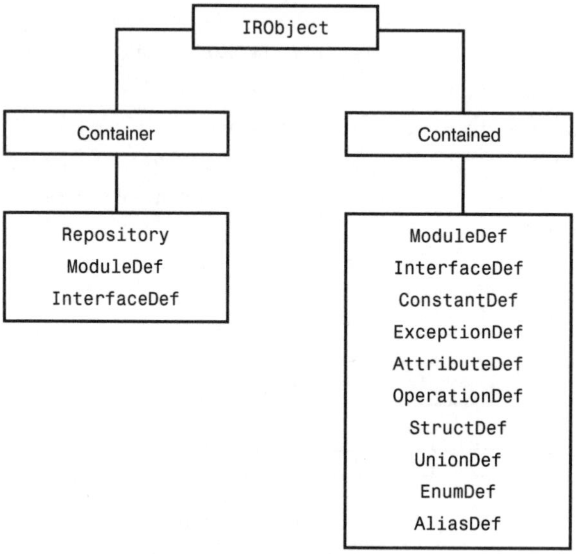

FIGURE 24.2
The `IRObject` *object model.*

IRObject

Container

Contained

Repository
ModuleDef
InterfaceDef

ModuleDef
InterfaceDef
ConstantDef
ExceptionDef
AttributeDef
OperationDef
StructDef
UnionDef
EnumDef
AliasDef

```
interface IRObject{
    readonly attribute DefinitionKind def_kind;
    void destroy();
};

typedef sequence<Contained> ContainedSeq;

interface Container:IRObject {

    ContainedSeq lookup(in ScopedName search_name);

    ContainedSeq lookup_name(in Identifier search_name,
                    in long levels_to_search,
                    in DefinitionKind limit_type,
                    in boolean exclude_inherited);

    struct Description{
        Contained contained_object;
        Definition kind;
        any value;
    };

    typedef sequence<Description> DescriptionSeq;

    DescriptionSeq describe_contents(
in DefinitionKind limit_type,
in boolean exclude_inherited,
in long max_returned_objs
);
```

```
    ......
    ......
    ......
};
```

The `lookup()` operations are the important operations on the `Container` interface. It is possible to look up a `Contained` object by passing either a relative or an absolute name to a `Contained`. Remember that a `Container` can essentially contain a `Contained`.

The `contents()` allow you to retrieve entire sets of `Contained` objects from a container. The first parameter, `DefinitionKind`, is the parameter that enables you to retrieve some or all of the contents of a container. Each of the `Contained` objects has it own `DefinitionKind` ID. For instance, `_dk_Module` is the ID for `ModuleDef`. If you specify `_dk_all`, all the `Contained` objects at that position are retrieved. If, on the other hand, you want to retrieve only operations, you can set the `limit_type` variable to `_dk_operation` so that the `ContainedSeq` will only contain operations if any are found.

`lookup_name()` enables you to locate a `Contained` object by name within a container. Again, the other parameters are essential to make a search more efficient; for example, the first parameter enables you to specify the depth of the search to be conducted, the `limit_type` plays the same role as it does with `lookup()`, and the last parameter can be set to false (in this case, the IR would search for registered `IRObjects` in the inherited interfaces).

Finally, the `describe_contents()` provides you with a sequence of `Descriptions` of the `Contained` objects. The `described_contents()` are a combination of the IR client calling `contents()` and then each of the content objects, iteratively invoking `Contained:describe()`, retrieving all the essentials of the results in a tidy array of the `Container:Description struct`. The following code shows the `Contained` interface:

```
interface Contained:IRObject{

    attribute RepositoryId id;
    attribute Identifier name;
    attribute VersionSpec version;
    readonly attribute Container defined_in;
    readonly attribute ScopedName absolute_name;
    readonly attribute Repository containing_repository;

    struct Description {
        DefinitionKind kind;
        any    value;
    };

    Description describe();
    .......
    .......
};
```

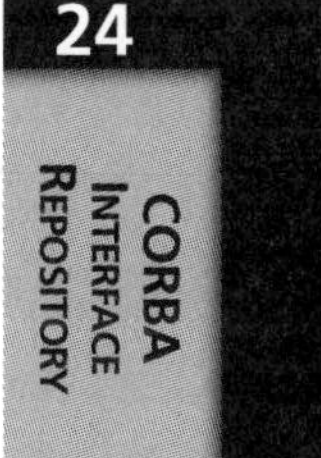

When the Container object has returned either a Container:DescriptionSeq or a Container:ContainedSeq sequence, the Contained interface protocol can be used to drill down to the details of the IRObject that is contained.

The describe() is the key operation to invoke on a Contained object. Every IRObject has a description attached to it if it is a Contained object. Again, you can use the kind (_dk_operation, _dk_module, and so forth) to figure out how to extract the value that is a CORBA.Any type.

Along with describe(), the various accessor methods for the attribute provide you with enough information to determine what the Contained object is.

Essentially, all the components of a repository are subclasses of either Container and/or Contained. The relationship is the same as shown in Figure 24.2.

We will only look at ModuleDef, InterfaceDef, and OperationDef for brevity. For more information on the various API, consult either the CORBA 2.*x* specification or your favorite ORB reference manual.

The ModuleDef Interface

The module is both a Container and a Contained. As a Contained, it can be part of a repository or other modules. As a Container it can hold constants, aliases (typedefs), exceptions, interfaces, and other modules. All the operations specified in the superclass are available to the ModuleDef.

The most essential method to invoke on an instance of ModuleDef is Contained.describe(). It returns a Contained.Description struct. It will define a kind as dk_module, and its value will point to a ModuleDescription struct:

```
struct ModuleDescription {
    identifier name;
    RepositoryId Id;
    RepositoryId defined_in;
    VersionSpec version;
};
```

For instance, the name will give you the name of the module, and the defined_in will indicate where it is Contained.

The InterfaceDef Interface

Like the ModuleDef, the InterfaceDef is also a subclass of Container and Contained. The following is a partial listing of this interface:

```
interface InterfaceDef:Container,Contained,IDLType{

    attribute InterfaceDefSeq base_interfaces;
    boolean Is_a(in RepositoryId interface_idl);

    struct FullInterfaceDescrition{

        Identifier name;
        RepositoryId id;
        RepositoryId defined_in;
        VersionSpec version;
        OpDescriptionSeq operations;
        AttrDescriptionSeq attributes;
        RepositoryIdSeq base_interfaces;
        TypeCode type;
    };

    FullInterfaceDescription describe_interface();

    . . . .
    . . . .
};
```

Within its protocol, it specifies an operation named `describe_interface()`. It returns a `struct FullInterfaceDescription`. It also provides you with a sequence of operations that are `Contained` within the interface as well as attributes.

The `OperationDef` Interface

The `OperationDef` interface is derived from `Contained`. This means that it can only be a contained object. It might be handy to think of the parameters as something that are contained in an operation. But this is not the case. All the parameters, the return types, and the exceptions raised by the operations make up an atomic whole. The interface is shown here:

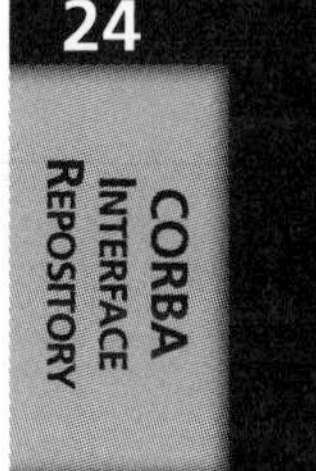


```
interface OperationDef:Contained{

    readonly attribute TypeCode result;
    attribute IDLType result_def;
    attribute ParDescriptionSeq params;
    attribute OperationMode mode;
    attribute ContexSeq contexts;
    attribute ExceptionDefSeq exceptions;
}
```

The attributes that are specified enable you to determine an operation in its entirety (except for the semantics of the what the operation will do!).

The params is defined as a sequence of ParameterDescriptions. This structure is given here:

```
struct ParameterDescription{
    identifier name;
    TypeCode type;
    IDLType type_def;
    ParameterMode mode;
};
```

The identifier gives you the name of the parameter, the TypeCode to the underlying TypeCode, and TCKind to specify the type of parameter; the ParameterMode gives you the direction in which the parameter is passed. Because the OperationDef is also a Contained, you can treat it as one by invoking Contained.Describe on it. It will return a Description struct with the following information that is represented as a struct. The kind will be dk_operation, and the value will hold a CORBA.Any pointing to an OperationDescription struct:

```
    struct OperationDescription{
        Identifier name;
        RepositoryId id;
        RepositoryId defined_in;
        VersionSpec version;
        TypeCode result;
        OperationMode mode;
        ContextIdSeq contexts;
        ParDescriptionSeq parameters;
        ExcDescriptionSeq exceptions;
    };
```

Using the Interface Repository

The following example illustrates how the Interface Repository can be used to read in an interface and write to a file locally.

The example uses the Dynamic.dii interface that we specified for using Dynamic Invocation Interfaces (DIIs). The example uses VisiBroker for Java. The following section illustrates some of the issues dealing with VisiBroker's Repository.

Using the VisiBroker Repository

The VisiBroker Repository can be started by executing the the irep application. Its command line is shown here:

```
syntax: irep [-console] IRName [File.idl]
```

The `irep` can be started either as a console application or be run in its own GUI. The GUI is shown in Figure 24.3. VisiBroker allows any number of repositories to be run. You can do that by providing a name to the repository. The repository can be loaded with an interface during startup by providing a `File.idl` parameter. So if you want to start the repository with `dii.idl`, use the follwing command:

```
syntax: irep SOAR dii.idl
```

The Repository should be populated with the interfaces. VisiBroker provides a utility named `idl2ir`. This tool can be used to update the repository.

```
Syntax: idl2ir [-ir name] [-replace] name.idl
```

The `idl2ir` can be used to update a specific IR by specifying a name for the IR. If the repository already contains the interface, an exception will be thrown. If you want to replace a particular interface, use the `-replace` flag. Updating the repository with `dii` is shown here:

```
syntax: idl2ir -ir SOAR -replace dii.idl
```

Reading Information from the IR

The following example illustrates how the IR can be used. The example builds a simple IR reader. The example will not attempt to do anything fancy—just read an interface that is defined in a module. Listing 24.2 shows the code for the example.

LISTING 24.2 IR READER CLIENT

```
package Dynamic;
import org.omg.CORBA.*;
import org.omg.CORBA.InterfaceDefPackage.*;
import org.omg.CORBA.TypeCodePackage.*;
import java.util.*;
import org.omg.CORBA.Repository;


public class IRClient {

  FullInterfaceDescription InterfaceDescription;
  org.omg.CORBA.Repository repository;
  org.omg.CORBA.ORB orb;
  private int _indent = 0;

  public IRClient(String[] args) {
```

continues

LISTING 24.2 CONTINUED

```
    if ( args.length == 0 ) {
      System.out.println(
        "Usage: Java Dynamic.IRClient Fully Qualified Interface Name");
      System.exit(1);
    }

    orb  = org.omg.CORBA.ORB.init();
    repository = org.omg.CORBA.RepositoryHelper.bind(orb);

    InterfaceDef idef = InterfaceDefHelper.narrow(
                              repository.lookup(args[0]));

    if(idef==null){
      System.out.println("Defenition Not Found");
      System.exit(1);
    }

    InterfaceDescription = idef.describe_interface();
    ReadInterface();
  }

  public static void main(String[] args) {
    IRClient iRClient = new IRClient(args);
  }


 protected void ReadInterface(){
      OperationDescription[] operations = InterfaceDescription.operations;
      StringBuffer line = new StringBuffer();
      line.append("interface " + InterfaceDescription.name + " {\n");
      for(int j = 0; j < operations.length; j++){
        ParameterDescription[] arguements = operations[j].parameters;
        line.append("\t");
        line.append(typecodeToString(operations[j].result) + " " +
                                     InterfaceDescription.operations
[j].name + "(" );        for(int k = 0; k < arguements.length; k++){
           line.append(getParameterMode(arguements[k].mode) +
                       typecodeToString(arguements[k].type) +
                       " " + arguements[k].name
                       );
           if(k<arguements.length-1)
              line.append(", ");
        }
        line.append(");" + "\n");
      }
      line.append("};" + "\n");
      System.out.println(line.toString());
  }
```

```
String getParameterMode(ParameterMode kind){
    String returnString = null;
    switch(kind.value()){
      case kind._PARAM_IN:{
         returnString = "in ";
         break;
      }
      case kind._PARAM_INOUT:{
         returnString = "inout ";
         break;
      }
      case kind._PARAM_OUT:{
         returnString = "out ";
         break;
      }
    }
    return returnString;
  }

  String typecodeToString(TypeCode kind){
  String ret = null;

  switch(kind.kind().value()){
    case TCKind._tk_void:
      ret = "void";
      break;
    case TCKind._tk_short:
      ret = "short";
      break;
    case TCKind._tk_long:
      ret = "long";
      break;
    case TCKind._tk_float:
      ret = "float";
      break;
    case TCKind._tk_double:
      ret = "double";
      break;
    case TCKind._tk_objref:
      try{
        ret = kind.name();
        break;
      }
      catch(BadKind bk){break;}
    case TCKind._tk_struct:
       try{
        ret = kind.name();
        break;
      }
```

continues

LISTING 24.2 CONTINUED

```
        catch(BadKind bk){break;}
      case TCKind._tk_string:
        ret = "string";
        break;
      case TCKind._tk_sequence:
         try{
          ret = kind.name();
          break;
        }
        catch(BadKind bk){break;}

      default:
        break;
      }
      return ret;
    }

    private String toIdl(org.omg.CORBA.IDLType idlType) {
      org.omg.CORBA.Contained contained =
               org.omg.CORBA.ContainedHelper.narrow(idlType);
      return contained == null ?
      idlType.type().toString() :
      contained.absolute_name();
  }

}
```

When the reference to the Repository is retrieved using the `bind` call, the constructor for the class uses the following line to construct an instance of `InterfaceDef`:

```
InterfaceDef idef =
InterfaceDefHelper.narrow(repository.lookup(args[0]));
```

The name that is passed into the command line must be a fully qualified name to an interface. So if you want to look up the `dii` interface defined in the `Dynamic` module, it can be done by invoking the class with the following syntax:

```
syntax: Dynamic.IRClient Dynamic.dii
```

Ensure that the interface has been loaded into the VisiBroker Repository. This can be determined by issuing the next code, typing in the name of the interface in the repository browser.

The reading of the interface is done in the `ReadInterface()` method. It acts on an instance of `FullInterfaceDescription`. This is a `struct` that contains all the information that is required to determine the interface:

```
struct FullInterfaceDescrition{

        Identifier name;
        RepositoryId id;
        RepositoryId defined_in;
        VersionSpec version;
        OpDescriptionSeq operations;
        AttrDescriptionSeq attributes;
        RepositoryIdSeq base_interfaces;
        TypeCode type;
    };
```

The first member of the `struct` provides us with the name of the interface. The attributes and the operations members encapsulate a sequence of operations and attributes that are defined in the interface.

Because we are dealing only with interfaces, it is not necessary to consider the module. For this reason, the first `for` loop just iterates over the length of the operation sequence:

```
for(int j = 0; j < operations.length; j++){
        ParameterDescription[] arguements =
   operations[j].parameters;
        line.append("\t");
        line.append(typecodeToString(operations[j].result) +
   " " +
   InterfaceDescription.operations[j].name + "(" );
. . .
. . .
```

The first `for` loop also prints out the return type by using a `typecodeToString()` method.

The second `for` loop iterates over the parameter list. The list of parameters can be retreived by invoking `operations[j].parameters`. During iteration, `operations[j].parameters` prints out the parameters in the operation with their mode of passage and their names and types:

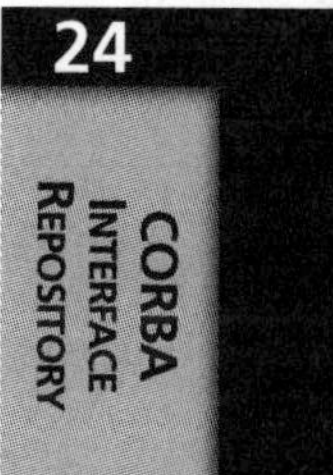


```
for(int k = 0; k < arguments.length; k++){
           line.append(getParameterMode(arguments[k].mode)
 + typecodeToString(arguments[k].type) +
 " " + arguments[k].name
   );
```

Internally, the implementation uses a string buffer to hold an expanding string. At the end of the process, its contents are printed to the system output terminal, as shown in Figure 24.3.

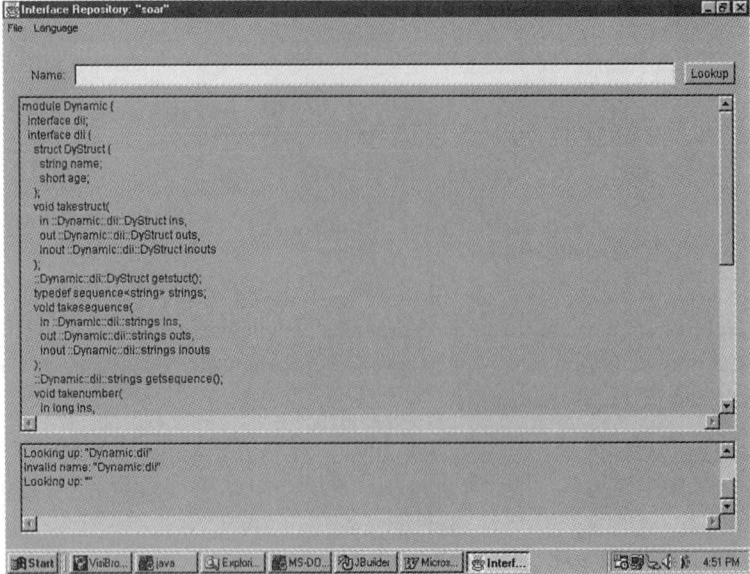

FIGURE 24.3
The systems output terminal.

Summary

The Interface Repository is a runtime database that can contain interface definitions in machine-readable format. Any aspect of an interface can be recorded in a Repository. When recorded, a client can use standard IR API to read and/or modify various parts of an interface.

One way such a technology can be used is by next-generation CORBA application builders that can enable developers to build drag-and-drop CORBA applications. It is also useful for Dynamic Invocation Interfaces. A DII client can use the IR to introspect the interface and dynamically construct an invocation in memory and make this invocation. A word of caution, though. IR does not contain meta-interface information. By that, I mean that the IR does not contain any information that describes the semantics of an interface. That is something that probably will be available in the next couple of decades.

CHAPTER 25

CORBA Dynamic Invocation Interfaces

IN THIS CHAPTER

CORBA has always been about compromises. For an organization as large as Object Management Group (OMG), compromises are the only way such a body can go forward with the standardization process for distributed systems architectures. The core CORBA specification is perhaps the most striking feature of such a process. The *C* in CORBA stands for *Common*; as such, it is a compromise that involves CORBA supporting two types of distributed object interactions: direct, or static, and indirect, or dynamic.

Static invocations are generally the most common way in which CORBA applications are built. This type of invocation involves a client being statically linked to a client-side stub. This type of invocation is generally faster because the application knows the methods that it needs to invoke on the server side. However, even the best-designed distributed object applications suffer from one drawback. This can be characterized as a coupling of interfaces. Object-orientation, at the most basic level, is about representing a model in terms of interfaces (read *encapsulation*). I call it the *interface representation* paradigm. Objects are different from the older ways of building systems. The old paradigm can be thought of as *data representation*. The two paradigms are related in that the complexity of data representation systems led to efforts to manage this complexity through data hiding—encapsulation, to be more precise (see Figure 25.1). Over time, this led to a full-blown paradigm known as object-oriented systems.

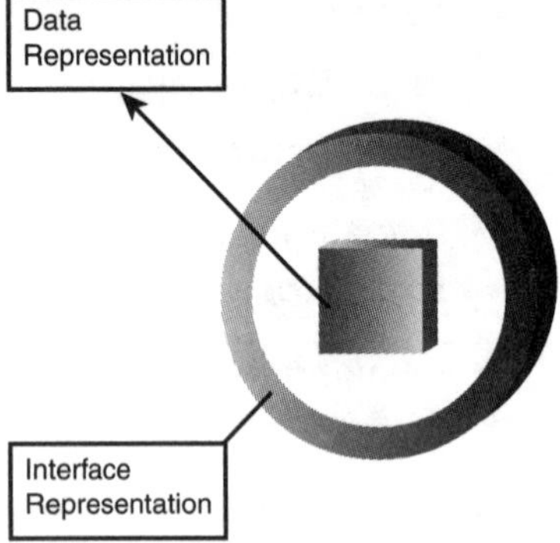

FIGURE 25.1
The paradigm shift.

From this perspective, the evolution of software engineering can be viewed as a series of paradigms that reduces interdependencies between the subcomponents of a software solution. The current paradigm through encapsulation decreases interdependencies by hiding the data representation behind interfaces. The logical question to ask then is: What if the interfaces change? The answer would provide an indication to the next paradigm that will emerge in software engineering. I would call such a paradigm *semantic representation*. The contours of such a shift are already emerging. Figure 25.2 shows a schematic of these paradigms in relation to each other.

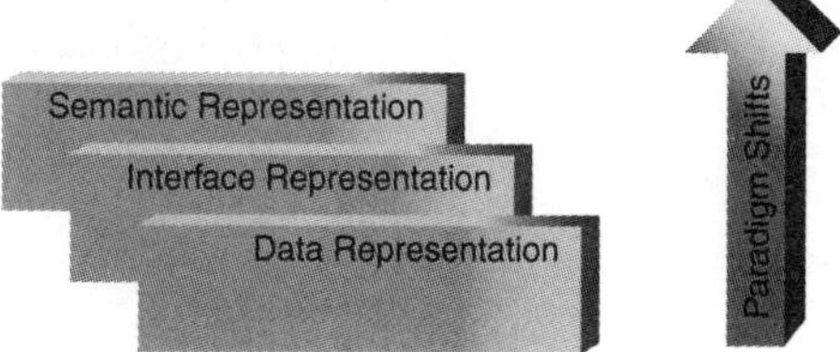

FIGURE 25.2
Semantic representation paradigm.

CORBA Dynamic Invocation Interfaces (DII) is one of the outlines of such a paradigm change. Changes in software engineering occur when an older paradigm is no longer sufficient to deal with the complexity of the solutions that the paradigm help create. It is safe to assume that the semantic representation paradigm will occur when the number of interfaces a system has to support cannot be managed by the same technology that created it. The "Object World Wide Web" might represent such a system.

DII is the prototype of the next paradigm. As it is currently conceived, the evolving paradigm does not have any mechanism for representing interfaces; it does, however, provide an outline of what such a technology might look like.

DII allows an application to have as few interdependencies as possible. Through DII, a client can construct an invocation during runtime and use the ORB to marshal and demarshal an invocation during runtime. DII uses `CORBA::Any` and the associated `CORBA::Typecode` extensively.

Using Dynamic Invocation Interfaces

You use the following steps to make a dynamic invocation. Essentially, a client needs to interact with an instance of the `CORBA::Request` object. Using this object, a client can construct a runtime operation, set the arguments and return types, and then make the invocation:

1. Obtain an object reference to the target object on which a client wants to makes the invocation. This can be accomplished using either a bind, the interface repository, or the IOR.
2. Initialize a `Request` object for the target object. This involves retrieving the `Request` object and setting the parameters and/or return values for the request.
3. Invoke the `Request`. This invocation can be synchronous or asynchronous. If it is the former type, the client has to wait for the return of the call. The latter type enables the client to continue with its execution.
4. Retrieve the result when the invocation returns.

The illustration of DII uses the following interface. The `dii` interface seeks to use a number of interfaces with parameters and return types, both primitive and complex types:

```
module Dynamic {
  interface dii {
    struct DyStruct {
      string name;
      short age;
    };

    void takestruct(
       in DyStruct ins,
       out DyStruct outs,inout DyStruct inouts);

    dii::DyStruct getstruct();

    typedef sequence<string> strings;

    void takesequence(
      in strings ins,
      out strings outs,
      inout strings inouts
    );

    strings getsequence();

    void takenumber(
      in long ins,
      out long outs,
      inout long inouts
    );
    long getnumber();
    void takestring(
      in string ins,
      out string outs,
      inout string inouts
    );

    void takestring(
       in string ins,
          out string outs,
       inout string inouts
    )

    string getstring();

    void takereference(
      in Dynamic::dii ins,
      out Dynamic::dii outs,
      inout Dynamic::dii inouts
    );
```

```
    Dynamic::dii getreference();
  };
};
```

The implementation uses VisiBroker For Java 3.3. The interface is compiled using the `-portable` flag:

```
prompt$> idl2java -portable -no_tie -no_comments dii.idl
```

Implementing the `dii` Interface

The fact that the client uses DII has no implication for how the `dii` interface is constructed. The server in this case (see Listing 25.1) can be implemented as in Chapter 5, "Java/IDL Mapping."

LISTING 25.1 DYNAMIC OBJECT IMPLEMENTATION

```
package Dynamic;
import java.io.*;
import java.util.*;

public class dynamic extends Dynamic._diiImplBase {

  FileOutputStream logFile = null;
  PrintWriter ios = null;
  Date now = new Date();
  java.lang.String[] returnStrings = null;
  Dynamic.dii insreference= null;

  public dynamic() {
  }

  public dynamic(String name) {
    super(name);
     try{
      logFile = new FileOutputStream("Log.dat",true);
      ios = new PrintWriter(logFile,true);
    }
    catch(IOException e){
      System.out.println(e.toString());
    }
    ios.println(new String(
        "[Logfile]:Dynamic Started " + now.toString()));
  }
  public void takestruct(
    Dynamic.diiPackage.DyStruct ins,
    Dynamic.diiPackage.DyStructHolder outs,
```

continues

LISTING 25.1 CONTINUED

```
  Dynamic.diiPackage.DyStructHolder inouts
) {
  String retname = ins.name + "out and inout add";
  int retage = ins.age + 20;

  String message = "takestruct() Called IN Parmam is: "
     + ins.name + " " + new Integer(ins.age).toString();
  ios.println(new String("[Logfile]:Dynamic " + message));

  outs.value = new Dynamic.diiPackage.DyStruct();
  outs.value.name = "OUT STRUCT NAME";
  outs.value.age = (short)4450;

  message = "takestruct() Called OUT Parmam is: "
     + outs.value.name + " "
     + new Integer(outs.value.age).toString();
  ios.println(new String("[Logfile]:Dynamic " + message));

  int inoutage = inouts.value.age;
  String inoutname = inouts.value.name;

  message = "takestruct() Called INOUT Parmam is: "
     + inoutname + " " + new Integer(inoutage).toString();
  ios.println(new String("[Logfile]:Dynamic " + message));

  inouts.value.name = retname;
  inouts.value.age = (short)retage;

}

public Dynamic.diiPackage.DyStruct getstuct() {
  String message = "getstuct() Called";
  ios.println(new String("[Logfile]:Dynamic " + message));
  return new Dynamic.diiPackage.DyStruct("
     Return Name",(short)44);
}

public void takesequence(
  java.lang.String[] ins,
  Dynamic.diiPackage.stringsHolder outs,
  Dynamic.diiPackage.stringsHolder inouts
) {

  returnStrings = new String[ins.length];
  outs.value = new String[ins.length];
  for(int i = 0; i< ins.length; i++){
    String message =
      "takesequence() Called IN PARAM IS: " + ins[i];
    ios.println(new String("[Logfile]:Dynamic "
```

```
      + message));
    outs.value[i] = new String();
    outs.value[i] = ins[i] +
      new Integer(i+i).toString();
    message = "takesequence() Called OUT PARAM IS: "
      + outs.value[i];
    ios.println(new String("[Logfile]:Dynamic " + message));
    inouts.value[i] = ins[i] +
      new Integer(i+i*2).toString();
    message = "takesequence() Called INOUT PARAM IS: "
      + inouts.value[i];
    ios.println(new String("[Logfile]:Dynamic "
      + message));
    returnStrings[i] = new String(ins[i]);
  }
}
public java.lang.String[] getsequence() {
    String message = "getsequence() Called";
    ios.println(new String("[Logfile]:Dynamic "
      + message));
    return returnStrings;
}

public void takenumber(
  int ins,
  org.omg.CORBA.IntHolder outs,
  org.omg.CORBA.IntHolder inouts
) {
   String message = "takenumber() Called IN Param: "
     + new Integer(ins).toString();
   ios.println(new String("[Logfile]:Dynamic "
     + message));
   outs.value = ins + 100;
   message = "takenumber() Called OUT Param: "
     + new Integer(outs.value).toString();
   ios.println(new String("[Logfile]:Dynamic " + message));
   inouts.value = outs.value + 100;
   message = "takenumber() Called OUT Param: "
     + new Integer(inouts.value).toString();
   ios.println(new String("[Logfile]:Dynamic "
     + message));
}

public int getnumber() {
  String message = "getnumber() Called";
  ios.println(new String("[Logfile]:Dynamic " + message));
  return 1001;
}
public void takestring(
```

continues

LISTING 25.1 CONTINUED

```
    java.lang.String ins,
    org.omg.CORBA.StringHolder outs,
    org.omg.CORBA.StringHolder inouts
  ) {
    String message = "takestring() Called IN Param " + ins;
    ios.println(new String("[Logfile]:Dynamic " + message));
    outs.value = ins + " outString";
    message = "takestring() Called OUT Param " + outs.value;
    ios.println(new String("[Logfile]:Dynamic " + message));
    message = "takestring() Called OUT Param " + inouts.value;
    ios.println(new String("[Logfile]:Dynamic " + message));
    inouts.value = outs.value + "inoutString";
  }
  public java.lang.String getstring() {
    String message = "getstring() Called";
    ios.println(new String("[Logfile]:Dynamic " + message));
    return new String("Returning String");
  }
  public void takereference(
    Dynamic.dii ins,
    Dynamic.diiHolder outs,
    Dynamic.diiHolder inouts
  ) {
    insreference = ins;
    String message = "takereference() Called IN Param "
        + ins.toString();
    ios.println(new String("[Logfile]:Dynamic "
        + message));
    outs.value = this;
    message = "takereference() Called OUT Param "
        + outs.toString();
    ios.println(new String("[Logfile]:Dynamic "
        + message));
    message = "takereference() Called INOUT Param "
        + inouts.toString();
    ios.println(new String("[Logfile]:Dynamic "
        + message));
    inouts.value = this;
  }
  public Dynamic.dii getreference() {
    String message = "getreference() Called";
    ios.println(new String("[Logfile]:Dynamic "
        + message));
    return this;
  }
}
```

The code has no complexity whatsoever. The only novel feature is that instead of outputting a client request to the system output terminal, the application uses a log file that is constructed with the constructor. The following code snippet initializes the log file:

```
logFile = new FileOutputStream("Log.dat",true);
     ios = new PrintWriter(logFile,true);
```

Other than this bit, the rest of the code is very standard and simple. So let's get to the implementation of the client. Nevertheless, before that we have to implement a server to host the interface implementation.

Implementing the Dynamic Server

The server implementation is standard, as most are (see Listing 25.2).

LISTING 25.2 DII SERVER

```
package Dynamic;n

public class DynamicServer {

  public DynamicServer(String[] args) {
    org.omg.CORBA.ORB orb = org.omg.CORBA.ORB.init(args,null);
    org.omg.CORBA.BOA boa = orb.BOA_init();
    Dynamic.dii dynamicObject = new Dynamic.dynamic("DynamicServer");
    boa.obj_is_ready(dynamicObject);
    System.out.println(dynamicObject + " is ready.");
    boa.impl_is_ready();
  }

  public static void main(String[] args) {
    DynamicServer dynamicServer = new DynamicServer(args);
  }
}
```

The server is called `DynamicServer`. The client we are going to build will be using the low-level bind call. This name, `DynamicServer`, is the one that the client is going to use to acquire the object reference.

The Dynamic Client Implementation

As indicated earlier, the client has to take a number of steps in order to make the invocation.

The sum of the code the client contains is a bit too much; I am going to break it up into a number of clients, each client making just two invocations. The `dii` interface that is implemented by the server contains the following set of operations:

- `struct` operations—The `struct` operation performs `in`, `out`, and `inout` on a `struct` that is passed back and forth between the client and server:

  ```
  void takestruct(in DyStruct ins, out DyStruct outs,
   inout DyStruct inouts);
  dii::DyStruct getstuct();
  ```

  The `struct` is defined as follows:

  ```
  struct DyStruct {
        string name;
        short age;
      };
  ```

- Sequence operations—The sequence operation does the same as the `struct` in the following operation:

  ```
  typedef sequence<string> strings;

  void takesequence(in strings ins,
  out strings outs,inout strings inouts);
      strings getsequence();
  ```

  The sequence operation uses a sequence of strings as parameters. The `getsequence()` returns a `struct`.

- String operations—This operation handles all aspects of string handling:

  ```
  void takestring(
        in string ins,
               out string outs,
              inout string inouts
            )

      string getstring();
  ```

- Primitive operations—Just as with the string operations, the code for dynamically handling any primitive is pretty much the same:

  ```
  void takenumber(
        in long ins,
        out long outs,
        inout long inouts
  );
  long getnumber();
  ```

- Object reference operations—These operations pass and return object references:

  ```
  void takereference(
        in Dynamic::dii ins,
        out Dynamic::dii outs,
  ```

```
          inout Dynamic::dii inouts
        );

        Dynamic::dii getreference();
```

Let's construct a client. Because the client differs very little from other CORBA clients, I shall show the initialization code just once (see Listing 25.3).

LISTING 25.3 DII CLIENT

```
package Dynamic;
import org.omg.CORBA.*;

public class DynamicClient {
  static org.omg.CORBA.Object DynamicObject;
  static org.omg.CORBA.ORB orb;

  static{
    orb = org.omg.CORBA.ORB.init();
    DynamicObject = orb.bind("IDL:Dynamic/dii:1.0",
                        "DynamicServer", null, null);
  }

  public static void main(String[] args) {
    DynamicClient dynamicClient = new DynamicClient();
  }

  public DynamicClient() {
    //The implementations to be placed here.
  }
}
```

The first thing the implementation should do is acquire an instance of `CORBA::Object` representing the remote object. The following code does this by using `bind()`:

```
DynamicObject = orb.bind("IDL:Dynamic/dii:1.0",
                        "DynamicServer", null, null);
```

The ten operations (two of each type) can be placed in the client's constructor. I have chosen to isolate them in separate methods:

```
    //Struct Operations
    makeStructCall();
    getStructCall();
    //Sequence Operations
    makeSequenceCall();
    getSequenceCall();
    //Primitive Operations
    makeNumberCall();
    getNumberCall();
```

```
//String Operations
makeStringCall();
getStringCall();
//Object reference Operations
makeReferenceCall();
getReferenceCall();
```

The first thing all these methods should do is acquire an instance of the `Request` class. There are three ways the request object may be retrieved. All three are specified on the `CORBA::Object` interface. The `CORBA::Object` has been initialized statically:

```
import org.omg.CORBA.Request;

public Request _request(String operation);

Request _create_request(Context ctx,
    String operation, NVList arg_list,
    NamedValue result);

Request _create_request(Context ctx,
    String operation, NVList arg_list,
    NamedValue result,
                        ExceptionList exclist,
                    ContextList ctxlist);
```

The three operations enable three ways to construct a request. The first creates a request by passing a string. This string represents the name of the operation on the server-side interface. After the request has been initialized in this manner, all the arguments and returns, if any, must be initialized before the request can be made.

The other two methods in the previous code snippet work with `NVList` and `NamedValues`. The `NVList` represents the parameter list of the operation, and the `NamedValues` contains the return types. If the last two operations are used, the `NVLIst` and the `NamedValue` must be initialized before the `Request` object is constructed. The `NVList` and the `NamedValue` objects do not have constructors, so they cannot be constructed in the usual manner. Invoking the appropriate method in the ORB can initialize these objects. These are `ORB.create_list` and `ORB.create_operation_list` for `NVList` and `ORB.create_named_value` for `NamedValue`.

For the purposes of this chapter, let's use the first mechanism to create a `Request` object. As mentioned, after the `Request` object has been created, the parameters have to be initialized. Parameters, when passed dynamically, have to be converted to `org.omg.CORBA.Any`. The `Any` type does not have a constructor. The `CORBA::Any` type can be created by invoking `ORB.create_any()`.

Invoking struct Operations Dynamically

In the following code listing, the implementation will use DII to dynamically make the call on the server; more specifically, the DII will be used to construct the invocation.

The first method is `makeStructCall()`. This method invokes the `takestruct()` operation on the `dii` interface. The code is shown in Listing 25.4.

LISTING 25.4 CONSTRUCTING `structs` DYNAMICALLY

```
private void makeStructCall(){

    Request request = DynamicObject._request("takestruct");

    Dynamic.diiPackage.DyStruct inStruct =
new Dynamic.diiPackage.DyStruct();
    Dynamic.diiPackage.DyStructHolder inOutStruct =
          new Dynamic.diiPackage.DyStructHolder();
    Dynamic.diiPackage.DyStructHolder outStruct =
new Dynamic.diiPackage.DyStructHolder();

    inStruct.age = 22;
    inStruct.name = "Koolaire";

    inOutStruct.value = new Dynamic.diiPackage.DyStruct();
    inOutStruct.value.age = 55;
    inOutStruct.value.name = "INOUT VALUE";

    outStruct.value = new Dynamic.diiPackage.DyStruct();
    outStruct.value.age = 0;
    outStruct.value.name = "";

    Any In = request.add_in_arg();
    Any Out = request.add_out_arg();
    Any Inout = request.add_inout_arg();

    Out.type(Dynamic.diiPackage.DyStructHelper.type());

    Dynamic.diiPackage.DyStructHelper.insert(Out,
                                  outStruct.value);
    Dynamic.diiPackage.DyStructHelper.insert(Inout,
                                inOutStruct.value);
    Dynamic.diiPackage.DyStructHelper.insert(In,inStruct);

    request.invoke();
```

continues

LISTING 25.4 CONTINUED

```
    outStruct.value =
           Dynamic.diiPackage.DyStructHelper.extract(Out);
    inOutStruct.value =
           Dynamic.diiPackage.DyStructHelper.extract(Inout);

    System.out.println(outStruct.value.name);
    System.out.println(inOutStruct.value.name);
  }
```

The `Result` object is constructed by invoking the `_request` on an instance of `org.omg.CORBA.Object`:

```
Request request = DynamicObject._request("takestruct");
```

The operation to invoke on the server side is named `takestruct`. After the `Request` object has been created, the three parameters have to be initialized. All three parameters are passed as `org.omg.CORBA.Any`. The `in` parameter is mapped to the Java final class. The `OUT` and `INOUT` are mapped to holder classes.

The `takestruct` operation now has to be initialized for the parameters:

```
Any ins = request.add_in_arg();
     Any outs = request.add_out_arg();
     Any inouts = request.add_inout_arg();
```

These lines create instances of `org.omg.CORBA.Any` as placeholders for any parameters. The `add_in_arg()` creates a placeholder for an `in` parameter, the `add_out_arg()` for the `out` parameter, and the `add_inout_arg()` for the `inout` parameter.

The `Request` interface also specifies interfaces to pass named parameters in an invocation.

After the placeholders are initialized, the `CORBA.Any` type has to be initialized. This is accomplished by inserting a type into `CORBA.Any`. These functions are always found in the `Helper` functions generated by the IDL pre-compiler. The insertion of a client type into `CORBA.Any` is shown in the following code:

```
Dynamic.diiHelper.insert(ins, inReference);
     Dynamic.diiHelper.insert(outs, outReference.value);
     Dynamic.diiHelper.insert(inouts, inoutReference.value);
```

All the `Helper` classes have these functions. They convert a type into `CORBA.Any`. In the preceding code, the `inReference`, `outReference.value`, and `inoutReference.value` types are converted into `CORBA.Anys`.

If you think about it, the server will face a subtle problem with just this code. The `out` parameter is initialized on the server side and passed back to the client. The `struct` that is passed contains a string. The size of this string can be determined only at runtime, because internally the string object is a pointer to a character array.

The server will receive only a CORBA.Any, which is a void pointer. Other than this, the server has no information to determine the type it is expected to initialize and pass back. It could have the void pointer, in theory, point to any location in memory.

In essence, the CORBA.Any is not just a void pointer; it contains a crucial piece of information called the CORBA.Any.TypeCode that unambiguously represents the type of CORBA.Any that is being passed around. CORBA.Any and CORBA.Any.TypeCode are provided in the appropriate Helper classes. For our purposes, the TypeCode support is found in the Dynamic.diiPackage.DyStructHelper class. The Any placeholder has to contain the TypeCode as well. This is done in the following line of code:

```
Out.type(Dynamic.diiPackage.DyStructHelper.type());
```

As for the in and inout parameters, because the client has initialized them, the server has the required information to determine what to pass back.

CORBA.Any is now completely initialized and ready to be passed into the server dynamically. At this point, the Request object is ready to be invoked. The operation has been named, and all the parameters have been initialized. The actual invocation is made on the following line:

```
request.invoke();
```

The request is dynamically marshaled and passed into the server object for execution. Now there is the small matter of trying to figure out what the server has passed back in the out and inout over to the client. The types are now CORBA.Any. They need to be converted back to the appropriate types. This is accomplished by using the very same Helper class that was used to convert the type into a CORBA.Any. The code is shown here:

```
outStruct.value =
     Dynamic.diiPackage.DyStructHelper.extract(Out);
     inOutStruct.value =
          Dynamic.diiPackage.DyStructHelper.extract(Inout);
```

Essentially, that is all there is to dynamic invocations. The rest of the implementation will not be discussed in as much depth, except when something new needs to be explained.

The second operation that is to be implemented is the getStructCall() method. This method needs to dynamically handle a struct that is being returned as a result of the invocation:

```
private void getStructCall(){
    Request request = DynamicObject._request("getstuct");
    request.set_return_type(
       Dynamic.diiPackage.DyStructHelper.type());
    request.invoke();
```

```
    Dynamic.diiPackage.DyStruct result;
    result = Dynamic.diiPackage.DyStructHelper.
extract(request.return_value());    System.out.println("RETURN STRUCT: AGE
" +
        new Integer(result.age));
    System.out.println("RETURN STRUCT: NAME " +
        result.name);

  }
```

The code is very similar to the implementation that was detailed in the `makeStructCall()` method. In the preceding code, the `CORBA.Any` that is being returned is set to the right `TypeCode` in the following line:

```
request.set_return_type(Dynamic.diiPackage.DyStructHelper.type());
```

Invoking Sequence Operations Dynamically

The two operations that handle sequence operations, `getSequenceCall()` and `makeSequenceCall()`, are illustrated in this section. Listing 25.5 shows the `makeSequenceCall()` method.

LISTING 25.5 CONSTRUCTING SEQUENCES DYNAMICALLY

```
private void makeSequenceCall(){
    Request request =
 DynamicObject._request("takesequence");

    java.lang.String[] inSequence;
    Dynamic.diiPackage.stringsHolder outSequence;
    Dynamic.diiPackage.stringsHolder inoutSequence;

    inSequence = new String[2];
    outSequence = new Dynamic.diiPackage.stringsHolder();
    inoutSequence = new Dynamic.diiPackage.stringsHolder();
    outSequence.value = new String[2];
    inoutSequence.value = new String[2];

    for(int i = 0; i < inSequence.length; i++){
       inSequence[i] = "INSEQUENCE STRING " +
new Integer(i).toString();
       outSequence.value[i] = "OUTSEQUENCE STRING " +
new Integer(i).toString();
       inoutSequence.value[i] = "";
    }
```

```
    Any In = request.add_in_arg();
    Any Out = request.add_out_arg();
    Any Inout = request.add_inout_arg();

    Out.type(Dynamic.diiPackage.stringsHelper.type());
    Inout.type(Dynamic.diiPackage.stringsHelper.type());

    Dynamic.diiPackage.stringsHelper.insert(In,inSequence);
    Dynamic.diiPackage.stringsHelper.insert(Out,
                                   outSequence.value);
    Dynamic.diiPackage.stringsHelper.insert(Inout,
   inoutSequence.value);

    request.invoke();

outSequence.value =
Dynamic.diiPackage.stringsHelper.extract(Out);
    inoutSequence.value =
Dynamic.diiPackage.stringsHelper.extract(Inout);

    for(int i = 0; i <  outSequence.value.length; i++)
        System.out.println(outSequence.value[i]);

    for(int i = 0; i <  inoutSequence.value.length; i++)
        System.out.println(inoutSequence.value[i]);
  }
```

The implementation of the sequence parameter follows along the same lines as the steps necessary to handle `struct` objects. First the `Request` object is created. Then the parameters to be passed are created and, if necessary, they are initialized. `CORBA.Any` placeholders for parameters are set up on the `Request` object depending on the directions the parameters are passed. If required, the exact type of the `CORBA.Any` is added as well, invoking the appropriate method on a `Helper` class. After the `Request` object has been prepared, the `invoke()` method is called on it. On the method returning, the `extract()` method on the correct `Helper` class is used to convert the returned `Any` (as `out` and `inout`) to the appropriate type.

The `getSequenceCall()` on the client side is constructed along similar lines, as shown in Listing 25.6.

LISTING 25.6 MAKING SEQUENCES DYNAMICALLY

```
private void getSequenceCall(){
     Request request =
DynamicObject._request("getsequence");
request.set_return_type(orb.create_sequence_tc(0,
```

continues

LISTING 25.6 CONTINUED

```
    orb.get_primitive_tc(
          org.omg.CORBA.TCKind.tk_string)));
    request.invoke();
    String[] result;
    result = Dynamic.diiPackage.stringsHelper.extract(
 request.return_value());

    for(int i = 0; i < result.length; i++)
      System.out.println("RETURN SEQUENCE: " + result[i]);
 }
```

The singular difference in this implementation is the setting of the return type on the `Request` object:

```
request.set_return_type(orb.create_sequence_tc(0,
     orb.get_primitive_tc(
           org.omg.CORBA.TCKind.tk_string)));
```

The return type is in essence an array of `String` objects. The string object is considered to be a primitive, so the implementation does not have to use a holder class to construct the return `CORBA.Any` or its `TypeCode`.

Invoking String and Primitive Operations Dynamically

The code for handling strings and primitive types is essentially the same. You encountered some of the issues relating to strings earlier in this chapter when you saw how to handle sequences of strings. The two methods that pass strings and primitives in parameters are implemeted in `makeNumberCall()` and `makeStringCall()`. Return primitives and strings are handled in the `getNumberCall()` and `getStringCall()` implementations. The actual mechanism is illustrated in Listing 25.7.

LISTING 25.7 MAKING STRINGS AND NUMBERS DYNAMICALLY

```
public void makeNumberCall(){

    int inNumber = 1001;
    IntHolder outNumber = new IntHolder();
    IntHolder inoutNumber = new IntHolder();
    inoutNumber.value = 1002;
    inoutNumber.value = 0;

    org.omg.CORBA.Request request =
DynamicObject._request("takenumber");
```

```
    Any ins = request.add_in_arg();
    Any outs = request.add_out_arg();
    Any inouts = request.add_inout_arg();

    ins.insert_long(inNumber);
    inouts.insert_long(inoutNumber.value);
    outs.insert_long(outNumber.value);

    request.invoke();

    outNumber.value = outs.extract_long();
    inoutNumber.value = inouts.extract_long();

    System.out.println("INOUT PRIMITIVE: " +
new Integer(inoutNumber.value));
    System.out.println("OUT PRIMITIVE: " +
  new Integer(outNumber.value));
  }

  public void getNumberCall(){

Request request = DynamicObject._request("getnumber");
request.set_return_type(orb.get_primitive_tc
 (org.omg.CORBA.TCKind.tk_long));
    Request request = DynamicObject._request("getnumber");
    request.set_return_type(orb.get_primitive_tc(org.omg.CORBA.
TCKind.tk_long));
    request.invoke();

    request.invoke();

    int ReturnPrimitive = 0;
    ReturnPrimitive = request.return_value().extract_long();
    System.out.println("RETURN PRIMITIVE: " +
new Integer(ReturnPrimitive));
  }

  public void makeStringCall(){

    String inString = new String("IN STRING");
    StringHolder outString = new StringHolder();
    StringHolder inoutString = new StringHolder();
    outString.value = "";
    inoutString.value = "INOUT STRING";

    Request request = DynamicObject._request("takestring");

    org.omg.CORBA.Any ins = request.add_in_arg();
```

continues

LISTING 25.7 CONTINUED

```
    org.omg.CORBA.Any outs = request.add_out_arg();
    org.omg.CORBA.Any inouts = request.add_inout_arg();

    outs.type(orb.get_primitive_tc
 (org.omg.CORBA.TCKind.tk_string));

    ins.insert_string(inString);
    outs.insert_string(outString.value);
    inouts.insert_string(inoutString.value);

    request.invoke();

    outString.value = outs.extract_string();
    inoutString.value = inouts.extract_string();

    System.out.println("INOUT STRING : " +
 inoutString.value);
    System.out.println("OUT STRING: " + outString.value);
  }

  public void getStringCall(){

     Request request = DynamicObject._request("getstring");
     request.set_return_type(orb.get_primitive_tc
(org.omg.CORBA.TCKind.tk_string));
     request.invoke();
     String returnString;
     returnString = request.return_value().extract_string();

     System.out.println("RETURN STRING : " + returnString);
  }
```

The implementations of string and primitive operations follow, on average, a similar pattern. As a representation, you will explore only two methods: `makePrimitiveCall()` and `getStringCall()`.

In `makePrimitiveCall()`, the `Request` object is first constructed as usual. The `Request` encapsulates the `takenumber()` operation on the server side. The operation takes three parameters, all of them `CORBA::Longs`. The parameters to the operations are initialized as shown in the following code:

```
Any ins = request.add_in_arg();
Any outs = request.add_out_arg();
Any inouts = request.add_inout_arg();

ins.insert_long(inNumber);
inouts.insert_long(inoutNumber.value);
outs.insert_long(outNumber.value);
```

In this instance, CORBA.Any.TypeCode is not required, because the amount of memory required for CORBA.Long is specified, and the associated marshaling can be unambiguously handled by the code generated for DII.

After the arguments are constructed and initialized, the invocation is made with request.invoke(). The out and inout parameters are retrieved by the following code:

```
outNumber.value = outs.extract_long();
     inoutNumber.value = inouts.extract_long();
```

The implementation for makePrimitiveCall() follows along similar lines. The difference is that CORBA.Any.TypeCode needs to be added for the out parameter, because the server needs to know how to handle this type correctly.

In the getStringCall(), the implementation enables the client to dynamically invoke the corresponding operation getstring() on the Dynamic.dii interface. The code is standard as for other implementations. The difference is in how the return type is set up. Because the return type is CORBA.Any, the correct CORBA.Any.TypeCode is passed on so that the cast from CORBA.Any to java.lang.String happens correctly:

```
request.set_return_type(orb.get_primitive_tc(
org.omg.CORBA.TCKind.tk_string));
```

Invoking Object Reference Operations Dynamically

Operations involving object references can also be constructed dynamically. These operations can have object references passed in all three directions—in, out, and inout—and can handle return types. The two methods dealing with object references are makeReferenceCall() and getReferenceCall(). The issues related to dynamic operations that involve object references are very similar to implementations dealing with parameters that involve allocation of memory that can only be determined during runtime. Because parameters are passed as CORBA.Any, the associated Helper classes are used to convert an object reference type to CORBA.Any and back. These classes handle the allocation of memory correctly for you.

The implementations for the two methods are illustrated in Listing 25.8.

LISTING 25.8 CONSTRUCTING REFERENCES DYNAMICALLY

```
public void makeReferenceCall(){

     Dynamic.dii inReference = new Dynamic.dynamic();
```

continues

LISTING 25.8 CONTINUED

```
     Dynamic.diiHolder outReference =
new Dynamic.diiHolder();
     Dynamic.diiHolder inoutReference =
new Dynamic.diiHolder();

     Request request =
DynamicObject._request("takereference");

     Any ins = request.add_in_arg();
     Any outs = request.add_out_arg();
     Any inouts = request.add_inout_arg();

outs.type(Dynamic.diiHelper.type());

     Dynamic.diiHelper.insert(ins, inReference);
     Dynamic.diiHelper.insert(outs, outReference.value);
     Dynamic.diiHelper.insert(inouts, inoutReference.value);

     request.invoke();
     System.out.println("OUT REFERENCE : "
+ outReference.toString());
     System.out.println("INOUT REFERENCE : "
+ inoutReference.toString());
  }

  public void getReferenceCall(){

    Request request =
DynamicObject._request("getreference");

    request.set_return_type(Dynamic.diiHelper.type());
    request.invoke();

    Dynamic.dii returnReference;
    returnReference =
Dynamic.diiHelper.extract(request.return_value());

    System.out.println("RETURN REFERENCE : "
+ returnReference.toString());
  }
```

The code in the `makeReferenceCall()` is very similar to the code for handling `struct` parameters dynamically. The `Request` object is constructed. Calling the appropriate `Request` interface operation sets the `CORBA.Any` placeholders for the parameters. If an `out` parameter cannot be correctly identified by the server for runtime memeory allocation, the `TypeCode` is set. If you are dealing with native IDL types then, the `CORBA.Any.Typecode` is formally specified. If they are user-defined types, as is in the case of `out`, the correct `TypeCode` should be set for the `CORBA.Any`. The setting of the `TypeCode` is shown here:

```
outs.type(Dynamic.diiHelper.type());
```

The `getReferenceCall()` needs to correctly convert the returning `CORBA.Any` to the right type. This is accomplished as you would handle an `out` parameter:

```
request.set_return_type(Dynamic.diiHelper.type());
```

With the ten methods laid out in this chapter, you should be able to handle any combination of parameters dynamically and synchronously.

Summary

Dynamic Invocation Interfaces (DII) are the other half of the CORBA way of doing things—compromises. Together with Static Invocation Interfaces, you have the *Common* in CORBA. As more and more complex distributed systems are built, the property that has been the strength of object-oriented technology, encapsulation, will become strained. Encapsulation is the mechanism by which interdependencies between the components that make up a system are kept to a minimum.

When the minimum is not enough, meaning when the complexity of a solution grows beyond the confines of the original problem into a matrix client/server problem, clients should be capable of making dynamic requests on the server. This enables a server-side interface to be changed without disrupting existing solutions.

CHAPTER 26

Developing CORBABean Wrappers

In This Chapter

Object-oriented (OO) systems are in the process of maturing. There was a time when you dealt with OO by dealing with issues such as classes and objects. Over the last few years, the paradigm has matured into a more robust worldview.The worldview is very simple and elegant. It is based on the premise that complex software systems can be built like a child building something using LEGO bricks, through a process of assembling blocks with a standard interface. Such a worldview is known as *component-based application development*. The main difference between a normal object and a component is that the former is just a runtime instance of some class. A component can also be an object that is an instance of some class, but it differs in one essential manner: Components are usually restricted to a standardized convention in describing the interface.

Like your LEGO bricks, a component model also has a standard interface that enables the rest of the world to interact with it in a standard manner. Such interactions could involve GUI-based workbenches that enable a developer to drag and drop components from a pallet to construct an application. They could be one of those expensive CASE tools that enables animation of a model using prebuilt components to display the various interactions.

There are two popular component models in the industry right now: MS Component Object Model–based components and JavaSoft's JavaBeans component model. At one level, both are competing platforms for developing components, but both vendors have technology that enables you to integrate one in the other. In this chapter, we shall consider only the JavaBeans model for building components. CORBA as a solution is used mainly to solve problems that involve integrating systems across operating systems and platforms, such as an NT-based client being serviced by a UNIX server and so on. Java is inherently a multiplatform technology; this enables Java solutions to have both source code portability as well as bytecode portability. This makes Java ideal for building CORBA solutions.

In that context, it is also beneficial if systems architects could rely on a multiplatform component model as well. Hence, JavaBeans makes the ideal component model for building CORBA components. Before we look into the relationship between CORBA and JavaBeans, let's take a brief tour of the JavaBeans component model.

The Simple JavaBeans Component Model

The JavaBeans component model is very simple. At its foundation, building a JavaBean component can be accomplished with just two steps:

1. A JavaBean component is a Java class that is provided with a default constructor.
2. Every property of a Java class that you want to expose as a property of the component you are creating should be provided with accessor and modifier methods.

For example, the following is a legal JavaBean component:

```
public class Date{
                private String date;
                public date();
                void setdate(String date){
                        this.date = date;
                }
                String getdate(){
                        return date;
                }
};
```

That's all it takes to create simple JavaBean components. Of course, most components will not be so trivial. The JavaBean component model offers a flexible architecture to extend and add more power of expression to your components. For the most part, CORBA components encapsulated as JavaBeans do not require all the features of the JavaBean model. CORBA components require only the simpler aspects of the bean model, because the JavaBean model is squarely aimed at the client side. The JavaBean model is designed to enable client-side use of Java a little more easily.

More importantly, most of the existing Java classes could already be JavaBean components because you probably followed good class design conventions, providing a default constructor and accessor and modifier methods for all your attributes.

In addition to the simple requirements of a default constructor and the accessor and modifier functions that a Java class needs to become a bean, it could support the following to become more sophisticated:

- A customizer class to enable a developer to modify sets of properties as a whole.
- Accessing properties through property editors and property sheets.
- Support for events.
- Support for introspection to enable a JavaBean-aware toolkit to discover the internals of a class at runtime.
- A `BeanInfo` class, to specify information such as what property sheets and customizers can be used with a JavaBean. You can also add information for icons as well.
- Persistence through serialization.

The tricky part about using any of these features is the art of figuring out when and why to use them when you build your bean. A complex JavaBean would support the entire range of auxiliary JavaBean support through property sheets, customizers, `BeanInfo` classes, and introspection. But for the most part, simple JavaBeans would not require all these auxiliary classes. The same can be said about CORBA beans. For most requirements, the basic requirements for JavaBeans is all that you would have to support. At most, you would also add event supports.

The server-side problems are to be addressed through another architecture that is based on JavaBeans. It is called the Enterprise JavaBeans model (EJB). The EJB model is based on the JavaBean model itself, but for building server-side components. EJB components can be considered as components very much like CORBA components, except they define a set of interfaces that a potential EJB component needs to support. EJB implementations currently use RMI protocols for distribution, but JavaSoft is currently extending to add support for IIOP as well. When this does occur, we will have a CORBABean model for components.

Let's look at the client-side beans model as it is aimed at IDEs. IDEs are critical to CORBA if it is to survive the sustained attack it will come under from other distributed component models. CORBA components wrapped as JavaBeans enable developers to use CORBA in the drag-and-drop, click-and-connect environments that JavaBeans are capable of providing. This enables you to add JavaBean-wrapped CORBA objects to a component pallet to allow a developer to simply drag and drop these components to build a GUI.

The following example will help illustrate how a simple JavaBean component can be built. We are going to take a simple CORBA interface and wrap it inside a JavaBean. The following IDL interface is used as an example:

```
module CorbaBean{
    interface CoffeeMachine{
        void setSwitchOn(in boolean value);
        void setCoffee(in string brew);
        void setTimer(in long time);
        void brew();
    };
};
```

The three operations could have been specified as read-only operations. In that case, the resulting Java interface would have been incompatible with the JavaBean model. Therefore, the IDL interface was specified so that the resulting interface would be JavaBean-compatible. In the example, the three methods, `setSwitchOn()`, `setCoffee()`, and `setTimer()` correspond to three modifier methods for three encapsulated properties of a bean. `get` and `set` methods result from specifying attributes in your interfaces.

Unfortunately, the accessor and modifier functions mapped from attributes are not JavaBean-compatible. You have to specify the accessor and modifier operations directly in your interface itself. For example, consider the following IDL interface:

```
interface Date{
       attribute string date;
};
```

This interface will generate the following Java code when it is run through a JavaIDL pre-compiler:

```
public class date extends _DateImplBase {
  String date;
  public date (java.lang.String name) {
    super(name);
  }
  public date() {
    super();
  }
  public void date(
    java.lang.String date
  ) {
    this.date = date;
  }
  public java.lang.String date() {
    return date;
  }
}
```

This class does have a default constructor. Most important are the accessor and modifiers. IDL attributes generate accessor and modifier methods, but these are just a set of overloaded methods with the same name as the attribute itself. JavaBean requires the class to be as follows:

```
public class Date{
               private String date;
               public date();
               void setdate(String date){
                       this.date = date;
               }
               String getdate(){
                       return date;
               }
};
```

Run the preceding interface through the Visigenic idl2Java pre-compiler with the following command:

```
prompt$> idl2Java -no_tie -no_comments coffeemachine.idl
```

The implementation of the `CoffeeMachine`, as shown in Listing 26.1, is straightforward. The object of the exercise is not to show how the CORBA component can be implemented, but how it can be wrapped as a JavaBean component.

LISTING 26.1 `CoffeeMachine` **IMPLEMENTATION**

```
package CorbaBean;
public class CoffeeMaker extends CorbaBean._CoffeeMachineImplBase {
  boolean SwitchOn;
  String Coffee;
  int Timer;

  public CoffeeMaker(java.lang.String name) {
    super(name);
  }
  public CoffeeMaker() {
    super();
  }
  public void setSwitchOn(
    boolean value
  ) {
      if(SwitchOn != value)
        SwitchOn = value;
  }
  public void setCoffee(
    java.lang.String brew
  ) {
      if(!SwitchOn)
        Coffee = brew;
  }
  public void setTimer(
    int time
  ) {
      if(!SwitchOn)
        Timer = time;
  }

  public void brew() {
Syste.out.println(Coffee " is brewing for " + Timer + " Seconds");
  }
}
```

At this point, there is nothing special about our component. The next step is to add support for beans. This has been partially done though the accessor methods that our component already supports. This support can be augumented by adding support for editors and the `Beaninfo` class to the component.

JavaBean Properties and Editors

Properties are named attributes that a bean supports. You provide support for properties through accessor and modifier methods. A JavaBean differs from other Java classes primarily through the support of `get` and `set` functions for its properties. Before going into how these properties can be changed from the outside, let's look at the various kinds of properties that a bean can support.

Simple Property

Simple properties are the ones that are directly accessible through the `get` and `set` methods that you provide. In the preceding example, the `CorbaBean.CoffeeMaker` supports three simple properties: `SwitchOn`, `Coffee`, and `Timer`. These three are only provided with modifier methods that a client can use.

The JavaBean model specifies additional ways of exposing properties.

Indexed Properties

Indexed properties are really like simple properties except that there is a sequence of such properties. In this case, the index is used to refer to the correct property element within the sequence. Such a property mechanism can be used when a JavaBean component refers to a whole series of properties. The following is a snippet of code that shows how such a set of properties could be used:

```
private String indexedProperty; //Property declaration

String[] getindexedProperty();
void setindexedProperty(String[] indexedProperty);
```

The preceding are `get` and `set` methods for the entire array of properties. When the developer needs to access or modify just one property from an index, the following methods can be used:

```
String getindexedProperty(in index);
void setindexedProperty(in index, String value);
```

Bound Properties

Bound properties are properties that generate events when the states of these properties are altered. Such a mechanism can be used for a bean with bound properties to notify other beans when a property is changed. For such a bean to generate events when a bound property changes, it must implement the `Java.beans.PropertyChangeListener` interface.

Bound properties are useful if you want to tie state-dependent subcomponents together. This means that when one component changes its state, it triggers the change of state in a dependent object and so on. In the preceding interface implementation, the `Timer` can be considered as a bound property. When the `Timer`'s state violates a certain constraint—in our case, when the timer expires—the bean should trigger an event to notify interested parties that the timer has expired.

Constrained Properties

Constrained properties are an extension of bound properties. Like the bound properties, a constrained property also notifies interested listeners that the state of a component has changed. The listener, in turn, can raise an exception, vetoing a potential change. Such an architecture enables you to couple an arbitrary number of components together purely in terms of their internal state transitions.

The event that is generated by a component is the `vetoableChange` event. On receiving the event, if the listener needs to veto the change of state, the listener can throw the `Java.beans.PropertyVetoException` to veto the change of event.

We will not try to build a fully fledged JavaBean component. Keet in mind that JavaBeans is a client-side component model. As such, supporting the entire JavaBean model might be unnecessary for CORBA components. But aspects of the model can be used to make the components you build a bit simpler to understand. This simplicity enables us to use CORBA components inside an IDE. At the most basic level, properties are the only things that a bean needs to support. Beyond that, anything that you provide is a bonus. I always try to hook up events to properties. They are a much better way for components to modify or access properties than with `get` and `set` methods.

JavaBean Event Model

Events are the notification mechanism used by the JavaBeans components. Of course, they don't really have to be JavaBeans to support events; a plain Java class can send and receive events. The critical aspect of understanding JavaBeans is that the JavaBeans components are all just Java classes, except a rigorous and precise but simple design strategy is imposed on them. Events are one such constraint.

There are a number of things that a component needs to accomplish in order to support events:

- An event object
- An event listener

- An event source
- An interface that enables you to tie up an event listener to an event source

In order for a component to become a listener, all it has to do is support the interface supplied. As for a component to become a source of the event, a component could fire an event object. The example that we built earlier will now be extended using events. Listing 26.2 shows the `BrewEvent` class.

LISTING 26.2 `BrewEvent` **CLASS**

```
package CorbaBean;
import java.util.*;

public class BrewEvent extends EventObject {
  String event;
  public BrewEvent(Object source, String msg) {
    super(source);
    event = msg;
  }

  public String toString(){
    return event;
  }
}
```

The `BrewEvent` class extends the `Java.util.Event` class. Any class that is used as an event object needs to do this. The class itself provides two methods: a constructor and an overriding of the `toString()` method from the `Java.lang.Object.toString()`. The event itself is encapsulated in a `String` object. Listing 26.3 shows the `BrewListener` interface.

LISTING 26.3 `BrewListener` **INTERFACE**

```
package CorbaBean;

import java.util.*;

public interface BrewListener extends EventListener {
  public void Brewing(BrewEvent e);
}
```

Objects that need notification when a state transition in a component occurs have to implement the preceding interface. This enables the class that generates the event to notify the class that implements the listener interface that a state has changed. The server will pass an event object into the `Brewing()` method to the listener that could encapsulate an event in the CORBA component.

The event objects enable the CORBA component to notify listeners when a remote client makes an invocation on the server component. Thus, the various GUI components that make up the server can be tied together using the event model. The `CoffeeMaker` implementation can now be extended to support our event model, as shown in Listing 26.4.

LISTING 26.4 `CoffeeMaker` IMPLEMENTATION WITH EVENTS

```
package CorbaBean;
import java.beans.*;
import java.util.*;

public class CoffeeMaker extends CorbaBean._CoffeeMachineImplBase{

  boolean SwitchOn;
  String Coffee;
  int Timer;
  private transient Vector brewListeners;

  public CoffeeMaker(java.lang.String name) {
    super(name);
  }
  public CoffeeMaker() {
    super();
  }
  public void setSwitchOn(
    boolean value
  ) {
      BrewEvent event = null;
      if(SwitchOn != value){
        SwitchOn = value;
        event = new BrewEvent(
       this,"Coffee Machine Is Switched On.");
      }
      else
        event = new BrewEvent(
       this,"Coffee Machine Is Switched Off.");

      fireBrewing(event);
  }
  public void setCoffee(
    java.lang.String brew
  ) {
      if(!SwitchOn){
        Coffee = brew;
        BrewEvent event = new BrewEvent(this,brew +
" Coffee Has been Selected");
        fireBrewing(event);
      }
  }
```

```
  public void setTimer(
    int time
  ) {
      if(!SwitchOn)
        Timer = time;
  }
  public void brew() {
      BrewEvent event = new BrewEvent(
                this, "Coffee Is Brewing");
      fireBrewing(event);
  }

  public synchronized void removeBrewListener(BrewListener l) {
    if (brewListeners != null
       && brewListeners.contains(l)) {
      Vector v = (Vector) brewListeners.clone();
      v.removeElement(l);
      brewListeners = v;
    }
  }

  public synchronized void addBrewListener(BrewListener l) {
    Vector v = brewListeners == null ? new Vector(2) :
                       (Vector) brewListeners.clone();
    if (!v.contains(l)) {
      v.addElement(l);
      brewListeners = v;
    }
  }

  protected void fireBrewing(BrewEvent e) {
    if (brewListeners != null) {
      Vector listeners = brewListeners;
      int count = listeners.size();
      for (int i = 0; i < count; i++)
        ((BrewListener) listeners.elementAt(i)).Brewing(e);
    }
  }
}
```

In the preceding implementation, the component fires an event whenever the remote client makes an invocation on the server object. In our context, the GUI will acknowledge the events by displaying them in some widget.

The class can fire an event whenever it chooses. To do so, the class first constructs an event object. It does so as shown in the following code snippet:

```
event = new BrewEvent(this,
"Coffee Machine Is Switched On.");
```

An event object is constructed with a string message. The object is of the type `BrewEvent`. After the object is constructed, it needs to fire the event at the listener. These listeners, of course, implement the `BrewListener` interface. Two methods enable a listener to register its interest in `BrewEvents`: `addBrewListener(BrewListener l)` and `removeBrewListener(BrewListener l)`. The `addBrewListener(BrewListener l)` method is used to register the interface, and the `removeBrewListener(BrewListener l)` method is used when an interface needs to deregister with the component.

Internally, the class uses a `Java.util.Vector` to hold the interface instances that are interested in being notified. The following is the code that implements the event firing:

```
protected void fireBrewing(BrewEvent e) {
    if (brewListeners != null) {
      Vector listeners = brewListeners;
      int count = listeners.size();
      for (int i = 0; i < count; i++)
        ((BrewListener) listeners.elementAt(i)).Brewing(e);
    }
  }
```

The code essentially consists of the component iterating over the contents of the `Vector` object and invoking the `Brewing()` method on the `BrewListener`. Thus, through a process of callbacks, the listeners are notified when the state of the component changes.

Using the CorbaBean

The previous code only implements events to couple various components. In our case, we will use the events to couple our GUI for the CORBA component with the GUI. The code is shown in Listing 26.5.

LISTING 26.5 JAVABEAN USER INTERFACE

```
package CorbaBean;
import java.awt.*;
import CorbaBean.*;
import com.sun.java.swing.*;
import java.awt.event.*;

public class CoffeeFrame extends JFrame {
  JScrollPane jScrollPane1 = new JScrollPane();
  JTextArea EventListerDisplay = new JTextArea();
  JButton StartButton = new JButton();
  CoffeeMaker coffeeMakerComponent = new CoffeeMaker("CoffeeMaker");

  public CoffeeFrame() {
    try  {
      jbInit();
```

```
    }
    catch (Exception e) {
      e.printStackTrace();
    }
  }

  public static void main(String[] args) {
    CoffeeFrame coffeeFrame1 = new CoffeeFrame();
  }

  private void jbInit() throws Exception {
      coffeeMakerComponent.addBrewListener(
               new CorbaBean.BrewListener() {
      public void Brewing(BrewEvent e) {
        coffeeMakerComponent_Brewing(e);
      }
    });
    this.getContentPane().setLayout(null);
    jScrollPane1.setBounds(new Rectangle(9, 12, 378, 202));
    StartButton.setText("Start");
    StartButton.setBounds(new Rectangle(294, 222, 90, 27));
    StartButton.addMouseListener(new java.awt.event.MouseAdapter() {
      public void mouseClicked(MouseEvent e) {
        StartButton_mouseClicked(e);
      }
    });
    this.getContentPane().add(jScrollPane1, null);
    jScrollPane1.getViewport().add(EventListerDisplay, null);
    this.getContentPane().add(StartButton, null);
    setVisible(true);
  }

  void coffeeMakerComponent_Brewing(BrewEvent e) {
     EventListerDisplay.append(e.toString() + "\n");
  }

  void StartButton_mouseClicked(MouseEvent e) {
      CorbaBeanServer server = new CorbaBeanServer(
               EventListerDisplay,coffeeMakerComponent);
      Thread thread = new Thread(server);
      thread.start();
  }

  class CorbaBeanServer implements Runnable{

    org.omg.CORBA.BOA boa = null;
    JTextArea display;
    CorbaBeanServer(JTextArea display,CoffeeMaker coffeeMakerComponent){
      this.display = display;
```

continues

LISTING 26.5 CONTINUED

```
      org.omg.CORBA.ORB orb = org.omg.CORBA.ORB.init();
      boa = orb.BOA_init();
      boa.obj_is_ready(coffeeMakerComponent);
      display.append(coffeeMakerComponent + " is ready.\n");
    }

    public void run(){

       try{
       boa.impl_is_ready();
     }
     catch(org.omg.CORBA.SystemException e){
       display.append(e.toString() + "\n");
     }

    }
  }
}
```

This listing consists of two classes. The first is the GUI class itself, which is named `CoffeeFrame` and is a subclass of `JFrame`. The second class is the CORBA class that is implemented as a thread. `CoffeeFrame` is mostly user interface–related. However, in the next sections, I discuss how the GUI can be coupled with the CORBA bean.

The GUI uses Java inner classes to construct the `BrewListener` interface:

```
coffeeMakerComponent.addBrewListener(
    new CorbaBean.BrewListener() {
      public void Brewing(BrewEvent e) {
        coffeeMakerComponent_Brewing(e);
      }
    }
);
```

The callback interface is implemented in the following manner:

```
void coffeeMakerComponent_Brewing(BrewEvent e) {
     EventListerDisplay.append(e.toString() + "\n");
  }
```

The method just updates the display when a remote client alters the state of the CORBA component. The GUI is also the CORBA server. Because the server blocks when the `impl_is_ready()` method is called, it is run on a thread. The server implementation is shown in Listing 26.6 for completion.

LISTING 26.6 CORBABeanServer IMPLEMENTATION

```
class CorbaBeanServer implements Runnable{

    org.omg.CORBA.BOA boa = null;
    JTextArea display;
    CorbaBeanServer(JTextArea display,CoffeeMaker coffeeMakerComponent){
      this.display = display;
      org.omg.CORBA.ORB orb = org.omg.CORBA.ORB.init();
      boa = orb.BOA_init();
      boa.obj_is_ready(coffeeMakerComponent);
      display.append(coffeeMakerComponent + " is ready.\n");
    }

    public void run(){

       try{
       boa.impl_is_ready();
     }
     catch(org.omg.CORBA.SystemException e){
       display.append(e.toString() + "\n");
     }

    }
  }
}
```

The server code executes on a thread. The server itself is launched by the GUI in response to a mouse click on a button. The bean model is not used with the client. Therefore, the client is very similar to the ones that we have built before, as shown in Listing 26.7.

LISTING 26.7 CorbaBean CLIENT IMPLEMENTATION

```
package CorbaBean;

public class CorbaBeanClient {

  public CorbaBeanClient() {
   org.omg.CORBA.ORB orb = org.omg.CORBA.ORB.init();
   CoffeeMachine coffee =  CoffeeMachineHelper.bind(orb,"CoffeeMaker");
   coffee.switchOn(true);
   coffee.selectCoffee("Java");
   coffee.setTimer(5001);
   coffee.brew();
   coffee.switchOn(false);
  }
```

continues

LISTING 26.7 CONTINUED

```
  public static void main(String[] args) {
    CorbaBeanClient corbaBeanClient = new CorbaBeanClient();
  }
}
```

The client is a straightforward implementation. It sequentially invokes the server interface. What should be happening on the server side is that when an invocation comes into the component, the component generates an event that is delivered to the GUI component. In Figure 26.1, that is precisely what is happening.

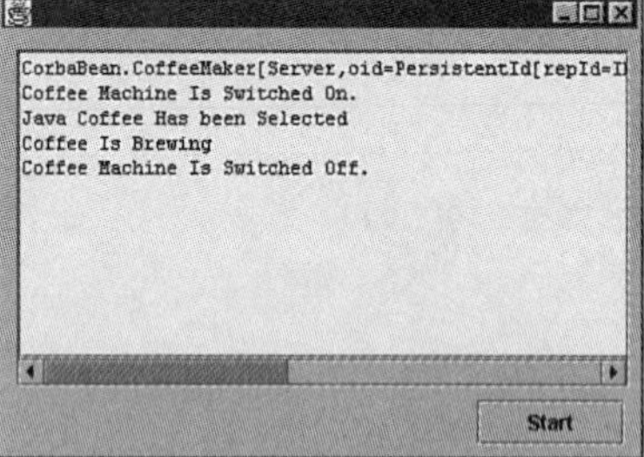

FIGURE 26.1
The CORBA client user interface.

The `BeanInfo` Class

All the information about a component's properties, methods, and events can be exposed to a development environment through a `BeanInfo` class. It is the `BeanInfo` class that enables you to specify which properties, events, and methods you would like to expose for a bean.

The class `Java.beans.SimpleBeanInfo` can be used as a template to construct a `BeanInfo` class. There are a number of `SimpleBeanInfo` methods that can be implemented by your component:

- `getPropertyDescriptors()`
- `getEventSetDescriptors()`
- `getMethodDescriptors()`
- `getBeanDescriptor()`
- `getDefaultPropertyIndex()`
- `getAdditionalBeanInfo()`
- `getDefaultEventIndex()`
- `getIcon(int)`
- `loadImage(String)`

The degree of implementation depends on the sophistication of your bean. The first three methods are the most crucial. With these three methods, the internals of a JavaBean component can be exposed through its `BeanInfo` class. These methods enable you to expose the properties, events, and methods of the bean, respectively. A tool can then introspect the bean and publish the descriptors in the editors that accompany the IDE that enables you to use a bean.

Implementing a BeanInfo Class for the CoffeeMaker

The class shown in Listing 26.8 implements the `BeanInfo` class for the `CoffeeMaker` bean. This enables an IDE to understand our bean, so to speak.

LISTING 26.8 `BeanInfo` CLASS

```
package CorbaBean;

import java.beans.*;

public class CoffeeMakerBeanInfo extends SimpleBeanInfo {
  Class beanClass = CoffeeMaker.class;
  String iconColor16x16Filename = "icon.gif";
  String iconColor32x32Filename;
  String iconMono16x16Filename;
  String iconMono32x32Filename;


  public CoffeeMakerBeanInfo() {
  }

  public PropertyDescriptor[] getPropertyDescriptors() {
    try  {
      PropertyDescriptor _coffee = new PropertyDescriptor(
               "coffee", beanClass, null, "setCoffee");
      _coffee.setDisplayName("Coffee");
      _coffee.setPropertyEditorClass(CorbaBean.CoffeeList.class);

      PropertyDescriptor _switchOn =
        new PropertyDescriptor("switchOn", beanClass, null,
"setSwitchOn");
      _switchOn.setDisplayName("Power");

      PropertyDescriptor _timer = new PropertyDescriptor(
                         "timer", beanClass, null, "setTimer");
      _timer.setDisplayName("Timer");
```

continues

LISTING 26.8 CONTINUED

```
      PropertyDescriptor[] pds = new PropertyDescriptor[] {
        _coffee,
        _switchOn,
        _timer,
      };
      return pds;
    }
    catch (IntrospectionException ex) {
      ex.printStackTrace();
      return null;
    }
  }

  public java.awt.Image getIcon(int iconKind) {
    switch (iconKind) {
    case BeanInfo.ICON_COLOR_16x16:
      return iconColor16x16Filename !=
          null ? loadImage(iconColor16x16Filename) : null;
    case BeanInfo.ICON_COLOR_32x32:
      return iconColor32x32Filename !=
          null ? loadImage(iconColor32x32Filename) : null;
    case BeanInfo.ICON_MONO_16x16:
      return iconMono16x16Filename !=
           null ? loadImage(iconMono16x16Filename) : null;
    case BeanInfo.ICON_MONO_32x32:
      return iconMono32x32Filename !=
            null ? loadImage(iconMono32x32Filename) : null;
    }
    return null;
  }
}
```

The `BeanInfo` class overrides the `getPropertyDescriptors()`and the `getIcon()` methods. The former method specifies the kinds of methods the `CoffeeMaker` bean supports. To assist in this, it uses a `Property Editor` class that is explained in the next section. The code for the property editor will be shown there as well. The `getIcon()` method loads a simple GIF file that represents the icon of the component when it is added to a pallet of an IDE bean builder.

Property Editors and Property Sheets

Property editors are the primary interface through which a developer could modify the default state of a JavaBean component. Each property that can be edited has its own property editor. it is the type that determines the kind of property editors that are available.

If a BeanInfo class is not provided for a bean, the development environment generates a default BeanInfo class for the bean using introspection. On the other hand, if a BeanInfo class is provided for the bean, the tool uses that class to generate an editor.

Using introspection, the tool generates the appropriate editor based on the type of property it is dealing with. Beyond the basic type that corresponds to the primitives, a developer needs to provide a custom property editor for types that are beyond a primitive type.

The BeanInfo class that we discussed before uses a property editor that is more specific that the one the default editor provides. The editor provides a set of values for the Coffee property of the bean. This property can only be a certain value that is specified in the Editor class. The code for the Property Editor class is shown in Listing 26.9.

LISTING 26.9 CoffeeMaker PROPERTY EDITOR IMPLEMENTATION

```
package CorbaBean;

import java.beans.*;

public class CoffeeList extends PropertyEditorSupport {

  private static String[] tagStrings =
              { "Jarro", "Calistor", "Havana", "Rim", };

  public CoffeeList() {
  }

  public String[] getTags() {
    return tagStrings;
  }

  public String getJavaInitializationString() {
    return "\"" + getAsText() + "\"";
  }

  public void setAsText(String text) throws IllegalArgumentException {
    setValue(text);
  }
}
```

The Coffee property, which is encapsulated by a String object via this editor, can have only four values, which are returned as an array of Strings. These show up as a drop-down combo box in the property sheet that the IDE provides. Property editors are best used if the value of a certain property is atomic. However, it is also conceivable that an atomic property is a derived property that is computed from a combination of multiple properties. Under these circumstances, you need to provide a customizer to set the derived property.

Summary

The JavaBean component model is a crucial breakthrough in the evolution of object-oriented systems to the next level of abstraction, which is based on components instead of classes. The JavaBean component model is inherently simpler than the older component models that came before it, because it does not take a lot of work to turn an existing Java class into a component.

One of the ways in which the JavaBean model can be leveraged by CORBA development is to use JavaBean as a mechanism to integrate in a cohesive manner the requirements of a GUI on the server side. This can be accomplished in a clean and nonintrusive manner by using various structural design patterns that promote decoupling. The JavaBean model, at its heart, is a set of design patterns, with the added benefit of the model being a standard as well.

As much as possible, design your server components with the plugs that enable it to be integrated into a GUI using the JavaBean model. Such a strategy will ultimately promote cleaner layers of abstractions that should ease your maintenance problems.

Appendixes

PART VI

IN THIS PART

APPENDIX

CORBA API Reference

IN THIS APPENDIX

The core API that is exposed by an ORB implementation is explained in this appendix. Only CORBA-compliant APIs are explained. For the proprietary extensions various vendors make to an ORB, it is best to refer to the appropriate manuals.

The BOA API Reference

The following interface specifies the functionality that the BOA exposes:

```
pseudo interface BOA (
Object create(in ReferenceData id,
       in InterfaceDef intf,
       in ImplementationDef impl);
void dispose(in Object obj);
ReferenceData get_id(in Object obj);
void change_implementation(in Object obj,
       in ImplementationDef impl);
       Principal get_principal(in Object obj,
       in Environment env);
void impl_is_ready(in Object obj,
       in ImplementationDef impl);
void deactivate_impl(
       in ImplementationDef impl);
void obj_is_ready(in ImplementationDef impl);
void deactivate_obj(in Object obj);
};
```

CORBA::BOA::change_implementation()

`CORBA::BOA::change_implementation()` enables the change of the implementation that is associated with an object. The `CORBA::ORB::setServerName()` function can be used to modify the implementation for all objects created by a server. This means that all objects in a server can be referred to by the name of the server.

CORBA::BOA::create()

`CORBA::BOA::create()` can be used to create a new object reference. This function does not create an object. This means that a call to this method assumes that the object already exists in a server.

CORBA::BOA::deactivate_impl()

When a server is ready to receive invocations from the client, it goes into a blocked call that is initialized by the `impl_is_ready()` method.

When the server is ready to shut down, it can deactivate the resources that it initialized by the `impl_is_ready()` call. The server can accomplish the deactivation by calling deactivate_impl() and passing the server name in the parameter impl. Invoking the deactivate_impl() causes impl_is_ready() to return from its blocked state.

CORBA::BOA::deactivate_obj()

As with the BOA, an implementation can notify the BOA that an object reference is ready for interaction with a client. This occurs when an implementation requires informing the BOA that it has completed the initialization of the implementation. When the server needs to deinitialize the implementation, it can call the deactivate_obj to remove the object from the request pool.

CORBA::BOA::dispose()

CORBA::BOA::dispose() invalidates the object reference.

CORBA::BOA::get_id()

CORBA::BOA::get_id() returns the identification information of the object obj that was initialized when the CORBA::BOA::create() was called.

CORBA::BOA::get_principal()

CORBA::BOA::get_principal() enables information about the client to be returned by the ORB. This information relates to the client that made the current invocation on the server object.

A server application can call this member function when processing an operation call from a client.

CORBA::BOA::impl_is_ready()

The impl_is_ready() method is at the heart of CORBA. This is the main method that is invoked when all the initialization is completed. This method blocks until the deactivatate_impl() is invoked that causes this method to return. When this method is invoked, it informs the ORB that the implemention is ready to receive invocations from the client.

This method blocks the server until an event occurs, handles the event, and reblocks the server to await another event. The impl_is_ready() function returns only under the following circumstances:

- A timeout occurs.
- An exception occurs while waiting for or processing an event.
- The function CORBA::BOA::deactivate_impl() is called.

CORBA::BOA::obj_is_ready()

The `obj_is_ready()` method is called when the initialization of the object is completed and it is ready to receive requests from the client. As with `imp_is_ready`, this method enables a service to remain active as long as the following conditions do not occur:

- It calls `CORBA::BOA::deactivate_obj()`.
- The call to `obj_is_ready()` times out.
- An exception is raised.

The CORBA::Object API

`CORBA::Object` is the base class of the IDL C++ classes. All objects are either directly or indirectly subclasses of this class. As such, all the methods that are available in this class are available in all the classes. Keep in mind that an instance of this class is available at both the client side (as a proxy) and at the server side (as a concrete object). The interface as defined by CORBA follows:

```
interface Object {
boolean is_nil();
Object duplicate();
void release();
ImplementationDef get_implementation();
InterfaceDef get_interface();
Status create_request(
in Context ctx,
in Identifier operation,
in NVList arg_list,
in NamedValue result,
out Request request,
in Flags req_flags);
};
```

CORBA::Object::_duplicate()

`CORBA::Object::_duplicate()` is called whenever the reference count of an object needs to be incremented. This might be necessary when a copy of an object reference needs to be passed back to a client.

CORBA::Object::_get_implementation()

`CORBA::Object::_get_implementation()` enables a client to retrieve the name that is used to register a service with the Implementation Repository.

CORBA::Object::_get_interface()

`CORBA::Object::_get_interface()` returns the interface that is registered with the Interface Repository. On returning the `interfacedef`, the client can construct the interface and make invocations on it dynamically.

CORBA::Object::_hash()

Every object reference that is constructed by an application has an object identifier associated with it. This identifier remains unique throughout the lifetime of the object reference. When using this method, it is conceivable that two separate and different object references may provide the same hashed value. If this is the actual case, the two object references in question are different objects.

CORBA::Object::_is_a()

`CORBA::Object::_is_a()` is useful when there is ambiguity over an inheritance hierarchy.

CORBA::Object::_is_equivalent()

`CORBA::Object::_is_equivalent()` is useful in determining whether two object references are equivalent. Two objects are equivalent if they have the same object reference, or they both refer to the same object.

CORBA::Object::_nil()

`CORBA::Object::_nil()` can be used to initialize a null reference to an object reference.

CORBA::Object::_non_existent()

`CORBA::Object::_non_existent()` can be used to see whether an object reference is present in a server. This method is invoked on the client side and is useful in determining whether the real object exists.

CORBA::Object::_request()

`CORBA::Object::_request()` can be used to dynamically construct an invocation on the server. This method can be extremely useful if the target operation is known beforehand.

CORBA::ORB

CORBA::ORB provides a set of functions that enable you to control an ORB from both the client side and the server. Some of these operations include support for an application to convert object references to a string (IOR) and back to an object reference. The full interface that is CORBA-compliant follows. After the interface, I discuss briefly the more important APIs of this interface:

```
// Pseudo IDL
// In module CORBA
pseudo interface ORB (
typedef sequence<Request> RequestSeq;
typedef sequence<string> arg_list;
typedef string OAid;
BOA BOA_init(inout arg_list argv,in OAid boa_identifier);
string object_to_string(in Object obj);
Object string_to_object(in string str);
Status create_list(in long count,out NVList new_list);
Status create_operation_list(in OperationDef oper, out NVList new_list);
Status get_default_context(out Context ctx);
Status create_environment(out Environment new_env);
Status send_multiple_requests_oneway(in RequestSeq req);
Status send_multiple_requests_deferred(in RequestSeq req);
boolean poll_next_response();
Status get_next_response(out Request req);
};
```

BOA BOA_init(inout arg_list argv,in OAid boa_identifier)

BOA BOA_init(inout arg_list argv,in OAid boa_identifier) initializes a server's connection to the Basic Object Adapter (BOA). The BOA controls the lifecycle of a server process.

string object_to_string(in Object obj)

string object_to_string(in Object obj) converts an object reference into a string. This string is the IOR for an object.

Object string_to_object(in string str)

When an IOR is constructed, it can be converted back to an object reference using this operation. The string_to_object() returns an instance of CORBA::Object. This object reference has to be narrowed to the required object.

```
Status create_list(in long count,out NVList new_list)
```

`Status create_list(in long count,out NVList new_list)` can be used to construct an argument list for Dynamic Invocation Interfaces (DIIs). The `NVList` object returned from the server can contain an argument that makes up the parameters of a DII invocation. It returns true if successful or false if not.

Status create_operation_list(in OperationDef oper, out NVList new_list)

`Status create_operation_list(in OperationDef oper, out NVList new_list)` returns a list of an `NVList`, in the parameter list, initialized with the argument descriptions for the operation specified in `OperationDef`.

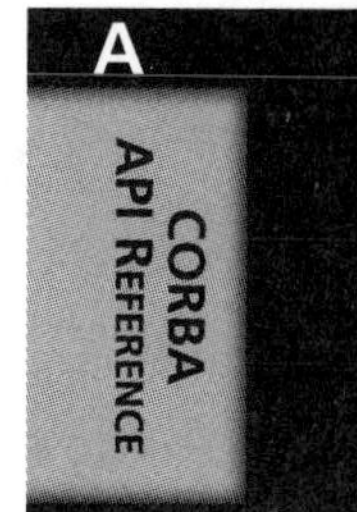

Status get_default_context(out Context ctx)

Use `Status get_default_context(out Context ctx)` to retrieve the context attached to a process. It returns a Boolean `typedef` whether it is successful or not.

Status create_environment(out Environment new_env)

`Status create_environment(out Environment new_env)` can be used to create an `Environment` object. The `Environment` object is used to transfer errors between clients and servers.

CORBA::Request

The interface `CORBA::Request` provides all the support required for Dynamic Invocation Interface (DII). DII enables an application to send requests to an interface without actually knowing anything about the interface during compile-time. The pseudo interface for this object follows. The request object is constructed by the client and issued to the ORB to make a remote invocation on a server object:

```
pseudo interface Request {
readonly attribute Object target;
readonly attribute Identifier operation;
readonly attribute NVList arguments;
readonly attribute NamedValue result;
readonly attribute Environment env;
attribute Context ctx;
```

```
Status invoke();
Status send_oneway();
Status send_deferred();
Status get_response();
boolean poll_response();
};
```

Status invoke()

`Status invoke()` instructs the ORB to make a request on a target object using DII. This method assumes that the operation itself has been properly constructed before the invocation can be made.

Status send_oneway()

`Status send_oneway()` enables the construction of an operation that can be invoked on the target as a `oneway` operation. A `oneway` operation enables a client to make an asynchronous operation on the server object. Like the `invoke()` method, the operation itself must be constructed properly before the invocation is made.

Status send_deferred()

`Status send_deferred()` enables the construction of an operation that can be invoked on the target as a `oneway` operation. A `oneway` operation enables a client to make an asynchronous operation on the server object. Like the `invoke()` method, the operation itself must be constructed properly before the invocation is made.

Status get_response()

`Status get_response()` enables the client to determine the outcome of an operation that has been made on the server object. It returns only when the request has completed.

boolean poll_response()

If the client made an invocation on the server object using `send_deferred()`, `boolean poll_response()` can be used to determine the outcome. The function returns immediately. If the operation has completed, the result is available in the `Request`.

CORBA::Principal

Class `CORBA::Principal` implements the IDL pseudo interface `Principal`, which represents information about principals that are the client. The information encapsulated in the `Principal` object can be used to provide authentication and access control.

TIE and BOA

In This Appendix

You should understand the essential difference between TIE and Basic Object Adapter (BOA), because it has consequence on the overall design and extensibility of a solution. The role of these components is to relate an IDL interface to its implementation. Most implementations of CORBA provide the BOA approach as well as the TIE approach. The interesting thing about these mechanisms is that they can be mixed so that an implementation can use both TIE and BOA.

BOA approaches are by far the most favored approach taken by most implementers. I believe this is mainly because most documentation and examples seem to deal exclusively with BOA-based approaches.

The BOA Approach

BOA support is usually generated by default, but for some CORBA implementations, you have to explicitly request the IDL pre-compiler to generate BOA support. BOA works by inheritance. The IDL pre-compiler generates the plug that binds an implementation to the generated mapping classes. This plug is the BOA class that your implementation class has to inherit.

All the examples in this book use the BOA model to implement the services and servers. Let's go over the process of showing how the BOA can be used.

The following example uses the `Factory` interface from Chapter 23, "CORBA and Design Patterns":

```
module Patterns {
    interface abstractFactory{

        Object create();
                void destroy();
    };

    interface concreteFactory:abstractFactory{

                struct Struct{
                   short number;
                };
                readonly attribute long identifier;
                Struct getStruct();
    };
};
```

After the interface has been pre-compiled, it has to be implemented. If you choose to use the BOA method, you have to subclass from the `[Name Of the interface]ImplBase`.

This class is generated by the pre-compiler. In the case of the `Factory` interface, there are two `ImplBase` classes that are generated, one for each interface in the module:

```
public class concreteFactory_i extends Patterns._concreteFactoryImplBase
..

public class abstractFactory_i extends Patterns._abstractFactoryImplBase
..
```

It is the `ImplBase` classes that are the key to the BOA method of using CORBA.

The `ImplBase` classes are generated for the module that you define. Here is the definition of the `*ImplBase` class:

```
abstract public class _concreteFactoryImplBase extends
       org.omg.CORBA.portable.Skeleton implements
Patterns.concreteFactory {
```

There are two pieces to the preceding class; the first is that it implements the Java interface mapping that corresponds to the IDL interface. The second is that the class extends the `Skeleton` class. The `Skeleton` class on the server side is the component that marshals and demarshals incoming invocations from the client side.

A class that extends the `*ImplBase` class automatically acquires all these functions. All that the deriving subclass has to do is override the methods that are specified in the interface. This is shown in Listing B.1.

LISTING B.1 BOA `Factory` COMPONENT

```
package Patterns;
public class concreteFactory_i extends Patterns._concreteFactoryImplBase {

  private Patterns.concreteFactoryPackage.Struct a_struct = new
Patterns.concreteFactoryPackage.Struct();
  private org.omg.CORBA.BOA boa_ = null;

  public concreteFactory_i(java.lang.String name, org.omg.CORBA.BOA boa) {
    super(name);
    a_struct.number = 10010;
    boa_ = boa;
  }

  public concreteFactory_i(org.omg.CORBA.BOA boa) {
    super();
    a_struct.number = 10010;
    boa_ = boa;
  }
```

continues

LISTING B.1 CONTINUED

```
  public Patterns.concreteFactoryPackage.Struct getStruct() {
    return a_struct;
  }

  public org.omg.CORBA.Object create() {
    return this;
  }

  public void destroy() {
   boa_.deactivate_obj(this);
  }

  public int identifier() {
    return a_struct.number;
  }
```

This is all that is required to implement the BOA model in a object.

The TIE Approach

TIE achieves the same result as BOA, but through using delegation instead of inheritance. Under C++, TIE is achieved by using a macro to "tie" together an implementation and the mapping. One of the prime reasons for using TIE instead of BOA is that TIE is considered more flexible because it enables a developer to have multiple implementations for the same interface.

The process of implementing a TIE model is given in Listing B.2. The first thing you have to do is pre-compile the interface. The TIE model is implemented by overriding the `*Operations` interface that is generated by the pre-compiler.

The `Factory` interface has a corresponding TIE interface, `Patterns.abstractFactoryOperations`. In order to implement the TIE, you must implement the interface shown in Listing B.2.

LISTING B.2 TIE `Factory` COMPONENT

```
package Patterns;

public class TieFactory implements Patterns.abstractFactoryOperations{

  private Patterns.concreteFactoryPackage.Struct a_struct = new
Patterns.concreteFactoryPackage.Struct();
  private org.omg.CORBA.BOA boa_ = null;
```

```
  public TieFactory(org.omg.CORBA.BOA boa){
    a_struct.number = 10010;
    boa_ = boa;
  }

  public org.omg.CORBA.Object create(){
    return this;
  }

  public void destroy(){
    boa_.deactivate_obj(this);
  }

  public Patterns.concreteFactoryPackage.Struct getStruct(){
    return a_struct;
  }

  public int identifier(){
    return a_struct.number;
  }
}
```

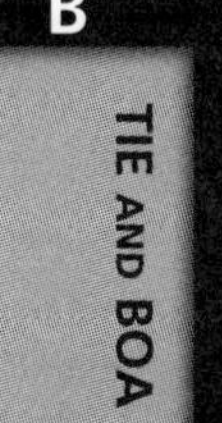

Because the `*Operations` interface is an extension of the `AbstractFactory` interface, the implementation of `abstractFactoryOperations` must implement all the methods that are specified in both the interfaces.

The basic difference should be clear. I have specifically used the example of Java in the preceding example, because Java makes the distinction between classes and types and that is essentially the difference between BOA and TIE.

APPENDIX C

Orbix and MFC

IN THIS APPENDIX

In this appendix, you look at how to use Orbix and the Visual C++ environment together so that they can be used productively.

Starting an Orbix/MFC Project

This project uses the following interface:

```
module mfc{
    interface authenticator{

        exception authenticationException{string reason;};

        struct user {
            string name;
            string pwd;
        };

        void authenticate(in user aUser) raises (authenticationException);

    };
};
```

This interface naturally consists of two projects: one for the server side and the other for the client side. The server side uses a normal console application. The client side uses MFC to implement the application.

The Server-Side Interface Implementation

The implementation of the server-side interface is very straightforward. The main purpose in this appendix is not to emphasize this implementation but to show how to build the client side. Here is how the server-side interface is implemented:

```
#include <iostream.h>
#include "authn.hpp"

void mfc::authenticator_i:: authenticate (const mfc::authenticator::user&
aUser, CORBA::Environment &IT_env) {

   cout<<aUser.name<<endl;
    cout<<aUser.pwd<<endl;
}
```

The logic of the implementation is limited to just outputting the parameter to the standard I/O. The server implementation is also very straightforward:

```
#include <iostream.h>
#include "authn.hpp"

void main(){
   mfc::authenticator_var authenticate;

  try {
    CORBA::Orbix.impl_is_ready("Signer");
  }
    catch (CORBA::SystemException &sysEx) {
    cerr << "Unexpected system exception" << endl;
    cerr << &sysEx;
    exit(1);
  } catch (...) {
    cout << "Unexpected exception" << endl;
    exit(1);
  }

  cout << "server exiting" << endl;

}
```

The server code consists of initializing the `mfc::authenticator` class and informing the BOA that the implementation is ready to receive invocations.

Register the server using the Orbix Server Manager or the `putit` utility. When registered, the server runs as shown in Figure C.1.

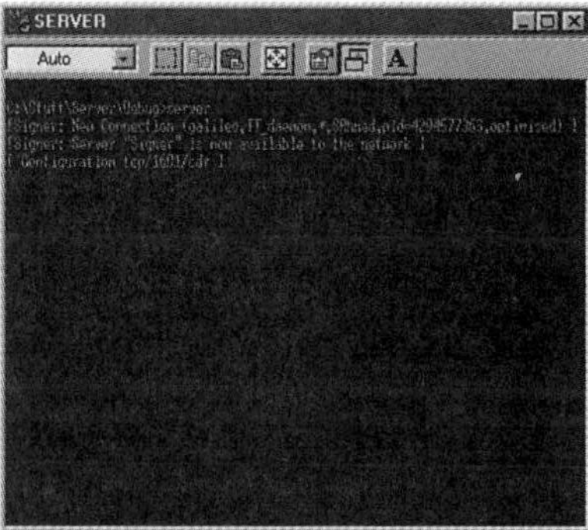

FIGURE C.1
The authentication server.

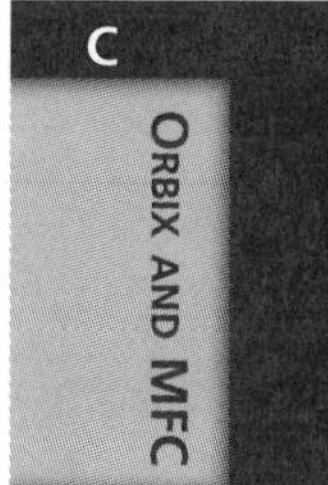

Building the Client

The client is built using MFC. Orbix 2.3c provides a Visual C++ add-on wizard to assist in the generation of MFC-based projects. Take the following steps to create an Orbix/MFC project:

1. Select the MFC/Win32 Console Orbix Wizard from the Projects tab of the New dialog that appears when you create a new project, as shown in Figure C.2.

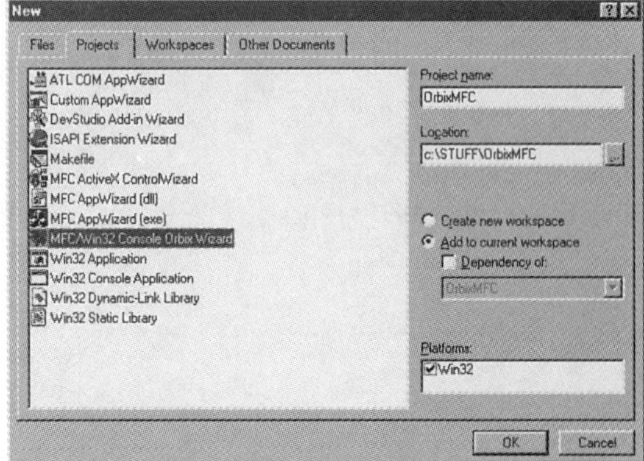

FIGURE C.2
Orbix/MFC Wizard, page 1.

2. Insert the IDL file that was specified. Then instruct the Wizard to generate support for the client side. This operation is shown in Figure C.3.

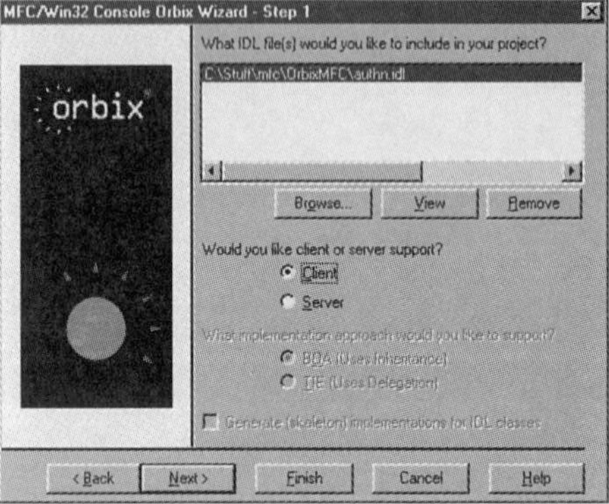

FIGURE C.3
Orbix/MFC Wizard, page 2.

3. When step 1 is done, you will be presented with a dialog box in which you can decide whether you want an MFC window application or a console application. For this example, use the MFC application. The window is shown in Figure C.4.
4. Decide whether you want a full-blown MFC application with its own windows. This example uses a simple dialog box to build the application. The choice is shown in Figure C.5.

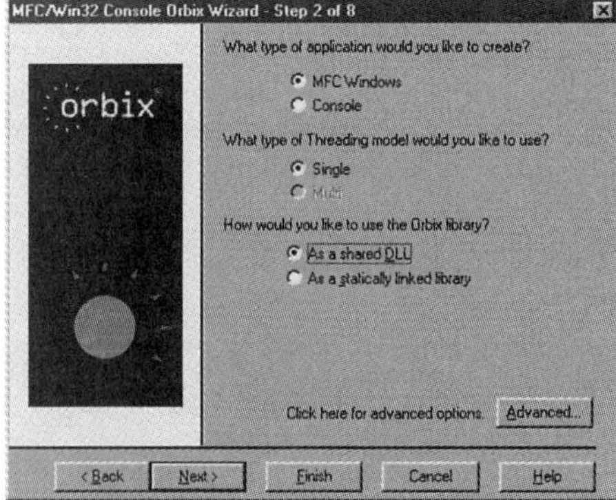

FIGURE C.4
Orbix/MFC Wizard, page 3.

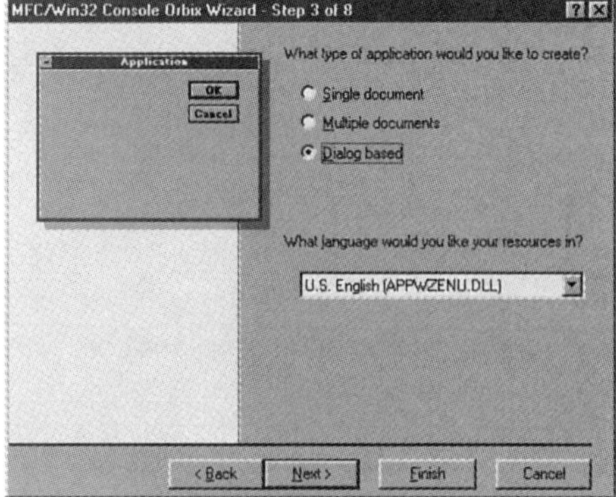

FIGURE C.5
Orbix/MFC Wizard, page 4.

The application will not use all the fancy options that MFC provides. For instance, you can add support for multidocument interface–based UI or add support for databased. For the present exercise, we will just stick to the basics. Therefore, all the other options are turned off.

When the required files have been generated, switch to the resource pane. Select the dialog folder to open the `IDD_ORBIXMD_DIALOG` resource. Add two text box and two button controls to the form so that the end result looks like Figure C.6. The object is to allow someone to use the form as a password requestor dialog for an application.

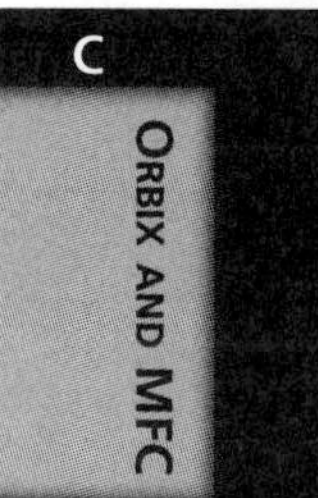

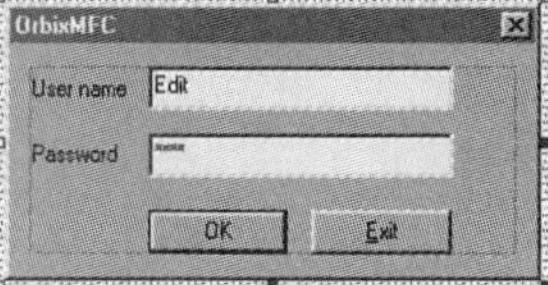

FIGURE C.6
MFC dialog building in progress.

The second TextField is a password field so that when the user enters some information, the text is replaced with asterisks.

Modification to the application is made to the COrbixMDApp class. Therein, the following code is added to the InitInstance() method:

```
BOOL COrbixMFCApp::InitInstance()
{

    COrbixMFCDlg dlg;
    int nResponse = dlg.DoModal();
    try{
        mfc::authenticator_var remoteObject =
mfc::authenticator::_bind(":Signer");
        mfc::authenticator::user_var User;

        if (nResponse == IDOK){
                User->name = dlg.m_name;
                User->pwd = dlg.m_pwd;
                remoteObject->authenticate(User);
        }
    }

    catch (CORBA::SystemException &sysEx) {

        cerr << "Unexpected system exception" << endl;
        cerr << &sysEx;
        exit(1);
    }

    return FALSE;
}
```

This implementation is not radically different from other client implementations except that the implementation is encapsulated in an MFC method.

After the code is entered, all you have to do is compile and link it.

Summary

Orbix 2.3 has taken another step toward closer integration with Microsoft Visual C++ with the addition of improved support for MFC. MFC is, by far, the most-used class library on the market. Despite CORBA's cross-platform support, it seems likely that CORBA is going to be most heavily adopted in Microsoft environments.

Therefore, it seems necessary to have MFC integration as painless and effortless as possible. As the example in this appendix illustrates, this is now possible.

INDEX

A

B

M

N

O

P-Q

R

S

T

U

V

W-Z

Sun Microsystems, Inc.

Binary Code License Agreement

READ THE TERMS OF THIS AGREEMENT AND ANY PROVIDED SUPPLEMENTAL LICENSE TERMS (COLLECTIVELY "AGREEMENT") CAREFULLY BEFORE OPENING THE SOFTWARE MEDIA PACKAGE. BY OPENING THE SOFTWARE MEDIA PACKAGE, YOU AGREE TO THE TERMS OF THIS AGREEMENT. IF YOU ARE ACCESSING THE SOFTWARE ELECTRONICALLY, INDICATE YOUR ACCEPTANCE OF THESE TERMS BY SELECTING THE "ACCEPT" BUTTON AT THE END OF THIS AGREEMENT. IF YOU DO NOT AGREE TO ALL THESE TERMS, PROMPTLY RETURN THE UNUSED SOFTWARE TO YOUR PLACE OF PURCHASE FOR A REFUND OR, IF THE SOFTWARE IS ACCESSED ELECTRONICALLY, SELECT THE "DECLINE" BUTTON AT THE END OF THIS AGREEMENT.

1. **LICENSE TO USE.** Sun grants you a non-exclusive and non-transferable license for the internal use only of the accompanying software and documentation and any error corrections provided by Sun (collectively "Software"), by the number of users and the class of computer hardware for which the corresponding fee has been paid.
2. **RESTRICTIONS.** Software is confidential and copyrighted. Title to Software and all associated intellectual property rights is retained by Sun and/or its licensors. Except as specifically authorized in any Supplemental License Terms, you may not make copies of Software, other than a single copy of Software for archival purposes. Unless enforcement is prohibited by applicable law, you may not modify, decompile, reverse engineer Software. Software is not designed or licensed for use in on-line control of aircraft, air traffic, aircraft navigation or aircraft communications; or in the design, construction, operation or maintenance of any nuclear facility. You warrant that you will not use Software for these purposes. You may not publish or provide the results of any benchmark or comparison tests run on Software to any third party without the prior written consent of Sun. No right, title or interest in or to any trademark, service mark, logo or trade name of Sun or its licensors is granted under this Agreement.
3. **LIMITED WARRANTY.** Sun warrants to you that for a period of ninety (90) days from the date of purchase, as evidenced by a copy of the receipt, the media on which Software is furnished (if any) will be free of defects in materials and workmanship under normal use. Except for the foregoing, Software is provided "AS IS". Your exclusive remedy and Sun's entire liability under this limited warranty will be at Sun's option to replace Software media or refund the fee paid for Software.

4. **DISCLAIMER OF WARRANTY.** UNLESS SPECIFIED IN THIS AGREEMENT, ALL EXPRESS OR IMPLIED CONDITIONS, REPRESENTATIONS AND WARRANTIES, INCLUDING ANY IMPLIED WARRANTY OF MERCHANTABILITY, FITNESS FOR A PARTICULAR PURPOSE, OR NON-INFRINGEMENT, ARE DISCLAIMED, EXCEPT TO THE EXTENT THAT THESE DISCLAIMERS ARE HELD TO BE LEGALLY INVALID.
5. **LIMITATION OF LIABILITY.** TO THE EXTENT NOT PROHIBITED BY LAW, IN NO EVENT WILL SUN OR ITS LICENSORS BE LIABLE FOR ANY LOST REVENUE, PROFIT OR DATA, OR FOR SPECIAL, INDIRECT, CONSEQUENTIAL, INCIDENTAL OR PUNITIVE DAMAGES, HOWEVER CAUSED REGARDLESS OF THE THEORY OF LIABILITY, ARISING OUT OF OR RELATED TO THE USE OF OR INABILITY TO USE SOFTWARE, EVEN IF SUN HAS BEEN ADVISED OF THE POSSIBILITY OF SUCH DAMAGES. In no event will Sun's liability to you, whether in contract, tort (including negligence), or otherwise, exceed the amount paid by you for Software under this Agreement. The foregoing limitations will apply even if the above stated warranty fails of its essential purpose.
6. **Termination.** This Agreement is effective until terminated. You may terminate this Agreement at any time by destroying all copies of Software. This Agreement will terminate immediately without notice from Sun if you fail to comply with any provision of this Agreement. Upon Termination, you must destroy all copies of Software.
7. **Export Regulations.** All Software and technical data delivered under this Agreement are subject to US export control laws and may be subject to export or import regulations in other countries. You agree to comply strictly with all such laws and regulations and acknowledge that you have the responsibility to obtain such licenses to export, re-export, or import as may be required after delivery to you.
8. **U.S. Government Restricted Rights.** Use, duplication, or disclosure by the U.S. Government is subject to restrictions set forth in this Agreement and as provided in DFARS 227.7202-1 (a) and 227.7202-3(a) (1995), DFARS 252.227-7013 (c)(1)(ii)(Oct 1988), FAR 12.212 (a) (1995), FAR 52.227-19 (June 1987), or FAR 52.227-14(ALT III) (June 1987), as applicable.
9. **Governing Law.** Any action related to this Agreement will be governed by California law and controlling U.S. federal law. No choice of law rules of any jurisdiction will apply.
10. **Severability.** If any provision of this Agreement is held to be unenforceable, This Agreement will remain in effect with the provision omitted, unless omission would

frustrate the intent of the parties, in which case this Agreement will immediately terminate.

11. **Integration.** This Agreement is the entire agreement between you and Sun relating to its subject matter. It supersedes all prior or contemporaneous oral or written communications, proposals, representations and warranties and prevails over any conflicting or additional terms of any quote, order, acknowledgment, or other communication between the parties relating to its subject matter during the term of this Agreement. No modification of this Agreement will be binding, unless in writing and signed by an authorized representative of each party.

For inquiries please contact: Sun Microsystems, Inc. 901 San Antonio Road, Palo Alto, California 94303

JAVA™ DEVELOPMENT KIT (JDK™) VERSION 1.2

SUPPLEMENTAL LICENSE TERMS

These supplemental terms ("Supplement") add to the terms of the Binary Code License Agreement ("Agreement"). Capitalized terms not defined herein shall have the same meanings ascribed to them in the Agreement. The Supplement terms shall supersede any inconsistent or conflicting terms in the Agreement.

1. **Limited License Grant.** Sun grants to you a non-exclusive, non-transferable limited license to use the Software without fee for evaluation of the Software and for development of Java™ applets and applications provided that you: (i) may not redistribute the Software in whole or in part, either separately or included with a product. (ii) may not create, or authorize your licensees to create additional classes, interfaces, or subpackages that are contained in the "java" or "sun" packages or similar as specified by Sun in any class file naming convention; and (iii) agree to the extent Programs are developed which utilize the Windows 95/98 style graphical user interface or components contained therein, such applets or applications may only be developed to run on a Windows 95/98 or Windows NT platform. Refer to the Java Runtime Environment Version 1.2 binary code license (http://java.sun.com/products/JDK/1.2/index.html) for the availability of runtime code which may be distributed with Java applets and applications.
2. **Java Platform Interface.** In the event that Licensee creates an additional API(s) which: (i) extends the functionality of a Java Environment; and, (ii) is exposed to third party software developers for the purpose of developing additional software

which invokes such additional API, Licensee must promptly publish broadly an accurate specification for such API for free use by all developers.

3. **Trademarks and Logos.** This Agreement does not authorize Licensee to use any Sun name, trademark or logo. Licensee acknowledges as between it and Sun that Sun owns the Java trademark and all Java-related trademarks, logos and icons including the Coffee Cup and Duke ("Java Marks") and agrees to comply with the Java Trademark Guidelines at http://java.sun.com/trademarks.html.
4. **High Risk Activities.** Notwithstanding Section 2, with respect to high risk activities, the following language shall apply: the Software is not designed or intended for use in on-line control of aircraft, air traffic, aircraft navigation or aircraft communications; or in the design, construction, operation or maintenance of any nuclear facility. Sun disclaims any express or implied warranty of fitness for such uses.

The OA Group is a European organization of 125+ people, dedicated to training, mentoring project teams, and the analysis, design, and development of systems and architectures using object-oriented technology (OOT), and specifically Open Standards. In this regard, the OA Group considers CORBA and Java to be the most important platform and set of technologies with which to build a robust and open architecture in the market today.

With offices in the Netherlands, Germany, Russia (R&D), and Belgium, the OA Group is one of the largest players in the Distributed Object Computing (DOC) market and a leading provider of CORBA and Java services and legacy system integration. The OA Group is an active member of the Object Management Group. In March 1998, we were awarded the status of Sun Authorized Java CenterT.

Partners in Training and Consulting:

In order to build appropriate solutions, the OA Group has effective working relationships with Sun, Oracle, Netscape, Inprise, Iona Technologies, and CMG. We work with these partners to understand and integrate their offerings with existing architectures or with new applications.

Services:

The OA Group was one of the first firms that became involved in OOT software development and services and over time has developed four areas of expertise:

- OOT training and upgrading of engineering skills
- OOT mentoring and consulting
- Project management and implementation
- Building high-end systems for large networks, embedded or real-time applications

The OA Group's project-based consultancy practice includes the development of an architectural framework for object-oriented (OO) projects, project workshops in which practical skills in implementing the chosen architecture are transferred, project mentoring, and knowledge transfer by means of courses. We also have experience with many different OOT products and solutions and are able to help clients with specific tool training and tool choice.

The OA Group applies expertise in handling all issues pertaining to OOT within a company's architecture. We believe in open systems and standards. CORBA and Java are therefore of particular importance in our philosophy.

Suhail M. Ahmed is the technical manager within the OA Group and performs senior consultancy work in the field of OOT.